THE ECONOMY OF INDONESIA

Selected Readings

THE ECONOMY OF INDONESIA

Selected Readings

Edited, with an introduction, by

BRUCE GLASSBURNER

CORNELL UNIVERSITY PRESS

Ithaca and London

First published 1971

International Standard Book Number 0-8014-0600-5
Library of Congress Catalog Card Number 77-127777

PRINTED IN THE UNITED STATES OF AMERICA
BY THE COLONIAL PRESS, INC.

To Innosanto Nagara

In Memoriam

Everett D. "Red" Hawkins died on August 31, 1970, while this book was in production. His contribution to the volume consisted not only of his chapter on labor organization in Indonesia but also of active support of the entire project in his capacity as Chairman of the Indonesia Seminar of the Southeast Asia Development Advisory Group. The editor wishes to express his gratitude for this contribution and his grief at the loss of a friend and associate of nearly fourteen years.

Preface

Because of the preoccupation of Indonesian economists with immediate policy problems of their country, and because of the minor role to which the economics profession of the world has relegated Indonesia and the limited accessibility of the nation in recent years to those few economists who have a research interest there, the flow of published materials on the Indonesian economy has been thin. This collection of articles and papers brings together a number of significant, widely scattered short works. But this sort of compilation would be useful even if the amount of recent research on the Indonesian economy were much greater than it is.

The articles were chosen with a view toward giving the historical record of economic performance and economic policy since Indonesia achieved independence in late 1949. At the same time the objective was to convey as well as possible the sectoral and institutional structure of the economic system. Two kinds of problems emerged in the process of making these selections. First, the period of the Sukarno years (1958–1965) was one during which economic data became increasingly difficult to acquire, in large measure because of the deterioration of the statistical reporting apparatus of government and also because economists, whether Indonesian or foreign, were not encouraged by government. Since 1965, despite considerable recovery of the reporting system, good data have remained hard to get. Hence updating of articles has not been easy, and in several cases it has been impossible. The reader is therefore advised to take careful note of publication dates.

The second problem has been the deep involvement of Indonesian economists since 1965 with the immediate problems of economic policy. While this has meant a huge gain in the quality of decision-making in this area—a gain which the editor, as an economist, can only applaud—it has drastically restricted academic research. The recent prominence of Indonesian economists in public affairs gives a general impression of ubiquity, but in fact they are a very small, excellent group of professionals, much too busy to contribute recent material to a book of this nature. Hence, they are seriously under-represented here. Their capacities have been utilized to the full in recent years; indeed they have been called upon to play so many roles of high responsibility that they have been stretched thin in each area. They not only must teach large university classes (indeed, many teach in several universities); they are also being asked to sit in the cabinet, the parliament, and the planning council. At the same time they have voluntarily undertaken a campaign of public education in economic affairs through a barrage of newspaper and magazine articles, public speeches, and interviews. Finally, they man the economics research institutions. In view of this overwhelming set of responsibilities it is remarkable that their contribution to research is as impressive as it is.

The editor is grateful to the Southeast Asia Development Advisory Group, which provided financial assistance and is, essentially, the sponsor of the work. Thanks are also due to Abdolhossain Zahedani, the author's graduate assistant, for his valuable help of all kinds.

BRUCE GLASSBURNER

Hong Kong
February 1971

Contents

The Authors

ALI WARDHANA is Professor of Economics at the Fakultas Ekonomi of the University of Indonesia, and Minister of Finance of the Republic of Indonesia.

H. W. ARNDT is Professor of Economics at the Research School of Pacific Studies, the Australian National University.

LANCE CASTLES, formerly a Research Assistant in Economics at the University of Indonesia, Lecturer in Indonesian Studies at Melbourne University, and Research Assistant in Economics at the Australian National University, is presently a Ph.D. candidate at Yale University.

J. PRICE GITTINGER is an economist and member of the staff of the Economic Development Institute at the International Bank for Reconstruction and Development.

BRUCE GLASSBURNER is Professor of Economics at the University of California, Davis.

The late E. D. HAWKINS was Professor of Economics, the University of Wisconsin, at the time of his death on August 31, 1970.

ALEX HUNTER is an economist and Professional Fellow at the Institute of Advanced Studies, the Australian National University.

J. A. C. MACKIE is an economist and Research Director of the Centre of Southeast Asian Studies at Monash University, Clayton, Australia.

INGRID PALMER is Fellow of the Centre for South-East Asian Studies at the University of Hull.

KARL J. PELZER is Professor of Geography and Director, Southeast Asia Studies, at Yale University.

David H. Penny is Fellow of the Research School of Pacific Studies at the Australian National University.

Mohammad Sadli is Professor of Economics at the Fakultas Ekonomi of the University of Indonesia, and Director of the Department of Foreign Investment of the Republic of Indonesia.

THE ECONOMY OF INDONESIA

Selected Readings

PART I

THE ECONOMY AND ECONOMIC POLICY: GENERAL AND HISTORICAL

Indonesia has fascinated and attracted Westerners for many centuries. It was "the fabled wealth of the Indies," in large measure, which led to the age of exploration, the discovery of America, and the spread of colonialism. The Portuguese arrived in the Moluccas in 1510, in search of spices for European markets. The Spanish, British, and Dutch soon followed. By the end of the sixteenth century, Dutch traders were dominant in the Indies. Early in the seventeenth century the Dutch East India Company extended its activities beyond trading and acquired territorial possessions not only in the Moluccas but also in Java and Sumatra, and the area became known as the Dutch East Indies.

The Company remained a dominant force in the economy until its charter was revoked in 1798, at which time the Dutch government assumed its functions and responsibilities. Aside from the British interregnum during the Napoleonic Wars, the Dutch government remained in power until the Japanese occupation of World War II (1942–1945). Indonesia proclaimed her independence on August 17, 1945, and, after four years of war and negotiation with the Dutch, achieved formal recognition of her sovereignty in late 1949.

Dutch economic exploitation of the Indies is one of the few examples of economically successful colonialism which the history of Western expansion into Asia, Latin America, and Africa provides. The East India Company succeeded largely by means of shrewd and ruthless dominance of export trade. In the nineteenth century, however, the colonial government relied heavily for forty years (1830–1870) on the "Culture System," which required Javanese farmers to produce profitable export commodities (mainly coffee, sugar, and indigo). Deliveries of these commodities were, in effect, a form of land taxation, for which there was only a legalistic *quid pro quo*.[1] Although the "Culture System" was an economic success, it nevertheless came under increasing political criticism in the 1850's and 1860's in the Netherlands. The Agrarian and Sugar Laws of 1870 ostensibly eliminated this taxation in kind and replaced it with a free market system. The earlier success of the "Culture System" was dwarfed by the boom of the last thirty years of the nineteenth century. Dutch capital responded enthusiastically and established a new pattern of plantation agriculture which came ultimately to dominate the export sector of the economy. Indonesian smallholders, therefore, lost relative importance as exporters and accordingly failed to improve their economic status; the overt exploitation of the "Culture System" was replaced by the market dominance of Dutch private enterprise.

In the Netherlands, therefore, colonial policy continued to be the subject of critical discussion; liberals argued that economic liberalism alone was insufficient, as it failed to lead to recognizable improvement in the quality of life of the indigenous Indonesian people. Indeed, as the population of Java grew, the possibility of retention of established living standards seemed threatened. In 1901, therefore, a new policy was initiated, especially oriented toward the welfare of the indigenous peoples. New efforts were made in the areas of education, health, public works, and agriculture. This reorientation of colonial policy, called the Ethical Policy, did not alter economic trends in any drastic way. The rate of inflow of Dutch and other European capital continued to grow, and the rate of growth of the indigenous population also accelerated. Perhaps the most significant shift in the pattern of economic development in the early decades of the twentieth cen-

[1] Deliveries were prorated against "land rents," which were claims by the government on landholders. Rents were considered due to the government as owner of all land—a system introduced from India by Governor Raffles during the interregnum.

tury was the shift of the growth impetus from Java to Sumatra, as Java became increasingly crowded and less capable of producing export surpluses.

The depression of the 1930's brought the long economic growth trend to a virtual halt. Loss of European markets forced a new interest in production for internal markets, as export surpluses were no longer available to cover the deficit in domestic production of consumer goods—the deficit of food, in particular. Policy now became oriented toward increased food production and domestic industrialization, especially on Java. Thus, as World War II approached, "a viable pattern of trade and specialization" was developing, with Java producing rice and manufactured goods for shipment to the outer islands (most notably Sumatra) in return for primary products and as partial compensation for her export deficit.[2]

The economy was turned even more intensively inward by the Japanese occupation, and economic growth was further inhibited. Interisland trade (which had expanded rapidly in the 1930's) was sharply reduced, and resources theretofore devoted to export production were diverted to food production for local consumption —a process already well underway on land previously devoted to sugar. The four ensuing years of struggle for independence afforded no opportunity for reconstruction. Hence, in late 1949, as the Indonesians celebrated their new-found independence, the economy which they inherited was a very badly damaged one, and one which was still of "colonial structure"—that is, dominated by export-oriented foreign enterprises in the modern sector and peasant agriculture in the traditional sector.

The articles in this volume are almost entirely concerned with the attempt at development of the economy since independence. This attempt has, obviously, been a struggle against great odds. It was an economy which had not grown significantly for two decades and was now in the hands of leaders with little or no experience in government. At the time of the present writing (early 1969), it cannot be said that the society has met the challenge with success. Per capita income in 1969 is probably no higher than it

[2] Douglas S. Paauw, "From Colonial to Guided Economy," in Ruth McVey, ed., *Indonesia,* Human Relations Area Files, New Haven, 1963.

was thirty years previously. This judgment cannot be made with any high degree of certainty, as statistics in Indonesia represent one of the most seriously underdeveloped aspects of her economic system. Most observers agree, however, that by the 1950's per capita income had returned roughly to prewar levels, while aggregate economic growth between 1958 and 1965—the years of Sukarno's "Guided Economy"—was probably insufficient to match the rate of population growth.[3]

There have been three phases in the history of Indonesia's economic policy since sovereignty was transferred in late 1949. From 1950 through 1957, parliamentary democracy was given a futile trial (eight cabinets served in those eight years). Policy in those years not only lacked continuity but was inhibited, on the one hand, by the (still great) strength in the economy of foreign and Chinese private business interests and, on the other, by the political risk involved in taking steps which would serve those interests.[4] In 1957 and 1958, President Sukarno moved into a position of greatly increased political strength and into dominance over economic policy. Following a short-lived (and entirely unsuccessful) rebellion by liberal-led elements against the Sukarno government in early 1958, the president moved to implement his *konsepsi*—his conception—of "Guided Economy." Aside from an aversion for market processes and foreign enterprises (most of which had been expelled by the time of the rebellion), the conception offered little guidance. The policies of the ensuing years reflected this aimlessness, and the economy's performance deteriorated, as shown most dramatically in rapidly accelerating hyperinflation and balance-of-payments deficits.

The "Guided Economy" period came to an end in September 1965, with the failure of an allegedly communist-led attempt to assassinate several of Indonesia's most prominent military leaders. The military, suspecting President Sukarno of complicity in the

[3] See, for example, Benjamin Higgins' sketch, entitled "Indonesia: The Chronic Dropout," in his *Economic Development,* rev. ed., W. W. Norton, New York, 1968.

[4] See the editor's "Economic Policy-Making in Indonesia 1950–1957," Chapter 2, below, for development of this thesis.

plot, deprived him of his powers and established a cautious regime under General (now President) Suharto. This government has placed heavy reliance on a small group of Western-trained economists, who have sought stability and a new basis for growth in fiscal balance, foreign aid, foreign private investment, and the dismantling of most of the control system. The aid-giving governments and private investors have both responded with enthusiasm, and in 1968 the inflation seemed at last under control. Good crops made a major contribution in 1968, but 1967 was a bad crop year, giving the regime a serious setback. Indigenous industry remains slow to respond, and the economic upswing from the depths into which the Sukarno regime had taken it is still more hope than reality. The hope remains alive that the regime's "New Economic Policy" will have a favorable effect if it is given the necessary political breathing space. At present, however, it is impossible to disagree with Benjamin Higgins' judgment that "Indonesia must surely be accounted the number one failure among the major underdeveloped countries."

The Natural Resource Base

Indonesia must, indeed, be regarded as a major nation. This is a large country, both geographically and demographically. Her total land area is approximately one-third that of the United States, but only China, India, and the U.S.S.R. are larger in Asia. This land, divided into thousands of islands, is spread over 3,400 miles east to west and 1,000 miles north to south. The nation's population and economic activity, however, are concentrated on the large islands of Java and Sumatra and (much less) on Borneo (Kalimantan) and Celebes (Sulawesi).

The equator bisects the archipelago, a fact which explains much about Indonesia's climate and agricultural resources. The monsoons govern her cropping patterns: the winds are wet and westward in December, January, and February; dry and eastward in June, July, and August. The dry season is wet enough to allow double- and triple-cropping in much of the most heavily cropped

[5] Higgins, *op. cit.,* p. 678.

areas, however. The natural vegetation of the islands is tropical rain forest, and the soils are generally lateritic. The high level of precipitation causes rapid soil-leaching. Rainfall on Kalimantan and most of Sumatra exceeds eighty inches annually, while most of Java receives between sixty and eighty inches. Thus the soil is generally poor except in those areas which have experienced recent volcanic activity or are irrigable from rivers draining volcanic areas. These conditions have led to shifting cultivation practices in large parts of Sumatra and Borneo. Java is the island best endowed with fertile soil, which explains the concentration of continual-cropping on that island, and also explains the extremely high concentration of population there. Rubber trees thrive on relatively poor soils in a tropical climate, as do other perennials such as coconut and oil palms. Most of Indonesia's land area remains heavily forested, despite serious deforestation in certain localities (the lesser Sunda islands, in particular).

Although Indonesia is relatively well endowed with valuable exportable minerals, such as petroleum, tin, and bauxite, she does not have a wide variety of large, known deposits of minerals usable as industrial raw materials. Hence her eventual industrial development will inevitably remain dependent on her ability to trade. She has no high-grade iron ore deposits and no coking coal. Indonesia has proven petroleum reserves in excess of nine billion barrels, and petroleum exports are the mainstay of her balance of payments. Production of petroleum is growing well, and a wave of enthusiastic exploration is now underway. Hopes are high that proven reserves will be expanded greatly in the near future. A variety of other types of minerals, such as sulfur, nickel, and manganese, are known to exist in the islands, but thus far only small-scale activity has been associated with them.

As an archipelago, Indonesia is endowed with seaways between major islands and major cities. Unfortunately, however, much of her coastal area is fringed by reefs or mangrove swamp, and she has relatively few natural harbors. Siltation and lack of maintenance in recent years have increased shipping hazards and costs in such important ports as Djakarta, Belawan Deli, and Palembang. Thus, even though Indonesia's natural resource base may be described as good by comparison with such countries as Japan or India, it certainly falls short of making her the land of infinite potential she is often considered to be in the popular view.

Problems of Human Resources

Indonesia's situation with reference to human resources reflects the shortcomings of her resource base and the legacy of colonialism. Not only are her people very badly undertrained and undereducated, but they are also very badly distributed geographically. Two Indonesians out of three live on the island of Java, where the average density of population in 1968 approached 550 per square kilometer[6]—more densely populated than the Netherlands, Japan, or East Pakistan. Indonesia as a whole, however, has a population density of about 59 per square kilometer—roughly that of the state of Illinois, and less than half that of India. All major islands other than Java, Madura, and Bali are well below that average. Sumatra had (in 1968) approximately 38 persons per square kilometer, Sulawesi had 43, and Kalimantan only 9.

This uneven distribution pattern has, for many years, made interisland migration attractive to governmental authorities, but it has persistently failed to be attractive to large numbers of Javanese, Sundanese, Madurese, and Balinese, despite governmental inducements. Between 1951 and 1959, the Transmigration Service sponsored 221,500 outmigrants from Java, Madura, and Bali, or only an average of 24,600 persons a year. And while at least that many more may be presumed to have moved without government sponsorship, the most optimistic estimate of outmigration (perhaps 75,000 per year) is dwarfed by the current annual natural increase of Java's population of at least 1,300,000. Thus, without dramatic success in the near future with transmigration and birth control, the nation may face an unmanageable demographic crisis.

The interisland demographic imbalance described above all but obscures another very serious aspect of the nation's population distribution, namely, that between urban centers and rural

[6] The 1961 census showed the density of population of Java and Madura as 477 per square kilometer. A conservative projection at 2 percent per annum to 1968 yields a density of 550. The same method of estimation is used for the other density figures used in this paragraph.

districts. While the intercensal growth of total population (1930–1961) was 55 percent, that of the twenty-one major Indonesian cities (those with 100,000 population or more in 1961) grew, over the same time period, 393 percent.[7] Djakarta, in particular, has swelled quite unmanageably. From a modest-sized city of a little more than a half million persons in 1930, she had become a sprawling metropolis of nearly three million in 1961.[8] In terms of total population, Indonesia ranks fifth among the nations of the world, with at least 108 million in 1966.[9]

Ethnic Problems

The ethnic composition of Indonesia's population is of great interest and economic significance. While there are literally hundreds of distinct ethnic and lingual groupings in the Indonesian population, they group into four broad categories of economic significance, namely, the Chinese minority; the Hinduized inland community, based on wet-rice culture; the trade-oriented, strongly Islamic coastal peoples; and the tribal groups of the mountainous interior regions (mainly in the outer islands).[10] Of these the second are by far the most numerous. It is the Chinese, however, who pose the most difficult problem for the nation because of their vastly disproportionate share of economic power. They are only about 2.5 million in number. Of these, perhaps one-third hold Indonesian citizenship, although probably that proportion would be larger if the Indonesian government had been more receptive to them since independence. However, the failure of the Chinese community to become integrated with the *asli* (indigenous) Indonesians is a major source of social and political friction. Not more than half of the ethnic Chinese are considered *Peranakan Ti-*

[7] Karl Pelzer, "Physical and Human Resource Patterns," in McVey, *op. cit.*, Table 2, p. 19.

[8] *Ibid.*

[9] Widjojo Nitisastro's low range estimate for 1966 was 108 million. His high range estimate was 109.2 million. By 1971, Dr. Widjojo gives 119.3 million and 121.7 million as his lower and upper estimates, respectively. These figures are taken from Table 73 of his book, *Population Trends in Indonesia,* Cornell University Press, Ithaca, N.Y., 1970.

[10] Cf. Hildred Geertz, "Indonesian Cultures and Communities," in McVey, *op. cit.*, pp. 24–96.

onghua, or Indonesians of Chinese descent. The remainder are *Totok,* or those primarily oriented toward China. In any case, in time of stress the distinction is all but ignored by the majority in the *asli* community. In part, this unhealthy situation is the legacy of the colonial regime, which fostered the special economic and social position of the Chinese. It did so by encouraging the Chinese traders in their development of a position of great strength in the "middle trade." Chinese owners of small- and medium-sized businesses built and ran the financial and trading network between the *asli* cultivator and the Dutch trading companies. Also, the Chinese, to a far greater extent than the Indonesians, were taken into positions of supervisory responsibility within the Dutch companies themselves. In the rural districts, the Chinese built a position of dominance in retail and other petty trade, in rice-milling, and in rural finance. With the departure of the Dutch companies in 1957, the Chinese community became the strongest element in the economy, aside from the government itself. As the economy generally faltered under President Sukarno's leadership, the Chinese lost heavily, financially, and were subjected to harassment and occasionally expulsion, particularly in the villages and rural areas. During the bloody aftermath of the attempted political *coup* in 1965, the situation deteriorated still further for many Chinese. In many localities the purge was much more anti-Chinese than anticommunist. Untold thousands were killed. However, the economic position of strength held by the Chinese has by no means been destroyed. In part, this is due to Chinese cleverness in masking their activities behind "Ali-Baba" business fronts (*Ali* is the *asli* figurehead; *Baba* is a pejorative for Chinese). The events of the recent period of trial, however, may have convinced large numbers of Chinese that they have no choice but to strengthen their exposed position by adding substance to interethnic economic and social connections. Indeed, in the long run there appears to be no other satisfactory solution. An attempt at mass repatriation to China in 1959 indicated clearly that it could be a solution for only a very small minority of Chinese; migration elsewhere seems even less likely to be a solution for a large number. From the point of view of some leaders in the present Indonesian government, the Chinese community's entrepreneurial talent and control of resources is seen as a force to be harnessed as much as a threat. Moderates hope for some *modus vivendi* of the sort which has evolved in Malaysia or in Thailand.

Education

The policy of the colonial government toward the education of the indigenous peoples was largely permissive. A thin but excellent network of primary, secondary, and higher educational institutions was built, and although they existed primarily to educate Dutch children for eventual advancement to Dutch universities, the local population was not formally excluded. Nor was any major attempt made to encourage large numbers of indigenous Indonesians to school themselves. As a result, the nation faced independence with a severe shortage of adequately educated political leaders and bureaucrats. The new government gave education first priority and expanded the entire school system very rapidly. Their success, as measured by the decline in illiteracy, was dramatic; indeed, that success is without doubt the most encouraging aspect of Indonesia's efforts at development. However, in the haste to expand education, little thought was given to appropriate design of the education system, and the present set of institutions is largely an obsolete version of the system built by the Dutch for their own children. Little has been done to raise the level of technical expertise of the Indonesian worker and farmer; and far too many secondary school and university graduates are suited only for white collar employment by government and business. This is a common story in low-income countries, particularly those which have had a long colonial history.

The Size and Structure of the Economy

There are no satisfactory data on the size of the Indonesian economy. Since independence, little work in depth has been done on the national income accounts, and excessive faith has had to be put in estimates done largely by foreign advisers on relatively short-term assignments. The first of these was the work of S. D. Neumark, published in 1954.[11] Since then, Muljatno and Baran-

[11] Biro Perantjang Negara, *The National Income of Indonesia, 1951–52,* Djakarta, 1954.

ski have attempted extensions of the Neumark estimates.[12] and Pillai has undertaken a more fundamental attempt at construction of a set of national income accounts.[13] Most recent estimates are extrapolations of the Pillai data, which were computed for 1958–1962. These extrapolations have been badly hampered by the severe budgetary constraints which have been placed, until quite recently, upon the Central Bureau of Statistics and by the virtual meaninglessness to which all value data were reduced by the hyper-inflation. Thus any estimate made in the past four or five years is little better than a guess, and not surprisingly the range has been wide—from $6.0 billion for the year 1968, in an unofficial Planning Council paper, to $11.8 billion for the same year by a U.S. government agency. At all events, per capita income in Indonesia, measured in U.S. dollars, is probably not higher than $100, and in the estimation of most observers it is less than that.

Not surprisingly, there has been little growth of national product over the last decade, apparently not quite enough to maintain per capita real incomes (Table 1).

Table 1. Index of per capita national product, at constant prices, 1959–1967

Year	Index (1958 = 100)
1959	98.2
1960	96.7
1961	98.4
1962	95.7
1963	93.1
1964	95.3
1965	95.8
1966	96.4
1967	98.6

Source: Nugroho, *Indonesia Facts and Figures*, Djakarta, 1967, Table 8.3, p. 540.

The nadir was reached in 1963, and there has been a slow but steady recovery since that year. Preliminary indications are that

[12] Muljatno Sindudharmoko, "Persoalan Pendapatan Nasional di Indonesia," *Ekonomi dan Keuangan Indonesia* (*EKI*), vol. 10, no. 8, August 1957, pp. 527–542.

[13] K. N. C. Pillai, *National Income of Indonesia, 1958–1962,* Central Bureau of Statistics, Djakarta, 1965.

1968 was a substantially better year than 1967, primarily due to improvement in agriculture;[14] hence for the first time per capita national product has probably gone above that of the 1950's in the decade of the 1960's.

Stagnation in overall production has been matched by lack of progress in the process of transformation. The structure of the economy in terms of composition of output has been virtually static since 1958. And, insofar as growth of the manufacturing sector relative to agriculture is a measure of success, there appears to have been gradual retrogression, as is shown in Table 2.

Table 2. Percentage distribution of national product by industrial origin, at 1960 prices, 1958–1964

Item	1958	1959	1960	1961	1962	1963	1964
Agriculture	50.5	52.2	52.4	50.2	53.5	51.4	51.5
Mining and quarrying	2.5	2.8	3.1	3.0	3.2	3.3	3.3
Manufacturing	13.2	12.6	12.3	12.9	12.7	12.5	12.0
Construction	1.8	1.8	1.8	1.8	1.8	1.9	1.8
Electricity and gas	0.2	0.2	0.2	0.2	0.2	0.3	0.3
Transport and communication	3.0	3.2	3.4	3.3	3.4	3.5	3.3
Wholesale and retail trade	14.9	14.5	15.2	16.8	15.5	16.9	17.3
Banking and other financial intermediaries	0.7	0.8	0.8	1.0	0.8	0.7	0.8
Ownership of dwellings	1.9	1.9	1.9	1.9	2.0	2.0	2.0
Public administration and defense	6.6	5.3	4.1	4.4	2.2	2.8	3.0
Services	5.5	5.6	5.6	5.5	5.8	5.8	5.7
Net domestic product	100.8	100.9	100.8	101.0	101.1	101.1	101.0
Net investment income	−0.8	−0.9	−0.8	−1.0	−1.1	−1.1	−1.0
Net national product	100.0	100.0	100.0	100.0	100.0	100.0	100.0

Source: Nugroho, *op. cit.*, Table 8.5, p. 542.

More recent data on occupational distribution than those given in Table 3 are not available to the editor, but one can infer from the output shares that no radical change is taking place. With less

[14] "Far Eastern Roundup," *The Far Eastern Economic Review,* October 31, 1968, cites the authorities of the International Monetary Fund as reporting "a great improvement" economically. Also the same periodical, dated September 26, gives a preliminary estimate for 1968 rice production by the ministry of agriculture of 10.6 million tons—360,000 tons above the 1968 target.

than 30 percent of the total employed population engaged in non-agricultural pursuits, Indonesia presents the classic picture of the underdeveloped economy. Given rapid rural-urban migration, it is evident that urban unemployment must be increasing with alarming speed. As early as 1961, the urban rate of unemployment

Table 3. Percentage distribution of employed persons ten years and older, by industry, 1961

Sector	Percent
Agriculture, forestry, and fishing	71.9
Mining and quarrying	0.3
Manufacturing	5.7
Construction	1.8
Utilities	0.1
Trade, banking, and insurance	6.7
Transport, storage, and communication	2.1
Services	9.5
Others (residual)	1.9

Source: Nugroho, *op. cit.*, Table 2.64, p. 111.

was reported as being 8.5 percent (vs. 4.9 percent in the rural sector). The overall rate of unemployment was reported as being 5.4 percent.[15] As indicated in the editor's article "Indonesian Economic Policy after Sukarno" (below, Chapter 13), the challenge of labor absorption in the economy is staggering. Not only is the labor force growing at a very rapid rate (the natural rate of population growth is a good first approximation), but also a large idle pool existed from the start (estimated as being 2.16 million in 1966). The magnitude of the unused labor pool is only roughly indicated by the data on overt unemployment, however. There is also a large and growing reservoir of disguised unemployment of which we have no estimates to any degree of statistical significance. The rough figure which has been adopted by Indonesian government officials, however, is 20 percent of the total labor force. The unemployment problem is worst among the young members of the labor force. The urban unemployment rate in the 15–19 age group

[15] Nugroho, *Indonesia Facts and Figures,* Djakarta, 1967, Table 2.59, p. 106.

was reported in the 1961 census to be 25.3 percent, and evidence indicates that there has been a considerable increase in that figure since that time. For the near future it is impossible to expect that economic growth will absorb all of the new entrants to the urban labor force. The best that may be hoped for is a reduction of the rate of its increase.

International Trade

As a colony, Indonesia was pre-eminently an exporting economy. In 1925, for example, the value of exports was 36 percent of domestic product.[16] Since the mid-1950's, however, exports have generally not amounted to as much as 10 percent of gross domestic product, perhaps falling as low as 5 percent. The bulk of this decline has been in smallholders' production of exportable agricultural commodities. Plantation exports have also declined relative to total production, but less seriously. Some indication of the severity of the decline in the postwar years may be seen in the dollar value of exports. At the height of the Korean War boom, Indonesia exported nearly $1.30 billion worth of goods. By 1962, this had dwindled to $664 million. Imports have declined also, but to a lesser degree, and quite erratically. Accordingly, the balance of payments has fluctuated widely, with the largest deficit ($521 million) having been reached in 1961. In the 1960's, large deficits have become normal, external indebtedness has mounted alarmingly, and the foreign exchange reserve has virtually disappeared (in March 1967, the reserve had fallen to $17 million). In 1967, the nation's total scheduled debt payments for the period 1967–1984 were $2.42 billion, or nearly three years' total export earnings. Rescheduling of the debt is a clear necessity and is being accomplished incrementally; new schedules have been drawn up by international agreements for three successive years.

In recent years, rubber and oil have produced approximately 70 percent of total export earnings, and while petroleum production and earnings have mounted steadily, rubber earnings have fallen despite increases in volume of exports by weight. Thus Indonesia has suffered seriously for her failure to diversify her

[16] Paauw, *op. cit.*, p. 182.

pattern of exports. Tin, which never recovered from the damage done to the mines during World War II, and which accounts for about 6 percent of the value of exports, has considerable potential for expansion. No other individual item accounts for as much as 5 percent of the total earnings.

The state of world markets has had something to do with the problem in which Indonesia finds herself in international trading, but it is likely that misguided economic policy is at least as significant. The heart of this problem has been the maintenance of official exchange rates which were grossly unrealistic, undervaluing foreign exchange so seriously that domestic producers of exportable commodities were forced to divert resources to other activity, or to export illegally. There is a good deal of indirect evidence that both lines of escape have been taken. The Suharto government has virtually abandoned pegged pricing of foreign exchange in the hope that rationalized prices will lead to a production response and to an increase of legal versus illegal exports.[17] Such responses take time, however, and, because of data lags, it is not yet known how effective these measures can be. At all events they are permissive measures.

Indonesia's economic problems are vast, and her means for dealing with them are modest. Whether or not a nation so beset can generate a satisfactory upward trend of economic growth remains to be seen. A study of the articles compiled in this volume will give the interested reader a basis for judgment in this matter.

[17] See the editor's "Pricing of Foreign Exchange in Indonesia, 1966–1967," Chapter 12, below.

CHAPTER 1

The Indonesian Economy, 1950–1963*

J. A. C. MACKIE

The economy of independent Indonesia has contrasted strikingly with that of the colonial era, particularly, of course, since the nationalisation of Dutch businesses in 1957–1958 and the severe inflation which has developed since that time. To describe these changes is relatively easy, to explain them far less so, for they are the outcome of a complex series of processes. The aim of this article will be to depict the main outlines of the economic scene rather than to analyse the details. But I will attempt to draw together illuminating figures and statistical series where they are obtainable in order to dispel the idea that we can only make broad generalisations, without much quantification, about an economy in such turmoil as Indonesia's. A greater sense of proportion can be maintained by a judicious use of the statistics which are still available to us.

The colonial economy was characterised by extremely low wages and costs; by high efficiency in the plantation sector and heavy investments (mainly Dutch-owned) in mining and tertiary activities, such as trading services and communications; and above all by a stable currency system and a remarkable ability to adjust to changes in world market conditions.[1] Since 1950, the situation

* Reprinted from Dietmar Rothermund, ed., *Studien zur Entwicklung in Sud und Ostasien,* Neue Folge, Teil 3 (Indonesien), Metzner, Frankfurt, 1964; by permission of the author and publisher.

[1] These features of the colonial economy are well illustrated in G. C. Allen and Audrey Donnithorne, *Western Enterprise in Indonesia and Malaya,*

has been tragically reversed in each of these respects. A major factor responsible for the change has been the perennial inflation, generated largely by political pressures associated with the so-called "revolution of rising expectations." Without doubt, aspirations towards the fruits of independence have frequently exceeded the abilities and resources available to achieve them. Many of Indonesia's recent difficulties can be attributed in large part to elementary technical or administrative shortcomings. But behind the superficial disorganisation there are also more basic structural problems and political complications.

Some of these problems were becoming critical even in colonial times. The most serious of them arose from the threat of over-population, especially on Java where the population has increased from about nine to sixty-three million in little over a century.[2] (Indonesia's total population numbered ninety-seven million at the 1961 census; the rate of growth is about 2.2 percent per annum.) There were three possible solutions: transmigration of surplus rural population to the less developed outer islands, raising agricultural productivity through extension services to peasants, and, most appealing to modernising nationalists, industrialisation. (A fourth solution, birth control, has received almost no attention whatever in Indonesia.) None offered a single way out or an easy one, for all required large amounts of capital which could not be raised within Java itself. Hence the basic political

---

Allen and Unwin, London, 1957. The only good accounts of resource development in recent years, apart from the annual Bank Indonesia Reports (Bank Indonesia, *Report of the Governor,* Djakarta. Cited hereafter as *Bank Indonesia Report*) which were invaluable during the years 1950–1960 until they ceased publication, are the chapters by Karl J. Pelzer and Douglas S. Paauw, referred to below, in Ruth McVey, ed., *Indonesia,* Human Relations Area Files, New Haven, 1963.

[2] The population problem is analysed on the basis of the 1961 census figures by Pelzer, "Physical and Human Resource Patterns," in McVey, *op. cit.,* pp. 13–23. A clear formulation of the population problem which has lost none of its relevance with the passage of time was given by H. de Meel, "Demographic Dilemma in Indonesia," *Pacific Affairs,* vol. 24, 1951. For an informed Indonesian view of the problem, with an interesting argument on the question of birth control, see Mohammad Sadli, "Indonesia's 100 Millions," *Far Eastern Economic Review,* April 4, 1963, pp. 21–23.

problem of independent Indonesia is this problem of acute unbalance arising out of the uneven rate of economic development in the past; Java had experienced nearly 150 years of intensive Dutch rule and investment by the time independence came, the outer islands (apart from a few enclaves), barely fifty. Java's agricultural land had been almost fully occupied by 1900, when its population was less than thirty million; the Dutch were aware of the problem of "diminishing welfare" even before the end of the nineteenth century. Today, although Java is more intensively endowed with overhead capital investment in the shape of communications facilities, electric power, towns and schools, per capita incomes there are generally lower than in the other islands, and it is a net importer, whereas most of them are net exporters. Elsewhere, intensive economic development, with its consequent "population explosion," goes back only 60 to 100 years and is today continuing with better prospects. Large areas of Sumatra, Borneo, and the eastern islands have not yet been opened up (although much of this land is not suitable for intensive agriculture and certainly cannot sustain high population densities such as Java's, which often exceed 800 and sometimes reach 2,000 per square kilometre), despite local overpopulation in relation to resources in some parts.[3] This unbalance gives rise to severe political tensions over the creation and distribution of financial resources for government-sponsored development; the absence of a clearly defined political solution has, moreover, obstructed economic progress in recent years. Yet there is no prospect of a solution to the population problem until substantial economic development has been achieved in both Java and the other islands.

Indonesia's changing position in the international trading system since the war has created another set of problems for her. After the disruption of depression, war, and revolution, there was little chance that she would recover the markets for some of her former staple exports (i.e., sugar, tobacco, coffee), while other products could only have been restored to their old levels by dint

[3] Pelzer, *loc. cit.* The most striking case of local overpopulation outside Java, in the Toba highlands of North Sumatra, is admirably described in Clark Cunningham, *The Postwar Migration of the Toba-Bataks to East Sumatra,* Southeast Asia Studies, Yale University, New Haven, 1958.

of substantial new investment, especially on estates. That soon proved to be out of the question for various political reasons. Only in rubber and oil was there a major increase in exports, but both these were rather special cases for reasons to be outlined later. Consequently, Indonesia's economic strength as a major source of supply for various raw materials has deteriorated during the 1950's, while other nations have established themselves in world markets as competitors.[4] To some extent, this was inevitable in view of changing world trade patterns, or could only have been prevented by vigorous and successful adjustments; but much of the loss could have been avoided if strong governments had followed different policies. More seriously, no new source of export earnings has been developed at all. Despite the common belief that Indonesia is lavishly endowed with natural resources, she has lost many of the natural advantages she had over her competitors in the prewar era of low costs and high efficiency. During the years 1950–1955, reasonable progress was being made in restoring output of most export products (and of foodstuffs) after the wartime damage. The economy was expanding at a low but steady rate of growth despite constant pressures towards inflation, while standards of living were widely felt to be higher than before the war.[5] After 1957, however, many things began to go wrong, first because of more rapid inflation (aggravated by the regional political crisis of 1956–1958), then because of the setbacks resulting from the seizure of Dutch plantations and businesses in 1958, and between 1959 and 1963 because of the cumulative disruptions to which the economy was subjected as the government struggled to maintain it on an even keel by means of a desperate series of temporary expedients.

[4] No comprehensive study has been made of recent changes in Indonesia's place in world commodity markets, although some scattered suggestions are contained in Allen and Donnithorne, *op. cit.,* Chaps. 3–7, 14, covering the years up to 1953 only. The deflection of trade from the Netherlands and the attempt to bypass Singapore would merit closer study.

[5] Paauw, "From Colonial to Guided Economy," in McVey, *op. cit.,* pp. 202–203, assesses per capita consumption levels since independence; Paauw discusses the statistical basis of the output estimates in the preceding section, pp. 189–200, and accepts estimates of the average rate of growth at somewhere around 5.1–5.5 percent per annum prior to 1958.

Great differences between the periods before 1957 and since are clearly apparent in any study of Indonesia's postwar economy, yet there is much continuity between the two. Our general picture of the productive sector in recent years must be based largely on an extrapolation of trends for the earlier period, for which our information is better and the pattern of change clearer. Nationalisation of Dutch enterprises from December 1957, constituted a revolutionary move from the legal and political viewpoints, but its economic consequences have only gradually become apparent. Until then, independence had not fundamentally changed the status of Dutch capital, except insofar as its profitability and future prospects were declining. Foreign enterprise was still widely regarded as the key to maintenance of export earnings and to new investment in plantation agriculture, oil, or industry, which had been one of the remarkable features of Dutch colonial rule. Governments and politicians were generally unsympathetic to the needs of foreign enterprises, but all governments down to 1957 tacitly accepted the need for them; public utterances against foreign capital were much milder than the policies actually pursued. The turbulent "take-overs" of 1957 (almost certainly not intended by the government in the form they took) meant, however, that there was no going back to a "liberal" economy. Private foreign capital was not likely to be invested in Indonesia after that.[6] And for various reasons of domestic politics, pressures towards a more thoroughly "socialist" reordering of the economy now began to prevail under President Sukarno's slogans of a "Guided Economy" and "Socialisme à la Indonesia."

Many of the economic troubles of the last five years have been due to the mistakes, oversimplifications, and excessive enthusiasms associated with this program and its complete rejection of anything that smacks of "free-fight liberalism" and capitalism. We will return to these in due course. But few basic structural changes

[6] A small amount of private foreign capital has been invested since 1958 in oil and other mineral exploitation projects and some "production-sharing" projects in industry; but none appears to have gone into agricultural investment, to which earlier-draft foreign-investment bills had assumed a significant inflow. Foreign credits on a government-to-government basis had been preferred by President Sukarno.

in the economic pattern have yet occurred. In most important respects, economic life continues as it did and, to describe it, we may best start with a general account of the major spheres of production.

The Production Record

Probably about 85 percent of Indonesia's 100 million people live in Indonesia's 48,000 rural villages or in towns of less than 10,000 persons.[7] Agriculture is their mainstay, although not all villagers own land or participate in the cultivation. Overpopulation has driven many to seek a livelihood from any available source—petty commerce, minor carrying services, tilemaking, building, handcrafts, etc. In some areas, as much as half the population is landless, while even the majority of landowning families may own less than a quarter hectare of *sawah* (wet-rice land).[8] Consequently, many peasants must have a secondary occupation, and it is almost impossible to trace a clear division of occupations within the villages or even between many of the villagers and the townsmen.

According to an estimate of Indonesia's gross national product made in 1952, agriculture made up slightly more than half the total figure of Rp. 81.6 billion at 1952 prices." [9] Peasant food

[7] The 1961 census reveals that nearly 10 percent of the total population lived in cities of over 100,000 inhabitants. I have not been able to make a calculation of the total in the medium-sized towns, but a rough calculation made in 1956, with very tentative criteria of what might be considered a "town," gave a figure slightly below 15 percent for the undeniably "urban" population. This may be a trifle low, but the increase in size of small towns appears not to have been as rapid as that of the major cities.

[8] Pelzer, "The Agricultural Foundation," in McVey, *op. cit.,* p. 126, reprinted as Chapter 4, below. For a case study of a thickly populated Central Javanese village see Widjojo Nitisastro, ed., "Some Data on the Population of Djabres, A Village in Central Java," *Ekonomi dan Keuangan Indonesia* (*EKI*), vol. 9, no. 12, December 1956.

[9] The basic postwar calculation of Indonesia's national income for 1951 and 1952 was made by Daniel Neumark in his article "The National Income of Indonesia, 1951–52," *EKI,* vol. 7, no. 6, May 1954, pp. 348–391. Revisions and later projections of the Neumark estimates have been made by Muljatno of the State Planning Bureau, the 1953–1954 figures being published in *EKI,* vol. 13, 1960 (in Indonesian). Attempts to convert these rupiah aggregates

crops were estimated at 37 percent of the total (Rp. 30 billion), peasant cash crops at 9 percent (Rp. 7.6 billion), livestock, fisheries, and forestry at about 8.5 percent, while plantation crops were assessed at about 3 percent. The figures are necessarily conjectural and provide a very slippery basis for inferences about the proportion of national income which goes to the "rural" sector as against the urban. Prima facie they suggest a distribution of national income that is unfavorable to the rural sector, insofar as it is justifiable to infer that nearly 40 percent of the national income is being earned in the nonrural sector, i.e., by about 15 percent of the population living in towns; there is ample corroborating evidence for this, despite scattered signs of higher consumption levels in the villages than before the war. On the other hand, direct taxation of peasants has been much lower than in colonial times. An overvalued exchange rate has been equivalent to a tax on export produce and so falls heavily on peasants of some areas, particularly in the outer islands. But there are too many variations from one region to another, and between social groups in single villages, to permit firm generalisations about a "rural" or "nonmonetised" sector in Indonesia. We have no statistical data on degrees of monetisation. Only about 20 percent of rice production is thought to enter the market, which implies greater home consumption of the major foodstuff than is found in India. On the other hand, products which are sold on the commercial market are produced over a very wide geographical area, and one would expect a higher proportion of peasants to receive part of their income in cash than in India.[10]

The rural villages have been partly cushioned against the adverse effects of inflation over recent years by a rise in rice prices at a rate roughly approximating the general rise in prices. Hence

---

into terms of dollars or other currencies can be misleading, since the rates of exchange vary for different transactions and over time.

[10] For some suggestive observations about the degree of monetisation in India, see Wilfred Malenbaum, *Prospects for Indian Development,* Free Press of Glencoe, New York, 1962, pp. 137–147. The estimate of rice entering the market in Indonesia is given in Leon A. Mears, *Rice Marketing in the Republic of Indonesia,* Pembangunan, Djakarta, 1961, p. 4, which contains much useful material about the rice economy.

it is often asserted that Indonesia has been able to withstand the damaging effects of inflation better than a more highly monetised economy would have by turning in on this vast "self-sufficient" sector. There may be a grain of truth in this, but some fallacious conclusions are sometimes drawn about the burden of inflation on peasants as compared with urban wage-earners on relatively fixed incomes. We do not have enough clear evidence to justify a broad assertion that the former have suffered less than the latter, since the distribution of wealth between poor and relatively rich has been a crucial (but unknown) factor in each case. It is significant that there is no evidence of a flowback of population from the overcrowded towns to the villages, as there was in the Depression. The drift is still towards the towns and diversified opportunities. One suspects that inflation is having a regressive redistributive effect in both sectors: wealthier peasants are better able to buy up lands of failing marginal producers and to benefit by selling their surplus rice at a high price, while poor peasants actually have to buy foods; wealthy town merchants and officials gain windfall profits from their control over scarce import goods, while the urban poor become impoverished. We simply do not know how far the processes of impoverishment and enrichment have gone in either sector.

Investment generated within the village economy is another subject about which only rough guesses can be made. Many observers have formed the impression that Indonesian peasants have a readier propensity than Indian peasants to introduce new methods or crops, to expand their production, and to undertake village community development projects.[11] In 1955, the authors of the Five Year Plan guessed that small-scale improvements of village facilities through village labour could amount to Rp. 1.5 billion

[11] This impression was reported to me by Indian advisers on community development attached to the State Planning Bureau in Djakarta in 1956. Comparing my own impressions of Indonesia with Kusum Nair's admirable report on rural development prospects in India (*Blossoms in the Dust,* Duckworth, London, 1961), I would infer that, although there is too much diversity in both countries to permit safe generalisations, the propensity to introduce more rewarding techniques would generally be stronger in Indonesia. But we need a Kusum Nair to document this.

per annum. In the years to which their calculations referred, food production had certainly been increasing slightly from the war-time low to about the 1940 levels in 1954. A period of stagnation in production followed until the end of the decade, although there are signs that the rice harvest has begun to increase again recently with some stimulus from a government campaign to encourage the use of fertiliser. One gets the impression that small-scale rural investment has also dwindled in recent years, and certainly been counterbalanced by tragic disinvestment due to floods, erosion, and deterioration of irrigation systems, without any compensating large-scale improvements. The Community Development Program introduced in 1956 is almost forgotten. It is quite likely that the inflation and disturbances of recent years have directed the attention of enterprising peasants towards buying up land or other tangible assets, rather than towards the risks of agricultural experiment and improvement. Yet one is constantly coming across instances of peasant initiative on a small scale in many parts of Indonesia (individual more often than cooperative), and one should not be tempted to think of the rural sector as inert and changeless. In appropriate circumstances, dramatic improvements could still be expected through the flowering of peasant aspirations towards a better life.

Because Indonesia's population has been increasing faster than her production of foodstuffs and exports during the past two decades, it is frequently assumed that consumption levels and standards of living must have declined. Indonesians generally deny this, however, or, at least, they did before the inflation became acute in 1961–1962. To illustrate that they have been better off since independence than they were under the colonial regime (materially, as well as spiritually) they point to demonstrable rises in the domestic consumption of sugar, tea, and coffee; to more widespread consumption of the most favoured cereal, rice; and, to greater availability of bicycles, radios, and similar goods in the villages, not to mention more schools, more books, relatively cheaper transportation, lower direct taxes, and the many psychological accompaniments of independence. How even the distribution of these benefits has been is another matter. We simply do not know how the living standards of the landless peasants or the kampong dwellers of the big towns compare with colonial times; we do know that there are vastly more people in both categories for reasons which are only partly the fault of recent Indonesian governments. It may well be the case that substantial improvements in living standards have been enjoyed by relatively small groups, while a much larger segment of society has imperceptibly experienced some decline; but it would be difficult to assess this in quantitative terms and certainly misleading to infer from it that only a small urban elite has had any benefit from the fruits of independence.

Consumption has also taken a perceptibly higher portion of the national income than in colonial times, while investment and depreciation provisions have declined to a tragic degree. The proportion of national income channelled into new investments and profit remittances out of Indonesia was frequently very high in colonial times, although exact figures are again hard to obtain.[12] Since independence, profit remittances have received only a tiny fraction of available foreign exchange, while new investment has been confined virtually to the oil companies and, with less productive effect, the government. Disinvestment, through failure to provide against depreciation, has been allowed to go to alarming lengths.

To give a more precise picture of changes in the gross national product in Indonesia, some of its major components and the production trends within each will now be described. The statistics available can generally be taken as fairly reliable, although, with some margin of error in the case of peasant crops, it is unwise to draw any elaborate inferences from them without corroboration. Only a few of the most important export commodities will be discussed, although Indonesia produces an impressive range of

[12] J. J. Polak, *The National Income of the Netherlands Indies, 1921–39*, Institute of Pacific Relations, New York, 1942, p. 65, gives figures of dividend remittances to the Netherlands and capital inflow for new long-term investments; but these included two boom-and-slump periods which are not necessarily typical of the earlier period of heavy Dutch investment in the colony. In any case, the figures could not be converted into a ratio of profit and capital formation into national income, unless more was known about distribution of aggregate income within the colony.

other exotic products from pepper, spices, tapioca, and sago to bauxite, coal, and jungle products. The value of these is relatively small, however, and their relevance to the immediate problems of restoring export income insignificant in comparison with Indonesia's traditional sources of wealth, on the basis of which the colonial economy was developed.

Rice and Other Foodstuffs

Rice production rose considerably in the early years after independence, with a 30 percent increase between 1950 and 1954. Some of this was due to the conversion of former sugar-growing lands to rice, some also to further increase in double-cropping, which has been increasing throughout this century; however, it is generally accepted that the limits to this have been reached. Between 1954 and 1957, rice production declined slightly on the main islands of Java and Madura; on the other islands some increase in area cultivated took place, but not sufficient to compensate. There has been a slight improvement since 1958, but there seems to be no doubt that population increase must be outstripping food production. Imports have been stepped up sharply to over 600,000 tons per annum since 1956 (and 962,000 in 1960). Other foodstuffs such as maize, cassava, and sago have shown minor increases in output, but they are not important enough to modify the general picture, although in some areas they are major subsidiary crops or even, towards eastern Indonesia, the staple foods. Rice is said to be more widely consumed than before independence, however, and is almost universally the preferred food. Flour is imported mainly for urban consumption. For 1961 and 1962, rice production has been given as 8,350 and 9,200 thousand metric tons, and imports mentioned at about one million tons in both years (slightly more in 1961).[13]

Rice-yields range around twenty quintals per hectare in most of

[13] Mears, *op. cit.*, p. 213; Central Bureau of Statistics, *Statistik 1956*, Djakarta, p. 113; Central Bureau of Statistics, *Statistical Pocketbook of Indonesia, 1961*, Djakarta, pp. 53, 116; Pelzer, "The Agricultural Foundation," in McVey, *op. cit.*, p. 131; and Economist Intelligence Unit, *Three Monthly Economic Review*, Indonesia, May 1963, p. 4. A table headed "Rice Production and Imports, 1951–1962," which appeared in the original article has been deleted.—Ed.

Indonesia's main producing areas, except Bali which has distinctly higher yields.[14] These yields are about the same as those of other Asian countries, excluding Japan where they are twice as high. But they certainly could be substantially higher if peasants used more fertiliser; at present only a handful do so, and fertiliser imports go mainly to the estates. In 1961, the government promoted an intensive "Rice Self-sufficiency" campaign by establishing a series of "paddy centres" which would provide loans for fertiliser (which was to be specially distributed to the centres), better seed, and credit to combat the *idjon* (crop-mortgaging) system. That particular campaign was unsuccessful, owing to a disastrous drought during the planting season and widespread misappropriation of funds at the local level. Even so, production rose in 1962, and there is no insuperable reason why the objective of self-sufficiency should not be reached, provided the economy offers the appropriate stimuli and services to the producers.

Government policy on rice-purchasing has been one factor in the way of increased production, since the price offered has generally been below market prices, and indirect pressure has had to be applied to ensure a supply.[15] Only about 10 percent of the harvest is purchased by the government. The original purpose of government-purchasing (before 1950) was to guarantee minimum purchase prices to the peasant and maximum retail prices to the consumers; it began before the war when rice-milling capacity was expanding rapidly and millers were applying heavy financial pressure on peasants to ensure supplies from them, but with wartime shortages the government gave more stress to maintaining a reserve of rice for emergency distributions. The political necessity for the latter has become more and more important in recent years, while the aim of ensuring a fair minimum price to peasants to safeguard them from the price fluctuations, which speculative purchasers are better able to exploit, has had to fall into second place because of inadequate revenues to constitute a

[14] Mears, *op. cit.*, pp. 217–228.

[15] *Ibid.*, pp. 18–25, 428–435, relates the history of government rice-purchasing policy. A more recent study is contained in Sadli, Ismael, and Kardiat, *Pembelian Padi Pemerintah, 1961,* Lembaga Penjelidikan Ekonomi dan Masjarakat, Universitas Indonesia, 1961.

subsidy. Peasants will willingly offer rice to the government purchasing agents at the low government price only at moments when market prices are as low, so they are getting less and less protection from speculative purchasers. In fact, it has even become difficult for the government to ensure its essential needs for emergencies (except through imports, largely through surplus rice from the U.S.A.) without applying pressure on the farmers. This, in turn, can only have a disincentive effect on production in the long run, unless a market price is paid.

Rubber

Since the introduction of *hevea braziliensis* in the first decade of this century, rubber has boomed in Indonesia to replace the old staples, coffee and sugar, as the main source of the country's export earnings. Although production had to be restricted owing to world market saturation in the two prewar decades, demand for rubber has been buoyant since 1950 (apart from a slight recession after the Korean boom), and Indonesian production has been spectacularly higher than before the war.

However, a declining trend has definitely been discernible in the last few years, and there are sadly few signs of immediate improvement. Indonesia has been surpassed, as the world's greatest producer of rubber, by Malaya, whose extensive and efficient replantings of high-yielding stocks on peasants' smallholdings, as well as estates, stand out in sharp contrast with the old and badly maintained trees of Indonesia's smallholders and with the low rate of replanting on her estates. The distinction between the estate sector and smallholdings, both in size of units and type of legal tenure, is very clearly marked in Indonesia in contrast with Malaya, where there is a gradual spread from smallholdings through small estates to huge units. Until very recently, there were few small estates in the 50–500 acre range in Indonesia, hence almost no possibility for a wealthy smallholder to rise up the ladder of estate ownership (Table 1.1).

Smallholders' Rubber

Over 25 percent of Indonesia's foreign exchange earnings has come from smallholders' rubber in the postwar years, more by value than from estate rubber (despite its much lower quality and price) and far more by volume. This is the only sector of the economy, other than the rather special case of the oil industry, where a substantial increase over prewar production has occurred.

Table 1.1. Exports of rubber

	Smallholder		Estate	
Year	Metric tons (thousands)	Rupiahs (billions)	Metric tons (thousands)	Rupiahs (billions)
1938	146		157	
1951	579	1.7	214	0.8
1952	477	2.5	312	2.3
1953	395	1.2	315	1.6
1954	496	1.9	265	1.2
1955	477	3.0	262	2.0
1956	429	2.4	260	1.8
1957	418	2.3	261	1.7
1958	377	1.7	223	1.2
1959	485	3.1	233	1.6
1960	388	2.7	190	1.5

Source: Compiled from Central Bureau of Statistics, *Statistik Konjunktur*, Djakarta, Table C.8, *passim* (monthly series).

The following figures for 1961 and 1962 are informative but not directly comparable; *International Financial Statistics*, September 1963, pp. 148–149, gives an index for volume of rubber exports at 112 and 114 for the two years on a base year (100) of 1958. The values of estate rubber exports were $122 million and $102 million, of smallholder rubber exports $183 million and $197 million, both categories well below the levels of 1959 and 1960.

Note: (1) Rupiah value in the table above has been expressed at the 1952–1959 rate of Rp. 11.4 per $U.S. (2) Smuggled rubber would not be included in these figures, but underdeclared rubber would be, although at a low assessment of value. Although estimates of the loss through smuggling and underdeclaration have often been given as 10 percent of total earnings from rubber, I am sceptical whether the loss has constantly been so high. (3) About 1 or 2 percent of total production is consumed in domestic industries (mainly by a few tyre factories).

Unfortunately, however, the increase is mainly attributable to the abnormally depressed market for rubber before the war and to high postwar prices. Little of it is due to postwar planting or new-found enterprise. On the contrary, experts have been afraid for some years now that Indonesian smallholders' production must soon collapse. Over wide areas the trees are old and badly maintained. Methods of tapping and processing (into blankets or crepe rubber rather than the more desirable smoked sheets) are crude and wasteful. Peasants are inclined towards 'slaughter-tapping' when prices are high, and to neglect the trees at other times when their labour is more profitably disposed elsewhere (with adverse effects on the yield and, supposedly, the life of the tree).[16]

The age of rubber trees in this sector is probably the major unknown factor responsible for this paradox. Most are believed to be about or above forty years old, which is usually quoted as the maximum productive life of a tree. But both propositions are questionable. It is known that large areas of rubber were planted by smallholders in three periods of high prices: 1910–1912, 1915, and 1924–1927. It is commonly said that little has been planted since then, but some observers believe that peasants may have taken the initiative of planting high-yielding stock during the past twenty years on a wider scale than we have realised. Government measures to promote replanting have not been successful (as they have in Malaya). But the whole question is still most obscure.

Smallholders' rubber is grown mainly in the Djambi and Palembang areas, also in Tapanuli and Kalimantan (west and south), but hardly at all in Java or the copra-growing islands of the east. Little of it is consumed domestically. Most of it is shipped to Singapore, where the poorer grades are remilled before re-export. An attempt to promote remilling within Indonesia failed, although the technical requirements are not complex. The nature of the collecting and export trade, predominantly in the hands of local Chinese, makes smallholder rubber one of the easiest products (along with copra) to smuggle out to Singapore or Malaya, where it is sold at a more advantageous rate of exchange. The volume of smuggled rubber (including some from estates also)

[16] K. D. Thomas, *Smallholders' Rubber in Indonesia,* Lembaga Penjelidikan Ekonomi dan Masjarakat, Universitas Indonesia, 1961, gives the fullest information on these problems.

has never been satisfactorily estimated, but it is probably not as great as reports often suggest.

Estate Rubber

There were 716 separate rubber plantations in production in 1956, covering approximately 586,000 hectares.[17] Only seventy-nine of these (generally small ones) were owned by Indonesians; most were Dutch, British, or American. The major rubber estate area lay south of Medan on the east coast region of Sumatra, while in the hilly regions of Java, a few less productive estates were scattered. Since 1957, the Dutch estates have been run by a government corporation known as PPN (Government Estates Central) which now controls approximately half the area of plantation rubber in Indonesia.

Since the initial Korean boom and recovery period of expansion in rubber plantation output from 1950 to 1953, estate production has showed a persistent tendency to fall. Various factors have played a part in this, many of them afflicting most other forms of plantation enterprise as well.[18]

a) The ageing of trees and low rates of replanting before about 1958 have been most important. Rubber trees are considered exhausted after forty years, and their yields fall off after twenty-five, but most estate planting in Indonesia had been done before 1930 and by the mid-1950's; it was not uncommon for a company to have 60 percent of its trees over thirty years old.[19] The Depression and war-revolutionary years had checked replanting, and after independence most foreign companies were waiting for assurances about the length of future tenure to be allowed them before they

[17] *Statistical Pocketbook of Indonesia, 1961,* p. 64. Estate rubber conditions in one area are described by Dahlan Thalib, "The Estate Rubber Industry of East Sumatra," in Douglas S. Paauw, ed., *Prospects for East Sumatran Plantation Industries: A Symposium,* Southeast Asia Studies, Yale University, New Haven, 1962. Allen and Donnithorne, *op. cit.,* pp. 117–127, 134–138, deal with problems confronting foreign estates in the early 1950's, most of which still persist.

[18] Allen and Donnithorne, *op. cit.,* Chap. 3.

[19] *Ibid.,* p. 135.

undertook major, expensive replanting programs. Many leaseholds in the North Sumatra area were due to expire in the 1960's, and government statements about future leases envisaged shorter periods than the companies considered acceptable. Consequently, replanting rates were probably less than 2 percent of the total planted area during the early 1950's, although normal estate practice is to maintain a 4 percent schedule. Paradoxically, some improvement in estate replanting rates appears to have occurred towards the end of the decade; foreign companies were obliged by law to replant, and the nationalisation of Dutch estates eliminated the uncertainty over tenure there. Nevertheless, there have been disturbing signs since 1961 that government estates are not receiving adequate funds to maintain the high replanting rates they achieved around 1960.[20]

b) Insecurity of tenure was bound to inhibit estate investment and efficiency in other ways besides replanting. Research activities fell behind during the 1950's, and it was Malaya which took the lead in developing the revolutionary new high-yielding clones, although Indonesia had earlier been far ahead of Malaya in techniques and efficiency of production. Recently, she has been importing high-yielding stocks from Malaya, but these are not necessarily ideal for the very different geographical conditions in Sumatra and Java. The tenure of foreign estates was finally settled on the basis of the 1960 Agrarian Law, but on terms even less advantageous to the estates than those they were resisting five years earlier, i.e., "exploitation rights" with a maximum of twenty years future currency (and an average probably well below fifteen), but with immediate surrender of one-third of their concessions. Unless there is a sharp change in government policy within that period, it seems unlikely that foreign companies will be able to operate under such restrictive conditions.

c) Squatters on estate lands, who moved in during the war and have since proved almost impossible to eject, also constituted a

[20] For some details of replanting rates in 1960, see J. A. C. Mackie, "Indonesia's Government Estates and Their Masters," *Pacific Affairs,* vol. 34, 1961, p. 349. The optimistic impressions about these estates which I gained at the beginning of 1961 were not sustained by reports received two years later.

serious nuisance in the early 1950's. They did not upset rubber plantations as seriously as the delicate balance of nature on Medan's tobacco lands, since they generally congregate on the fringes of plantations or along small streams which are, in any case, not very suitable for rubber trees, which need well-drained soil.[21] But they aggravated the problem of illegal tapping and damage to trees, while creating a major political embarrassment to both government and estate owners. Deforestation, the silting of rivers and drainage canals, and a steadily rising water table along the low coastal lands of East Sumatra are also diminishing the value of large areas. In the foothills of East Sumatra and West Java, insecurity due to armed rebels has been a serious disturbance in limited areas, although the over-all effects of the 1958–1961 rebellion on rubber production have often been exaggerated.

d) Labour problems were a serious discouragement to foreign estates early in the 1950's, although they have been less troublesome in recent years since the right to strike on "vital" enterprises was introduced. Demands for higher wages coincided with a decline in productivity in a dramatic reversal of prewar patterns. But in recent years the plantations have had a stronger bargaining position, despite current low money wages, because they do provide a substantial real wage in food and housing (much greater in Sumatra than Java, where the labour supply is, of course, much greater). Paradoxically, Sumatran plantations have been short of regular labourers in recent years, owing to disruption of the old estate-sponsored migration schemes from Java. One new difficulty has been a decline in productivity and work discipline owing to the disincentive effects of a fixed, low wage structure which reflects the government's reluctance, as an employer of estate labour, to let its own costs rise. A recent tendency towards reliance on contract labour on government estates in Sumatra is also threatening the traditional efficiency of plantation agriculture there.[22]

e) Staff problems have made it difficult, first, for the foreign

[21] Karl J. Pelzer, "The Agrarian Conflict in East Sumatra," *Pacific Affairs,* vol. 30, 1957, pp. 151–159. See also the three case studies in Paauw, *Prospects for East Sumatran Plantation Industries.*

[22] Donald Blake, "Labour Shortage and Unemployment in North East Sumatra," *Malayan Economic Review,* vol. 7, October 1962, pp. 110–111.

companies to maintain the high prewar levels of technical competence and, recently, for the government estates to fill the gaps left by the departed Dutch. Few Indonesians had been promoted beyond the rank of *mandur* (field overseer) under the colonial regime. Even in the 1950's Dutch companies were generally reluctant to carry out Indonesianisation, still promoting very few Indonesians into the higher echelons and arguing, rather tendentiously, that few suitably qualified Indonesians were available. To curb their preference for employing Dutchmen, the government retaliated by making it difficult for them to get entry visas. This was considered a serious problem by Dutch estate owners in the early 1950's. The slow rate of Indonesianisation has left a disastrous legacy since 1958 in the paucity of Indonesians with sufficient managerial experience and technical training to be ready for the promotions to senior jobs. In the circumstances, the new managers performed quite commendably, but excessive bureaucracy and deteriorating conditions have evidently undermined their morale recently.

f) High company taxes and ever-increasing delays in the remission of profits constituted a formidable discouragement to new foreign investment from about 1953.[23] Consequently, plantations concerned themselves more with quick returns and minimising costs, rather than assuring long-term efficiency. On the other hand, if they did acquire large rupiah balances which could not be remitted abroad, it often made sense to invest them in replanting in the hope of ultimate benefit; some companies were replanting quite extensively early in the decade; others had to be forced to do so. Unfortunately it cannot be said that government ownership has reversed the trend towards disinvestment, since the government itself has been desperate to wring short-term revenues out of its plantations and has spared relatively little capital for investment. The notion that plantations are *ipso facto* very profitable underlies a commonly held belief that they can be made to yield

[23] Allen and Donnithorne, *op. cit.*, p. 135, illustrate the situation in 1954; only in 1962 were remittances of profits earned in 1958 completed for all foreign companies, although the amounts of foreign exchange required are not substantial.

very large revenues to the government—a sharp contrast with colonial assumptions.

Petroleum

This is the only sector of the economy in which substantial new investment has taken place (alongside some disinvestment as well), and a steady postwar increase of production has been maintained.[24] During the war, all of the seven oil refineries operating in 1941 were severely damaged. Immediately afterwards, the Dutch colonial government encouraged the rapid restoration of three of these which now process the bulk of Indonesia's oil: the Stanvac and Shell refineries at Palembang (South Sumatra) and the Shell refinery at Balikpapan (East Kalimantan); minor installations under government management at Pangkalan Brandan (North Sumatra) and Tjepu (East Java) do not yet handle great quantities. Crude oil has also been produced and exported in steadily increasing quantities by Caltex at Pakanbaru (Central Sumatra) since 1952. The latter was the only one of the three big foreign companies to experience such favourable fortunes in the postwar decade. The others faced an uncertain future whose outlines have only become a little clearer since their oil agreement with the government in June 1963. Shell and Stanvac negotiated in vain throughout the 1950's for new concessions (convenient to their old installations) which they needed to continue operations in Indonesia. Their prewar concessions under the old colonial Mining Law had been well worked over, and little scope remained for new development. Stanvac has been importing between 2 and 3 million tons of Middle Eastern crude oil annually to keep her Palembang refineries at capacity. Even the steadily expanding output of the new Caltex fields is expected to reach its peak in a few years. In the meantime, the company is under pressure to build a refinery, which will presumably entail the further obligation to supply the home market at artificially low prices. Hence a tug-of-war between the established companies and the government has

24 Allen and Donnithorne, *op. cit.*, pp. 174–180, describe the broad prospects of the three main companies after the war. Scattered information on later developments can be found in *Petroleum News*, ANTARA, Indonesia, 1961 (bi-weekly).

been continuing for a decade, with the government latterly negotiating concessions with various newcomers to the field on terms more favourable to itself as a means of persuading the Big Three.

Actually, the oil industry's contribution to Indonesia's foreign exchange needs is much less than gross export values would suggest. In recent years, about $80 million has been available for financing other imports after the net proceeds have been offset by the costs of imports within the oil industry, by payments for domestic consumption, and by the companies' share of the proceeds.[25]

The agreements between the government and the oil companies have been extremely complicated and secret, although conforming broadly until recently to something like the 50:50 division of profits between company and host government which has prevailed elsewhere in the oil world. Renegotiating the agreements was complicated by indecision over the new Mining Law until 1960, by political uncertainty, by the effect of inflation on company costs and the pegged prices of petrol and kerosene on the home market, and by the growing tangle of import, export, and exchange taxes which cut across the complex financial agreements signed in 1954 to replace the old "let-alone" agreements signed by the Dutch government. The government was, in any case, restrained by a parliamentary resolution of 1951 from extending any existing concessions until parliament had approved a new Mining Law. This had not been done when negotiations for a new financial agreement got under way in 1959; but, in the meantime, the oil companies had been squeezed severely by the inflation, especially the two supplying the domestic market, where prices were barely allowed to rise for fear of political repercussions. Hard bargaining ensued until June 1963. The long-awaited Mining Law of 1960 declared that no new concessions would be granted and that holders of existing concessions would be permitted to retain them for short periods only. In future, only state-owned agencies would be responsible for oil development, but these would be permitted to utilise the services of foreign com-

[25] A table, headed "Oil Production and Export," which appeared in this article as originally published, has been deleted.—Ed.

panies on a "contractor" basis; the existing companies were offered some prospect of priority of selection as contractors. But still no agreement was reached on the financial arrangements; Indonesia was pressing for a formula nearer to 60:40, while the companies were determined to ensure terms which would be proof against inflation. In 1962, Indonesia signed "contractor" agreements (allegedly on terms nearer to the 60:40 ratio) with three new American companies. Only after very stubborn negotiations, in which both sides seem to have employed "brinkmanship" to the full, was agreement finally reached in Tokyo in June 1963.[26] The financial provisions do not appear to be essentially different from those prevailing earlier, and whether they conform to a 60:40 or 50:50 division of profits is itself a highly abstruse question. The companies are to continue supplying the Indonesian market in proportion to their total production, a formula which may bear heavily on Caltex. The major innovation has been acceptance of a formula under which the refining, distributing, and marketing installations of the companies will be nationalised (and paid for in hard currency) by Indonesia over the next fifteen years.

Sugar

Until a few decades ago, the country's chief plantation commodity and main source of Java's fabulous wealth, sugar, has declined in importance so much that it produced only about 3 percent of exports during the postwar decade. In 1961, sugar even had to be imported. Today the prospects of substantially restoring earlier levels of production are discouraging, although some expansion beyond recent levels should not be impossible.[27]

The factors responsible for this decline may be listed in a rough order of magnitude.

a) The number of mills in production was sharply reduced (temporarily) by the Depression and by the damage inflicted dur-

[26] Informative accounts of the Tokyo agreements are given in the *Economist,* London, June 8, 1963, and *Three Monthly Economic Review,* July 1963, pp. 5–6.

[27] On the sugar industry, generally, see Allen and Donnithorne, *op. cit.,* Chap. 4, and Pelzer, "The Agricultural Foundation," in McVey, *op. cit.,* pp. 141–146, reprinted as Chapter 4, below.

ing the Japanese occupation (when some mills were used to grind cement) and the revolution. Although the number of mills in operation since 1950 has been roughly the same as in the prewar decade, historical accidents, and not just considerations of efficiency, have determined which have survived. The formerly rich sugar-growing area of Jogjakarta was for years without any milling facilities and had to rely on expensive transport of cane to other areas. Many mills have been inadequately supplied with spare parts, and equipment costs have risen greatly. For these and other regions, the famous efficiency of prewar times has declined sadly.

b) Yields per hectare of cane cultivation have fallen from about 160 to between 100 and 130 quintals. The proportion of "tebu rakjat" (cane grown by peasants independently of the mill and sold to a mill for processing) has risen steadily from an insignificant prewar quantity to 25 percent in 1955 and 42 percent in 1958; but the loss of efficiency from this method is considerable. In colonial times the mill manager possessed great influence over the local population and on the civil servants to ensure that the best land be planted with sugar and that labour be available at crucial periods (during the harvest campaign or the planting and weeding seasons, for example). But, significantly, they have lacked this influence since 1950, while more profitable, alternative uses of their land and labour have presented themselves to the peasant. Much higher incomes per hectare can be obtained from tobacco or rice-growing than from sugar. By 1960, the sugar mills' difficulties in renting land led the government, which now owns all the mills in Indonesia, to *enforce* sugar cultivation in regions where it was grown before the war.[28] This is most unpopular with peasants and is unlikely to solve the problem. The disastrous harvest for 1962, although largely influenced by the weather, seems to confirm this point.

c) Home consumption has increased about threefold since colonial times from about 15 percent to over 70 percent of the harvest. The domestic price has been kept low, more industries are

[28] Pelzer, *loc cit.;* Mackie, *op. cit.,* pp. 145–146. On the area under smallholder cane, see *Bank Indonesia Report* for 1959–1960, p. 170. A table presenting further detail on sugar production and export has been deleted.—Ed.

using sugar, and more people are undoubtedly consuming more sugar than they used to. Hence special problems arose in 1960 and 1962, when production was not sufficient to provide the normal domestic need for over 600,000 tons per annum.

d) International marketing prospects were gloomy in 1950 when Indonesia re-emerged on the world sugar market after the disruptions of a decade. The quota she was assigned in the International Sugar Agreement of 1950 on the basis of previous years' exports was only 350,000 tons, although special provisions were included in the agreement anticipating her recovery of her historic position as one of the world's major producers. Yet her exports have never since reached even the quota set. Just as the long-term threat of synthetic rubber seems to have paralysed the will of many Indonesians to compete in that field, the loss of an unlimited world sugar market and her former advantages in this field seem also to have had an inhibiting psychological effect on many people. In fact, world production has expanded 30 percent above prewar levels while Indonesia's production has fallen by that amount.

Other Export Products

The changes which have occurred in Indonesia's other major export products will be summarised more briefly. In nearly every case, except tin, volume has been below prewar levels, and there has been no immediate prospect of substantial increase. Their yearly fluctuations have been relatively unimportant, compared with those of rubber and oil. During the broadly "normal" years of the mid-1950's, about 30 percent of Indonesia's export earnings was brought in by seven commodities: (1) tin, roughly 7–9 percent of total exports; (2) copra, 6–8 percent, until 1956 when it dropped to about 3–4 percent; (3) coffee, 3–4 percent; (4) tobacco, 3–4 percent; (5) palm oil and kernels, 3–4 percent; (6) tea, 3–4 percent; (7) sugar, 1–2 percent.[29]

Virtually all the tea, palm oil, and sugar can be regarded as plantation crops; many of the factors inhibiting reinvestment on

[29] Percentages computed from Central Bureau of Statistics, *Statistik Konjunktur,* Djakarta, Table C.8, *passim* (monthly); more precise percentages (generally lower than in the earlier years) for 1956–1960 are published in the *Statistical Pocketbook of Indonesia, 1961,* Table 50.38.

rubber estates applied to them also. Some coffee and tobacco (particularly the valuable Deli wrapper leaf) also came from estates, but relatively far less than in colonial times, less than 25 percent of each crop in recent years. Both are becoming smallholder crops. The area planted with all three crops was well below prewar levels, productivity (per hectare and per worker) was lower, oil palms and tea bushes were ageing, and there was no prospect of restoring prewar production levels unless the general outlook for foreign enterprises improved dramatically.[30]

Peasant production of export crops has therefore become relatively far more important than in prewar times, as, indeed, it had been tending to do since the beginning of the century. Some observers even speculated in the early years of independence that smallholder production might generally supersede the estates. Peasants are less handicapped by a top-heavy cost structure, and their lower productivity per hectare may not be an immediately serious drawback (although it would in overpopulated regions).[31] Certainly Indonesia's governments showed more favour in their export regulations to smallholders than to estates. But the record of smallholder production is little more encouraging than that of estates. The special case of rubber has already been explained. Copra, almost entirely a smallholders' crop, has been produced in quantities which early in the decade appeared to be 30 percent or more below prewar levels; recently the supply has fallen more disastrously because of shipping shortages in the eastern islands where most copra is produced. Amongst the many factors which explain the failure of smallholders' production in achieving a post-independence recovery seems to be the lack of constant pressure, which existed in colonial times, for peasants to maximise

[30] See Pelzer, *loc cit.;* and Sajuti Hasibuan, "The Palm Oil Industry on the East Coast of Sumatra," in Paauw, ed., *Prospects for East Sumatran Plantation Industries.*

[31] J. S. Furnivall, *Netherlands India,* Cambridge University Press, London, 1944, p. 320, tabulates an increase in peasant export crops from 10 to 37 percent of total exports between 1898 and 1929. The case for peasant production of export crops as against plantations is put forward, not entirely convincingly, in Erich H. Jacoby, *Agrarian Unrest in Southeast Asia,* 2d ed., Asia Pub. House, New York, 1961, pp. 72–73, 140.

their cash incomes (partly to pay taxes) even where the return on their labour was small; since independence, the tax inducement has diminished almost entirely, but other cash incentives have been undermined by the inflation and periodic shortages of consumer goods, especially in the remote areas. Tobacco production has increased rapidly as a peasant crop in recent years, because in this case the price has created a strong incentive. But the demand sustaining that price has come very largely from domestic cigarette consumption, rather than from export markets. It is, unfortunately, doubtful that the return to the peasant would have been so advantageous if he had depended on export markets at the overvalued official rate of the rupiah. In the case of coffee, which is both exported and consumed locally, we find that peasant production is slightly below prewar levels, but now much greater than estate coffee which is steadily declining. This accords with a long-term shift in the geographical distribution of coffee production, away from Java into rather remote areas of Sulawesi and South Sumatra.

Industry

According to the 1952 national income estimates, about 8 percent of the gross national product was derived from manufacturing industry, a figure which is probably overestimated. The bulk of it must be attributed to the amorphous and statistically unfathomed home industries employing less than ten workers. Establishments in the statistical categories "medium" and "large" yield adequate basic statistics, but the number of these establishments is not large.[32] In the textile industry (where most progress has been made), since the protective tariffs of the Depression years set it on its feet, approximately 20 percent of Indonesia's consump-

[32] In 1959, returns for 10,650 establishments employing 430,000 persons, of which those in the category of "large" establishments (i.e., with more than 50 workers or using motors of more than 5 horsepower, for which statistics are fairly reliable) numbered 1,690, with 289,000 workers; see Central Bureau of Statistics, *Perusahaan-Perusahaan Industry, 1959,* Djakarta. Neumark's estimate for industry is based on crude assessments of the total industrial labour force (including backyard industries) and assumed wages, so the margin of error is high; see *EKI,* vol. 7, 1954, pp. 374–375.

tion of woven cloth and 5 percent of her spun yarn was met from within the country in 1953. These proportions may have increased slightly until 1957, but since then the disruption of raw material imports has severely disturbed Indonesian domestic industry, presumably at all levels.[33] Only in a few minor commodities have Indonesia's infant industries been able to supply the entire domestic market. In no case can her manufacturing products hope to be exported, for costs are so high that few of her industries would survive without the effective protection provided by the complex system of import taxes.[34] The government has long been committed to a program of state-owned heavy industries which it is pursuing with the aid of foreign loans, e.g., the Gresik cement factory, a paper mill in Blabak, preparations for a fertiliser plant, and Russian-sponsored iron and steel. Such major investments are intended to provide the substructure on which a self-sustaining national industry may be built. But smaller investments in the light consumer goods industries, which have been left implicitly to private businessmen, only attained a modest volume even during the favourable years of the mid-1950's; since 1961 they seem to have almost dried up entirely because of the intense uncertainty of prices, supplies, and government regulations.

Tertiary Occupations

The numbers of people engaged in commercial transactions, transportation, finance, services of various kinds, government employment, and professions in Indonesia always seem very large, largely because of extensive disguised unemployment and overswollen towns. Superficial impressions of this kind can be mislead-

[33] Raw material imports and consumption give the most easily accessible rough index of industrial production in Indonesia; *Statistik Konjunktur,* May–June 1961, Table 9.A, pp. 57–61, gives a gloomy picture of the decline in 1958–1960, especially in the textile industry.

[34] Protective tariffs as such have not been a subject of dispute in Indonesia, since the incidental protective effects of import licensing and multiple exchange rates have had indiscriminately protective effects, usually manipulable by the industries affected. Batik cloth, which is the only Indonesian "manufacture" well known abroad, has to be smuggled out since its export is banned for various reasons, including the fact that the cloth itself is virtually subsidised under the multiple exchange rate system.

ing; by some measures the proportions of the work force engaged in these sectors are by no means large, even though labour-intensive patterns of organisation make good sense economically. Neumark estimated that about 30 percent of the national income emanated from these sectors, a relatively high amount when it is considered that most of it would be earned by town dwellers who would hardly constitute much more than about 15 percent of the population. (If the figures are reliable, they confirm the impression of relatively high urban incomes.) No safe conclusions can be drawn about the changes in numbers or incomes within these sectors during recent years. Since little new capital seems to have been invested in the well established, capital-intensive enterprises (indeed, the depreciation of old-established services and equipment has probably been most damaging in just these sectors) any increase in numbers employed has almost certainly not been a sign of improved services, and productivity has almost certainly declined; the same can probably be said of the governmental sector, where various brakes on personnel expansion have been applied, although not entirely successfully. On the other hand, the distribution of employment opportunities and incomes amongst more and more participants, even to the point of what seem to be absurdly small economic units, seems to be occurring in the sphere of services and urban employment, just as it has in many overcrowded Indonesian villages.[35] It is quite likely that increasingly large numbers of people are drawing increasingly small incomes from participation (with a bare minimum of capital or prior provision of skills) in tertiary occupations.

Policies and Plans

How have Indonesian governments approached the problems of restoring the economy after its wartime damage and of stimulating economic growth in new fields? It is striking that most discussions of Indonesia's economic future have been couched in broadly "socialist" terms, or have at least paid lip service to socialist ideals;

[35] The expression "shared poverty" has been coined for this phenomenon by Clifford Geertz; see his "Religious Belief and Economic Behaviour in a Central Javanese Town: Some Preliminary Considerations," *Economic Development and Cultural Change,* vol. 4, no. 2, January 1956.

the meanings attached to those phrases, however, have always been vague, while in actual practice Indonesian governments have been reluctant to disrupt the thoroughly "capitalist" economic structure inherited from the colonial regime until 1958. Since 1959, "Socialisme à la Indonesia" has acquired the force of an official ideology, and the condemnation of "free-fight liberalism," now a term of execration, has been expressed in actions as well as words. We will see later that the pressures and limitations of practical politics have generally had greater influence than abstract theories in determining Indonesia's economic policies. But socialist aspirations have so pervaded discussion of policy alternatives that it has been politically out of the question for even the most undoctrinaire of governments and ministers to flout them or attempt to give absolute priority to rapid restoration of production along austere, businesslike lines, as recommended, for instance, by Dr. Schacht in 1951.

If we try to analyse what Indonesians have meant by the term "socialism," two elements stand out. First, for some it has meant little more than "Indonesianisation"—breaking the grip of foreign capital, mostly Dutch and Chinese, over the trading and industrial sectors and plantation agriculture. Whether this was to be done by state nationalisation or by the creation of an Indonesian business class was, for a long time, an unresolved argument. Capitalism was identified with the hated colonial economic structure; to be "progressive" in the modern world meant, in some sense, to espouse "socialism," i.e., state controls, planning, and, in theory at least, the notion of equality. Laissez-faire government policies were bound to leave the foreigners in a dominant position.

In the second place, great stress has been put on "collectivist" organisation of the economy, on the "family principle," or the "*gotong rojong*" (mutual assistance) method of performing certain agricultural tasks in the villages (and hence on the rejection of individualism, private self-interest, and the profit motive). Cooperatives were regarded as an excellent expression of Indonesian social ideals, which devalue the bourgeois virtues of thrift and provision for the future.[36] On the other hand, it is noteworthy

[36] See Geertz, *op. cit.,* on social values in Java. Cf. Mohammad Hatta, *The Cooperative Movement in Indonesia,* Cornell University Press, Ithaca,

that collective farming has almost no advocates, even among the communists. One even hears frequent complaints that the peasants are not "cooperatively minded." In fact, the peasant economy is intensely individualist and mercenary; after all, village *pasar* (markets) reveal the working of the forces of supply and demand in their most naked form with intense bargaining for almost every transaction. But solid, practical considerations reinforce these socialist attitudes at the government level. A large state sector is unavoidable for various reasons; even laissez-faire Dutch economists accepted that. There are only the embryonic Indonesian "middle class" and the very few rich landlords or prosperous peasants who might serve as agents of private capital accumulation. The Dutch and Chinese domination of the monetised sector virtually stifled Indonesian enterprise, and even the "indigenisation" policies of the last ten years have barely broken the grip of the latter. When the Dutch plantations and businesses were taken over in 1957–1958, there was virtually no alternative to state ownership, so that a substantial shift in the balance of power took place, whose consequences we will examine later.

As an example of the verbal dialectics made necessary by Indonesia's fervent commitment against capitalism and a "liberal" economy, we should notice some Indonesian reactions to an often quoted clause from the Constitution (Article 33); the clause reads, "The economy shall be organised as a joint endeavour based on the principle of the family relationship."

Innumerable words have been devoted to the task of interpreting this Article. A former prime minister, Mr. Wilopo, offered a characteristic interpretation at a university seminar on the subject.[37] "The term 'joint endeavour' (*usaha bersama*) conveys the idea of a form of enterprise that is quite distinct in character from private enterprise: in the latter all decisions are in the hands of the entrepreneur and all the worker's life and work depends on the employer. . . . Our ideal is of a type of enterprise in which . . .

N.Y., 1957, for an advocacy of cooperatives as a form of discipline and training in the ways of a modern economy.

[37] Wilopo and Widjojo Nitisastro, *The Socio-Economic Basis of the Indonesian State,* Cornell Modern Indonesia Project (translation series), Cornell University, Ithaca, N.Y., 1959, p. 5.

the term 'based on the principle of the family relationship' signifies a basis of collective responsibility directed towards achieving a common effort which will achieve progress for each participant." He admitted that the Article did not formulate any specific principle which could constitute a definite line of action, but he urged full support for the (antiliberal) principle implicit therein, with the proviso that additional clauses should be devised to reinforce Article 38 "making impossible all methods of abuse of economic power." Against this characteristically formal and legalist approach to the problem, an able young economist* replied that Wilopo's interpretation was self-contradictory on the role of private enterprise in the new society and that Article 38 could only be interpreted to mean social control of abuses of economic power, not complete rejection of private enterprise. In seeking an acceptable interpretation of the Article, specific roles for private, public, and cooperative enterprise must be worked out. But even he accepted the necessity of doing this within the broadly "antiliberal" framework of the Constitution's vague clauses on social justice.[38]

In the early years of independence, Indonesian governments took steps to give content to the aspirations embodied in the Constitution by beginning to lay the foundations for a large public sector. A few struggling Dutch estates and industrial enterprises were purchased and put under a Government Estates Central (Pusat Perkebunan Negara or PPN) and a new semiautonomous Industrial Bank (Bank Industri Negara or BIN). Until 1958, neither of these had grown sufficiently to make any significant difference in the distribution of economic power between foreigners and Indonesians, or even to pose any threat of this.[39] Nor were they promising examples of public enterprise in action. Only two large investment projects were pioneered by BIN: the Gresik cement plant (set up with a U.S. Export-Import Bank loan and supervision, with quite successful results) and a spinning mill at Tjilatjap, which was expensive and poorly run. No significant

* The "young economist" was Widjojo Nitisastro, now Director of the National Planning Council of the Republic of Indonesia.—Ed.

[38] *Ibid.*, pp. 13–15, 20.

[39] Bruce Glassburner, "Problems of Economic Policy in Indonesia, 1950–1957," *EKI*, vol. 13, July–August 1960, pp. 302–321.

new investment in the all-important field of export agriculture took place, until the sudden nationalisation of Dutch enterprises in 1957–1958 left the government with so much of the nation's productive apparatus in its hands that it was compelled to approach the problem more directly.

Wherever possible, various other piecemeal policies were pursued in the early 1950's to nurture Indonesian enterprise. Demobilised soldiers were assisted to set up small businesses on co-operative lines, especially in the saw-milling industry. The Small Scale Industrialisation Plan was a well conceived attempt to provide simple pieces of equipment to backyard manufacturers on a loan basis with easy repayments; it succeeded in a few cases, but was discredited in time by poor departmental administration and the losses incurred. Another attempt was made to assist particular groups of small industries by establishing "Production Centrals" (*Induks*) which would disseminate better materials and techniques, or eliminate the dependence on Chinese "middlemen" (a favourite target of resentment and source of hope for great savings). Again, few of these were successful and only slight progress was made in building up small industries to reduce Indonesia's heavy dependence on imported manufactures.[40]

It can be seen that these hesitant attempts to establish new productive potential were not confined to the state sector, but also embraced small private (Indonesian) enterprises. So, too, did the most important and controversial of the government policies aimed at changing the economic structure—those embraced by the term "Indonesianisation." In 1950, import licences in certain restricted categories of easy-to-sell goods were reserved solely for Indonesian importers, under the so-called *benteng* system.[41] This was frankly intended to promote native Indonesian businessmen, in effect

[40] A gloomy picture of the progress of industrialisation up to 1954 is given by Sumitro Djojohadikusumo, ed., "The Government's Program on Industries," *EKI*, vol. 7, no. 11, November 1954. See also *Bank Indonesia Reports* from 1955–1956 to 1959–1960 for some euphemistical accounts of difficulties confronting industry.

[41] The *benteng* system is most fully described in John O. Sutter, *Indonesianisasi, Politics in a Changing Economy, 1940–1955,* Data Paper no. 36, Department of Far Eastern Studies, Southeast Asia Program, Cornell University, Ithaca, N.Y., 1959, pp. 1017–1029.

excluding Chinese who had acquired Indonesian citizenship, although the regulations did not specifically exclude the latter. However, in time Chinese importers learned to operate through puppet Indonesian licence holders who became known as "briefcase importers." The *benteng* principle was later extended in scope, culminating in a scandalous system of "special licenses" governing many types of import during a period of severe foreign-exchange stringency in 1953–1954. Yet the effect in shifting the bulk of import trade from the hands of the Dutch "Big Five" was barely significant. Nor did many of the 5,000 or more Indonesian beneficiaries from these licenses manage to establish themselves in the import trade as a result of these opportunities to reap almost assured profits. In 1955, it was estimated that only a few hundred were conducting any real business at all. Government policy hardened against this group in later years, and in 1959, after the take-over of the "Big Five," private importers (including Chinese) were excluded from all but 20 percent of this lucrative business. Even so, the issue is still unresolved, and there are signs that failures in the government trading companies have recently raised the hopes of national businessmen that they may yet inherit the Dutch legacy.

A less controversial means of assisting "*nasional*" businesses was the expansion of credit through the three major state banks and the mushrooming private banks. This policy was pursued most vigorously in 1956, when the inflationary effects of such a policy seemed less threatening than before; it was checked the following year, and subsequent manipulation of credit policy (a major inflationary factor in 1960–1961) has been for the benefit of state enterprises rather than private. Credit policy aroused heated political arguments—less about the principle of aiding private Indonesian capitalists than about the parties they belonged to! But its economic benefits were meagre.

The Five Year Plan

No systematic approach to the problem of stimulating economic development was attempted until the Five Year Plan, 1956–1960, was drafted late in 1955, after several years of preparatory study by the National Planning Bureau under Ir. Djuanda. The plan's main rationale was to build up within the public sector the essential basic industries, utilities, and services which would sustain and stimulate further investment in the private sector. Estimates were made of the capital investment that could be anticipated, without inflation, in the two sectors over the five year period —approximately Rp. 2.5 billion per annum in each, plus another Rp. 1.5 billion of village investments through self-help projects. The plan itself was essentially an arrangement of priorities for expenditure in the public sector. It made virtually no attempt to regulate the private sector, in this respect being much simpler than the Indian plans, which have been concerned to regulate the allocation of resources in the latter sphere. A few broad guidelines for future investment were laid down: mining and heavy industries to belong to the public sector, light industries to the private, etc. But there was little attempt to draw these lines sharply or to indicate priorities for the few private capitalists wondering where they should invest, which some of them, paradoxically, seemed to want. This laissez-faire quality of the plan became a ground for later criticisms that it was merely a coordination of departmental programmes, without any positive objectives.[42]

Up to a point this was true. The major purpose of the Five Year Plan was to estimate, on the basis of earlier trends, how much finance would be available for government spending, without resort to deficit financing except on a modest scale. Development projects devised by the ministries were then ranked according to priorities worked out more or less by rule of thumb in the Planning Bureau to maximise quick productive returns. A few large projects in the irrigation, power, industry, and mining fields would, if carried out, have had a direct impact on production; the rest of the outlays were devoted to auxiliary services, research, educational activities, etc. By 1960, quantitative "targets" for production of rice, rubber, and certain industries were set, but these were not tightly related to any calculations of how the plan would lead to increased out-

[42] A good outline of the Five Year Plan and its preparation is given by Benjamin Higgins, *Indonesia's Economic Stabilisation and Development*, Institute of Pacific Relations, New York, 1957, pp. 40–53. The official version is summarised as "A Study of the Indonesian Economic Development Scheme" in *EKI*, vol. 10, September 1957, pp. 600–642.

put. They were merely extrapolations from reasonable guesses about likely rates of increase. So too were the calculations of the modest increases in national income that were expected—about 3 percent per annum, which would yield only a 6.5 percent rise in per capita incomes over the five year period, since a population increase of 1.7 percent per annum was accompanying it. There were no specific plans relating to export trade policy or ways to increase the foreign exchange earning capacity of the plantations, although it was assumed that these earnings would increase.

The whole plan depended on the avoidance of inflation and the continuation of the rising production trends of 1951–1956. Both assumptions collapsed in 1957, when political turmoil and sharply accelerated inflation (with a 30 percent per annum increase in money supply from 1957–1961, then a much higher rate) threw all development plans and the budget into confusion. Some of the projects continued, but the entire budgetary process fell into disarray, and the Five Year Plan had become almost irrelevant by 1958. It is, however, interesting as an example of official economic thinking in the mid-1950's, before the dramatic leap towards a "Guided Economy" in 1959–1960, and as a realistic estimate of the resources available for development.

The Nationalisation of Dutch Enterprises

The seizure of all Dutch properties in Indonesia in December 1957 occurred suddenly, and, regardless of its revolutionary effects on economic life, without any prior planning except perhaps in the mind of President Sukarno and a few youth leaders around him.[43] The government seems to have been taken by surprise by what happened and initially divided in its assessment of the appropriate response. Once the deed was done, however, there was little choice but to proceed with nationalisation and accept the vast new responsibilities of managing these productive and trading enterprises within the state sector despite the paucity of experienced technicians and managers. To hand them over to Indonesia's private businessmen was almost out of the question; not

[43] For a brief account of the "take-over" process, see Mackie, *op. cit.*, pp. 340–343.

only were these embryonic capitalists politically unpopular, their commercial record had also been disastrous in most cases.

The consequences of this decision were momentous. It virtually put an end to earlier notions that private foreign investment would contribute to the development of Indonesia's economy, except in a few special cases like oil and minerals. (Some foreign estates and companies remained, of course—mainly British and American, and even some Anglo-Dutch companies like Shell and Unilever; but their position was now far less secure than it had been and only the oil companies were investing new capital in Indonesia.) It also paved the way towards a much more "Socialist" approach to economic problems through direct governmental intervention, since the previous reasons for reluctance to discourage foreign capitalists no longer existed. There was also a psychological effect—a sense of daring, confidence, and revolutionary fervour after such a big step towards becoming masters in their own house. The doctrines of a "Guided Economy," "Socialisme à la Indonesia," and the rejection of "liberal thinking" all flourished with very little dissent in 1958–1960. Government intervention in economic life increased vastly. The Eight Year Over-all Development Plan of 1960, superseding the now irrelevant Five Year Plan, marked the apotheosis of the new political economy.[44]

There were also two more profound but diffuse consequences. Such a transfer of property was bound to have some political repercussions within Indonesia, to which we will return later. Moreover, the historic pioneering or entrepreneurial function of the Dutch enterprises would now have to be assumed by government agencies if the long-term structural problems of the Indonesian economy were to be solved. Until 1957, there had been no encouraging sign that any other elements in the society were emerging to take over this function, no sign where new sources of investment or new forms of production might be found. To this extent

[44] On "Socialisme à la Indonesia," the reader should combine the analysis by Paauw in "From Colonial to Guided Economy," in McVey, *op. cit.*, pp. 206–214, with Herbert Feith's handy discourse on ideology and symbols in "The Dynamics of Guided Democracy," also in McVey, *op. cit.*, pp. 366–395.

the foreign estates had remained as essential props of the old economic structure on which governments depended heavily, too, for foreign exchange earnings and tax revenues, but for which it felt little direct responsibility. After 1958, that responsibility was to be sheeted home to it. Governments were now directly implicated in the effects of their policies on the productive process in a way which they had never been between 1950 and 1957. If the new public enterprises failed, the price would have to be borne by the state budget in the last resort. It might have been hoped that this challenge would have compelled governments to give high priority to the problems of setting the new enterprises on their feet. Unfortunately it must be said that the acceleration of inflationary pressures and disruption of the economy over the last five years have made it practically impossible for the government estates and trading companies to function efficiently or profitably. Some of the reasons for this will become apparent in the pages following.

The Eight Year Plan

In 1959, an entirely different National Planning Council, a political rather than a technical body, set out to devise a new and more fundamental plan appropriate to the new era of "Socialisme à la Indonesia." The Eight Year Over-all Development Plan of 1960, which was hastily thrown together and endorsed unanimously by the People's Consultative Assembly, was based on quite fantastic assumptions to justify, in theory, government expenditures of Rp. 30 billion per annum on development projects, again *without* inflation and without increased taxation.[45] (This was twelve times the annual sum regarded as a safe maximum in 1956, although prices and budgets had risen by less than half that multiple.) The economic development projects listed for inclusion were, to a large extent, those included in the original Five Year Plan, supplemented by grandiose schemes for "spiritual and mental development" as well, but this time without any assessment of

[45] Paauw, *op. cit.*, pp. 222–231, has given the most coherent account of the Eight Year Plan; Don D. Humphrey (leader of the 1961 U.S. Survey Mission to Indonesia) has made some trenchant comments in "Economic Planning in Asia: Indonesia," *Asian Survey*, vol. 2, no. 10, December 1962, pp. 12–22.

priorities or indication how they would be assigned. That was left to President Sukarno, who was designated administrator of the plan with the requirement that parliamentary approval must still be sought for each project, which meant that the crucial decisions had still to be made. The plan was no more than a symbol of approval and authority for a vast portmanteau of projects intended to please everyone. It was not a rational allocation of scarce resources, desperately scarce though all critical resources were.

This appears to have been the symbolic function of the Eight Year Plan—to win consensus by avoiding the painful choice of priorities. Enormous stress was put on national determination and will, on the national ideals which must be realised. Agreement about a distant vision was politically more urgent than argument about the paths immediately ahead. It did not matter that the arithmetic underlying the esimate of Rp. 30 billion per annum bordered on fantasy. Various ministers were hoping to win control over the effective execution of the plan and use it their way, some as an instrument of personal power, others to save the rational elements in it and ensure that at least the more sensible and urgent of the "list A projects" would be carried out.

Again, this plan is more interesting as a revelation of Indonesian political processes than as an exercise of the economist's craft. Budget revenues of Rp. 30 billion were allocated for it in 1961, but the new spurt of inflation in 1962–1963, coinciding with vast expenditures on the 1962 West Irian campaign and an austerity budget in 1963, seems to have doomed the 1960 plan to irrelevance just like the Five Year Plan. By 1963, stabilisation had displaced development as the watchword, and the problem of merely checking inflation began to seem insuperable for political reasons if not economic ones.

The Instruments of Economic Policy

Although in their attempts to resist inflation and to develop the economy since 1950, Indonesian governments have utilised most of the orthodox instruments of economic control, such as fiscal policy, monetary policy, trade controls, wage and price regulations, etc., their reliance on a few vital regulators and taxes has been very striking. On the other hand, monetary policy has rarely been an influential weapon against inflation (and only occasionally a serious contributor to it); some taxing powers have been disastrously neglected and even direct price controls over a few essential commodities have proved sadly ineffective in the face of steady inflation.

The effectiveness of the weapons available to governments to control a "guided economy" has, paradoxically, diminished over the past decade as the problem of curbing inflation has overshadowed almost all other considerations of economic policy. Budgetary stringency has meant that governments have not had sufficient resources to intervene successfully through their own agencies in the public sector in order to raise production. Anti-inflationary measures have therefore depended almost entirely on a combination of budgetary policy (since deficits have been the primary cause of inflation) and import regulation. These two regulators are themselves interdependent, since import taxes yield such a great part of government revenues. (On the expenditure side of the budget it has been politically impracticable to attempt major cuts.) The most serious weakness in a situation like this is that too many purposes have to be fulfilled through import taxes —raising revenue, manipulating general price levels through the flow of goods, adjusting the price and supply of goods to different elasticities of demand, protecting local industries while ensuring their supplies of raw materials and capital goods, preventing political unrest. The result has been that highly complex multiple rates of exchange have grown up, only to be slashed aside periodically when the system becomes unworkable. On the other hand, direct taxes have constituted a diminishing proportion of the total revenue, since they have rarely been adjusted to the new inflationary conditions, as our discussion of the tax structure will show. Taxes on personal incomes and corporations are not significant economic regulators as they are in more sensitively balanced economies. Fiscal devices such as subsidies and protective tariffs have only occasionally and marginally been important. Budget deficits have become endemic partly because it is difficult to reduce expenditures radically; therefore attention has had to be concentrated on the revenue side. And, with the steady growth of inflation, attempts to maintain control over prices and wages have been effective only in distorting the cost structure, not in checking the basic problem. Credit expansion or contraction has been increasingly overshadowed as a factor governing the supply of money by the budget deficits. Whereas quite fine adjustments of several such economic regulators could be relied on to maintain approximate stability in the early 1950's, sledgehammer blows have become increasingly necessary in recent years—vastly wider spread of tax differentials between luxury imports and necessities; massive prepayment requirements of importers; a "monetary purge" to reduce the money supply in 1959; sudden levies on owners of houses and motor cars in 1962; drastic rundowns in the foreign exchange reserves, followed by alarming dependence on foreign aid subvention. Reliance on financial "gadgetry" to stave off one looming crisis and win breathing space till the next has so occupied the economic departments of the government since 1957 that only on rare occasions (e.g., the brief resumption of large-scale development outlays in 1961) have they had the time, resources, and room to manoeuvre needed for tackling broader problems.[46]

Inadequacies in the tax system help to explain why so much reliance has had to be put on import levies.[47]

Three features of the revenue from various taxes are striking:

1. Taxes falling on imports and exports have generally accounted for 50 to 60 percent of total revenues. Ease of collection is a decisive factor here; direct taxes are difficult to collect and create political difficulties, whereas trade tax levied at harbours, or excise levied at the point of production, are relatively easy, and less damaging politically, since consumers will blame the importer, as well as the government, for price increases. But the result is that any adjustments of foreign trade regulations must be

[46] Documentation for these rather sweeping generalisations will emerge in the following pages; comparison may be made with Higgins, *op. cit.,* Chap. 1, for an illustration of the much more varied techniques available to governments in the 1952–1955 period.

[47] An excellent survey of the tax structure in Indonesia is given in Douglas S. Paauw, *Financing Economic Development: The Indonesian Case,* Free Press, Glencoe, Ill., 1960, Chaps. 4–6 and Appendix B–C. For a more technical analysis of the administration of the taxes, see M. D. Dris, "Taxation in Indonesia," *EKI,* vol. 11, August–September 1958. A table, headed "Revenue from Various Taxes" has been deleted.—Ed.

devised so that no serious loss of revenues to the government occurs.

2. Direct taxes have been far less important than indirect. Company tax contributes the biggest share here, with income tax following. But, with inflation, the relative proportion of each has declined, since adjustments of the scale of these taxes have been few and lagged far behind price rises. Income taxes were originally levied only from relatively high income groups, and, although many more incomes must now fall within those brackets, the numbers assessed appear not to have risen comparably. Direct taxation in the rural sector has been particularly light. The main burden of providing direct taxes has fallen on the capital-intensive sector; foreign enterprises and national businessmen are too easily distinguishable and too vulnerable politically to be able to evade taxes easily. The failure to raise a greater proportion of revenue by direct taxation in the rural sector is one of the most glaring weaknesses of the present system.

3. The diversity, obsolescence, and multiplicity of taxes has meant that high administrative costs have frequently been coupled with rather low revenue yields. Few taxes have been abolished since 1950, despite the "colonial" stigma on many. Only one major increase in rates of direct taxation has occurred—a very unpopular one in late 1959, soon after the "monetary purge." (Trade taxes have been very frequently adjusted, however.) An example of obsolescence is the "Development Tax," introduced by the beleaguered Jogja Republic in 1947 as 10 percent of all hotel and restaurant charges; it is almost impossible to police effectively amongst innumerable small enterprises with rudimentary account books, if any.

The immobility of the tax structure is therefor a serious handicap to effective anti-inflationary action. It seems that governments are reluctant to do more than tinker with some of the obvious anomalies, since any attempt to overhaul this historical ragbag of taxes radically would require, implicitly at least, some choice of where increased tax burdens must fall. The National Planning Council shirked this issue entirely in 1960 with the assertion that taxes must not be increased, because the people could not afford to pay and that inflation must be avoided because of the suffering it caused. Twice, in moods of belt-tightening determination, governments have decreed heavy impositions broadly on "the wealthy," but without much distinction between sources of incomes.

Income tax could certainly yield far greater revenues than it has. There was an actual decline in the number of assessments recorded between 1952 and 1955, despite inflation of cash incomes. The obligation to make tax returns evidently applies only to people who have been issued with the appropriate forms by the taxation authorities, and it was difficult for them to chase up self-employed persons. Incomes under Rp. 5,000 were assessed on "external signs of prosperity"; only those above (i.e., most middle and senior government servants and employees of big corporations) were taxed at source of wages. At 1954 rates of exchange, Rp. 5,000 represented about $450 (U.S.). The rates percent of income levied at that time were:

Income in rupiahs	*Tax in percent of income*
3,000 or less	0
3,000–50,000	3
50,000–100,000	22
100,000–300,000	36
300,000–500,000	57
500,000–1,000,000	64
1,000,000–2,000,000	70

Between 1951 and 1955, an estimated 91 percent of all assessed incomes fell in categories below Rp. 5,000, yielding an average of only Rp. 17.5 (about $1.5). This is fantastically low, even when we take into account that the tax is used partly as a supplement to the company tax. Small personal businesses which do not keep records are reached by income tax only; those which do by company tax, so that it does not include one lucrative set of incomes.[48]

Inadequate collection of direct taxes in the rural sector has perhaps the most intriguing political implications. Without doubt, tax levels here represent a far lower fraction of peasant incomes now than in colonial times; Paauw estimated in 1954 that taxes stood at 500 percent of their prewar levels but cash incomes were

[48] Dris, *op. cit.*, pp. 44, 49; Paauw, *op. cit.*, p. 248.

2,000 percent. The Dutch system certainly bore unduly heavily on the poor, but inflation of cash incomes has steadily eroded the relative burden.[49] There appears to be still considerable taxable capacity here, if only it can be tapped effectively. (Producers of export crops are, indeed, burdened by imports on foreign exchange earnings, like the PBE of 1957–1959, and, in the last resort, by the multiple exchange rate created by import taxes, although few understand the arithmetic of these.) But Paauw found that, quite apart from the low rates of taxation prevailing, the central taxation service was not an efficient instrument of tax collection at the village level. He advocated far greater descentralisation of the responsibility for both collecting and utilising minor tax revenues to autonomous local units, so that local officials would see the benefits of their efforts and so have greater incentive to improve collection than they had when it seemed that all revenues merely flowed back to Djakarta. The only account we have of the procedure for assessing the major tax on agricultural yields within the village reveals that the central taxation office depends heavily on the cooperation of village officials, who have vested interests in understanding incomes there.[50] How to decentralise this system, or devise another, is itself an explosive question, however.

Two Persistent Economic Ills: Inflation and Black Market Foreign Exchange Rates

Since these two phenomena have overshadowed Indonesian economic life from 1950, some of the short-range policies applied towards them need to be understood. The long-term problems involved in their solutions raise even more complex and basic questions about how production is to be increased and the economy restructured; they entail also political questions about the values and social structure of Indonesia's various communities and about the role of ideology in the search for new solutions. But these questions are outside our province here.

[49] See Douglas S. Paauw, "The Role of Local Finance in Indonesian Economic Development," *EKI,* vol. 8, January 1955, pp. 2–24.

[50] Widjojo and Ismael, *The Government, Economy and Taxes of a Central Javanese Village,* Cornell Modern Indonesia Project (monograph series), Cornell University, Ithaca, N.Y., 1959, pp. 21–28.

Inflation

Prices have risen in very close conjunction with the increase in volume of money since 1950, and the latter figure has been influenced predominantly by budget deficits, with credit expansion occasionally playing a small part. That, at its simplest, is the problem of inflation in Indonesia.[51]

Put differently, Indonesia's postwar inflation may be seen as a problem of excess demand—"too much money chasing too few goods"—since the increase of cash-purchasing power has not stimulated a proportionate increase in the supply of goods and services. In the early 1950's, excess demand arose from several sources: (1) from the sudden rise of export incomes during the Korean boom, which generated unfulfilled demand for local products (rice, sugar, etc.) and imports, and created high expectations about income levels which could not be sustained when the boom collapsed in 1952; (2) from wage increases, which were successfully demanded by militant trade unions between 1950 and 1953, to the detriment of some export industries which were then burdened with rising costs—since then, however, wage increases have lagged far behind price rises on the whole and can hardly be considered a major inflationary force; (3) from the increase of demand elsewhere in the economy, either through budget deficits or excessive credit creation or even through wasteful investment, all of which have contributed in Indonesia, although the former has dominated the picture.

Hopes that the aggregate supply of goods would increase and thus relieve inflationary pressures have constantly recurred in Indonesian discussions of the problem. Our survey of the production record reveals how vain these hopes have proved, except for some increase in food production in the early 1950's from the abnormally low postwar levels. Even here a ceiling was reached by about 1955, and subsequent increases have been small and hard-won. The volume of imports, the second major component in aggregate supply, has been far below 1951–1952 levels ever since the Korean boom, except in 1956.

[51] A table entitled "Money Supply, Deficits and Price Levels, 1951–1961," has been deleted.—Ed.

On a brief historical survey of the main factors causing inflation, we may notice that the initial push was given by the buoyant export incomes created by the Korean boom, which rapidly pushed up prices of domestic and imported goods, thus upsetting the severely deflationary policy pursued in early 1950.[52] Growth of bank credit and budget deficits (which have become endemic with the one exception of 1951) were also contributory factors, although not nearly as serious as they were to become after 1952, since the high level of imports helped to check price increases. The need to curb imports rigorously for the sake of balance-of-payments equilibrium after 1952 weakened this compensating instrument, just when the extravagant budget deficits of 1953–1954 began to constitute the major inflationary force. (Attempts to stimuate production and exports by various direct "inducement" devices in these years actually aggravated the problem by proliferating government controls and corruption with disincentive effects on investment in productive fields.) A spectacular, but brief, attack on inflation was launched in August 1955, with the so-called "Sumitro reforms" which relaxed import controls, cut away much of the corruption surrounding the complex trade regulations, and reduced liquidity by demanding heavy prepayments of importers. The speculative hoardings of 1954–1955 were forced onto the market, and prices fell dramatically, especially of textiles. However, liberalisation could only last as long as the foreign exchange reserves were buoyant; Sumitro was aided by a fortuitous jump in rubber prices late in 1955, so that exports were increased greatly, continuing at a high level well into 1956, even after a change of government. By the middle of 1956, however, import controls were again necessary, along with stimulation of some exports whose costs of production were exceeding world market prices. Nevertheless, prices were generally stable through 1956 and inflation seemed, for the first time, to be briefly under control.

In 1957, a new and more persistent phase of inflation set in, however, as a result of vast budget deficits incurred in the attempt to overcome the political crisis created by regional dissidence. Henceforth deficits were to swell the volume of money by about

[52] For a more analytical account of inflationary pressures in the 1950–1957 period, see Paauw, *Financing Economic Development,* Chap. 2.

30 percent per annum until 1962–1963 when the rate stepped up sharply to 100 percent per annum. A disguised devaluation, the BE system, also pushed up import costs and hence prices. Then in 1958, export levels collapsed about 20 percent after the seizure of Dutch estates and imports for 1958–1959 were cut back by more than 33 percent of the previous two years. Prices rose steeply in 1959 as the volume of money doubled within two years. Various liquidity-reducing devices failed to check the speculative tendencies these circumstances encouraged, and, in August 1959, the government attempted a drastic "monetary purge" which cut the volume of money in circulation from Rp. 34 billion to 21 billion. Prices fell for a few months because of the liquidity crisis which followed, but the disruption was so great that the government had to let out vast credits of its own agencies simply to keep going.[53] Within six months the volume of money was back to its former level, and prices were rising again. A determined effort to curb expenditures in 1960, coupled with import relaxation in August 1960, did bring some check to price increases in 1960–1961; "hot money" was soaked up to some extent by the creation of a new high rate of exchange for control-free luxury imports (at Rp. 200 per dollar, compared to an official rate of 45), and the foreign exchange reserves, carefully husbanded through 1959 to their highest level in mid-1960 since 1952, were drawn down steadily through 1961.

Prices again stabilised in early 1961, and the prospects were briefly encouraging again; the political disruptions of 1957–1958 were at last over.[54] But the volume of money was boosted in the

[53] The "monetary purge" is discussed at length by Ralph Anspach, "Monetary Aspects of Indonesia's Economic Reorganisation in 1959," *EKI,* vol. 13, January–February 1960, pp. 2–47.

[54] A brief survey of anti-inflationary policies in 1960–1961 is contained in "Humphrey Mission Report," pp. 97–108 (officially entitled "Indonesia: Perspectives and Proposals for U.S. Economic Aid," *Report to the President by the U.S. Economic Survey Team to Indonesia, 1962,* published by Southeast Asia Studies, Yale University, New Haven, 1963). Developments since 1961 must be traced rather sketchily from the *Three Monthly Economic Review* or the *Far Eastern Economic Review Yearbooks* for 1962 and 1963. Some useful figures still appear in the International Monetary Fund's *International Financial Statistics,* Washington, D.C., although generally after long delays.

second half of the year as the government undertook lavish development expenditures in conformity with the Eight Year Plan program of Rp. 30 billion per annum, which was to be financed by a deficit, compensated by drawing down the exchange reserves. On top of this came heavy military expenditures in 1961–1962 for the West Irian struggle and a disastrous drought in late 1961, which set back an ambitious program aimed at self-sufficiency in rice. Rice prices spiralled alarmingly in late 1961. The volume of money reached Rp. 68 billion and then doubled in the course of 1962. Foreign exchange reserves had been run down almost to zero by 1962, and, although imports for that year remained well above the 1958–1960 average (thanks largely to foreign aid receipts), inflationary pressures could no longer be cushioned by running down reserves. In 1963, it was clear that unless stabilisation could be achieved, the economy would be far more vulnerable to inflationary upsets than it had been in the earlier years when the impact had been cushioned somewhat.

Eliminating, or at least reducing, government deficits is obviously the first requirement if inflation is to be checked. Indonesian politicians know this well enough and talk about it a good deal, but the political problems involved are so alarming that they often take refuge in other rationalisations (e.g., that the "real" solution, which therefore deserves priority, is increased production, therefore more public investment). Some attempts at increasing government revenue have been made, notably in 1960, when the deficit was kept surprisingly low as a result of tax increases. But unless public expenditure can be pruned drastically, particularly on the armed forces, no solution is foreseeable, especially as the tax revenue from foreign trade must shrink with the decline in exports. Yet the only major attempt to reduce government expenditure in 1952, ended in disaster for the government responsible, while in more recent years vested interests in lavish and lax government expenditures have become entrenched in the political system.

By 1963, cabinet ministers were talking in terms of three years being needed to bring the situation under control. They are probably right in perceiving that there is no panacea for the budget deficit or for inflation in general. Piecemeal financial reforms may have a perceptible effect, as they did in 1960, if they are applied with determination, although inflationary pressures have intensified and the government's resources to combat them have diminished seriously since then. Production of export crops fell sharply by 20 percent in 1962, and the prospects of any significant increase in nonfood production are not bright. The utilisation of army units for developmental work in the villages has received a great deal of attention recently. It may well prove a useful psychological safety valve, as a means of associating the army with the villagers and of postponing the necessity to demobilise the overlarge (350,000 strong) army. It may even help to open up some land for development outside Java or bring isolated villages in Java into contact with the market by improving roads and bridges. But its immediate impact on national output will not be sufficient to offset the inflationary effect of the huge budget deficits.

In the long run, it is essential to increase production, of course, and this will require substantial new investment, although the more immediate priority is to raise the present low rates of utilisation of existing productive resources. To do this, one of the most urgent needs is to disentangle the chaotic cost structure which has been created by piecemeal regulations and abortive attempts to hold down prices artificially. A laissez-faire economy is obviously out of the question, but more purposeful utilisation of the price mechanism is essential.

The Foreign Exchange Rate and the Black Market

As the value of the rupiah has depreciated with the inflation since 1950, two formal devaluations and numerous modifications to the "effective" rate of exchange for importers and exporters have occurred. In fact, the "par" rates have generally not applied to the majority of foreign exchange transactions, for which a complex set of "multiple exchange rates" has been built up through various steeply graded taxes on imports and exports (or sometimes subsidies on the latter). The grossly overvalued par rates have not been an accurate token of the rupiah's purchasing power and have generally applied only to capital and payments transfers—and, even then, usually with some additional taxes pushing up the effective rate for the purchaser of foreign exchange. As can easily be imagined, the whole system operates as a huge set of disguised taxes and subsidies, of which the ultimate burden falls on producers of export commodities.[55]

The black market and gold rate for the rupiah generally fluctuated in the vicinity of 300 percent of the official effective export rate until about 1958.[56] The disparity increased fantastically in 1959–1960 to nearly ten or twelve times the latter rate, then settled back to 400–500 percent through 1960 and 1961 before spiralling up again in 1962–1963. The explanation for the 1959–1960 jump is easily pinpointed as a flight of Chinese "hot money" at a time when Chinese small shopkeepers were being driven out of the villages and the formerly lucrative opportunities for utilising surplus cash in importing were being closed to private businessmen. Although this was, in effect, capital flight, which has been going on throughout the past decade, the grossly inflated demand for black market foreign currency soon spent itself. It is noteworthy that no devaluation has ever eliminated the disparity (although an uncertain waiting period with low black rate usually follows), because of a constant demand for foreign exchange which cannot be obtained through official channels, particularly for profit remittances and capital repatriation. On the other hand, the demand is not unlimited and merely speculative against a depreciating rupiah, for it sometimes pays to buy black market rupiahs in order to purchase export commodities. Not enough is known about the extent of the foreign exchange loss through black market operations, but it certainly represents a net drain, not compensated by any significant inflow of private capital.

The multiple exchange rate system is a mechanism for adjusting supply and demand for foreign exchange through official channels by means of differential rates or taxes for different transactions.

[55] For a fuller treatment of this problem up to 1960, see W. M. Corden and J. A. C. Mackie, "Development of the Indonesian Exchange Rate System," *Malayan Economic Review*, vol. 7, April 1962, and Chapter 12, below.

[56] Until early 1961, the black market rate of the rupiah was published in *Statistik Konjunktur*. Since then, newspapers have been forbidden to publish the rate, and it has been necessary either to follow the Hong Kong market rate in the *Far Eastern Economic Review* or to consult *Pick's Currency Yearbook*.

Even when Indonesia had a fairly simple system of trade taxes in 1950–1952, the superimposition of a negotiable foreign exchange certificate which exporters could sell to importers created the characteristic feature of a multiple rate system; it was so devised that exporters effectively received Rp. 7.6 per dollar, while importers had to pay Rp. 11.4. Since this meant that the rupiahs obtained from $1,000 worth of export produce would only suffice to obtain two-thirds that value in imports, the system ultimately operated as a redistribution of income away from the exporter.

Indonesia's system became far more complex when import taxes known as TPI (*Tambahan Pembajaran Impor*) were imposed in August 1952 after abolition of the 1950–1952 certificate system. Imports were divided into four categories ranging from essential to luxury goods; in order to choke off demand for luxury and inessential goods, only essentials were tax-free, less essential goods paid 100 or 200 percent of the par rate, and "luxuries" were prohibited. These categories were modified several times between 1952 and 1960, but the essential principle remained and has, indeed, been continued in a slightly different form since 1961. However, the bulk of Indonesia's imports (about 80 percent under the initial 1952 classification) were in the lowest category, so that their effective rate was generally close to the overvalued par rate. Rice, cotton cloth, baby milk, medicines, newsprint, and books have generally carried little or no tax, because the political consequences (and the impact on cost of living) of higher taxes would be too dangerous. When the effective rate for these is considered in relation to either the black market rate or a hypothetical "real" or single equilibrium rate, at which the supply and demand for foreign exchange would balance, it is clear that lightly taxed imports were, in effect, being subsidised. The subsidy was paid not by the high duty imports, which were too limited in quantity to yield substantial sums, but by exports.

Attempts to bring the supply and demand for foreign exchange into balance through a market system of fluctuating rates have been attempted on several occasions. The most comprehensive attempt to attain stability in this way was the 1957–1958 *Bukti Ekspor* (BE) system, under which the exporter received a negotiable certificate to the face value of his export and sold it to importers who likewise had to produce BE certificates to the equivalent value of their foreign exchange needs. The exporter had to pay a 20 percent tax on his proceeds, but otherwise no attempt was made to load the transaction against him. The rate was entirely set by the daily market, and in theory exports would be stimulated and imports checked if the price rose in response to demand for foreign exchange, with the result that equilibrium should be attained automatically. However, the system turned out to have a built-in tendency toward *disequilibrium,* since demand constantly exceeded supply. Importers knew that even if prices rose they could always sell goods so long as a high volume of money sustained internal demand and shortages of goods persisted. They would suffer losses if the BE price subsequently fell, but this never happened. The rate drifted from 210 percent of par in July 1957, to 332 percent in March 1958 (giving effective rates of Rp. 18.4 to 30.3 per dollar), when the government stepped in and "froze" the rate. Eighteen months later it devalued the currency directly to Rp. 45 per dollar.

The principle of fluctuating rates was also attempted (momentarily only) in 1950 under the first certificate system and, for a part only of export earnings, under the 1956 BPE system and the 1962 SIVA system. The latter seems to have been conceived mainly as a stimulant to exporters, who now obtained a negotiable certificate for 15 percent of their earnings, which importers could buy to conduct imports without resort to all the usual controls. Again, after a hesitant start, the market rate of the SIVA drifted away from thirteen to over thirty times the par value. In May 1963, the SIVA was abolished and an entirely new system introduced at a newly effective rate of Rp. 315 per dollar plus import taxes.[57]

No single stabilising device has succeeded in holding the external value of the rupiah. Consequently, the government has had to rely increasingly on direct controls over import applications and on various *ad hoc* measures to choke off the demand for foreign exchange. In recent years, Indonesian governments have been more and more occupied with the sheer mechanics of safe-

[57] *Three Monthly Economic Review,* July 1963, pp. 1–3.

guarding their gold and foreign exchange holdings, to the exclusion of more basic economic problems. The decline of these reserves in 1961–1962 from around $300 million to nearly zero leaves Indonesia facing its most intractable problems yet.

Can we draw any conclusions about the future from this account of past trends? Will economic deterioration continue to a point of complete collapse or may we expect Indonesia's revolution to reach a Thermidorean stage where the drive towards *Umwertung aller Werte* will be restrained by forces compelling restraint and consolidation? Speculation about these issues becomes deeply involved in problems of political analysis, of course. But the economic framework may prove decisive for two reasons. The first is that, although Indonesia's economy has proved remarkably resilient to the shocks and strains of the last six years, there are reasons for thinking that the limits of flexibility are being approached in 1963, primarily because of the deteriorating foreign exchange situation. If Indonesia's capacity to import declines substantially below the quite high levels of 1961–1962 (as it well may, although probably not to a crippling extent unless all foreign aid dries up), radical changes in the tax structure will be necessary if the central government is to maintain the financial resources and hence the power (of both allocation and coercion) which it has had available over recent years. The political consequences could be far-reaching.

A second reason why the economic framework may limit the unfolding of political forces is related to a point raised earlier about the consequences of the transfer of Dutch properties in Indonesia. The immediate social and political consequences of this great shift in property relations were minor because the estates were nationalised rather than passed on to a class of "national capitalists." The new elite of managers and technicians in the new government estates and trading corporations, who came into prominence alongside the other contenders for elite status (civil servants, party leaders, and army officers), were, however, the least influential politically because so many of its members had been employees of Dutch firms. In the long run, the influence of this managerial elite seems bound to increase because of its indispensibility and its close association with the wealth-producing apparatus of the state. So far there has not been much indication that the government's economic policies have reflected the concerns of the men responsible for producing the foreign exchange and tax revenues. Effective power has remained with political leaders who have given secondary consideration, at most, to the nation's economic problems. About three years ago, it seemed reasonable to expect that the "administrator" types among the several elite groups might draw together in asserting the interests of the productive sector for which they were primarily responsible, as against the politicos and ideologues. Such a polarisation does not seem to have occurred.[58] There are too many divergences of interest within the governing elites and still too fragile a link between property and the men in charge of it. The crudely Marxist assumptions we can often make with a fair degree of truth about the relationship between property ownership, political power, and government policies simply have not applied in Indonesia. Before 1957, this could largely be attributed to the dominance of Dutch and Chinese capital, to the extraordinarily wide dispersion of property ownership within the Indonesian population, and to the lack of cohesive or organised economic interest groups. Since 1958, the first of these factors has been replaced by a dominating state sector. Burnham should be our mentor rather than Marx in such a situation, but he is just as irrelevant. Only a precise and intricate analysis of many factors in the power structure will give any persuasive answers—but not persuasive predictions.

It is hard to see how any stability can be achieved in the Indonesian economy or in the polity until such time as the controllers of property are brought into much closer relationship with the determining (and maintaining) of economic policy. It does not seem to me to matter greatly whether this should be achieved within an economy with a dominant public sector and strongly socialist ideology (of a Russian or Yugoslavian hue—the latter very fashionable these days—or distinctively Indonesian) or whether private enterprise will yet win greater scope for itself because of the poor record of the state corporations in the last

[58] I advanced an argument along these lines in "Indonesia's Government Estates and Their Masters," *op. cit.*, pp. 354–357.

few years of turbulent inflation. (There have been some intriguing indications that the pendulum may now be swinging back from its 1958–1962 trend towards state dominance simply out of a realisation that it is, in fact, politically easier to control private enterprise than state corporations.) In any event, it is clear that Indonesia's revolution has not yet worked itself out to a point of new sociopolitical equilibrium any more than economic equilibrium.

CHAPTER 2

Economic Policy-Making in Indonesia, 1950–1957*

BRUCE GLASSBURNER

The period beginning in December 1949, with the transfer of Dutch sovereignty over the East Indian Islands to the government of the United States of Indonesia and ending in December 1957, with the so-called "take-over" of Dutch-owned business property seems clearly destined to become one of those times of struggle and crisis which historians of the nation will analyze and re-analyze over the generations, interpreting and reinterpreting the known facts as the perspective of time changes. We are, of course, still much too close to that period to be able to understand its historical significance at all well. It is nevertheless of great importance to make an effort to understand the recent past in a highly dynamic situation such as that which now exists in this new nation.

It is the intent of this article to analyze the period in terms of just one aspect—namely, the making and implementation of economic policy—not only because the author is an economist rather than a historian or political scientist, but also because the disappointing record of economic policy during that period clearly reflects the underlying political conflict which eventually resulted in the drastic action of December 1957. This record, therefore, makes the dramatic attempt at reordering which is now in progress

* Reprinted with permission of the University of Chicago Press and the editors of *Economic Development and Cultural Change,* from the January 1962 issue of that journal.

in the nation somewhat more easy to understand than is possible if it is viewed only as a series of current events.

I would like to begin this analysis of the period by asserting that, from the point of view of economic policy, the years 1950 to 1957 in Indonesia are best understood as years of a hopeless losing battle on the part of a very small group of pragmatically conservative political leaders against an increasingly powerful political opposition of generally radical orientation.

This statement, while it is my own way of putting the point, is by no means entirely original. The same general idea has been more or less clearly stated by six other writers. In order to give proper credit where due, and to indicate clearly the eclectic nature of this analysis, it will be useful to look at the statements of this general hypothesis that have been made in several analyses of the Indonesian economic and political scene which have appeared in the last few years.

Dr. John Sutter, in his extensive, descriptive study of Indonesian economic policy,[1] sees the period as being divided into two parts, which are, roughly, the times of political ascendancy of two major factions in the struggle. The period of the first four cabinets, from December 1949, when Dr. Mohammed Hatta took office as prime minister, until June 1953, when the cabinet of Mr. Wilopo[2] fell, is referred to by Sutter as "the *Masjumi* period." He regards it as such in spite of the fact that Hatta and Wilopo were not members of the Masjumi political party, because, in his view, during this period the dominating outlook among members of the cabinet was the "Sjafruddin-Masjumi" outlook. (Mr. Sjafruddin Prawiranegara was first minister of finance and later the governor of the Bank of Indonesia. He was also quite consistently the Masjumi party's outstanding spokesman on matters of economic policy.)

The period following the fall of the Wilopo cabinet is referred

[1] John O. Sutter, *Indonesianisasi, Politics in a Changing Economy, 1940–1955,* Data Paper no. 36, Department of Far Eastern Studies, Southeast Asia Program, Cornell University, Ithaca, N.Y., 1959.

[2] The designation "Mr." (for *Meester in Rechten,* or Master of Laws) is a Dutch title, still widely used in Indonesia.

to by Sutter as "the PNI period";[3] it was dominated in outlook by "the less tolerant ultranationalist and socialist politicians." [4]

Although Sutter uses these labels as major time categories, he does not dwell on their significance at length, nor does he explicitly make use, except very occasionally,[5] of the idea of the conflict implied in the distinction as a means of analyzing the economic policies of the postrevolutionary period. Aside from the fact that he gives brief and casual treatment to this basic idea, it seems to me that he overemphasizes the importance of the Masjumi and the quite highly conservative (by Indonesian standards) Sjafruddin. The emphasis on Sjafruddin indicates a tendency on Sutter's part to regard the leadership of the earlier period as being more conservative in outlook than it really was, an emphasis which is necessary if his two periods are to be clearly distinct. This tendency to overemphasize the differences in the ideological orientation of the leadership of the two periods is also reflected in his reference to the leadership of the "PNI period" as being in the hands of "socialist politicians," when in fact, socialism is basic to the political ideology of virtually all shades of the Indonesian political spectrum. It might be added that the use of the party labels is unfortunate, in view of the fact that by no means do all members of the Masjumi party think along the lines of Sjafruddin; Dr. Sukiman, who was prime minister from March 1951 to March 1952, appears to be one major exception. Similarly, the PNI has its "economics-minded" intellectuals, who fail to fit the description of "ultranationalist," Wilopo and Mr. Sumanang (Wilopo's minister of economic affairs) being important examples.

Benjamin Higgins has suggested terminology which describes the basic antagonism somewhat better than that of Sutter. Higgins suggests that "economics-minded" or "development-minded" persons struggled for power against a group he characterizes as "his-

[3] PNI are the initials of the *Partai Nasional Indonesia* (Indonesian Nationalist Party).

[4] Sutter, *op. cit.*, p. 1190.

[5] He does speak at one point of a tendency for the two sides to cancel each other out, "and [leave the] Government on a dead center of inactivity or . . . [following] the moderate rationalist-socialist middle course of which Djuanda and Sumitro were exponents." *Ibid.*

tory-minded."[6] The former turn out to be essentially Western-oriented, and the latter to be "a mixture of Communists and of a larger number who are nationalist, conservative (in Western terms), and isolationist."[7] The orientation of the latter group Higgins sees as being more militantly antiforeign and more concerned with the retention of Indonesia's traditional linguistic, cultural, and religious institutions. The main advantage of this terminology over Sutter's is that the awkward connection of such attitudes to party labels is avoided. The disadvantage is that the terminology is unfair to the radicals of the left who opposed the leadership and policies of the first four cabinets.

The same criticism can be made of the terminology used by John Meek, who feels that the split occurs between those emphasizing Indonesianization of the economy and those who emphasized economic development.[8] Meek makes the difference in orientation between the two groups the center of his analysis of economic policy from 1950 to 1954, concluding, incidentally, that those interested in Indonesianization first achieved considerably more success than the other group, in spite of the fact that four of the five cabinets in the time period which he analyzed were led by the group that have been referred to here as pragmatic conservatives. The main point, implicit in all of the writings thus far discussed, is that the group in opposition from 1950 to 1957 refused to accept the basic premise of the cabinet leadership, i.e., that the main outlines of the structure of the economy, both in terms of ownership and function, had to be lived with for a relatively long period of time, and that policy had to be designed to improve its functioning. This much can be accepted as correct, but it does not follow from this that demands for "completion of the revolution" in the economy and insistence on Indonesian control over economic institutions are to be regarded as backward-looking (as they are by both Meek and Higgins).

[6] Benjamin Higgins, *Indonesia's Economic Stabilization and Development,* Institute of Pacific Relations, New York, 1957, p. 103.

[7] *Idem.*

[8] John Paul Meek, *The Government and Economic Development in Indonesia, 1950–54,* Ph.D. thesis, University of Virginia, Charlottesville, 1956, microfilm, p. 185.

The most ambitious attempt to deal with the relationship of this conflict to economic policy is that of Hans Schmitt.[9] Schmitt sees the basic cause of economic and political strife in Indonesia as stemming from the economic interests of the "bureaucratic elite" of the Indonesian community, who were faced with a frustrating obstacle in the form of continued domination of the industrialized-commercialized sector of the economy by foreign interests, primarily Dutch. Schmitt bases his analysis on a drastic premise:

> It seems . . . plausible to argue that extensions in the capital stock enhance the power of those who control it. This is a consideration which leads to a contemporaneous conflict between interests of power and of consumption. Maximum consumption (and leisure) is apt to be in the immediate interests of people not in control of accumulated capital, and maximum investment of those that are. The rate of economic development would then reflect the balance of power between them. The rate is maximized, *ceteris paribus,* when one group is firmly in control and in fact sees its power enhanced by further accumulation. Unfortunately, neither has been the case in Indonesia, and this is reflected in the course of Indonesian monetary policy.
>
> The capital stock in Indonesia has been predominantly in the hands of foreigners, reflecting pre-war colonial conditions.[10]

The bureaucratic elite is not well identified by Schmitt, but from context it would appear to mean the broad mass of government employees and the government-created group of *nasional* (i.e., indigenous) entrepreneurs, the bulk of whom were importers. These people had considerable political power and little control over economic activity, and were, because of this, both desirous and able to raise their own standards of "consumption and leisure" by becoming economic parasites. Thus their interests were in direct conflict with "rational" economic goals, and they formed an intransigent opposition to cabinet-led attempts at fiscal retrenchment. Domestic inflation was in the interest of the importer group, for one thing, and, since government expenditure on a

[9] Hans O. Schmitt, "Monetary Policy and Social Conflict in Indonesia," Djakarta, 1958, multilithed. A later version of this paper was submitted as a Ph.D. thesis to the University of California, Berkeley, in 1959.

[10] *Ibid.,* pp. 1–14.

high level meant high government employment and also opportunities to favor interests in close relation to this elite, streamlining of government finance aroused ready opposition.

The Schmitt version of the conflict raises several difficult questions. First, one is inclined to ask why the early cabinets made any attempt at all to devise policies that would bring fiscal stability and economic growth. In connection with the Wilopo cabinet's retrenchment program, Schmitt is bothered by this question himself: "Since these interests [i.e., those challenged by the retrenchment policy] were those of the elite taken as a unit, . . . it is curious to find any political orientation developing at all that would be prepared to challenge them." [11] The answer which Schmitt found was that (a) the Masjumi party anticipated very wide popular support in the general elections, and could therefore ignore the interests of the elite, and (b) failing the materialization of popular support, the Masjumi felt confident of "the support which . . . [retrenchment's] proponents could muster in the army."

But this reply does not really answer the question. Why, even with popular and/or military support, should the Masjumi leadership wish to foster the interests of entrenched Dutch capital and ignore the interests of its countrymen? Masjumi party members were to be found in large numbers among the *nasional* importers, if not so strongly among the civil servants, all this aside from the fact that the cabinet in question was under the leadership of the "liberal" wing of the Nationalist party, not the Masjumi. Finally, what would motivate the army leadership to support fiscal retrenchment? Surely its leadership was no less nationalistic than that of the bureaucracy.

A second difficult question raised by Schmitt's formulation is that of the identification of the interests of the elite. As George Kahin has said:

> The Indonesian bureaucracy was not a harmonious and unified group . . . although the bureaucracy can be regarded as a force of some consequence in the Indonesian political scene, its impact has not been as great as might be expected on the basis of the high pro-

[11] *Ibid.,* pp. 3–18.

portion of the Western-educated Indonesian elite it has incorporated. Where the influence of its members has been felt, it has frequently been in terms of party advantage rather than calculated to promote views or interests of the bureaucracy as a whole.[12]

Thus, it appears plain that any attempt to explain the pattern of politics and economic policy in terms of a simple theory of economic interest runs afoul of the complexities of multiple economic interests, and the quite apparent presence in the community of elite group members who were interested enough in economic stabilization and development to make modest efforts at appropriate policy proposals, and even to fight for them politically to some extent.

But Schmitt's analysis contains a basically correct insight—namely, that the economic elements in the basis of power of the opposition to these cabinets and their policies, lay in the fact of the continued existence of an entrenched Dutch economic interest, and in the economic impotency of the Indonesian elite in general.

J. A. C. Mackie, in a recent article,[13] deals with the same issue in still different terms, though basically it is the same as the Schmitt analysis. Mackie says that the government in this period (1950–1957) did not represent "productive interests," but "consumers" instead. Hence, policy was not "productive." In the absence of a strong government, the "conditions appropriate to a free-enterprise deveolpment policy" could not be expected. This formulation, too, would seem to put the matter rather too firmly in terms of economic interest to avoid the problems of the Procrustean bed.

Last in this gallery of analysts of the schism of Indonesian leadership is Herbert Feith, who, in a remarkably fine M.A. thesis, has examined the problem entirely from the point of view of the political scientist. Feith, like Sutter, sees the period as being divided by the fall of the Wilopo cabinet. Until that event took

[12] George McT. Kahin, "Indonesia," in Kahin, ed., *Major Governments of Asia,* Cornell University Press, Ithaca, N.Y., 1958, p. 521.

[13] "The Political Economy of Guided Democracy," *Australian Outlook,* December 1959, esp. pp. 287–288.

place (June 1953), "the political elite was substantially united on fundamentals." [14] But by that time, according to Feith, a serious political polarization had taken place, and the failure of that cabinet swung control decisively to the other pole, i.e., to the "mass leaders." Before the pendulum swing, he argues, policy was largely in the hands of the "intellectuals" of the Masjumi, PNI, and Indonesian Socialist party (PSI).[15] The position of strength which this group held in 1950 was eroded by a continued discrepancy between expectations and performances, a discrepancy which was, in large measure, the result of the efforts of the so-called mass leaders themselves, who were able to make ready use of the anti-Dutch, antiliberal sentiments that were deeply rooted in the community. While Feith's analysis of the schism is far more complete than that of any of the others, it is primarily an analysis of political events and thus, properly enough, tends to place its relationship to economic policy in a position of secondary interest. Secondly, his emphasis on the intellectual leadership of the one pole and on the mass orientation of the other tends to prejudice the case against the latter.

The radical left and right do not entirely lack rationale for their positions, however alien their premises may be to Western observers. The Marxian point of view, for example, rests on the argument that the state is inevitably controlled by those who control the economy, and that private capital is inherently exploitative. Refusal to cooperate with governments which made even tentative gestures toward rehabilitation of the colonial economy was consistent with this argument, which, incidentally, originates with Western academics.

The radically conservative point of view is that Indonesian culture has been badly diluted by more than three centuries of

[14] Herbert Feith, *The Wilopo Cabinet, 1952–53: Turning Point in Post-Revolutionary Indonesia,* Cornell Modern Indonesia Project (monograph series), Cornell University, Ithaca, N.Y., 1958, pp. 210–211.

[15] In Feith's terminology, "intellectuals" are persons "of Western university or senior secondary education" (*op. cit.,* p. 19), and "mass leaders" are those whose positions of power rest on "narrowly political skills," rather than on any claim to administrative expertise or knowledge of government.

Western overlordship, and that the only hope of salvaging Indonesian institutions is to prevent their further dilution. The continued presence of Dutch business and government personnel meant to many Indonesians the continued existence of the colonial social structure, in which the Dutchman sat atop a pyramid whose base was "native." They hope to see free Indonesia develop her own institutions, "consistent with the Indonesian spirit." Pragmatically, the fact that the "mass leaders" were able to enlist mass support would seem to suggest that their political premises, if not their economic logic, might be more nearly correct for the longer view than those on which the leaders of the opposite pole felt compelled to operate.

To support my restatement of the idea that runs through all of these analyses in terms which seem to fit my problem best, it is necessary to start with the Round Table Conference held at The Hague in the autumn months of 1949. At that conference, the Netherlands agreed to grant Indonesia her sovereignty, politically, but at the same time established conditions in the agreement which were designed to preserve Dutch economic interests in the archipelago. The following are the relevant passages taken from the agreement:

Section A

Article 1

1. In respect of the recognition and restoration of the rights, concessions, and licenses properly granted under the law of the Netherlands East Indies (Indonesia) and still valid on the date of transfer of sovereignty, the Republic of the United States of Indonesia will adhere to the basic principle of recognizing such rights, concessions, and licenses. The Republic of the United States of Indonesia also recognizes, insofar as this has not been done, that the rightful claimants be restored to the actual exercise of their rights under the proviso referred to in the following paragraphs of this article. . . .[16]

[16] Article 1, paragraph 3, specifically qualified this paragraph to take account of the problem of squatters on estate lands, noting that removal of population from the lands might cause "too much unrest," and that each case must be judged on its individual merits in this regard.

Article 2

The rights, concessions, and licenses referred to in Article 1, paragraph 1, may be infringed only in the public interest, including the welfare of the people, and through amicable settlement with the rightful claimants, and if the latter cannot be achieved, by expropriation for the public benefit, such in accordance with the provisions of Article 3.

Article 3

Expropriation, nationalization, liquidation, compulsory cession, or transfer of properties or rights, shall take place exclusively for the public benefit, in accordance with the procedure prescribed by law and, in the absence of an agreement between the parties, against previously enjoyed or guaranteed indemnity to be fixed by judicial decision at the real value of the object involved, such in accordance with provisions to be prescribed by law.[17]

These provisions in the agreement were the basis of perpetuation of an economic system which even the most tolerant of Indonesian patriots must have found difficult to accept agreeably, for the degree of foreign domination of the economy (aside from peasant agriculture) was extreme. Nan Amstutz cites a prewar estimate that only 19 percent of the privately owned nonagricultural capital was in the hands of indigenous Indonesians, while 52 percent was held by Dutch owners.[18] In 1952, it was estimated that 50 percent of all consumer imports were still being handled by four Dutch firms, and 60 percent of exports by eight firms.[19] The bank of issue was a largely Dutch-owned corporation, controlled by Dutch officers. Private banking was largely in the hands of seven foreign banks, three of which were Dutch. Under such circumstances it is little wonder that even the moderate leaders

[17] Round Table Conference results as accepted in the second plenary meeting held on November 2, 1949, in the "Ridderzaal" at The Hague, published by the Secretariat-General of the Round Table Conference (no date), pp. 23–24.

[18] Nan G. Amstutz, "Development of Indigenous Importers in Indonesia, 1950–55," Ph.D. thesis, Fletcher School of Law and Diplomacy, 1958, p. 8.

[19] Meek, *op. cit.,* p. 168n.

felt that the Indonesian revolution had not yet entered its economic phase.[20]

Thus, the situation which confronted the economic leaders of the new national community was one which they inevitably had strong inclinations to change. It can be taken for granted that any successful Indonesian politician is, first of all, a nationalist, and secondly, a socialist.[21] The task, then, which the government faced in 1950 was to stabilize and expand an economy that was (a) foreign-dominated and (b) privately owned. They were expected to devise policy which, if successful, would benefit the interests of their ideological enemies at least as much as their allies and, anticipating the general elections, to attempt to gain the support of the politically sensitive part of the electorate—a group more radically inclined than they. Examined in retrospect, it is not surprising that they made so little progress in formulating successful economic policy. As Feith aptly puts it, "the fiery idealism of Jogjakarta and the days of guerilla fighting had to be accommodated in the Dutch-established structure of Djakarta." [22]

In terms of achieving that accommodation, it was fortunate that, in 1950, a virtual monopoly of economic expertise was held by sober-minded, Dutch-trained, pragmatic socialists. In the first four cabinets, only Hatta and Dr. Sumitro Djojohadikusumo were trained economists, but the general direction of their economic ideology was followed by several others whose experience and inclinations perhaps qualified them as economic experts, namely, Sjafruddin Prawiranegara, Djuanda Kartawidjaja, Jusuf Wibisono,

[20] Higgins, *op. cit.*, p. 102, quotes Hadji Agus Salim to this effect.

[21] The question often arises in discussions of Indonesian politics as to whether the nation's Communist party leadership is not perhaps communist first and nationalist second—and if then only as a matter of political convenience. Confronted by this question in personal conversation, a close associate of D. N. Aidit, Secretary General of the Indonesian Communist party, emphatically stated that Aidit has always said that he is a communist because he is Indonesian. It is fair to say, furthermore, that the party in Indonesia has taken a consistently nationalist position for many years—and particularly so after President Sukarno had assumed the position of prime minister.

[22] Feith, *op. cit.*, p. 3.

and perhaps others. Of this group, Sjafruddin was the one most clearly inclined to accept the circumstances and willing to make the necessary accommodation, while Sumitro was undoubtedly the least inclined in that direction. Sjafruddin's cautious variety of socialism was clearly stated by him in 1948 in the following words:

> The ideology which is suitable to our society is Religious Socialism, an ideology which is in harmony with the Constitution. Religious Socialism does not abolish individualism, individual initiative, and individual responsibility . . . Competition arising out of private initiative as such is not bad, but the contrary, because competition increases production and improves the quality of goods . . . Only at a certain stage does this liberal economy not increase production and is there a tendency to limit production. At that stage the government must intervene by nationalizing certain private enterprises or establishing enterprises itself.[23]

This was, indeed, the voice of conservatism. But the more dynamic, and, I think it is safe to say, more effective Sumitro took a position farther left and more clearly nationalistic:

> In general in the states of Asia, in my view, the effort to surmount stagnation and retrogression, and later to encourage increasingly fast development, must be planned and consciously arranged. Here comes to the forefront the state which takes the role of the pioneer in the process of development. It is a fact that, in the states of Asia, there are not yet, or not yet sufficient, groups of creative entrepreneurs from within the society itself . . . The state must play an important role, particularly in the beginning stage . . . unless development is to be left absolutely to the foreign entrepreneurs which are [now] in our countries . . . In my opinion, this last road is not the intention and goal of development which is desired in the states of Asia. Both for the creation of autonomous investment and of skills, the state must and can play an important role by means of direct or indirect policy.[24]

[23] Quoted from Kahin, *Nationalism and Revolution in Indonesia,* Cornell University Press, Ithaca, N.Y., 1952, p. 310. The original is Sjafruddin's pamphlet, *Politik dan Revolusi Kita,* Jogjakarta, 1948.

[24] Sumitro Djojohadikusumo, *Ekonomi Pembangunan,* Pembangunan, Djakarta, 1957, pp. 128–129 (my translation).

Six months after joining the Natsir cabinet, Sumitro more directly expressed his leftward, nationalistic bent in policy by directing the development of the Economic Urgency Program of 1951, a plan for quite extensive economic intervention in an attempt to establish indigenous industries.[25] And later, as minister of finance in two cabinets, Sumitro took drastic action to weaken the position of foreign enterprise. Sumitro, I think, represented more nearly than did Sjafruddin (Sutter's nominee for the guiding spirit), the attitude of the leadership group of the time, for even Sjafruddin's own Masjumi party proposed in 1950 a comprehensive, if cautious, program of nationalization for vital enterprises and was directly responsible for the nationalization of the Java Bank under the Sukiman cabinet (with Sjafruddin rather reluctantly replacing the Dutch president, A. Houwink). But whether the consensus among the leaders was nearer the views of Sjafruddin or those of Sumitro is really of little moment, for the range was not wide in view of the circumstances. The orientation of both of these men was at least nominally socialist and essentially pragmatic—toward making the system work. No cabinet undertook a major program of economic re-ordering. And it was Sumitro, whose inclinations were radical, who turned out to be the most ingenious at "tinkering around the edges" of the economic system.[26]

As for the persons charged with economic responsibility after the fall of the Wilopo cabinet, the possibility of their designing and implementing economic policy that was "rational" in terms of the existing economic system was almost nonexistent. There was no longer even a vague positively-oriented consensus, since they, in opposition, had repudiated the very steps that such rationality would call for. Ultimately, then, the only way out was

[25] Sumitro Djojohadikusumo, ed., "The Government's Program on Industries," *EKI* November 1954. While the plan was strongly interventionist, its impact on the structure of the economy was slight, since (as Sumitro's article shows) implementation of the program was never carried far.

[26] Sumitro and Sjafruddin debated their differences freely in newspaper articles, in books, and in Indonesia's economic journals (e.g., Sjafruddin's carefully considered annual reports as governor of the Bank Indonesia, *Bank Indonesia Reports,* 1951–1956, and Sumitro's collection of articles, *Persoalan Ekonomi di Indonesia,* Indira, Djakarta, 1953).

the radical way, namely, nationalization of the Dutch enterprises.

With this orientation toward the situation, let us now turn toward the pattern of economic policy. The appended table and the following discussion give a summary of that pattern.

The Hatta Cabinet[27]

The cabinet led by Dr. Mohammed Hatta has been the only one in Indonesia's political history to be led by a professional economist. Unfortunately, however, its focus was narrow and its view restricted very much to the short run. The primary concern of this brief cabinet was with political unification. At the time of the transfer of sovereignty (December 1949), the new nation was known as the Republic of the United States of Indonesia, a federation of sixteen states, of which the Republic of Indonesia was one. Over the following nine months these states merged with the Republic of Indonesia to become a "unitary state."

Despite this atmosphere of political defiance of Dutch advice and influence, the cabinet gave its attention to many matters of economic policy. The most important measure undertaken was an attempt at monetary reform through simultaneous currency devaluation and the literal cutting of the money supply in March 1950. The "money cut" involved the actual cutting in half of all Java Bank notes in denominations larger than 2.50 Indonesian guilders[28] and the reduction of all bank deposits larger than 400 guilders by half. Compensation for losses incurred in this purge were made in long-term government bonds.

The results of this reform were disappointing. President Houwink of the Java Bank claimed that the purge had reduced the money supply by 1.6 billion guilders—41 percent of the money supply! But, amazingly, the monthly data on money in circulation published by the Java Bank show a reduction from March to

[27] The following sections, summarizing the performances of the various cabinets, are largely the result of many hours of newspaper scanning undertaken by Wagiono, Ho Ing Thong, and Kenneth D. Thomas.

[28] The Indonesian currency was known as the guilder until the nationalization of the Java Bank on May 22, 1951, at which time the bank of issue became the Bank Indonesia, and the currency became the rupiah.

April of only 170 million guilders, and prices of food and textiles actually rose over the period.[29]

Aside from these quite drastic efforts at monetary and fiscal control, little else was undertaken during this cabinet's short tenure. Foreign assistance received during 1950 was larger than at any time from 1949 to 1954, reflecting, perhaps, Hatta's firm belief that the main sources of development capital must be foreign. Also, by the end of 1950, the bulk of Java's railway network had been placed under the operation of the Indonesian government, replacing the Dutch private owners.

The Natsir Cabinet

The first cabinet of the unitary Republic of Indonesia was led by Mohammed Natsir of the Masjumi party. This cabinet was probably the most distinctly dedicated toward action in economic affairs of any in Indonesian republican history. Sumitro was named minister of trade and industry, and Sjafruddin, minister of finance.

This cabinet was fortunate in taking over during the period of the full development of the Korean boom. It was thus blessed with very strong export demand, which provided at once a solution to the problem of the balance of payments, as well as a rising source of government revenue. The cabinet reacted to this situation by liberalizing imports as a means of keeping domestic prices down, raising standards of consumption, and encouraging the development of indigenous enterprise.

Credit was tight for the foreign-owned firms that dominated the economy, though easy for the burgeoning *nasional* firms. In an

[29] *The Java Bank, Report of the President and of the Board of Directors,* 1950–1951, p. 29. These annual reports will be cited hereafter as *Java Bank Report.* Schmitt argues (*op. cit.,* pp. 2–43) that the differential exchange rate system, which was introduced with the devaluation as a means of correcting the deficit in the balance of payments, counteracted both the money-reducing and the deflationary impact of the purge. While this system would indeed have this effect in a small way, no conceivable change in the trade balance could account for the huge discrepancy between the president's stated estimate of the reduction in money in circulation and the modest (4 percent) change shown in the monthly statistics. For this writer the discrepancy remains unexplained.

attempt to broaden the fiscal system, a 2.5 percent turnover tax was imposed. A combination of fiscal prudence and high revenues produced a sizeable budget surplus in 1951.

This cabinet also designed, but did not have time to initiate, an Economic Urgency Program. This was a highly nationalistic attempt to diminish the nation's dependence on foreign economic interests in several ways: by developing small, *nasional* (i.e., indigenous) industry to produce import substitutes in the hope of reducing dependence on foreign trade; by means of capital assistance to indigenous enterprise; and by restricting certain markets to indigenous sellers. The latter aspect of the program is often referred to as the "*benteng* program." [30] The Urgency Program was opposed from within the cabinet by Sjafruddin because of its highly nationalistic aspect.[31]

The "historical rights" to shares of the foreign exchange allocation which had been used by the Dutch government to re-establish the prewar pattern of trade were abandoned by the Natsir cabinet, since it was their avowed intention to change that pattern in such a way as to diminish the degree of foreign domination.

As a means of supporting the economic program, the government reorganized the *Bank Rakjat* (People's Bank) and directed its activities toward support of small business. At the same time the *Bank Industri Negara* (State Industrial Bank) was established to provide credit for reconstruction and development projects. The *Bank Negara Indonesia* was also greatly expanded and given the direct responsibility for providing capital for the *benteng* importers. Both the *Bank Rakjat*'s reorganization and the establishment of the *Bank Industri Negara* actually took place in April 1951, just after the fall of the cabinet on an issue of regional autonomy.[32] This was, clearly, a very active cabinet, but with only six months of life, it could make little genuine progress. It was followed by a cabinet divided in control between the Masjumi and the Nationalist parties, though still led by the Masjumi.

[30] *Benteng* is the Indonesian word for protected or fortified.

[31] *Java Bank Report*, 1951–1952, pp. 39–42.

[32] Although implemented late, the policy is properly called the Natsir cabinet's. Lags in implementation, e.g., in the case of the foreign investment law, often make responsibility for a particular policy difficult to assign. But in this case the responsibility belongs plainly to the Natsir cabinet.

The Sukiman Cabinet

The Sukiman cabinet served for ten months, from April 1951 to February 1952—a period of several significant landmarks in the economy's history. The finance minister was Jusuf Wibisono, and Wilopo was minister of economic affairs during most of this period. The most significant developments were the nationalization of the Java Bank and the collapse of the fiscal situation. The peak of the Korean boom was passed by mid-1951, and Indonesia's exports began to decline. The 1952 budget deficit was nearly three billion rupiahs, as compared with a surplus of 1.7 billion rupiahs for the preceding year. The deficit would have been larger still, had not a substantial revision of fiscal policy followed in the Wilopo cabinet later in the year.

The multiple exchange rate system which had been part of the fiscal trappings of the economic system since the reforms of 1950 was abandoned on the advice of Hjalmar Schacht, who had been invited to Indonesia by Sumitro as financial adviser. The "Sumitro Plan" for small industries was partially implemented during the same year. The *benteng* program was continued, but, as a result of less careful screening of applicants for import licenses, the proportion of legitimate importing businesses initiated declined, and the disastrous fate of the program was thereby foreshadowed.

The Sukiman cabinet fell in February 1952, over the issue of the signing of the Mutual Security Agreement with the United States.

After some political difficulty, the Wilopo cabinet was formed in early April 1952, with retrenchment as its initial economic theme. Sumitro returned to the cabinet, as finance minister, and Sumanang became minister of economic affairs. Despite heavy expenditure commitments which carried over from the Sukiman cabinet, the estimated 1952 deficit of Rp. 4 billion (as of June 1952) was pared down at the year's end to a realized deficit of slightly less than Rp. 3 billion. This was accomplished mainly by ingenious gadgeteering, particularly with the taxes and exchange regulations in the foreign trade sector, although some effort at austerity in government expenditure was made as well.

The most spectacular effort at economy was made in connection with "rationalization" of the army through modernization and manpower reduction. Conservative factions within the army combined with conservative political elements to oppose attempted renovation, resulting in the abortive effort on the part of the rationalization's supporters to force the issue by use of arms, in October 1952. The attempt failed, and the results were disastrous for the proponents of the rationalization as well as a blow to the cabinet leadership and their supporters. This fiasco, incidentally, is often pointed to by persons familiar with the Indonesian political scene as the actual turning point, rather than the fall of the cabinet, which came several months later.

Less spectacularly, but more significantly, the ministry of finance sought a budget for 1953 that would call for an aggregate reduction in government expenditures of more than Rp. 4 billion —more than 25 percent of total expenditures in 1952. Implementation would have resulted in the dismissal of at least 150,000 persons on the government payroll, according to an estimate by the ministry of finance.[33] In point of fact, expenditures were not greatly reduced, but the Wilopo cabinet actually succeeded in maintaining a deficit less than that which they had projected until June 1953, when the cabinet fell on the issue of use of force to remove squatters from Sumatran estate lands.

The First Ali Sastroamidjojo Cabinet

The fiscal stringency of the Wilopo cabinet was promptly abandoned with the accession of the first cabinet in free Indonesia's history that did not have Masjumi representation. This was the longest-lived cabinet of any which preceded Ir. Djuanda's[34] *Karja* cabinet of 1957–1959. From a fiscal point of view, this cabinet's first nine months were catastrophic. The government's debt was trebled and foreign exchange reserve was eliminated altogether.[35]

This unfortunate performance in the financial field was complemented by the open perversion of the *benteng* policy. Under the minister of economic affairs, Mr. Iskaq Tjokrohadisurjo, the

[33] Cited by Higgins, *op. cit.,* p. 10n.

[34] The title "Ir." (*Ingenieur*) is commonly used in Indonesia to designate persons holding degrees in engineering.

[35] Schmitt, *op. cit.,* pp. 3–48, Table 3.6.

issuing of licenses became primarily a means of financial support for the Nationalist party. The government was bitterly criticized for its fiscal failures, on the one hand, and its perversion of the *benteng* policy, on the other, and in November 1954, several major cabinet changes were made, including the replacement of Iskaq with Ir. Rooseno Surjohadikusumo. Reforms were immediately undertaken in the importers' screening process by Rooseno, but the reputation of the *nasional* importer group had been irreparably damaged. Thereafter little faith was placed in this means of displacing foreign enterprise.

The main efforts at restabilization following the November 1954 cabinet shake-up were directed toward import restrictions. These efforts met with considerable success. Efforts to curb the rise in the money supply, however, were less successful.

Although under the first Ali cabinet a draft bill on foreign investment regulations was brought forth, the general atmosphere and attitude of the government at the time was anything but congenial toward foreign enterprise. In particular, the abrogation of the trade policy section of the Round Table Agreement could be, and was, rather generally regarded as a negative gesture in this respect. Thus, the Ali government presented a confusing and disturbing face toward the supporters of private foreign enterprise in Indonesia.

But despite these policy failures, the cabinet successfully maneuvered its parliamentary strength until July 24, 1955, when the political repercussions of difficulties in the appointment of a new army chief of staff brought the government down.

The Harahap Cabinet

Following a cabinet crisis of less than three weeks, Hatta, as acting president, brought the Masjumi party back to government leadership by inducing Mr. Burhanuddin Harahap, the Masjumi parliamentary leader, to accept the position of prime minister. Sumitro Djojohadikusumo returned to the post of minister of finance.

This cabinet was generally recognized as an interim cabinet, in office to maintain government until the general elections, which were scheduled for the month of September 1955, and until a new parliament could be installed. In spite of this situation, or perhaps because of it, this cabinet was one of the most active and most successful in the field of economic policy. The confusing import certificate system was swept away, along with all special import taxes, and a relatively simple system of tax categories took their place, graduated according to the nation's need for the imported commodity to be taxed. The licensing system was depersonalized to eliminate corruption, and a new Foreign Exchange Board (BDP) was created to displace the old KPUI. Screening of *nasional* importers was improved, and an attempt was made to give the same privileges to all businessmen who were citizens of Indonesia, regardless of ethnic origin. This latter move was morally and economically laudable, but politically very dangerous, in view of the common fear of the traders of Chinese descent.

At the same time, importers were required to advance the full value of the goods they intended to purchase abroad at the time application was made for an import license. Importer's prepayments of this sort had been used by previous governments, but never so severely. The results of this rapid action were quickly in evidence. By November, the money supply had been reduced by nearly Rp. 600 million (almost 5 percent),[36] and prices of imported goods, which had risen nearly 13 percent in the first six months of 1955, fell almost 15 percent in the second half. The gold value of the rupiah rose by nearly 8 percent between April and September.[37] Food prices, however, continued to rise with increasing rapidity largely due to a very bad crop year.

Aside from this vigorous resumption of *ad hoc* fiscal discipline, the only major accomplishment of the Harahap cabinet was the decision to abrogate the Round Table Agreement unilaterally. This took place only a month before the cabinet returned its mandate, in March 1956.

The Second Ali Cabinet

Ali Sastroamidjojo returned to cabinet leadership in late March 1956, and it shortly became evident that his second term was to be little better than the first from the point of view of

[36] *Ibid.*, pp. 4–7.

[37] *Bank Indonesia Report,* 1955–1956.

economic policy, even though this time the Masjumi was to be represented.[38] Jusuf Wibisono, who had presided over the inflationary policies of the Sukiman cabinet as minister of finance, resumed the post.

The results were a prompt resumption of a large current budget deficit and an almost immediate crisis in foreign exchange. The shortage of foreign exchange, it should be noted, would have been much less a problem for Mr. Wibisono if it had not been for the eagerness with which Sumitro and his associates had increased imports in their enthusiasm for price reduction. However, the response of the government was feeble, and the crisis steadily deepened. A loan of $55 million from the International Monetary Fund was negotiated in August 1956, as a means of partial rescue.

Several important economic matters which had long been pending came to a head under this cabinet. One was the foreign investment bill, which was finally submitted formally to parliament. This was a limited accomplishment, however, since the bill was not actually passed until three years later.[39] The second was the abrogation of the debt to the Netherlands, signifying the end of all semblance of the economic agreement on which the transfer of sovereignty had been based.

The record of the second Ali cabinet, like the first, was a mixed one as far as its attitude toward foreign capital was concerned. The new export inducement certificates (*Bukti Pendorong Expor*) were issued to foreign as well as to Indonesian exporters, whereas in former versions of this scheme, the foreigners were excluded. Also, antistrike and antisquatter legislation was proposed by the government as measures to protect the estates, which were largely foreign-owned and operated.

Finally, the long-awaited Five Year Plan appeared in May 1956 and was approved by the cabinet in September. This plan, however, was the product of effort expended over four years and at least five cabinets. Little credit is due to the Ali cabinet for the timing of its appearance.

In February 1957, President Sukarno announced his famed con-

[38] This indicates, as the Sukiman cabinet's record had, that *Masjumi* participation was no guarantee of performance.

[39] With minor alterations.

ception of "Guided Democracy" in an atmosphere of virtual revolt. Incidents multiplied in the various provinces thereafter, and in March, the second Ali cabinet fell. Djuanda Kartawidjaja, the minister of planning in the second Ali cabinet, accepted the leadership of a nonparty "business cabinet" (or *Karja* cabinet, as it is often referred to in Indonesia)

The Djuanda Cabinet

The Djuanda cabinet had little opportunity to formulate new economic measures before the West Irian action of December 1957 ended the period which is under discussion here. It was mainly concerned with the rapidly deteriorating political situation which threatened to develop into civil war.[40] This challenge, however, was economic as well as political and military.

The most significant economic response on the part of the cabinet leadership was a new version of the exchange certificate system, known simply as the *Bukti Expor* or "BE" system. The essence of the system was that exporters were issued par value in certificates rather than currency in return for their foreign exchange earnings. At the outset of the program, these certificates were saleable for whatever the market would bring minus a 20 percent tax. Importers were required to present sufficient certificates of par value to cover any foreign exchange request. The effect of this measure was, of course, a *de facto* devaluation. The market value of the certificates had reached 332 percent of par value by April 1958, far in excess of the anticipated ceiling, when their price was pegged. This attempt to placate the exporting outer islands did not succeed as a political move, nor was it notably successful as an economic measure. However, the BE certificates were required for import as late as August 1959, when the system was abolished as part of a new monetary reform.[41]

[40] In fact, a "State of War and Siege" was declared just prior to the formation of the cabinet.

[41] Of course, the basic "liberal" aspect of the BE system had been abandoned in April 1958, when the upward spiral of the price of the certificates had been blocked by pegging. Between that date and August 1959, Indonesia was, in fact, operating with a multiple exchange rate system, the BE certificates only being excess baggage. This was apparently not clearly under-

The Djuanda cabinet also fought a hard but losing battle with government finance under the minister of finance, Sutikno Slamet. A halt was ordered in further hiring of government personnel, and an attempt was made at increasing general taxation. The result for the year, however, was a deficit of Rp. 5.5 billion, or nearly 22 percent of total government expenditures.[42]

A three-day national conference, or *Musjawarah Nasional* (Munas), was held in mid-September 1957. This conference was primarily political, being largely concerned with the attempt to re-establish the dual leadership of Hatta and President Sukarno as a means of reuniting the nation. However, there also emerged a suggestion of a program for regional autonomy in development of the economy and decentralization of foreign exchange control. A follow-up National Planning Conference (Munap), held in November 1957, set out this program more fully. Subsequent political events—the West Irian action and the open rebellion in Sumatra and Sulawesi—all but erased the memory of these proposals for the remainder of the Djuanda term of office.

On November 29, 1957, Indonesia's resolution in the United States General Assembly calling for cession of West Irian (West New Guinea) to the Indonesian Republic was defeated. In early December, there began a series of demonstration strikes against Dutch firms. One of these, at the Dutch interisland shipping company, KPM, turned into a worker coup of management prerogatives. Other worker groups followed suit in short order. During the next two weeks, under military supervision, the movement became a *de facto* expulsion of all Dutch management. The Djuanda cabinet neither sponsored nor resisted the "take-over" movement. There was little public criticism of the action of the army and the worker groups.

The Djuanda cabinet remained in office until the political reorganization of June 1959, at which time President Sukarno himself became prime minister, returning to the 1945 constitution of

---

stood in Djarkata prior to the 1959 money purge, judging from the heated attacks against the BE system on the part of businessmen, economists, and members of parliament.

42 Central Bureau of Statistics, Djarkata.

the revolutionary Republic as his legal basis.[43] Thus was the stage set for the development of "Socialisme à la Indonesia."

What general characteristics emerge from the pattern? First of all, it is very evident that, outside the financial fields, there wasn't much activity. There is a marked absence of policies that would have led to major changes in the economy. A glance down the lefthand column of Table 2.1 at the dates of the various cabinets gives one very quickly a good answer for that. There was not sufficient time to get very far with formulation of big plans.

More explicitly, there is no clear-cut, consistent march toward elimination of the Dutch economic interests. There are several moves in this direction: the *benteng* program, the Sumitro Plan for indigenous industries, and the abrogation of the Round Table Agreement. None of these made major inroads.

Also, there is no striding forward into socialism. Aside from the socialization of the Bank of Indonesia, there was only the taking-over of the railway companies, the utilities companies, and the establishment of a variety of government enterprises under the *Bank Industri Negara*—and perhaps a few others.

Aside from the Sumitro Plan, the Five Year Plan, and the suggestions for regional development that came out of the National Conference in 1957 (named here in order of decreasing degree of implementation), there has been no program for economic development.

Apart from three separate intervals of successful control of the budget and the balance of payments, fiscal irresponsibility is general. And these intervals provide the relief in the general picture, because otherwise, there is a marked sameness in the economic policy activities of cabinet after cabinet. These three cabinets, in which financial policy was quite successful, are the three out of the eight that are usually regarded by Western observers as the good ones. The main thing that all three had in common was the active participation of Sumitro. Two of them were Masjumi-led, one PNI-led. The outstanding failure in this respect, on the other hand, was the one PNI cabinet in which the Masjumi did not

[43] Ir. Djuanda is still often referred to, erroneously, as prime minister. He is now, in fact, the "first minister."

participate. At the same time, other cabinets, which did include Masjumi people (one, the Sukiman, was led by Masjumi), did not perform notably better.

Why, aside from the three almost quixotic attempts to deal with financial crises, did all cabinets do so little in any direction? If they were all nationalists, why did they not vigorously attack the vested Dutch interests? Since they all called themselves socialists, why was there no vigorous program of building of state enterprise? Why, when the more pragmatic intellectual clique was defeated, was there no clear repudiation of their policies and no marked swing to reflect the polar political swing which Herbert Feith finds?

The answer, I think, is simply that little else *could* be done so long as the economy retained its colonial pattern of ownership. The Indonesian leaders felt that they could not eliminate the Dutch owners and their administrative staffs because they had little or nothing to put in their place. There were no funds with which to compensate the nationalized owners; and there were no Indonesian experts to operate the firms. Practical policy thus called for attempting to build an Indonesian commercial and industrial economy alongside the foreign one. This huge task was attempted in only a small way, via the unfortunate *benteng* program, and through in-service training in the larger Dutch firms.

The same general problem arose in connection with building new state enterprise. The new capital was not available, nor was the expertise. In short, the legacy of colonialism paralyzed them.

The general fiscal irresponsibility stemmed from a variety of causes. Schmitt believes that the government lived with deficits because deficits were in the interest of the bureaucratic elite. Indeed, government employees could not accept retrenchment policies that would endanger or eliminate their jobs. However, it is dubious that inflation was in the interest of the dominant political group in general. More likely explanations are to be found in the archaic tax system, the inadequate civil service, the expensive defense establishment, and the anticolonial abandonment of taxation of landed interests. Sumitro's fiscal success was the result of ingenious financial "*ad-hocery*," to use Higgins' term. Most of his devices were once-over palliatives. Fiscal reform never came.

Also, there was always the threat of the general elections, the effect of which was to stifle inclinations toward action. Since no one really knew what the Indonesian electorate would respond to, the sensible tactic for any cabinet was to play it safe.[44] It has been suggested that the Harahap cabinet was an exception to this, having, apparently, staked a great deal on making the Masjumi appear to be the honest, expert party, cleaning up in the wake of the disastrous PNI cabinet of Ali Sastroamidjojo.[45]

Finally, there were the recognized facts that financial stability would serve the interest of the Dutch businessmen and bankers; that rehabilitation of the estates would serve the purposes of the Dutch plantation owners; and that a larger amount of produce had to flow through Dutch distribution channels and float in Dutch boats and ships. Or, if these improvements did not serve the Dutch, then they would serve the Chinese, if they did not serve both. The argument that they would also serve Indonesians was justifiably called *Kolonial denken,* a version of what Americans call the "percolator" or "trickle-down" theory.

Summarizing, I find several differences with other analyses of this period and these problems. First, viewing the situation in Indonesia historically, it is debatable whether the "pragmatic conservatives" can be regarded as correct in their attempt to live with the established economic structure. Secondly, these leaders, when in power, succeeded in making no great attempt at this accommodation because (a) their political opposition was too effective to permit it, and (b) their own ideological orientation, being nationalist and socialist, made them hesitant to move vigorously in that direction. Thirdly, Western observers generally have

[44] Regarding the elections from hindsight, apparently the electorate need not have been feared by national policymakers. Local issues seem to have determined nonurban voting patterns. But even if this had been understood beforehand by the leadership of the pragmatic conservatives, their actions would have been little, if any, less hampered, for the power of their opposition in parliament, the civil service, and the active political public was such that any major effort toward improving economic performance within the established structure could be defeated.

[45] The Harahap cabinet had only a few weeks in which to project this image prior to the elections, and most of the program necessarily was undertaken after it could conceivably have had any effect on their outcome.

Table 2.1. The pattern of economic policy, 1950–1957

Cabinet	Commercial, monetary, and fiscal policy	Nationalization	Assistance to indigenous business	Foreign investment	Other
Hatta (nonparty) 12/49–9/50	1. Money cut 2. Export certificates	Railways		$100 million U.S. loan	
Natsir (Masjumi) 9/50–3/51 (without PNI)	1. Tight credit (foreign banks) 2. BIN, BNI, and BR banks 3. Turnover tax 4. Extended free import list, "liberal" commercial policy 5. Tight budget 6. Some success with countercyclical policy		1. Industries program (Urgency plan) 2. *Benteng* 3. Abolition of "historical rights"	ECA agreement negotiated	Strike restrictions
Sukiman (Masjumi) 4/51–2/52 (cabinet including 5 Masjumi, 5 PNI)	1. Abandoned differential exchange rates 2. Large deficit in budget	Bank Indonesia nationalized 5/22/51	*Benteng* loosened	MSA agreement	1. Two-year agricultural plan 2. Emergency labor law
Wilopo (PNI) 4/52–6/53 (cabinet including 4 PNI, 4 Masjumi, 2 PSI)	1. Budget balance 2. Tight import restriction 3. Import prepayments		*Benteng* tightened	Much discussion, no great success	1. Army rationalization 2. Antisquatter action

Ali I (PNI) 8/53–7/55 (without Masjumi)	1. Large deficits in a. budget b. balance of payments 2. Trade policy section of Round Table Agreement abolished		1. Iskaq—very open-handed 2. Rooseno (11/54), began careful screening	Draft regulations on foreign investment	
Burhanuddin Harahap 8/55–3/56 (Masjumi = caretaker)	1. KPUI abolished; BDP established 2. Imports liberalized 3. Prepayments raised and advanced 4. Deficit in budget virtually eliminated		1. All Indonesian-owned businesses (*peranakan*) called *nasional* 2. General tightening of screening		1. Anticorruption drive 2. Round Table Agreement abrogated
Ali II (PNI) 4/56–3/57	1. Large budget deficits 2. Export certificates reintroduced 3. Proliferation of regulations		No major change	1. Foreign investment bill submitted to parliament 2. $55 million IMF loan	1. Five Year Plan completed 2. Debt to the Netherlands abrogated 3. Labor law a. Antisquatter b. Regional mediation boards set up
Djuanda (nonparty business cabinet) 3/57–8/59	1. *Bukti Expor* 2. Heavy import restriction	Dutch firms taken over, 12/57	Second Economic Congress—end of *benteng*		Munas and Munap—program for regional autonomy in economic development

tended to regard the political opposition to this group from a jaundiced point of view. Both strong nationalism and rapid socialization have their intelligent, intellectual proponents in Indonesia, as elsewhere. From the short-term point of view, their opposition had demonstrably unfortunate economic effects; if they had had the patience of Hatta, they could have perhaps seen their ends achieved by evolutionary means with much less political and economic disruption. But who is to say that Hatta's gradual way would involve less social cost, even if *all* costs were to be fully considered? And it is to be expected that Indonesians would count that part of the cost which the Dutchmen had to pay at a sharp discount.

Thus, it appears to this writer that Schmitt was basically right in asserting, in effect, that there was a one-way road to expulsion of the Dutch interests. Having accomplished that, however, Indonesia has by no means solved her economic problems. Indeed, she has created many in the process. Also, the divisive forces which emerged during the last ten years have raised such problems of security and political stability that it may be many years before an atmosphere can be established in which it will be possible to consider development of economic policy on anything but the crisis level. The most that can be said is that a major block was removed from the path of the policymaker with the crushing of Dutch economic interests in the West Irian action of 1957.

CHAPTER 3

Reflections on Boeke's Theory of Dualistic Economies*

MOHAMMAD SADLI

Reviewing Professor Boeke's conceptions on the highly controversial subject of "dualistic economies" is a somewhat slippery engagement, for Boeke used to blame his opponents for misinterpreting and mispresenting his ideas.

Being aware of this, the present writer can only try to minimize the risk by sticking close to Boeke's original wordings and by not trying to condense the exposition too much, for condensation often leads to a biased representation. On the other hand, Boeke's "dualistic theory" is perhaps not free from inconsistencies. This opinion is shared by Professor Higgins.[1] These inconsistencies have perhaps contributed much to the so-called misinterpretations.

Exposition of the Theory

What is Boeke's theory in essence? It is the following: "Social dualism is the clashing of an imported social system with an indigenous social system of another style. Most frequently the imported social system is high capitalism. But it may be socialism or communism just as well, or a blending of them." [2] The emphasis here

* Reprinted from *Ekonomi dan Keuangan Indonesia* (*EKI*), June 1957, by permission of the author. The editor has taken the liberty of making a number of minor editorial changes.

[1] B. H. Higgins, "The 'Dualistic Theory' of Underdeveloped Areas," *Economic Development and Cultural Change*, vol. 4, no. 2, January 1956, pp. 99–115.

[2] J. H. Boeke, *Economics and Economic Policy of Dual Societies*, Tjeenk Willink & Zoon, Haarlem, 1953, p. 4.

is on the clash between an imported and an indigenous social system of divergent character. The clashing societies have quite different value systems as well as other characteristics, which are dissimilar.

Boeke asserts, then, that "every social system has its own economic theory. A social economic theory is always the theory of a special social system. . . . Therefore the economic theory of a dualistic, heterogeneous society is itself dualistic. It has to describe and explain the economic interactions of the two clashing systems. . . . In so far it even will have to be three economic theories combined into one: the economic theory of a pre-capitalistic society, usually called primitive economies, the economic theory of a developed capitalistic or socialistic society, usually termed general economic theory or summarily social economic theory, and the economic theory of the interactions of two distinct social systerms within the borders of one society, which might be called dualistic economics." [3]

How are the two clashing societies different from each other so that two distinct economic theories have to be applied to them? According to Boeke, the "Western" economic theory is based upon the propensities of a Western society, which are: "(a) unlimited wants on the part of the economic subject; (b) money economy as the system under which the economic subject lives; (c) many-sided corporative organizations, on which the individuals base their economic activity. These fundamental principles are inextricably intertwined." [4] Boeke further describes the system of values under capitalism as one that "finds expression in rationalism, in the tendency to make self-interest our lodestar, in limitless multiplication of wants, in exchange, trade and traffic, in a sharp distinction between business and household and the continuous narrowing of the latter, in the commodity-character of all products, in a steady growing division of labor, with its counterpart: organization and planning, in contracts and in corporations." [5]

On the other side is the precapitalistic village society "with

[3] *Ibid.*, pp. 4–5.
[4] *Ibid.*, p. 10.
[5] *Ibid.*, p. 13.

their original and organic social ties, their traditional tribal system, their limited and modest needs, their principle of agricultural production for subsistence by independent families, their subordination of exchange as a means of satisfying wants, their lack of a spirit of profiteering, of competition, of organized enterprise, of professional trade, of capital, and of mechanized industry, with the irregularity of their exertions, with their subordination of the economic motive to—and blending with—all kinds of religious, ethical and traditional social motives; in short with the pre-capitalistic characteristics, these millions of small worlds may truly be said to make up a world of their own." [6]

This clash between the two societies (or economies) is not a temporary or transitional stage, but a lasting disequilibrium. "Social-economic dualism, far from being a passing phase the termination of which may be hastened by a western policy of integration, must be accepted as a permanent characteristic of a large number of important countries, permanent at least within a measurable distance of time." [7] This apparent permanence, if real, has far-reaching consequences on development problems. In fact, it almost excludes the possibilities of development. It conveys a very pessimistic outlook for modernization and the improvement of living standards. "I will expose no plans," says Boeke, "except to stress the need for a 'village restoration.' This restoration will not take place through a revival of the rural gentry, but must follow more democratic ways. New leaders must spring from the small folks themselves, and must be accompanied by a strong feeling of social responsibility in the people themselves." Just how all this is to be accomplished, Boeke does not say; "but the sphere of action must be small, the time slow, and the goal won by 'Faith, charity, and patience, angelic patience.' " [8]

Why does Boeke think that this dualistic disequilibrium situa-

[6] J. H. Boeke, "Oriental Economics," Institute of Pacific Relations, New York, 1947, mimeo., p. 3.

[7] J. H. Boeke, "Three Forms of Disintegration in Dual Societies," *Indonesië*, vol. 7, no. 4, April 1954, p. 294.

[8] J. H. Boeke, "Western Influence on the Growth of Eastern Population," *Economia Internazionale*, vol. 7, no. 2, 1954, pp. 336–339. Cf. Higgins, op. cit., p. 104.

tion will last? In the West, capitalism has also conquered a primitive and traditional realm. In the West, the mentality which prevailed in the urban centers penetrated rural society and revolutionized among the villagers not only principles of production but their whole conception of life. Where production had been carried on almost entirely for subsistence, with the sale of only small surpluses in the market, production for exchange became the rule. The farmer became entrepreneur producing in corporate connections. Rural industry developed as a fruit of the new intercourse between town and country; agricultural cooperation grew as a new plant from its roots; specialized enterprises were formed with separate market organizations; agriculturists imitated the technical principles of urban industry—mechanization, standardization, concentration, capitalization. These concepts became common property in rural society, as it adopted profit for its watchword, money and market for the base of its enterprise.

In this way, the old homogeneity in an economic sense between town and country was re-established on a new level, but at the cost of the traditional rural social structure. The town had conquered the country which absorbed the new conception of life; together they overran the ancient village organization.

"Such was the modern development in the West, in Europe, in the environment where the new social economic theory was born and bred and where it has its home. And because economists take the body of facts for their theoretic systems from the environment with which they are familiar, their predominant theories today fit exclusively this part of the world." [9]

This same evolution could not happen in the Eastern countries where dualism in the social structure is now prevalent. The main reason, says Boeke, is because in the West development was a "process of *endogenic* social progression; of *evolution*, [and] ultimately homogeneity will appear because one system, be it a mixture [of declining precapitalism and emerging young capitalism] penetrates through all the strata of society." [10]

In a dual society, on the other hand, one of the two prevailing social

[9] Boeke, "Oriental Economics," p. 1.

[10] *Ibid.*, p. 3. The italics and brackets are mine.

systems, as a matter of fact always the most advanced, will have been imported from abroad and have gained its existence in the new environment without being able to oust or to assimilate the divergent social system that has grown up there, with the result that neither of them becomes general and characteristic for that society as a whole. Without doubt the most frequent form of social dualism is to be found there where an imported western capitalism has penetrated into a precapitalistic agrarian community and where the original social system—be it not undamaged—has been able to hold its own or, expressed in opposite terms, has not been able to adopt the capitalistic principles and put them into full practice.[11]

A very important aspect of Boeke's theory is the permanent or stagnant character of the clash between the two societies; it is therefore very important to identify the reasons Boeke gave for it. He was not very explicit and elaborate about this matter, but we have inferred the following from his writings, which we have also quoted above.

First, perhaps because the modern organization is *imported.*

Second, perhaps because the modern organization is of the *high* capitalistic nature, in contrast with the young capitalistic system which absorbed the European village society in the last century. This reason is the same as the one Higgins gave for dualism: the coexistence of a very capital-intensive structure (the estates and mining industries) and a very labor-intensive indigenous structure, so that factor proportions in use are not always a reflection of factor proportions available. There is a sharp cleavage between the two economies. These are the "technical and economic reasons for dualism." [12]

Third, is perhaps that the precapitalistic society in the East, rooted in the villages, was not able or did not want to adapt (for some reason) to the "relatively modern, youthful and aggressive Western capitalism, established in Urban centers and it reacted passively: injured and weakened, unable to resist the Western forces. But their *number is too great* to permit a decisive outcome, and the battle drags on." [13] This third possibility is conceivably

[11] Boeke, *Economics and Economic Policy of Dual Societies,* p. 4.

[12] Higgins, *op. cit.,* pp. 112–113.

[13] Boeke, "Oriental Economics," p. 2; italics mine.

related to the first, but we have listed it nevertheless as a different cause since it can throw a clearer light on the process.

We want to examine a little further the highly crucial question of whether dualism is really an unavoidable and permanent phenomenon. But first it is necessary to examine what the products of interaction are between the two clashing societies with different values. Boeke is not very encouraging about this. The main theme he wants to convey is that the precapitalistic society fails to adapt fruitfully; instead it disintegrates and degenerates, its members becoming more and more the victims of misery and increasing poverty.

Indebtedness and *overcrowding* are the two major consequences resulting from the clash and the inability of the rural society to adapt. Boeke sees the working of Malthusian laws as inevitable. The tradition-bound, precapitalistic society is not willing to dispose of its ethic of having many children. This ethic was perhaps well suited to the previously agricultural society where, with plenty of land available, every hand was productive, and therefore welcomed; furthermore, families needed to have many children in the face of the high death rate. But presently, every temporary surplus is soon dissipated by the lowering of the death rate and the consequent rising of the net reproduction rate. "Colonization, emigration, industrialization, irrigation, agricultural improvement, and so on, are the symptoms among the people themselves of a growing realization of their own responsibility for the realization of the population problem. But these programs will never bring permanent relief and in this connection it ought to be mentioned that the pre-capitalistic forms of birth restriction, abortion and infanticide, again are spreading, and that especially abortion today is practiced universally in that part of the world." [14]

Rural indebtedness is the result of the incapability of the precapitalistic society to adapt itself to the economy of exchange.

Most of the people in the Orient depend on agriculture. This agriculture is for subsistence, in principle remains outside the system of exchange, and is not directed toward making money and profit. Never-

[14] *Ibid.*, p. 42.

theless people are increasingly obliged to incur money expenditures, with the penetration of their economy by Western capitalism in the shape of import products, transportation services, money interest, cash rents, and money taxes.

This discrepancy is the economic aspect of dualism. It causes a permanent shortage of money, and subjects the rural population to a constantly increasing burden of debt. The peasant is obliged to sell an ever larger part of his crop outside the village, although his produce is not suitable for this purpose and although, in point of fact, he needs it to feed his family; although the market prices are unfavorable; although he is inexperienced in marketing practices; and although only a fraction of the price paid by the consumers comes into his hands. Advantage, desire for profit, or commercial considerations have not counted in the choice of the crop and therefore cannot affect the value transaction either. When prices are low, a larger part of the crop will be sold than when prices are high; but correspondingly nobody will abandon his food crops because their cultivation has become unprofitable and the market price has dropped below production cost.[15]

The farmer thus becomes increasingly dependent upon the exchange market. At harvest time, he sells an increasing amount of his crop at low prices and has to buy part of it back during *patjeklik* (meager period before next harvest) at much higher prices. At the time of sowing and planting he also needs money to buy the seeds, perhaps also to pay help. At times, he is obliged to hold *slametans* (offering feasts) to celebrate a family happening such as birth, circumcision, marriage, or death. An important part of the consumption pattern of a village community is dedicated to this "social consumption," which is very inelastic to income fluctuation.

All this is good breeding ground for the moneylender—a very familiar character in Eastern villages. But the moneylender is generally not regarded as an usurer at all. Surely he is not a philanthropist either, but his function and services are needed in the present setting of a village community, as long as propensities are not changed and the proper institutions (village banks, etc.), are not adequately available to handle the demand for credit. Eco-

[15] *Ibid.*, p. 58.

nomically speaking, the problem of indebtedness is a circular problem: poverty increases the people's liquidity preference, thus the interest rate; scarcity of capital (and saving) limits the supply of it and forms another cause of high interest rate. In all, it is logical (and not specifically "Eastern") that interests are high. But this alone cannot fully explain the extent of rural indebtedness. The propensity to incur debt must have additional noneconomic causes; and Boeke is probably right in his assertion that the whole precapitalistic village atmosphere is not conducive to the growth of a spirit of "accounting-mindedness" among the farmers. The farmers are helpless against money. They have never learned to regard money as an accounting unit, or to count in terms of profit and loss. Money is for them just another precious good and, only incidentally, a good means of exchange. If a farmer incurs a debt he soon forgets about the principle, and he only worries about his interest obligations. The moneylender seldom reminds him of this principle; perhaps this is why the lender is usually not regarded as an exploiter (although in times of crisis and bitterness the villagers sometimes come to murder him), for all that he stresses is the pay of the interest. We find this mentioned again in Arthur Goodfriend's recent manuscript when he describes the death of a baby: "Neighbours dropped in to offer their condolences. Among the first was the money lender. He urged Djogo not to worry about the money he owed. 'Just try,' he said, 'to keep up the interest payments.' "[16] Meanwhile, an interest payment of 10 percent per month (more at times of inflation) is quite common for such advances.

The self-sufficient, precapitalistic village community has other values or propensities as well, which are of major importance for understanding Boeke's dualistic theory. Since production (on the farm) was regarded mainly for the provision of one's own wants (which are limited), outside labor, in town or on a plantation for instance, is never regarded as a permanent engagement. From the viewpoint of the farmers the income from outside labor is "marginal," just to acquire cash needed for paying taxes, buying kerosene, salt, textiles, etc. These additional expenses are limited; thus,

[16] Arthur Goodfriend, "Fifth Trip to Asia," unpublished manuscript.

as soon as the required amount of cash is earned, the propensity to work (outside) drops. This is the well-known phenomenon of the backward-bending supply curve of labor, experienced by many European employers.

When plantations raise wages, the result is frequently absenteeism, gambling, drunkenness, etc. This phenomenon occurs also in "contract coolie" communities. Contract coolies are laborers contracted from Java to work (full time) on plantations in North Sumatra. This paid labor is for them not a marginal occupation. Modern sociologists, therefore, would hesitate to present a single cause of explanation for this phenomenon. Barry Moore (in "Western Impact on Indian Society") remarks on this respect: "No firm facts are available that would enable us to determine whether the reduction of effort was due to cultural factors such as the absence of a tradition of frugality and hard work, to an abundant supply of labor, or to the fact that the work itself may actually be close to the limits of human endurance. Quite probably all three factors are at work in varying degrees at different times and places. Irrespective of the source of such attitudes there is some evidence that this range of alternatives is unsatisfactory to the (Indian) workers themselves."

Whether peculiar social values are the cause of backward-bending supply curves or not, one can point to economic reasons which, at times and places, have produced the same phenomenon. For instance, a rise in wages may not be matched by an appropriate increase in spending opportunities. Many Western-owned plantations are situated in remote parts of the countries. The supply of goods (which are income elastic) may be fixed by difficulties in transportation, purchasing, etc. Therefore, a rise in wages may temporarily mean nothing for the laborer for he cannot buy more goods. At worst, the local shopkeepers will increase the prices. It is therefore not surprising that workers find other outlets for their additional incomes, e.g., in gambling. In situations where the marginal utility of the extra money is very low, gambling is a way to increase it. Prostitution and other vices are in a sense industries with a more elastic supply curve in such isolated communities (especially in these contract coolie communities) where more innocent kinds of recreation industries are lacking.

On the other hand, the backward-bending supply curve of labor in a South American country is nicely neutralized by the distribution of a Sears Roebuck catalog and the procurement of the listed articles. This opportunity increases the alternatives for spending. Demonstration effects operate and result in the jacking up of the level of wants.

It is, at this stage, perhaps appropriate to point to some important phenomena of a rural economy, notably the potential existence of *spatial monopolies*. This is not the cause of the backward-bending supply curve at all, but it can strengthen it. The village community is dispersed; moreover, in those underdeveloped countries transportation facilities are inadequate. The people are poor and not able to overcome the friction of space. These are all building stones for a spatial monopoly held by the wholesale buyer of agricultural crops and by the distributor of imported commodities. In many Asian countries the two functions are embodied in the same merchant. The Chinese middleman-storekeeper is a well-known example, combining the functions of buying farm products, distributing necessities, and providing credit. For two or three villages there can be only one grocery store which combines all these functions. There is no room for a large number of these agents, thus preventing competition. At best, an oligopolistic situation exists, while the ethnicity of the storekeepers facilitates collusion vis-à-vis the atomistic farmers' group. This rural phenomenon of spatial monopoly is not restricted to the East; it is universal instead. Fifty years ago, the same situation of spatial monopoly existed in rural areas of the United States. The growth of the mail-order house has eliminated much of the monopoly power, but such an alternative is currently not available in many underdeveloped countries (except for the experiments with village cooperatives, which are on a much smaller scale). Under these conditions of spatial monopoly held by the (Chinese) storekeeper, chances are that the terms of trade for the farmers vis-à-vis these shopkeepers can never be favorable.

Under such conditions (and *ceteris paribus!*), Boeke might be right when he suggests that the only "relief for poverty" is going back to the old village pattern and avoiding the exchange economy. It is true that exchange increases welfare, for one can move up on a higher indifference curve, but between the farmer and the village grocer there is no true exchange. Because of the credit tie, the villager is compelled to sell his crop at prices fixed by the grocer and either take the articles in the store at their prices or leave them altogether; often he has no competing supplier. All this, incidentally, leads Hla Myint to observe that all that counts for the natives' welfare in these plural societies is the *internal* terms of trade (between farmer and wholesaler) and not the external terms of trade (between countries). The problem of breaking this monopolistic position of ethnic minority groups over the farmers is one of the most important socioeconomic problems of these countries.

The spirit of the precapitalistic village community which emanates from a system of self-sufficiency, and consequently limited wants and profit motives, is hardly conducive to social solutions such as industrialization and migration. As Boeke says: "In the main, the impediments to migration are social and psychological. The Asiatic, at least the Asiatic agriculturist, is an inhabitant of the plains and does not like mountain country; his duty to his ancestors binds him to his native soil; his communal sense binds him to his native village; he must have an opportunity to cultivate irrigated fields; he is more liable than are members of less conservative populations to suffer from change of climate; above all, he lacks *the spur of the spirit of enterprise and of the desire for profit because he is still guided by reliance on self-sufficiency.*" [17]

Such are the intrinsic characteristics of a precapitalistic society as Boeke described them. What happens if such a community has to deal with the imported capitalistic system? Frustration, disintegration, and poverty are inevitably the fruits of such a contact. "It isolates the individual, old and young, from the close community with family and village; forces on him all kinds of organizations imported from the Western world—organizations in which he does not feel at home and which, therefore, he makes use of only as an outsider, forbids and combats his social and religious customs,

[17] Boeke, "Oriental Economics," p. 45; italics mine.

takes a positive interest exclusively in his economic activities; and accentuates his economic wants without being able to procure for him the means, or strengthen such means as he has, to satisfy these wants. As a result, a sense of frustration and of poverty is awakened in the individual." [1]

Poverty and Its Relief

Boeke's diagnosis finds its climax in the therapy. The patient is incurably sick. All one can do is reduce the pain; if recovery comes, it will come but slowly. The root of all evil is "that *a precapitalistic society is driven further and further away into an exchange economy for which it is not fitted and which it cannot master.*"

It is impossible to transform small cultivators of food crops into commercial agricultural entrepreneurs, producing with profit for a ready market. It is impossible so to increase the productivity of the food crop cultures that they become a profitable business. It is impossible to thin out the crowded peasantry sufficiently to give it the necessary elbow room. It is impossible to create industrial means of existence to loosen a sufficient percentage of the cultivators from the land and so make room for a favorable division of the cultivable area, with land enough for each of the remaining peasants. Neither agricultural reforms nor resettlement nor industrialization are efficacious measures to arrest what Chinese authorities call rural bankruptcy.

It will be necessary to acquiesce in the immutability of the dualistic character of oriental countries, in the perpetuation of the subsistence economy of the rural masses. Once this view is accepted, it will be seen that these masses must be burdened as little as possible with money demands. Their selfsufficiency will have to be strengthened. Their need for products brought from outside, and especially imported products, will have to be reduced. In short, the illusion that the masses can be developed in a Western way to become a limitless market for Western industrial products will have to be abandoned. *The static, traditional character of precapitalistic society will have to be consolidated in contradistinction from the free, dynamic development in the capitalistic sphere. This dualism will have to be accentuated by respect for, and rehabilitation of, the oriental characteristics of the village community.*[19]

18 *Ibid.*, p. 13.

19 *Ibid.*, p. 68; italics mine.

The Evaluation of the Theory

It cannot be denied that Boeke's descriptions of the Eastern (or perhaps only the Javanese) village are in many instances true. Boeke knows a lot about the Javanese village life in the colonial period.

His desire to establish a special economic theory in explanation of these dual societies is perhaps valid, although many economists will deny this. It all depends upon how one understands economic theory. Any society, whatever it may be, must somehow meet three fundamental problems:

1. *What* commodities shall be produced and in what quantities?
2. *How* shall goods be produced?
3. *For whom* are goods to be produced? [20]

In a primitive society, custom may rule every facet of behavior. *What, How,* and *For Whom* may be decided by traditional ways of doing things. In a dictatorial system one central authority might decide upon these questions. On the other hand, in a "capitalist free enterprise economy" a system of prices (of markets, of profits and losses) primarily determines *What, How,* and *For Whom* goods and services shall be produced.

An economic theory can hardly be said to exist for a primitive and traditional economy if all decisions on allocation of resources and distribution of income are guided by fixed customs (which in practice perhaps never will occur). But what Boeke is interested in is the economic theory of a dualistic society, that is, of the clashing societies. Perhaps there can be room for a separate economic theory for such a community (explaining the mechanics of an equilibrium system), but if that economic theory has to explain the *What, How,* and *For Whom* of the society in question, then it is clear that Boeke did not succeed in developing such a theory. Perhaps Boeke was seeking too much. All he did essentially was to explain supply and demand behavior, e.g., the backward-bending supply curve for labor and the inelastic demand curves of people with "limited wants." Boeke explained much about the social

[20] See P. A. Samuelson, *Economics: An Introductory Analysis,* 7th ed., McGraw-Hill, New York, 1967, Chap. 2.

impact of a high capitalistic system upon a precapitalistic society, but this can hardly be called a separate economic theory.

Perhaps Higgins is essentially right when he maintains that the conventional economic analysis can adequately explain economic interactions in a dualistic society. The propensities in a dualistic society are different. Therefore, the supply curves of the factors of production and the demand curves of consumers can be explained in the light of these social characteristics; but once the proper curvature of the supply and demand schedules are established, conventional supply and demand analysis can adequately arrive at the equilibrium solution. Indifference curves between work (effort) and leisure may have a variety of shapes, and so also demand curves in relation to income and price changes. If the development of a specific consumption and demand theory for these dual societies is all that Boeke intended in creating a particular "economic theory," then such is his own right. But even in that case he did not go very far, and his theory *remained essentially static.* He probably could not develop a dynamic theory, since he believes in the permanency of dualism.

Wants are limited in a precapitalistic society, according to Boeke, and this is the cause of most failures in economic development. As long as wants are limited, we agree, no development can take place because this development is then simply not wanted or understood. Boeke himself admits that the wants of the natives can be increased by government action. But he condemns such action because it "accentuates his [the native's] economic wants without being able to procure for him the means." Once the scope of human (economic) wants can be broadened, however, the rigidity of Boeke's theorem is likely to fall apart. The indifference curves between effort and leisure may shift, and consequently the backward-bending part of the supply curve (of effort) may be pushed back to a region where it usually lies in conventional analysis.

What about the Malthusian phenomenon? This can spoil every improvement in living standards, as each increase in productive effort is soon dissipated by the increase in population. It is quite true that increase in wants alone cannot solve the problem. But these problems can be further taken care of by tools of modern economic analysis. The main problem is that of formation of scarce resources. If the rate of capital formation (complemented by adequate entrepreneurial and technical skills) lags behind population growth, then regression cannot be stopped. If the first is greater, then a positive rate of progress is achieved. One does not need to create a special economic theory for dualistic societies to explain these things.

A provocative aspect of Boeke's dualistic theory is the claim that this clash is permanent; at least there is no prospect for direct relief. This presumption is strategic in Boeke's theory because it leads to his conclusion that the Gandhistic prescription of "plain living and high thinking" is the only way out. Poverty cannot be transformed into material welfare. But since poverty is (according to Boeke) a psychological state of affairs (that is, people are poor because they *feel* they have far less than other people), it can be relieved by philosophical acceptance and the pursuit of high spiritual reflections.

It is understandable that most present-day Indonesians revolt against this prescription. Boeke is not very convincing. *The logical chain* which leads to a *clash* between the precapitalistic society and the imported high capitalistic society on the one hand, and the permanent character which he attributes to this clash on the other hand, are not very clear and convincing. As mentioned earlier, Boeke listed three (possible) causes: (1) because the capitalistic society is *imported,* (2) because the imported capitalistic system is of high capitalistic structure, and (3) because of the receiving, precapitalistic society is unable or unwilling to adapt, and is too big in number to give in and be assimilated. A deeper analysis of the working of these three causes is not given, and this is the unsatisfying part of it. It would be much more fruitful to leave the possibilities for adaptation, integration, or synthesis open, and to try to analyse what the particular problems would be for this process. We want to advocate this approach as being more significant than Boeke's approach of just staring at the clash. ("Dualistic theory is no more and no less than this clashing of the two communities," he once wrote in a letter).

The Process and Problems of Adaptation of Eastern Underdeveloped Countries

It is definitely not my purpose to present a theory of the process of adaptation and acculturation. The process itself is certainly very complex and not properly understood yet. But since we have engaged the main attack on Boeke's theories in this area, it is perhaps proper to say something about it. We want to state the problem specifically: what are positive (conducive) factors and negative (deterring) factors in the process of adaptation and acculturation?

First, there is the attitude of the "receiving" culture. Does it want or does it not want to acculturate? The appreciation of the receiving society for the giving country is important. The Chinese, for instance, always found their own culture superior to any of the "barbaric," intruding cultures, and this attitude certainly was a barrier to fruitful adaptation or acculturation.

Second, there is the scope and intensity of contact. If contact is widespread, it is almost certain that some acculturation will occur.

Third, the *Who* in this contact is important. If the contact group is not a social-leading group, or not a reference group, it is not likely that the acculturation will be diffused. On the part of the incoming culture, it is also of crucial importance who the contact persons are. If a bunch of shrewd traders were the representatives of the West, it is not likely that these people and their culture would find appeal.

The above are very general qualifications. Of course there are other factors which influence the process of adaptation; social factors are important, but we will deal with them later. The above mentioned qualifications are presented in advance to serve as a rough check list.

But before we go any further, we want to ask ourselves what type of social change is likely to occur in the present-day, underdeveloped countries. This course of change will reflect then what kind of adaptation and acculturation can be anticipated.

The underdeveloped countries are by definition poor, while productivity is low. What they want is development, a higher productivity, and consequently a higher standard of living. This can perhaps be debated by proponents of the Boeke school, but at present let us take for granted that all the efforts of Asian and other poor countries indicate that they want the above aims.

We assume that most of these underdeveloped countries start with a precapitalistic structure: small, self-sufficient production and consumption units. How is higher productivity to be achieved? Mainly in two ways: division of labor and roundabout (i.e., capitalistic) production methods. This entails specialization and a much larger output than the nation's own consumption potential. An exchange economy is thus required. An exchange economy stresses the importance of transport cost. Localization economies will give birth to towns, perhaps first as nodal points of exchange between agricultural areas and the outside world which provides the industrial goods. The first service industries will also tend to locate at these agglomeration points. If agricultural productivity increases, a potential market for domestic industries will arise, and consequently manufacturing industries will spring up.

Urbanization economies (i.e., the external economies achieved by the agglomeration of different industries in an urban center) will attract many industries. *Urbanization becomes thus a progressively dominant pattern of social and economic growth.* Such was the growth pattern of the West, of Soviet Russia, even of Japan, and will no doubt—that is, if one drops the belief that dualism is permanent—be the case in the present-day, underdeveloped countries of the East.

We repeat, the growth process is as follows: division of labor, specialization, capitalization, exchange, industrialization, and urbanization. Why do we stress this growth pattern? Because we want to pose this: that the cultural and social development has to follow the same path. The self-contained, precapitalistic village structure *must* give way for exchange economy, for the integration of village communities into larger economic units, for a national economy. The village economy must, at least in cases where it lies in industrial regions, ultimately be integrated with the urban economy in so-called urban metropolitan areas. These assertions are far removed from Boeke's thesis, which does not believe in the integration of village and town, etc.

We will not deny that the dualism (i.e., the clash) will disappear quickly once a deliberate modernization has been instigated. The process of acculturation and adaptation is bound to be a slow one; it can certainly not be achieved within one generation. On the other hand, the problem is not such that development will not occur *until* acculturation has been completed. There are theorists who claim that until rational behavior is completely adopted by all layers of an Eastern society, modernization will only retain a thin finish, not capable of further self-perpetuation or self-generation. These theorists used to point to the Japanese development as an example (or prediction?) of unstable modernization because the Japanese did not adopt the whole integrated spirit of the West; in their private life the Japanese are often still "medieval."

We do not think in these rigid terms. A mixture of old and new in the outlook of people can exist without doing the economic structure much harm. Although we believe that the society is a system and that everything is in equilibrium with everything else, we do not know yet how precisely this equilibrium works, and how far "substitutabilities" are possible. The Japanese have mixed a highly modern business life with a more backward rural life, a feudal pattern of social life, and even this mixture seems to facilitate rapid economic development.

It seems that life to some extent can be compartmentalized. Arthur Goodfriend tells about the Indonesian doctor who is a highly skilled physician, in the modern sense, but still believes in the apparently magical potencies of the *dukun* (a "witch doctor"). How is all this dualism possible without confusion? Perhaps because the different functions can be separated from each other: the office work of the Japanese businessman can be separated from his home life, the operation of the modern Indonesian doctor is separated from that of the *dukun*. The urban life can to some extent be distinguished from the rural life. The modernization of a backward country need not be the same in all compartments of social life. The approach for the rural sector must be different than for the urban sector. The urban sector must perhaps necessarily be the most "modern" sector of life. We will come back to this point shortly.

From the experience of countries such as Japan, Soviet Russia, Turkey, and others, we can probably adduce that social development can be "engineered" to accelerate the process. Social change must be wanted and deliberately instigated by a leading group within the community. The leading group is by definition a minority because we assume that the masses of people are (in the beginning) static and traditional in their outlook. It need not be a ruling elite, although chances for success are better if it is a ruling or leading one. This is because *social coherence* is of paramount importance in the process of social modernization. The more important is this social coherence for underdeveloped countries nowadays because they cannot hope for social development in isolation. Many of these countries are already plural societies where a common social and moral tie frequently does not exist. The importance of social coherence became the central point of Levy's study on the growth of Japan and China. China lacked the social unity whereas Japan had it, and this was perhaps a strategic factor in the success of the latter and the failure of the first. Says Levy: "In Japan the transition did not undercut the system of control over deviance or the possibility of highly controlled direction of the members of the society, as was the case in China."

"Control" in this respect is not to be interpreted in only its imperative meaning (although this element certainly exists), but in the society the spirit of "follow-the-leader" can be strong enough to stipulate the direction of the movement without force at all. The leading elite is here a so-called "reference group," and the sources of its authority can be various: it can stem from a long tradition of authority (the emperor in Japan, etc.), or it may result from a new ruling elite, who have replaced the old ruling class or estate by conquest, revolution, or otherwise. In this case, the loyalty of the masses is transferred automatically (because people are used to obedience). The Communist party in Soviet Russia and the colonial regimes in the East are perhaps good examples of this type of social stratification.

But why did Indonesia, India, Burma, etc., not develop socially (and economically) under colonial administrations? If we interpret this question only in its aspect of acculturation, we could probably use the check list mentioned in the beginning of this section, namely, attitudes, scope of contact, and nature of contact.

The attitudes of the natives and their imperial masters alike were perhaps not favorable. The intruding foreigners were not liked. It was very doubtful that the colonizers wanted the natives to be emancipated. Virtually no opportunity was given for the indigenous population to have a responsible share in the modern administration and economy. General education in the modern sense was not encouraged. Contact with the Western world was also very limited. Only a handful of Europeans were in the country, and they lived isolated in their own sphere. They kept their social distance because of a sense of superiority, and also as a part of their colonial policy. The Dutch with their containment policy deliberately kept the indigenous structure "intact" as much as possible, whereas the British imposed their common law upon the indigenous social structure which naturally did not foster acculturation. There has been some acculturation among the higher social classes (which had closer dealings with the foreign rulers as subrulers), but because of rather rigid class or estate distinctions there was very little diffusion down below.

We have already said that some fruitful, though limited, contact was maintained between Western officials of the colonial administration and the indigenous aristocracy (which was incorporated in the colonial regime). This is why most of the present-day national leaders in many of these Asian countries come from this same social class. But besides this contact there is not much to be proud of. Many Europeans who went to the East to try their fortune were not the best specimens, at least in the cultural sense, of the Western culture, although they may not have lacked the spirit of profiteering. The kind of acculturation which occurred in the colonial armies is certainly not the enlightening kind and was not altogether a blessing for the receiving countries.

The above is perhaps a further examination of Boeke's first case of dualism, namely that the high capitalism is *imported.* Because it is imported by a colonial power there is a negative (and perhaps hostile) attitude towards acculturation; the contact is limited and not of "high quality."

Boeke himself denied strongly that colonialism has anything to do with social dualism. On the contrary, he believes that the "enlightened" kind of colonial rule (the "ethical rule") is a blessing for this dualistic society. Says Boeke: "the Government has not shown itself a willing instrument of capitalistic interests but has acted as the protector and promotor of what it regards as Indonesian interests—as the interest of each part concerned in the country's industrial life, in its production in the widest sense. This is the new economic policy of the authorities, a policy in really grand style." [21]

Furnivall,[22] on the other hand, has another explanation of social stratification in which colonialism is certainly a cause. He does not think in terms of dualism and the clash of a precapitalistic and a capitalistic economy. Furnivall, instead, thinks in terms of "pluralism." Countries like the Netherlands Indies are typical of plural societies where the rulers and the ruled are of different races. The different societies within one country form closed worlds among themselves; they have their own value systems, and there is no "common will" except, possibly, in matters of supreme importance, such as resistance to aggression from outside. In economic life, this lack of a common will finds expression in the absence of any common "social demand" (Perhaps Furnivall's notion of social demand comes close to what we can call a social welfare function). The absence of this common (or median?) set of values for the plural societies makes the (economic) exchange relations between the constituent societies similar to those prevalent in international trade. One economist once put the difference between national and international trade like this: national trade is trade *among us,* international trade is trade *between us and them.* It suggests that in domestic trade (and in domestic affairs) the trading partners are not completely "homo economicus"-minded, that is, only having an eye for profit and not caring for the other man's welfare. The two trading partners are controlled by the same "social welfare function." In international trade such is far less the case. In plural societies the capitalistic class is more "rucksichtlos." The European or the Chinese in Indonesia is less restrained in exploiting the economically weaker indigenous population, because interracial moral restraint is often less severe, and

[21] Boeke, *Economics and Economic Policy of Dual Societies,* p. 228.

[22] J. S. Furnivall, *Netherlands India,* Cambridge University Press, London, 1944.

also because alien groups (e.g., the Chinese and Arabs in Indonesia), having no social responsibilities whatsoever in their pursuit of gain and profit (as long as they stay within the law), stand between the indigenous population and the colonial rulers. In these dependent countries there were no strong reference groups within the indigenous societies which could lead the process of adaptation. In Burma where such happened under King Mindon, it did not last long; it was soon crushed by the British.

Boeke would perhaps strongly object to this, arguing that in independent Japan, Thailand, present-day Indonesia, etc., this dualism still exists. We do not deny that the process of adaptation takes a long time, perhaps generations. But there is certainly an important difference between "dualism" in Japan and in Java. The process of modernization in Japan is unmistakably farther advanced than in Java, even though the Japanese farmer is still poor and still has to submit part of his harvest to landlords, government, and moneylenders. These are perhaps remnants of dualism, but it has also something to do with the development policy of the government (or the ruling class). Japan has managed its agricultural revolution, a phenomenon hardly imaginable under a dualistic situation as described by Boeke in Java. Boeke's dualism is static, hopeless. Japan's dualism is much more dynamic. Income per capita is still low, and rural exploitation is therefore still possible, but this income per capita is rising.

We have wandered a little from our central theme: the process of acculturation and adaptation. But we have perhaps picked up an important precondition (requirement) for successful adaptation (for economic development): the existence of a strong social will, sovereign enough within the community, borne by an elite which acts as a reference group. This social will is devoted to the sake of social development.

The social structure must be intact because social coherence guarantees the efficacy of authority of the leading elite. The leading elite, incidentally, must have the proper capacities to lead, to *innovate*. It must be flexible in the execution of its role; it must assume new roles where circumstances command; it must keep the system of social stratification open for new members who are better equipped for the new roles. It must in this way always be prepared to broaden its own base.

In the foregoing, we have asserted that the process of economic development leads ultimately to industrialization. An industrial culture is in essence an urban culture. In economic as well as in social processes we find many hen-and-egg phenomena. *These circular relationships can perhaps be used as a tool for social engineering.* We want economic welfare through economic development. This brings us ultimately to an urban civilization whether we like it or not. But once we accept this, can't we play with the reverse relationship? We create urban centers by putting industries in urban agglomeration. Can't we hasten the process of economic and social development by doing so? It is perhaps a somewhat wasteful way of proceeding, but "shock-treatments" are sometimes needed to break up "cakes of custom." There is a high correlation coefficient between urbanization and literacy, the use of mass media, impersonal relationships (contracts, etc.), the breaking up of extended family ties, rational behavior, etc. All these characteristics are the right properties for a developed exchange economy. We can probably conclude from this why social development was not so successful in the Netherlands Indies. Urban industries were not undertaken in any appreciable scope. The agricultural (estate) and mining industries are too dispersed, too rural, to convey a new spirit of modernization to the masses. And in the terms which Higgins used, the "population multiplier" was too small.

Seen from this standpoint, the craving of many underdeveloped countries for industrialization (complete with a steel mill!), for its own sake almost, comes into another light. Western economists are quick to condemn this and on good economic grounds. (Incidentally, a steel mill is now more of a market-oriented industry so that lack of domestic resources is no severe economic objection; the size of the market is the only limiting factor.) But these economists used to teach that industrialization must come by itself if productivity increases and markets widen. Productivity must be increased in line with comparative advantage. Industrialization is a result of development and not the reverse. But if industrialization, and consequently urbanization, can create the required propensities, at least the development of the required human factors can be fostered. And it is perhaps this human factor that is the most important in the process of economic development. How is it otherwise to be explained that Japan and Germany after being destroyed by the war can build up their economy so quickly, whereas certain underdeveloped countries cannot even use a credit line of $100 million from the EXIM-Bank in five years? Capital is perhaps not the scarcest resource in comparison with complementary human resources. An Indonesian official traveling in eastern Europe told this story of advice given by some people over there: "Western economists are bad advisors for you. They are not much different than the former colonial theorists. They always let you proceed cautiously, economically, which means very slowly. They criticize your plans for steel mills and stress that you limit your industrialization to small industries. We can give you only this advice: go ahead and industrialize your country as much as you can. Problems can be solved by doing!'

This advice is most likely also politically colored, but since it comes from a source which has the same problems as many underdeveloped countries on the other side of the fence, it sounds sympathetic and every grain of truth is eagerly appreciated.

One last word about Boeke's theory. In a descriptive sense it certainly contains a lot of truth. It is of crucial importance to take account of cultural and other human factors in dealing with development problems. For this he has made a great contribution. In fact his theory has been used by the colonial government and by the national government as well as serving as the base of a protectionist policy domestically. The farmer must be protected from expropriation of his land, indebtedness, and usury; the laborer from exploitation; the indigenous newcomer-businessman from murdering foreign competition. This kind of public policy is strongly recommended by Boeke himself, and one can read his public policy recommendations,[23] forgetting about his principal diagnosis and therapy. Protection is also needed for another purpose: to prevent social disintegration and to preserve social coherence.

[23] Boeke, *Economics and Economic Policy of Dual Societies,* pp. 230–320.

It looks as if Boeke himself wanted some of this social rehabilitation. One of the policies he stresses is village restoration. Village restoration (now called community development programs) is necessary, but certainly not in Boeke's sense. Time cannot be set back. The postwar Indonesian village has made some steps already in modernizing its community life. The authority stratification is restored and imbedded in the local community. But this is also what Boeke wants. The present-day Indonesian village, however, has gone farther. The village is incorporated into (or linked to) larger social units. Local chapters of the labor and farmers' unions, of political parties, cooperative movements, etc., are all new social innovations with the purpose of integrating the village unit with national units. This broadening of the village horizon is necessary, once we accept the progress of specialization, exchange, and widening of markets. The village cannot fall back upon its traditional pattern of self-sufficiency; instead it must be part of a wider market system, encompassing the country and the world.

As a postscript we want to end with the remark that we did not try to evaluate the political content of Boeke's dualism, although it might well be that this aspect is the root of dualism. If dualism was not created by colonialism, the latter certainly did strengthen it. Indonesian opponents simply believe that Boeke was providing a good theoretical (and thus respectable) excuse for perpetuating colonial policy in the then Netherlands Indies. Social science can not, as yet, prevent the wish from sometimes being the father of the thought.

PART II

AGRICULTURE

Indonesia, like most low-income, overpopulated nations, will succeed in the early stages of her development effort only if productivity per head can be raised in the agricultural sector—if only because the great preponderance of her population is engaged in agricultural pursuits. This is not to say, of course, that industrialization and urbanization (which is already advanced and the continuation of which is inevitable) are unimportant or inimical to the process of growth and development, but rather that failure to succeed in agricultural development will render the attempt at urban modernization futile. Shortages of food, fibre, and exportable agricultural produce will eventually turn the terms of domestic trade against the urban sector and generate greater scarcity of imported goods essential to urban development.

After two decades of independence, Indonesia remains seriously crippled by the failure of the agricultural sector to grow at a rate significantly greater than that of her population. In the late 1960's, the failure is being given explicit recognition, and new initiatives are being taken. The magnitude of the problem, however, is such that there is little immediate ground for optimism. The enthusiasm which grew from the success of the *bimas,* mass rice culture guidance program, in 1966, was dampened by relatively poor crops in 1967 and by the complexities of administering such a program on a large scale. The hopelessly depressed price of rubber on the world market in 1967 and 1968 has subdued hopes for quick recovery of either the smallholder sector or the estate sector in rubber production.

The *bimas* program, which is described very briefly in the paper by Penny and Gittinger reproduced in this section, is deserving of fuller treatment. A paragraph from the *Bulletin of Indonesian Economic Studies* provides the essential information:

The *Bimas* extension programme, which originated out of the Bogor Institute of Agriculture in the 1962–63 rice season in Java and was expanded on to a national scale in 1964–65, has proved beyond doubt that Indonesian farmers will respond well to agricultural extension if there are adequate supplies of fertilizer, insecticides and agricultural implements. In 1964–5 an average increase in rice output of more than 80 per cent was recorded from the 220 villages (11,000 hectares) served by the programme. In the following year output increased by an average of approximately 30 per cent on 220,000 hectares. It had been hoped to expand the programme to 750,000 hectares in 1967, but not enough foreign exchange for fertilizer import was made available to allow the target to be met, and the area to be covered was reduced to 480,000 hectares.[1]

The above description, which was written in early 1967 was followed a year later in the same bulletin by the following:

The Bimas program has been continued but it is not likely to be as effective as in previous years. The original sponsor, the Institute of Agriculture, Bogor, and most other universities have withdrawn, and the bulk of the extension work will now be done by field agents of the Department of Agriculture. These men will not live in the villages as the students had done. The Institute is no longer participating because the government has retained the link between agricultural extension (with credit, fertilizer, etc., supplied) and the government's rice buying program. With the former the farmers are provided with a real incentive to produce more, but the latter provides a disincentive.[2]

[1] D. H. Penny and Dahlam Thalib, "Survey of Recent Developments," *Bulletin of Indonesian Economic Studies* (*BIES*), no. 6, February 1967, p. 26.

[2] J. Panglaykim, D. H. Penny, and Dahlan Thalib, "Survey of Recent Developments," *BIES*, no. 9, February 1968, p. 29. L. A. Mears has analysed the program more thoroughly than any other author. See his "Report on Agricultural and Related Problems in Indonesia with Special Emphasis on Foodgrain—July, 1967," Agency for International Development, Djakarta, 1967, dittoed.

The background of the nation's agricultural problems is admirably set out below by Karl Pelzer's survey article. Penny and Gittinger offer a very informed, if somewhat controversial discussion of the issues on the uses of economics in agriculture and the economic behavior of the Indonesian peasant.

CHAPTER 4

The Agricultural Foundation*

KARL J. PELZER

Despite the Indonesian government's keen interest in industrialization, the economy of the archipelago is still basically agrarian. The primary production sector—which yields peasant food crops, smallholder and plantation export crops, livestock, fish, and forest products—provides well over half the national income and is a source of livelihood for more than 60 percent of Indonesia's gainfully employed inhabitants. By far the most important of its divisions is that of peasant food crops, which alone accounts for more than one-third of the national income. It is, however, as a supplier of tropical export crops that Indonesia is best known, for it is one of the world's leading producers in this field.

The archipelago's wealth in tropical agricultural commodities has been proverbial for many centuries. Spices, grown mainly in the Moluccas, began to attract traders to the archipelago as early as the beginning of the Christian era—at first from China and India, later from the Middle East and the eastern Mediterranean, and since the end of the fifteenth century from the western Mediterranean and northwestern Europe. During the past three centuries, the variety of Indonesia's agricultural export products has steadily broadened, in part as a result of an ever-widening world demand for tropical commodities and in part because of the successful introduction of exotic plants from other tropical areas. The

* Reprinted from Ruth T. McVey, ed., *Indonesia,* Human Relations Area Files, New Haven, 1963, by permission of the author, the editor, and the publisher.

Portuguese and Spaniards were responsible for the introduction in the sixteenth and seventeenth centuries of such important crops as maize (corn), cassava, sweet potatoes, tobacco, red pepper, and a host of fruits and vegetables. The coffee bush, brought to West Java by the Dutch in the seventeenth century, spread from there to other parts of the archipelago. Tea, cinchona, rubber, oil palm, sisal, abaca, and other less important economic plants reached the country in the nineteenth and twentieth centuries, during the heyday of Indonesian plantation agriculture.

The archipelago has owed its outstanding reputation as an exporter of tropical agricultural products in part to the fact that its topography provides enough diversity in altitude and therefore in climate to suit a wide range of economic plants. Moreover, parts of the country are endowed with highly fertile young volcanic soils and can thus support demanding crops. The majority of the Indonesian people are skilled and industrious cultivators who, though they possess a considerable degree of the conservatism characteristic of peasant societies, have successfully incorporated exotic crops into their agriculture. Finally, the agrarian, economic, and fiscal policies pursued by the Netherlands Indies government after 1870 encouraged the development of estate agriculture, attracting capital to this sector not only from the Netherlands but also from other European countries and the United States.[1]

The development of a plantation economy brought about the division of Indonesian agriculture into two major sectors: a highly scientific estate agriculture, extensive in its use of land and intensive in its use of labor[2] and capital; and a peasant agriculture, tradition-bound and—at least in Java—highly labor-intensive. The plantations, being capable of financing the construction and operation of factories, took over the cultivation of crops requiring complicated and costly processing, while the peasants concentrated

[1] During and shortly after World War I, American firms—such as the United States Rubber Commpany and Goodyear Rubber Company—had a far more encouraging reception in Indonesia, where they were able to lease all the land suitable for rubber cultivation that they wanted, than they did in the Philippines.

[2] Tea, sugar, and tobacco estates, in particular, are both labor- and capital-intensive.

on the production of domestic food crops and export crops which demanded little processing. In some cases peasants became satellite producers of such crops as tea and sugar, selling their output to nearby plantations for processing. Such products as palm oil, centrifugal sugar, and tea are typical plantation crops, while copra, spices, and kapok are produced by peasants; rubber and coffee take an intermediate position, being at home in both sectors. Between 1938 and 1958, some striking changes occurred, so that by now the peasant's share in the production of sugar cane, tea, and tobacco is markedly greater than it was in 1938.

While this division is the most obvious one in Indonesian agriculture, the peasant sector shows regional, organizational, technological, and orientational variations which permit further divisions such as: permanent-field agriculture, carried on in the densely populated parts of the country, versus shifting-field, or swidden agriculture, which is characteristic of the thinly settled regions; subsistence versus market or export-oriented agriculture; or irrigated-field versus dry-field cultivation.

Though the staple food of most Indonesians is rice, by no means all peasants are rice growers, and in several regions of the archipelago rice is not the principal food. Maize is the staple in parts of Celebes, Timor, Lombok, East Java, and Madura, while in recent years cassava has become the main source of starch for villagers in tertiary limestone regions of Java. Sago is the staple in parts of eastern Indonesia; most of it is obtained from spontaneous stands of the sago palm, although some ethnic groups such as the Toradja of Celebes also plant it as a crop.

In Java, peasant-held land which is cropped continuously is divided into three major categories: *sawah,* or irrigated land; *tegalan,* or unirrigated land; and *pekarangan,* compound or mixed garden land.[3] Intermittently cultivated land is known as *huma* in Java and generally as *ladang*[4] in the outer islands. Of these types

[3] While the term *sawah* is used throughout Indonesia, the terms *tegalan and pekarangan* are readily understood and generally used only in Java and Madura, since they refer to a type of land use best developed only by the Javanese and Madurese. Javanese settlers have carried tegalan and pekarangan cultivation into the outer islands, especially into South Sumatra.

[4] In parts of the outer islands the term *ladang* no longer refers exclusively

of cropland, sawah is the most highly prized, followed by pekarangan; teglan and ladang—unless planted with cash crops—are of lesser value. Of the more than thirteen million hectares of land in Java and Madura, about one quarter is occupied by sawah, suitable for the raising of wet rice, and somewhat over a third by tegalan, pekarangan, and fresh-water fish ponds. Agricultural land use in those islands has already passed its limits of safety. Java has been without arable forest land since before World War II, and inroads made since then in its forest reserves—which should cover 30 instead of the present 22.7 percent of the area—have caused erosion and flood problems which can be checked only by reforestation of the most exposed land. Consequently any expansion of the sawah cultivation can take place only at the expense of the tegalan area, and settlements can expand only by encroaching upon either sawah or tegalan.

In contrast, the outer islands, except Bali, have plenty of room for extension of the cultivated area. There only one percent of the land is devoted to sawah culture, which is important only in such small islands as Bali and Lombok and in relatively restricted areas of Sumatra, Borneo, and Celebes.[5] The size of the tegalan and pekarangan area of the outer islands is unknown; but in all probability it is not much larger than that of sawah, the prevailing type of agriculture in these territories being swidden cultivation.

Swidden agriculture is characterized by slash-and-burn clearing, by a rotation of fields rather than of crops, and by short periods of cropping (one to three years) alternating with long fallow periods—up to twenty years or more, but often as short as five years. Swidden cultivators prefer to lay out their temporary fields in forest areas. By now, however, there is relatively little primeval forest left in Indonesia, so that the swidden farmer normally clears

---

to temporary fields, or swidden, carved out of the forest but also to dry land which is in continuous use, either for the raising of annuals—land which the Javanese would call tegalan—or dry land which has been planted with tree crops, such as rubber or coffee.

5 Even though sawah culture is practiced in parts of Atjeh, Tapanuli, East Sumatra, the Minangkabau region of West Sumatra, and in the Javanese settlement districts of South Sumatra, sawah occupies only 1.8 percent of the total Sumatran area.

a parcel of second-growth forest (*belukar*) which may have been cleared innumerable times in the past. He may even have to turn to land covered with *alang* grass, which is far less fertile than that which has rested for several years under dense forest. The longer the fallow the larger the area needed to support a swidden cultivator, who on the average requires about ten times as much land as his sawah-cultivating counterpart in Java.

Swidden agriculture's requirement for extensive forest-fallow land renders somewhat deceptive the figure for land use in the outer islands; less than ten million hectares, or 7.3 percent of the land surface, are under dry-land cultivation. This represents only the land actually in production; to it should be added about 25 million hectares included under the headings "other forest areas" and "other land," for this inactive area is a necessary part of the swidden system.[6] This amount must be charged against the nonreserved forest areas, leaving 47.5 million hectares, or 35 percent of the area, permanently covered by nonreserved forests. Since a reduction of the forest cover much below 40 percent would involve serious risks to soil and water management, any large-scale expansion of cultivation in the outer islands requires the replacement of the present land-extensive swidden system by permanent-field agriculture. This has already become necessary in such densely settled sections of the outer islands as the coastal regions of East Sumatra and parts of South Sumatra.

Swidden agriculture is one of the world's least understood land-use systems and is often referred to in disparaging terms because of its "wastage" of cultivable land. As a matter of fact, in view of the low fertility of so many Indonesian soils, swidden cultivation is a rational system so long as the population density is low enough to permit fallow periods of sufficient duration to allow adequate recovery of soil fertility. Those who condemn the system also overlook the fact that it has played a very important role in the cultivation of smallholder rubber, which has spread with amazing rapid-

[6] This estimate is based on the assumption that five million hectares form the active ladang area, which is used for two years and then lies fallow for ten years. Therefore 25 million hectares under forest and grass fallow are the counterpart of 5 million hectares of currently cultivated ladang.

ity in the outer islands since about 1910.[7] *Hevea brasiliensis*—a tree which grows best in the humid tropics up to an elevation of about 600 meters—fitted perfectly into the swidden system, despite the early predictions of government officials and planters that it would require the kind of care that only a well-run plantation could give. Swidden cultivators of Sumatra and Borneo planted rubber in ladang which they had previously used for one of two plantings of food crops, instead of letting a nondescript belukar cover it. At the end of a seven-year period the swidden cultivator —with a minimum of care by way of an occasional slashing of undergrowth—had a valuable garden, capable of producing latex for forty years or more if properly cared for. After three or four such plantings, the shifting cultivator turned into a rubber grower who—with a favorable price ratio between rubber and rice—could thenceforth afford to purchase his rice from the Chinese buyer of his rubber. Other crops which fit easily into the swidden system are coconuts, coffee, and pepper. However, the world requirement for these crops is not as great as for rubber, and both coffee and pepper are more demanding in regard to soils, climate, maintenance, and harvest labor. They therefore never gained so wide a distribution or so great an importance in the rural economy of the outer islands as has the smallholder cultivation of rubber.

A similar development of smallholder cultivation took place in West Java in the eighteenth and nineteenth centuries, when swidden cultivators planted coffee on a large scale in their old huma. By the end of the nineteenth century, however, virtually all shifting-field cultivation had disappeared from that island,[8] for population pressure had forced the conversion of the available land to permanent-field systems. Because of the lack of any land surplus, peasants in Java cannot afford to convert tegalan into

[7] Jacob Ozinga, *De economische ontwikkeling der Westerafdeeling van Borneo en de bevolkingsrubbercultuur* (The Economic Development of West Borneo and Smallholder Rubber Cultivation), Zomer en Keuning, Wageningen, 1940, pp. 237, 262–265.

[8] Swidden cultivation in Java is still found only in relatively thinly settled portions of Bantam, in the western part of the island.

rubber gardens, for even though such a shift might bring greater eventual profit, it would mean foregoing any yield for at least six years—until the rubber reaches its producing stage. As a result, peasant agriculture in Java is almost wholly devoted to raising food crops for subsistence, while a good part of that on the outer islands shows a marked commercial bent. The social and economic consequences of this orientational divergence have had considerable effect on recent political relations between Java and the outer regions.

In Java, the average peasant cultivates less than one-half hectare of land, which may consist of sawah, tegalan, and pekarangan, or a combination of pekarangan with one of the other two. Even so small a farm is thus divided into several tiny parcels. If the land consists mostly of sawah which is irrigated by a modern system supplying water during both the rainy and dry seasons, two rice crops can be planted during the year. A cultivator whose sawah is watered by a peasant-designed irrigation system, or who must depend on rainfall alone, has no possibility of raising a second rice crop. He may, however, plant a less moisture-demanding, dry-season crop, such as soybeans, sweet potatoes, or maize. Tegalan, too, are often double-cropped—soil and moisture supply permitting—unless they are planted with a crop which requires more than four or five months to mature, such as cassava.

The practice of multiple-cropping has spread in Java ever since the nineteenth century, as the per capita supply of land shrank and the average farm size declined. By now at least one-fourth of the plowed land on this island is producing more than one crop a year. The construction of numerous modern reservoirs has played an important role in this intensification of cultivation. The sugar industry as well as the government has engaged in the provision of modern irrigation systems and storage dams, for sugar cane requires twelve to fourteen months to mature and demands a considerable supply of water during the dry season. In consequence, peasants in the sugar-producing areas are in a generally favorable position regarding water supply, though the Irrigation Service gives their fields lower priority than the sugar lands in distributing the available water.

The principal crop raised by the Indonesian farmer is rice, the staple food for most Indonesians. We do not know the exact origin of domesticated rice, but all evidence points to the Southeast Asian mainland as its home. From there, long before the beginning of the Christian era, its cultivation spread into Indonesia. It did not, however, extend to the easternmost parts of the archipelago: rice is not grown in West New Guinea; even in the Moluccas it is unimportant, sago palm being the staple item of diet. In Indonesia, as in other parts of the Asian tropics, many different varieties of paddy are cultivated in accordance with a wide range of ecological conditions. The two major classes are upland or dry rice, which depends on rainfall alone for its moisture needs, and lowland or wet rice, which requires an inundated sawah for its cultivation. Dry rice is far less important than wet rice in Indonesian agriculture: in 1960, approximately 1.3 million hectares of upland paddy were harvested, as against close to 6 million hectares of irrigated rice.[9] One-third of the rice area harvested in the outer islands is devoted to dry-rice varieties, which are suitable to swidden agriculture and require relatively little manpower to cultivate. They often produce less per hectare than lowland paddy, however, and on Java and Madura, where land and not labor is in short supply, wet cultivation accounts for about 93 percent of the rice area harvested.

Nonstaple food crops are referred to in Java as *polowidjo,* which indicates that they are subsidiary or secondary to rice. Over the last century secondary crops have come to play an important role in Java both as a part of the daily fare and as a source of cash. The major secondary crops are maize, cassava, sweet potatoes, taro, peanuts, soybeans, red (chili) pepper, and onions. Some of these are raised in tegalan the year round, others in sawah during the dry season. A failure of the secondary crops is fully as serious as is a poor rice crop, since they provide cash for the purchase of the daily food when the old rice crop has been consumed and the new one is still weeks away.

A further source of produce is the pekarangan which surrounds each house in the villages of Java and many homes in the towns. These gardens are carefully tended, well watered, and densely

9 Central Bureau of Statistics, *Statistical Pocketbook of Indonesia, 1961,* Djakarta, p. 51.

planted with a great variety of trees, bushes, and small plants. They are highly productive, and their leafy vegetables, pods, tubers, and fruits contribute greatly to the diet as sources of protein and vitamins A and C. Moreover, since there is always something to be harvested from the pekarangan, they provide a year-round source of cash.[10] Outside Java, pekarangan are best developed on Madura, Bali, and Lombok; they play a minor role elsewhere and are lacking completely in areas where swidden cultivation prevails.

According to surveys undertaken in 1957, 78 percent of sawah owners in Java had less than 0.5 hectare and 90 percent less than one hectare. Prewar village surveys have shown that many of the peasants who owned only tiny holdings were heavily indebted; they retained only a small share of the yield, the larger part going to moneylenders. At present the extent of rural indebtedness is unknown, since there are no official records; but it is clear that moneylenders exercise *de facto* control over a large share of the land by virtue of unrecorded agreements; thus peasants who appear to be independent and in control of their land are in reality sharecroppers. Peasants who depend upon the goodwill of their creditors are usually reluctant to volunteer information about their indebtedness for fear they will create difficulties for themselves if they speak frankly—especially if they have borrowed from one of the village officials. The moneylender-landlords, for their part, will not volunteer information, in order to avoid taxes. As a result, village records showing ownership of land do not reflect the true socioeconomic conditions in the rural areas.

According to investigations[11] conducted in a village of West Java by rural sociologists of the Agricultural College at Bogor, no less than 44 percent of the heads of households engaged in

[10] For a further description of the uses of pekarangan, see G. J. A. Terra, "Tuinbouw" (Gardening), in C. J. J. van Hall and C. van de Koppel, *De landbouw in de Indische archipel* (Agriculture in the Indies Archipelago), vol. 2A van Hoeve, The Hague, 1948, pp. 630–631.

[11] H. ten Dam, "Cooperation and Social Structure in the Village of Chibodas," in *Indonesian Economics: The Concept of Dualism in Theory and Policy,* van Hoeve, The Hague, 1961, pp. 347–382. A Dutch version was published in *Indonesië,* vol. 9, 1956, pp. 89–116.

agriculture had no land of their own; another 25 percent owned only a piece of compound land in the village, and 23 percent had less than one hectare of tegalan—not enough to provide a living. Thus no less than 92 percent of the families in the village were compelled to work full or part time as tenant farmers or agricultural laborers. Of the 8 percent that were independent, 6 owned from 1 to 5 hectares of land and 2 held more than 5 hectares. The leading families—i.e., those who owned more than five hectares—held about half the land in the village. For six months of the year they employed the landless to raise potatoes and cabbage on their tegalan; for the other half of the year these farmhands became sharecroppers, growing dry rice and maize on the same land. Similarly, a study of the *kabupaten* of Malang (East Java) showed that 16 percent of all heads of households were completely landless, 64 percent had insufficient land to support their families, and only 20 percent had enough to be independent.[12]

Social stratification in Javanese villages shows a correlation with the amount and kind of land owned. Villagers who hold both sawah and pekarangan—with a house on the latter—have a higher standing than do those who lack sawah but own some tegalan land and a pekarangan with a house. Below this group come those who have only a house plot in the village, and they in turn rank higher than villagers whose houses stand on someone else's pekarangan. The lowest group of all consists of those who possess neither land nor house but live as boarders in another person's home. The numerical proportion of these groups in a given village is an excellent indicator of the local population pressure on the land.

The great shortage of land in Java has given rise to a considerable degree of rural underemployment; living standards in the crowded villages are very low, and radical peasant associations have won considerable support there. Similar characteristics can be observed in many of the sawah districts of the outer islands, particularly in North Tapanuli, South Sumatra, and Lombok. By contrast, the peasants of the swidden regions, especially those who

[12] Don C. Bennet, "Population Pressure in East Java," Ph.D. thesis, Syracuse University, N.Y., 1957, p. 138.

own stands of commercial export crops, generally enjoy a higher income; what is most important, they still have room to expand the cultivated area in step with population growth.

Since sharecropping is so widespread a phenomenon on the Indonesian agrarian scene, the Sharecropping Law (no. 2/1960) promises to affect a very large percentage of the peasantry.[13] Its stated aims are to bring justice into the landlord-sharecropper relationship, to protect the weak sharecropper against the strong landowner, and to provide the sharecropper with adequate incentives for increasing production. The law authorizes the heads of the second-level, autonomous regions to fix the ratio by which the yield is to be divided; a nationwide minimum portion for sharecroppers has been set, however, at one-half the yield on sawah and two-thirds on tegalan. All sharecropping agreements between landowner and tenant must be registered; they may not involve more than three hectares per sharecropper and must be valid for at least three years for irrigated land or five years for unirrigated land. Agreements between moneylenders and peasant debtors must, according to the law, be concluded at the office of the village administration.

The Basic Agrarian Law (no. 5/1960) is also of great significance, for it replaces the previous colonial land laws and provides a keystone for future agrarian legislation. Whereas Netherlands Indies' laws had considered final ownership of land to rest with the state, the new legislation is based on the concept of private property. Individual hereditary right of ownership (*hak milik*), the basic land right recognized by the law, may be held only by Indonesian citizens. It is not absolute, since the state may regulate the use of land under its authority to administrate the country's natural resources in the national interest. The new act also recognizes *hak ulajat,* or the right of adat communities to dispose of land and other resources not yet encumbered by hak milik; the

[13] Sharecropping is known under various local names: *maro* or *mertelu* in Central and East Java, *nengah* or *djedjuron* in the Priangan district or West Java, *memperduai* in the Minangkabau area of West Sumatra, *tojo* in the Minahasa region of Celebes, and *njakap* in Lombok. In 1960, the ministry of agrarian affairs estimated 60 percent of all peasants to be sharecroppers.

state, however, reserves the power to override this right in carrying out development projects of national interest.

In order to assure hak milik to as many peasants as possible, the Basic Agrarian Law limits the amount of land which an individual may own under this right and forbids absentee ownership. The limits on such holdings have been determined according to population density, with a uniform minimum for subdivision of two hectares.[14] The stated purpose of this minimum limit is to ensure sufficient income to the Indonesian peasant and to prevent excessive fragmentation of holdings. Land in excess of the permissible maxima has been registered and is being taken over by the state for distribution among the landless rural population. Land reform committees have been established throughout Indonesia down to the third regional level (*kawedanaan*) to oversee this process; the fixing of the amount of indemnification to be paid the owners is left to the committees of the second (*kabupaten*) level. Whatever the specific amount, 10 percent is to be paid into savings accounts in the local bank for cooperatives, farmers, and fishermen, while the remaining 90 percent is to be issued in land reform bonds bearing a 3 percent interest rate and redeemable in twelve years. Those who benefit from the program must pay for the land they receive within fifteen years, during which period they must be members of a peasant cooperative.

Since the land reform program is still in its early stages, it is not possible to evaluate its success.* The ministry of agrarian affairs estimated that as a result of the various land reform provisions about a million hectares would become available for redistribu-

[14] The following maxima of sawah and dry land (*tanah kering*), based on population density by regencies, or kabupaten, are allowed:

Density per sq. km.	*Sawah*	*Dry land*
Less than 50 persons	15.0 hectares	20 hectares
51–250 "	10.0 "	12 "
251–400 "	7.5 "	9 "
Over 400 "	5.0 "	6 "

* The land reform program under the Basic Agrarian Law has had little impact outside the estate sector and can now (1970) be regarded as a dead letter.—Ed.

tion.[15] While this would certainly give relief to many peasants, it cannot provide them all with the two hectares envisioned as the nationwide minimum holding; indeed, no land reform program could accomplish this, for in Java there is simply not enough land to go around. The fact of the matter is that the problem cannot be solved by a redistribution of the land, but only by a redistribution of the population or by the creation of employment outside the agrarian sector—either of which would have to be accomplished on a truly massive scale.

One of the consequences of the rural overcrowding caused by population growth is that food production has not kept pace with the steady increase in spite of very intensive land use. Because of the lack of statistical data on peasant food crops in the outer islands prior to World War II it is not possible to compare prewar with postindependence food production for the country as a whole; but it is safe to assume that output in the latter period, while higher than that of colonial times, has declined relative to the total population. In Java, the chief area of overcrowding, production in 1960 was only slightly above the level reached in 1940, and the per capita supply of major foodstuffs—production minus seed—declined markedly. The low nutritional level resulting from the insufficiency of food production has concerned authorities ever since the beginning of the century. At present, the average Indonesian consumes only 2,125 calories a day, whereas the United Nations' Food and Agriculture Organization regards 2,300 calories as the desirable level.[16]

To help close the increasing gap between production and dietary need, Indonesia must import large quantities of rice and wheat flour, as well as protein foods and powdered and canned

[15] Decree of the minister of agrarian affairs, no. SK/509/Ka, August 22, 1961. This land is to be derived from the following sources: (1) lands in excess of the permissible maxima set by Act no. 56/Prp/1960; (2) lands of absentee owners; (3) former private estates and proprietary lands (*particuliere landerijen*); (4) former principality lands; (5) former plantation lands returned to the state; and (6) other lands directly administered by the state (speech delivered by the minister of agrarian affairs at the Conference on Village Community Development, August 10, 1961).

[16] Foreign Agricultural Service, U.S. Department of Agriculture, *The World Food Deficit: A First Approximation,* Washington, March 1961, p. 22.

milk. In 1959, rice imports amounted to 603,000 metric tons, or 11.5 percent of the value of all imports, as compared to an average of 240,000 tons (3.6 percent of total import value) in 1938–1940. Wheat flour imports averaged 132,000 metric tons in the 1955–1959 period, compared with an average of 94,000 tons in 1938–1940. Since Indonesia desperately needs its foreign earnings for capital goods and other nonagricultural essentials, it can ill afford its present purchases, much less an increase in the amount and range of its food imports. The government has therefore bent its efforts toward raising domestic supplies, concentrating on the chief staple, rice. In 1958, it prepared a Three Year Rice Production Plan, which aimed at achieving a production of 100 kilograms of rice per person a year—which, together with the equivalent of 60 kilograms of rice in the form of maize, cassava, sweet potatoes and other tubers, would bring Indonesia's per capita supply to a level deemed adequate by nutritionists.

The Three Year Plan consisted of a short-range program for the intensification of production on land already under the plow in Java and the outer islands and a long-range program of extension of the area under cultivation in the less populous parts of the country. Implementation of the short-range program centered on the establishment of paddy centers, which were to aid the peasants by providing them with improved seeds, fertilizer, and cash credit (see Table 4.1). The peasants who received this aid were expected to repay the centers in cash or in kind from their increased yield.[17] It was calculated on the basis of a pilot project that by 1961–1962 production would rise on the average by eight quintals of paddy (four quintals of milled rice), producing an additional 1,200,000 metric tons of milled rice. The plan foresaw Indonesian self-sufficiency in rice by the end of 1962,[18] but by the end of

[17] The original plan called for repayment to be made by delivery of from 5.5 to 6.5 quintals of paddy per hectare. However, some Central Java chapters of the Barisan Tani Indonesia (Indonesian Peasant Front, an association closely allied to the Communist party) objected to this on the grounds that it resembled the *idjon* system—i.e., moneylending in return for payment in kind at harvest time, a form of indebtedness with which the Javanese peasant was all too familiar. In late 1961, the government therefore began to allow repayment in cash, which the peasants preferred.

[18] This calculation was based on population estimates which were proved

Table 4.1. Summary of three year rice production plan

Category	1959–1960	1960–1961	1961–1962
Population*	90,330,000	91,956,000	93,611,000
Rice requirements, at rate of 100 kg. per capita yearly (metric tons)	9,033,000	9,195,000	9,361,000
Paddy centers			
Number of centers	42	125	500
Area to be affected (hectares)	100,000	500,000	3,000,000
Improved seed requirements (tons)	5,000	25,000	150,000
Fertilizer requirement (tons)	10,000	50,000	300,000
Paddy to be collected in settlement of credits: 6 quintals of stalk paddy per hectare (tons)	60,000	300,000	1,800,000
Mass intensification			
Area to be covered (hectares)	303,000	1,240,000	2,000,000
Improved seed requirements (tons)	3,200	60,000	100,000
Fertilizer requirement (tons)	30,300	124,000	75,000
Insecticide requirements			
Phosphorus, sulphur, aldrin (tons)	530	730	750
Endrin (liters)	56,250	112,500	112,500
Agricultural tools required			
Mattocks	200,000	250,000	550,000
High pressure pumps	1,500	1,500	400
Water pumps	200	500	1,000
Rice production target (tons)	8,780,400	9,061,000	10,050,000
Difference between rice requirement and production (tons)†	−516,000	−406,000	+387,000

Source: Planning Office, Department of Agriculture, *Three Year Rice Production Plan*, Djakarta, January 1, 1960.

* Census of October 1961 showed that Indonesia's population came close to 97 million rather than the 92 million estimated by planners.

† 3 percent allowed for waste.

1961, it was clear that this estimate had been unrealistic. Instead of the expected surplus of 390,000 tons of rice from the 1962 harvests, it is safe to assume a deficit of at least 1,000,000 tons for that year (see Table 4.1).

---

by the 1961 census to be in error by about 4 million. Rice needs were thus 400,000 tons more than initially calculated, and increased thereafter at the rate of 200,000 tons a year.

An important task assigned to the paddy centers was the collection of rice needed by the government for distribution to the armed forces, government employees, and estate laborers as well as for injection into the market in order to keep down its price for the consumer. As long as the difference between the government-controlled and free-market prices of rice was relatively small, the state was able to obtain a high percentage of its requirements (see Table 4.2). However, in 1960, prices began to soar on the

Table 4.2. Paddy purchased by the government in Java, 1952–1962 (metric tons of dry paddy in stalk)

Crop year	Quota	Purchased	Percentage collected
1952–53	800,000	495,724	62.0
1953–54	800,500	749,178	93.6
1954–55	994,000	791,743	79.6
1955–56	1,200,000	593,484	49.4
1956–57	800,000	514,006	64.2
1957–58	800,000	692,683	83.9
1958–59	900,000	324,687	36.0
1959–60	900,000	536,583	59.6
1960–61	1,000,000	544,804	54.4
1961–62	1,000,000	517,250	51.7
1962–63	1,400,000		

Sources: 1952–53 to 1956–57: Leon A. Mears, *Rice Marketing in the Republic of Indonesia*, Pembangunan, Djakarta, 1961, p. 162; 1956–57: Mears, *op. cit.*, Supplement, Table A-13a; 1958–59 to 1961–62: data obtained by correspondence with Central Bureau of Statistics.

free market, and the government was forced to offer the peasants one and a half meters of textiles at controlled prices in return for every half quintal of paddy in order to provide them with adequate incentive to deliver the rice quota. In 1961, free market prices of rice in Djakarta rose from Rp. 6.62 to Rp. 48.75; this increase, the product in part of serious drought, continued into 1962 and caused the government to fail in realizing its collection program.

It remains to be seen whether the paddy centers can play the role that is expected from them. On the one hand, average yields in Indonesia are very low, and it should be possible to increase them substantially by the use of better seeds, sufficient quantities of commercial fertilizers and pesticides, improvement of drainage and irrigation systems, and better preparation of the land. All of these remedies require sizable investments which the poverty-stricken peasants cannot afford. The aid provided by the paddy centers, if well administered and on a sufficiently large scale, should therefore do much to increase yields. So far, however, the centers have been handicapped by a lack of trained personnel, seed, and fertilizer. Moreover, the program requires the peasants to take the risks without assuring them a price which is in line with the cost of living; they therefore have little incentive to increase rice production for sale on the government-controlled market. At best, it appears inevitable that rice imports will have to be continued for at least another two or three years; and it may require the completion of some of the long-range programs for irrigation, swamp drainage, and fertilizer plant construction before self-sufficiency can be achieved.

Agricultural exports play a critical role in the Indonesian economy, for they provide approximately two-thirds of all foreign exchange earned. Production is divided between large-scale plantation enterprises and small peasant holdings. The area controlled by plantations has always been small relative to the economic importance of the estate sector: approximately 4.7 percent of Java and 1 percent of the outer islands (excluding West New Guinea) are devoted to this form of agriculture. Not even all of this limited area is under production, however. In 1958, only 828,000 of the 1,800,000 estate-controlled hectares were actually planted with cash crops, the rest being either occupied by squatters, in fallow, or still under forest cover. Estates are highly concentrated in the residency of East Sumatra, which accounts at minimum for about 53 percent of the plantation area and 46 percent of the land in production. This heavy concentration has given the region a vital importance in the Indonesian economy and at the same time has made it a center of conflict between peasant and planter interests.[19]

[19] Karl J. Pelzer, "The Agrarian Conflict in East Sumatra," *Pacific Affairs*, vol. 30, 1957, pp. 151–159, and Clark E. Cunningham, *The Postwar Migra-*

The oldest plantations in Indonesia, which were largely concentrated in the principalities of Central Java, date back to the early part of the nineteenth century. Between 1830 and 1870, estate agriculture received little or no encouragement from the colonial authorities, however. During this period the government relied on the compulsory production of export crops by the Javanese peasantry—the so-called Cultivation System. The Agrarian Law of 1870 provided for the gradual abolition of this system and opened the doors to plantation development in both Java and the outer islands. The planters were required, however, to lease the land on which they operated; unlike estate enterprises in most other parts of the world, those in Indonesia could not own land outright. Private ownership of land was restricted to ethnic Indonesians, and so no pattern of large land holdings by foreigners or Indonesians of foreign descent was established.

The only exception to this rule was a type of tenure, found mainly in West Java, which dated back to the period of the East India Company and the incumbencies of Governors-General Daendels and Raffles at the beginning of the nineteenth century. In order to raise ready cash the Company, and later the state, sold about 1.5 million hectares of land to private persons; and the owners of these "private estates" (*particuliere landerijen*) exercised seignoral rights over land normally held by the government.[20] Since the treatment of Indonesians living on these proprietary lands was all too often harsh and oppressive, the villagers in these areas frequently resorted to violence during the nineteenth century. In 1911, the Netherlands Indies government began the gradual repurchase of such lands,[21] but it was not until the passing of the Law on the Abolition of Private Estates in January 1958 that they completely disappeared.

---

tion of the Toba-Bataks to East Sumatra, Southeast Asia Studies, Yale University, New Haven, 1958.

20 Among the perquisites held by owners of private estates were the rights to collect one-fifth of crop yields, a fee on fruit trees and other profit-yielding trees and shrubs, a tax on land occupied by buildings, and a fee on land covered by fish ponds. They could also appoint village chiefs, approve elected village officials, and dismiss them from office.

21 The Dutch parliament had authorized the first repurchase of a private estate in 1910.

With this exception, plantations have operated in Indonesia under one of two types of leasehold. In Java, sugar and tobacco planters rented land from Indonesian villagers, being permitted to use in any one period only one-third of a village's sawah area for the raising of estate crops. After the harvest the land had to be exchanged against another third, this system of rotation being designed above all to prevent planters from gaining a permanent hold on village lands. Contracts were usually closed with the village heads rather than with individual peasants, thus strengthening traditional tendencies toward communal landholding; in the periodic reapportionment of plots to individual cultivators, the village heads assigned each claimant a parcel in each of the three sections into which the village sawah area had been divided in order to make possible rotational leasing by an estate. This type of lease could be concluded, in the case of a sugar plantation, either for a single occupation of sixteen months or for several occupations extending over a maximum of twenty-one and a half years.

The interests of planters and peasants interlocked under leaseholds of this kind; but since the planters were much stronger financially and organizationally than their peasant partners, the authorities developed a complicated set of regulations designed to protect the latter against abuses. Even so, the equity of the peasant-planter relationship was a subject of considerable controversy; it continues to be one even today, although the sugar and tobacco estates have since been transferred to public control by the Indonesian government.

Since perennial tree crops do not permit an interlocking of peasant and plantation agriculture, all other estates—tea, coffee, cinchona, rubber, and oil and coconut palm—have leased land under the second system of tenure. By the Agrarian Law of 1870, all land to which no Indonesian could prove ownership or use was deemed to be public domain; it could therefore be applied for by nonIndonesians—in particular planters and plantation enterprises—for lease under a 75-year contract (*erfpacht*), which allowed for the mortgaging and inheriting of the land. This system was first applied especially to Java and Madura. In the indirectly-governed parts of the outer territories, and especially in East Sumatra, plantation interests were able to obtain land from the local Indonesian rulers in the form of 75-year agricultural concessions; these were rather more favorable to the planters than the long leases of the directly-governed regions in that they did not give clear precedence to peasant claims on the land.[22]

In 1957, only a small portion of estate lands belonged to government-owned and -operated plantations. The seizure of Dutch enterprises in Indonesia began at the end of that year, however, and in 1959 all Dutch-owned concerns were nationalized, bringing some 542 plantations—held either as agricultural concessions or as long leases—under public administration.[23]

In 1960, the Basic Agrarian Law abolished the regulations which had governed estate holdings since 1870. Agricultural concessions and long leases were replaced by *hak guna-usaha*—right of exploitation—which can be held by Indonesian citizens or by corporate bodies established according to Indonesian law, domiciled in the country, and having made application for the conversion of their previous rights to hak guna-usaha by September 24, 1961. Exploitation rights obtained by foreign companies as a result of the conversion of previous rights are valid only for the remaining time of the original tenure and in any case for not more than twenty years.[24] Land newly given out under hak guna-usaha may be held for twenty-five years, and this limit may be

[22] For a detailed discussion of land laws established in the period of colonial rule, see J. G. W. Lekkerkerker, *Concessies en erfpachten voor landbouwondernemingen in de Buitengewesten* (Concessions and Long Leases for Agricultural Enterprises in the Outer Islands) Wolters, Groningen, 1928; and G. J. Nolst Trenité, "Agrarische regelingen (Agrarian Regulations), in van Hall and van de Koppel, *op. cit.*, vol. 1, pp. 286–309.

[23] Prior to 1959, there were thirty-five government-owned estates operated by PPN (Pusat Perkebunan Negara, or Government Estates Administration), a part of the ministry of agriculture. In 1959, the PPN-Baru (new PPN) was created to administer the plantations acquired in that year by nationalization; and in 1960 the two bodies were merged under the title PPN.

[24] The United States Rubber Company received exploitation rights for a period of twelve years with the understanding that further extension will be considered provided that the Company in the meantime undertakes research and development work. However, the Indonesian government insisted upon cession of no less than 30 percent of the planted area.

extended in cases where the crop planted requires several years before it begins to produce. Land held under hak guna-usaha may be inherited or otherwise transferred, and it may be mortgaged.

Since by the time the Basic Agrarian Law was passed all Dutch-owned plantations had been nationalized and were under PPN (Pusat Perkebunan Negara, or Government Estates Administration) management, the legislation mainly affected American, British, Belgian, and French concerns. Although most foreign companies applied for conversion of their agrarian rights to hak guna-usaha by September 1961, in late 1962 it is not yet known how much land has been returned to the government. The long-range future of foreign-owned plantations, however, is still uncertain, although the Indonesian government does not rule out further extension of the exploitation rights beyond the date of the current contracts. For years the authorities have insisted on the gradual replacement of foreign personnel by Indonesians and have accelerated this process by issuing entry and work permits to foreign employees sparingly. While this policy's aim of opening upper-level positions to Indonesian nationals is certainly justifiable, it has the unfortunate short-run effect of spreading still thinner the already scarce managerial, scientific, and technical skills available to the industry. The state-run enterprises are particularly ill-equipped in this respect, and unless they can be provided with competent staff, together with adequate funds, sufficient disciplined labor, and opportunities for expanding and replanting their crop areas, a further weakening of the plantation sector seems inevitable.[25]

Of the forty-odd commercial export crops grown in Indonesia, only eight—rubber, copra, sugar, palm oil, tobacco, hard fiber, coffee, and tea—are of major importance. In terms of quantity, agricultural exports reached their peak in 1928 with over five

[25] J. A. C. Mackie, "Indonesia's Government Estates and Their Masters," *Pacific Affairs*, vol. 34, 1961, pp. 337–360, gives an excellent account of PPN operations and a most informative summary of the many problems besetting the plantation sector. See also Douglas S. Paauw, ed., *Prospects for East Sumatran Plantation Industries: A Symposium,* Southeast Asia Studies, Yale University, New Haven, 1962. This symposium deals with the tobacco, palm oil, and rubber industries of East Sumatra.

million metric tons but declined markedly after that year. Both the plantation and the smallholder sector share in this trend, with the important difference that by 1960 the volume of plantation exports had shrunk to a mere 17 percent of that of 1928, while the volume of small holder exports had only declined to 56 percent of the 1928 level. Furthermore, while in 1928 the plantations accounted for 67 percent and smallholders for 33 percent of all agricultural exports, by 1960 the roles were almost reversed: smallholders furnished 62 percent and plantations only 38 percent. Except for rubber, all agricultural exports have fallen in volume; none, however, has declined so heavily as has sugar.

Sugar was king among Indonesia's plantation crops during the first three decades of this century; and since the sugar plantations are located in Java, that island in 1928 contributed more than half the value of all agricultural exports. In 1928, the industry reached its apogee; since then, except for a brief recovery in the late 1930's, it has been on the downgrade. During the depression of the 1930's, the number of sugar mills in Java declined from 180 to 94, only 84 of which were in operation in 1939. Sugar production was curtailed by more than 50 percent during World War II, and the land no longer needed for sugar cane was used for the growing of rice and other food crops. During the struggle for independence about half the sugar mills were destroyed as part of the Indonesian scorched-earth policy; some of them have since been repaired, and at present Java has fifty-four operating sugar mills. In the postrevolutionary period the sugar planters found themselves confronted both by a national government determined to wipe out the "colonial" aspects of the peasant-planter relationship[26] and by a peasant population well aware that the loss of two rainy-season crops and one dry-season crop was not adequately compensated for by the rental offered them. In 1958, following the seizure of all Dutch-owned enterprises in Indonesia,

[26] Among the measures taken by the Indonesian government to eliminate injustices in the sugar districts was the repeal of such regulations as a 1923 law forbidding the purchase of peasant-produced cane by the sugar mills, and a ruling of the prewar Irrigation Service discriminating against Indonesian canegrowers by allotting them less irrigation water during the dry season than was granted to European planters.

the administration of the sugar estates passed to PPN—the agency in charge of state-run plantations—and since then the sugar industry has been in public hands.

Despite the concentrated efforts of management in the post-revolutionary period, sugar production has not reached a level higher than two-thirds that of 1938. The area under cane for milling in sugar factories climbed slowly to a peak of 55,000 hectares in 1960—as against 85,500 in 1938—but the yields of cane per hectare declined seriously, falling from 164 quintals of raw sugar per hectare to 104 quintals in the same period.[27] At the same time, relatively low sugar prices caused per capita annual sugar consumption to increase; and this, coupled with the absolute increase in population and continuing low production, brought about a drastic curtailment of exports in 1958–1960. In 1961, shipments abroad were completely halted, although the International Sugar Agreement allowed for an export of 350,000 tons. In this manner Indonesia, thirty years ago one of the world's leading suppliers, has, at least temporarily, disappeared from the roster of sugar-exporting countries. As a matter of fact, the country at present has a shortage of sugar for domestic consumption, especially in the outer islands: In May 1962, the black market price of that commodity in Medan was reported to be Rp. 250 per kilogram. This circumstance has contributed to a rise in the production of types of sugar which are not processed by mills and therefore are not subject to government-set prices, such as non-centrifugal "cup" sugar and sugar made from the sap of the aren, lontar, and coconut palms.

The government has tried to increase sugar production in order to satisfy domestic needs and provide foreign exchange. Some of the factors contributing to the current depressed state of the industry are material or technical ones—poor seed cane, deteriorated irrigation systems, lack of fertilizer, poor cultivation and harvesting methods, and lack of labor, managerial, and scientific personnel. In addition, production is adversely affected by a conflict between peasant interests and government policy. The state wishes to keep sugar prices low as an anti-inflationary measure and in order to compete on the world market. To create ade-

[27] Bank Indonesia, *Report of the Governor,* 1958–1959, Djakarta, p. 197.

quate incentives by subsidy would be extremely expensive, particularly in view of the fact that recent rapid rises in food prices have made it increasingly profitable for the peasants to use their land for other crops. The government has therefore resorted to systems of "compulsory deliveries" and "compulsory surrender" of land for artificially low remuneration, which the student of Indonesian economic history will recognize as repetitions of eighteenth- and early nineteenth-century colonial policies. The land rentals paid by PPN are so low that the villagers have every incentive not to lease their land to the agency; when pressed, they try to make available only poor land, and that as late as possible in the planting season.

The Land Use Law (no. 38/1960) enables the state to compel peasants to forego the better financial returns which would result from planting "nonvital" crops such as onions or tobacco in the interest of "nationally vital" produce such as sugar cane. In 1961, it was ruled that peasants living in sugar districts were obliged to sell cane, which they raised for their own account, to the local sugar mill for the most unprofitable price of Rp. 25 per quintal.[28] In January 1962, the government issued a decree specifying the hectarage of sawah that must be planted with cane for delivery to the mills.[29] Should this regulation be completely implemented, the sugar cane area of 1962–1963 would exceed that of the immediate prewar period. At the same time, however, the government has shown a certain ambivalence in its policy of restoring the sugar production in its original area of concentration: in December 1961, for example, a high official of the department of agriculture declared that it would not be feasible to provide increasing amounts of land for sugar cane in Java, since the land was needed for other crops. In the future, he stated, it would be necessary to develop a modern sugar industry in the outer islands,

[28] Supreme War Administration Degree no. 4, 1961.

[29] Decree no. SK/XIV/1/KA, Djakarta, January 31, 1962. The regulation which was based on the powers granted by the Land Use Law, identified each mill and stated the amount of land to be planted with sugar, but left it up to the local and regional heads to establish the quotas for individual villages. The decree called for a total of 95,680 hectares to be planted in sugar, of which 77,340 were to be planted by the sugar plantations and 18,340 by peasants for delivery to the mills.

where it would be possible to mechanize cultivation and to permit the cane to ratoon, thus following the example of modern sugar industries outside Indonesia.[30]

Whereas centrifugal sugar production has thus far been exclusively a Javanese industry and has depended on the existence of plantations and their processing facilities, rubber growing has developed in both Java and the outer islands and has been both a plantation and an independent smallholder activity. Rubber entered the Indonesian economy at a time when Java's arable land was almost all in use and when the areas which had been declared public domain were for the most part already in the hands of European planters. In consequence, although about 40 percent of the estate rubber is located in Java only one percent of the smallholder rubber is grown there. Peasant cultivation of rubber—which, as we have seen, fitted swidden agriculture admirably—is located for 75 percent in Sumatra and 24 percent in Borneo.

In 1928, rubber was second to sugar as the most important agricultural source of foreign exchange, but during the depression it took the lead and has held it ever since, producing almost half the value of all Indonesian exports in 1959 and 1960. This expansion, coupled with the decay of the sugar industry, resulted in a reversal in regional contribution to the economy: Java, which at the beginning of the century produced about three-fourths the value of Indonesian agricultural exports—58 percent in 1928—has become an absorber rather than an earner of foreign exchange. This period also marked a general shift from plantation to smallholder cultivation as the chief source of production for export. Ever since the late nineteenth century, smallholders have contributed a steadily increasing share of Indonesia's agricultural exports, and their role could have been even greater during the colonial period had it not been for the government's policy of favoring planters over peasants.[31] Since the transfer of sovereignty,

[30] Speech by Amin Tjokrosuseno of the Department of Agriculture, delivered at the Conference on Sugar Production at Tjipajung in December 1961.

[31] This was particularly evident in the sugar and rubber industries. For the latter, see P. T. Bauer, *The Rubber Industry: A Study in Competition and Monoply,* Harvard University Press, Cambridge, 1948, pp. 208–215. Cases of favoritism were defended by Netherlands Indies' officials with the argument

the peasant sector's share of the value of agricultural exports has consistently exceeded that of the estates. This has further strengthened the predominance of the outer islands over Java as an earner of foreign exchange since, as we have seen earlier, the shortage of land hampered the development of smallholder enterprises there.

Although smallholder rubber production expanded steadily during the prewar period, in 1940 plantation exports were still twice the value of smallholder shipments. This figure, however, is somewhat deceptive as a measure of the relative size of the two sectors at the time. It would appear that even before 1941 smallholders already had a substantially larger amount of land under rubber than did the planters, but they were not permitted by the government to utilize their productive capacity to the same degree in implementation of the International Rubber Restriction Agreement of 1934.[32] With the termination of the restrictions on tapping, the smallholder came into his own and, producing far more rubber than the planter, has become the chief earner of foreign exchange.

Rubber plantations tend to produce steadily to their capacity, showing little fluctuation in response to changes in price. Since Dutch-owned estates were replanted extensively in the early 1950's with trees of a high-yielding variety, the output of the plantation sector should increase in the near future, provided obstacles to greater production can be kept to a minimum. In recent years, however, plantation production has been plagued by widespread theft, labor problems, lack of spare parts and new equipment, loss of land due to squatting, and losses of both equipment and

---

that the interests of the state were best served by a strong plantation industry capable of competing on the world market.

[32] Whereas the plantation rubber area is exactly known, the smallholder acreage has only been estimated on the basis of a census count of trees, undertaken in the late 1930's. A preliminary figure, based on the assumption that smallholders had planted 850 trees per hectare on the average, gave a total of about 700,000 hectares under peasant rubber; a second estimate, assuming a lower density of trees, indicated an area of 1,300,000 hectares. Whichever figure one accepts, it is apparent that the smallholder area was considerably larger than that of the estates. In allotting production quotas under the rubber restriction agreement, the Netherlands Indies' government favored the plantation by a ratio of 100:71.5.

rubber as a result of the rebellion of 1958. Moreover, plantations located in the neighborhood of extensive peasant-rubber areas are beset by labor shortages when rubber prices are high, since laborers—especially the casual workers, but also some of the regular force living on the estates—will move into the smallholder sector of the industry, where they can earn considerably more money by tapping on a share basis. As plantation wages have tended to lag behind the rising cost of living, laborers who have turned squatters find it more rewarding to raise food crops, for which they can get a good price, than to seek employment on a plantation. As a result, the labor shortage has become acute in East Sumatra, an area which is planted with no less than 43 percent of the country's estate rubber.[33]

Smallholders rarely tap all trees capable of producing latex; instead, their output fluctuates considerably. Variations in the course of a year of stable rubber prices are due to the fact that most smallholders do not devote all of their labor to rubber; they grow other crops, especially dry rice, and they may spend time fishing. There appears to be a connection between rubber output and rice prices: the rate of tapping falls off when rice prices are higher than those brought by rubber, and increases when the reverse is true. In the leading smallholder rubber districts of Sumatra and Borneo a shortage of tappers also handicaps production and is responsible for neglect of rubber gardens, poor tapping, and no tapping at all in inconveniently located gardens. Only when rubber prices are so high that additional tappers can be drawn from labor surplus areas and plantations by the offer of half and even two-thirds of the yield is full smallholder production realized. During the Korean war, which brought high world rubber prices, the smallholders produced record quantities, but since then their output has fallen off.

In recent years, with food prices greatly inflated and rubber prices kept low by means of foreign-exchange controls and overevaluation of the rupiah, the incentives for the smallholders to maximize production have been notably lacking. On the other

33 The virtual collapse of the old labor-recruiting organization which for many years imported laborers from Java also contributed to the development of a labor shortage.

hand, the great difference between the official and illegal currency exchange rates and the considerable portion of export earnings retained by the central government have made it tempting for merchants to purchase rubber and other smallholder export crops at inflated prices and to smuggle them into Malaya or the Philippines, keeping the foreign exchange for themselves or converting it into merchandise for black-market sale at home. This conflict between smallholder and commercial interests of the outer islands and the policies of the central government contributed greatly to the separationist tendencies which resulted in the rebellion of 1958. The restoration of central authority has not been accompanied by an improvement in the smallholders' position, and there is thus considerable danger that smuggling will continue or that the peasant will shift to the production of nonexport crops.

The position of peasant-grown rubber is further threatened by the fact that very few of the smallholdings are planted with high-yielding seed material—in contrast to the plantations, which by now have a considerable percentage of their land planted with selected and improved trees. Most smallholder gardens are thirty-five years old or over and are therefore in immediate need of replanting. But the peasants are reluctant to cut down trees as long as they are still producing latex, knowing that it takes at least six years for new trees to come into production. Replanting with high-yielding strains is imperative, however, because only such trees can produce efficiently enough to compete with synthetic rubbers, which have made great inroads into the natural rubber market in the postwar period.

If Indonesia is to maintain a market for its rubber, heroic measures for the planting of new lands and the complete replanting of the old stands should be undertaken over the next fifteen to twenty years. This is a huge task, considering the size of the area involved and the great organizational, financial, and labor investment which it will require. However, in view of the importance of rubber to the national economy, its capacity for yielding good returns even on relatively poor soils, and its perfect suitability to the ecology of Sumatra and Borneo, it would seem worthwhile for Indonesia to emulate Malaya in carrying out a large-scale program of extension and replanting of smallholder rubber.

The second most important smallholder crop is copra. This did not become an important export item until the last quarter of the nineteenth century, although the coconut palm is an ancient economic plant in the archipelago and is found wherever climate and soil permit. In the 1880's, coconut palms were planted extensively on Sangihe Island by smallholders, and coconut plantations were begun on the islands of Talisse and Kinabohutan, north of Celebes.[34] The coconut palm, however, never became a significant plantation crop; about 95 percent of the copra exports in 1939 were produced by Indonesian smallholders located above all in Sumatra and in Celebes or nearby small islands.

Commercial stands of coconut palm are planted in swidden areas, either in ladang under active use or in fields which have become overgrown with alang grass. For two to three years it is possible to plant upland rice, maize, pineapple, or robusta coffee between the young palms, and the return from these catch crops covers part or all of the cost of planting and maintenance until the trees begin to bear fruit. The palms usually number 100 to 120 trees per hectare; this area and density will produce on an average about 1,000 to 1,200 kilograms of copra a year. In view of the longevity of the palm it is extremely important that care be taken to select seed from high-yielding trees, since the difference in the number of nuts produced is very great between a poor and a good yielder. Since most of the palms now in existence were planted some sixty to eighty years ago there is a great need for rejuvenation of the coconut groves through replanting. Here, however, we meet a problem very similar to that besetting the smallholder rubber industry: the peasants are reluctant to cut down palms that are still yielding, even though production may have fallen off or the trees become so tall that harvesting is difficult.

Ever since the end of World War II Indonesia's copra exports have been considerably below prewar tonnage. To some extent this has been due to natural causes or neglect. For example, in the residency of East Sumatra extensive stands of palms died because

[34] S. J. Hickson, *A Naturalist in North Celebes,* J. Murray, London, 1889, pp. 72–73.

the land flooded, owing to the heavy silting of rivers which in prewar days had been regularly dredged. The rhinoceros beetle and other pests have also lowered production. In part, however, the fall in recorded exports has not reflected an actual decrease in production but a conflict between the smallholders and the central government similar to that noted in the rubber industry. The coconut growers of Celebes and the islands to the north have smuggled sizable quantities of copra to Davao and other ports of the Philippines, where they can obtain a good price in foreign exchange, rather than sell it to government buying organizations, which pay them too little and too late. It has been estimated that in some postwar years up to 300,000 tons of copra were taken out of Indonesia illegally. The coconut growers' discontent over government purchase policies contributed to Celebes' participation in the rebellion of 1958, during which time legal shipments came to a standstill. Since then, exports have been adversely affected by the shortage of shipping, which became acute following the withdrawal of the Dutch interisland fleet from Indonesian waters.

Livestock raising is important only in some of the lesser Sunda islands. However, some 70 percent of Indonesian cattle and buffalo are to be found in Java and Madura, where they are in the main kept as work animals on the farms. Since only about 5 percent of Java's land area is under grass, the peasant who owns a draft or meat animal is confronted by the problem of obtaining adequate quantities of fodder. Furthermore, as is so often the case in the humid tropics, the native grasses are notoriously low in nutritional value and production. Livestock holding in Java could be raised by the use of fodder crops of a higher yield and nutritive content and by the substitution of the cut-and-carry system for grazing, which causes losses due to the trampling of valuable fodder plants. Proper grazing methods and improved grassland management could also contribute substantially to greater meat production in the lesser Sunda Islands.

Because of the relative scarcity of livestock, meat is expensive and is consumed only in very small quantities by the average Indonesian. Protein intake is exceedingly low, having been estimated at 43 grams a day, as against a reference standard of 65 grams.[35] Even this figure, representing one of the lowest protein consumption rates in the world, may be too high, for Indonesia's usually optimistic Eight Year Development Plan envisaged an increase to only 48 grams by 1968.[36] Of this, it was hoped to realize only 8 grams in the form of animal protein, the rest coming from such vegetable sources as soybeans, peanuts, and bean sprouts.

A small portion of the animal protein that is consumed comes in the form of poultry and eggs, since villagers frequently keep fowl, which are not fed but allowed to scavenge. In general, however, the peasants cannot afford to consume such meat and dairy products as they produce but must market them. Fish, rather than such items, is by far the greatest source of animal protein in the Indonesian diet, and both deep-sea and inshore fishing are important industries throughout the archipelago. Deep-sea fishermen usually devote full time to this trade, while those working inshore waters tend to use fishing as a supplement to farming or some other economic activity. The number of both sailing and motorized fishing vessels expanded greatly in the 1950's;[37] a further increase in the number of motorized deep-sea craft is greatly needed in order to reach fishing grounds too far from land for sailing vessels to exploit without the catch spoiling before it is landed.

In addition to its sea operations, Indonesia also has important inland fisheries utilizing fresh water ponds, or *siwakan,* and salt water ponds, or *tambak,* for fish farming. Fish-pond farming is especially well developed by the Sundanese of the Priangan region

[35] *The World Food Deficit,* p. 22; and Erich W. Zimmerman, *World Resources and Industries,* Harper, New York, 1951, pp. 190–191.

[36] *Rantjangan Dasar Undang-undang Pembangunan Nasional-Semesta-Berentjana Delapan Tahun: 1961–69, Disusan oleh Dewan Perantjang Nasional Republik Indonesia* (Draft of a Basic Bill for an Eight Year National Overall Development Plan: 1961–69, prepared by the National Planning Council of the Republic of Indonesia), vol. 5, part 13, no publisher, Djakarta, no year, p. 2742.

[37] In 1951, Indonesia had only about 100 motorized fishing vessels; these increased to 1,462 by 1959. Between 1954 and 1959, the number of sailing vessels rose from 97,000 to 176,000. See *Statistical Pocketbook of Indonesia, 1960,* p. 84; and also *Indonesia-U.S. Cooperation: A Report, (October 1950–June 1955)*, United States Operations Missions in Indonesia with the cooperation of the Indonesian State Planning Bureau, Djakarta, 1955.

of West Java and by the Minangkabau in the highlands of West Sumatra. Lacking regular permanent fish ponds, Javanese peasants will also raise fish in their sawah if the water supply permits. In coastal regions of Java and Madura, mangrove swamps and young alluvial land not suited for crop production have been converted into salt and brackish water ponds on a large scale.

The total yield of Indonesian sea and inland fisheries in 1960 was about 760,000 metric tons[38]—410,000 from the seas and 350,-000 from inland waters—compared to a total 1940 production of 460,000 tons. Despite this increase, the present annual catch is insufficient to meet the need for fresh and preserved fish products. However, the government is well aware that a fuller utilization of Indonesian fish resources would increase the protein supply without necessitating the allocation of precious agricultural land for the raising of livestock; and with the help of foreign aid it has been endeavoring to improve the exploitation of both sea and inland fisheries.

Indonesia is dependent on its exports of commercial crops to provide it with much of its essential imports and development capital; at the same time it needs a high level of food crop production to avoid the utilization of foreign exchange for agricultural imports. As we have seen, the production of both food and export crops is at present in a somewhat parlous state. Food production has lagged behind population growth, while the export of all commercial crops except rubber has declined since the prewar period. Though rubber production has remained high, its future is threatened by competition from synthetics, which the smallholders in particular are in a poor position to withstand.

A real improvement in both commercial and food crop production cannot be achieved without considerable government investment, not only in the form of money and materials but also in terms of organizational and scientific skills. There is a great need

[38] Of this, Java and Madura produced 100,600 tons from sea and 113,000 from inland fisheries. Sumatran sea fisheries contributed 145,000 and inland fisheries 54,000 tons; Borneo 65,000 and 156,000; Celebes 36,000 and 22,000; the lesser Sunda Islands 21,000 and 2,000; and the Moluccas 42,000 tons from sea fisheries and none from inland ponds (*Statistical Pocketbook of Indonesia, 1961,* p. 83).

for the restaffing of the experiment centers which helped make Indonesian plantation agriculture famous before World War II, as well as for research in support of smallholder agriculture on a scale far larger than that undertaken in the colonial period. Technical and administrative skills are still very short in the state plantation sector and in the paddy centers; and the latter are further handicapped by their law-enforcing function, which makes it difficult for peasants to receive their advice and aid without suspicion. Above all, the peasants need education of the kind that will enable them to become better producers; there is a pressing need for an effective agricultural extension service which would establish a close link between the research and seed stations on the one hand and the smallholders engaged in cash and food crop production on the other. Granted that the Indonesian peasants are conservative, they are not so close-minded as to be unwilling to imitate convincing demonstrations which are in keeping with their economic resources and technical competence. Their conservatism is, in fact, largely a function of their economic position. Those who need help most badly are understandably the most reluctant to take risks and try out suggestions which have not been thoroughly tested in their locality, and it is therefore necessary that great care be taken in introducing innovations in such poverty-stricken areas as Java.

The Indonesian government is acutely aware of the need to raise agricultural production and has developed elaborate programs for this purpose. Thus far the plans have not generally been implemented in an effective manner. In part this failure has been caused by a lack of the funds, materials, and skills necessary to their execution. In part it results from the fact that programs developed in Djakarta often have proved unrealistic in terms of regional conditions or have been rendered ineffective by the many bureaucratic layers through which they must pass. We have noted, too, that in both food and export crop production there is a tendency toward conflict between the interests of the peasants and those of the central authority. The government, in sore need of revenue and foreign exchange, seeks to minimize the prices paid to the producers and to increase its control over crop production; the peasants seek to evade this by resorting to illegal marketing channels or by switching to the cultivation of noncontrolled crops. The political dangers of this situation have already been demonstrated by Sumatran and Celebes smallholder support of rebellion; but even from a purely agricultural point of view it has ominous implications. If the trend continues it may mean that peasants, though dependent on government assistance for the improvement of their crops, will become increasingly disinclined to accept state-sponsored aid and innovation. The already observable tendency to shift to the production of more profitable noncontrolled crops may lead to a neglect of those products most important to the economy and to a general disinclination to expand production beyond subsistence needs. The solution to the problem is not easy to foresee in view of the straitened circumstances of the government and its need for large quantities of foreign exchange and reasonably priced food for the burgeoning nonagrarian population. Nonetheless, if Indonesia's agricultural production is to expand in the future along rational lines, better regard for peasant interests would seem necessary.

CHAPTER 5

Economics and Indonesian Agricultural Development*

DAVID H. PENNY and
J. PRICE GITTINGER

The Place of Agricultural Economists

Economists, particularly good agricultural economists, are a scarce resource in Indonesia today. General economists in Indonesia rarely study agriculture, even though agriculture occupies 70 percent of the population and produces some 55 percent of the national income. Of the 34-man Economic Stabilization Board, a critical body at the present juncture, only one is an agricultural economist.

Good research agricultural economists can best be used, for the present, primarily to determine relationships between variables and, to a lesser extent, to estimate aggregates. Indonesian policymakers need to know the shape of economic, as well as other, processes at work in the agricultural sector; only later will it be necessary for them to know in some detail about totals and other quantities. They already know something about the totals—total production, total area, total exports, total imports, and the like. But knowing these things has given them little upon which to base programs to increase production. For example, some economists might think it worthwhile to calculate the price elasticity of supply for smallholder rubber; yet if it is easy, as we believe it is, to increase the supply of smallholder rubber by means of an

* Paper prepared for the Seminar on Technology and Science in Indonesian Development at the Center for Developmental Change, University of Kentucky, Lexington, Kentucky, May 21 through 27, 1967. Reprinted by permission of the authors and of the director of the seminar.

imaginative program (modeled after the *bimas* program, which uses college students studying agricultural curricula as extension workers), then there is little use in making a conventional study.[1]

For such purposes, economic analysis efforts should be ranked in the following order of priority: (1) formulation of effective agricultural development policies firmly rooted in economic realities; (2) research using the minimum of resources necessary to provide "directional" answers—that is, answers that point the way to program formulation without the much greater research effort needed to supply elegant academic details; and (3) only in last place, such matters as careful quantification of large samples yielding highly significant data which lead to quite precise quantitative statements on which to base policy formulation.

Economic analysis of the agricultural situation in Indonesia must first indicate the magnitude of the problem. It ought also to indicate in a general way what policy pattern is required if development is to occur. It should outline alternative economic policies in a form which can readily be used by policymakers and which will increase their awareness of the opportunity to use economic policy more effectively. Many policymakers lack a clear idea of economic processes in agriculture at the microeconomic level. In Indonesia, this lack of clear perception persists partly because there is not yet the "social control" which in other countries comes through farmers' organizations and lobbying activities. One result is that Indonesian policy still does not pay enough attention to creating an environment which will give farmers, and others, the opportunity to work to make themselves more prosperous. How many policymakers have ever met, talked with, and understood a farmer or a small trader? It is here that agricultural economists can make a substantial contribution.

Examples abound of how quite simple economic analysis can indicate policy directions. For instance, the ratio between the price of rice and the price of fertilizer remains today so unfavorable that few farmers can afford to use fertilizer, even when they know how to use it and are aware of what it can do. It can be readily demonstrated that it would be cheaper for the nation as a

[1] *Bimas* is an acronym derived from *bimbingan massal* meaning mass guidance.

whole to import fertilizer than to import rice (Sie did so as long ago as 1954,[2] and others have done so since). Unfortunately, the agricultural economists allowed a number of wrong conclusions to be drawn from this calculation. One such conclusion was that because importing fertilizer could be more profitable than importing rice, it could likewise be assumed that the actual profits would be the same as those calculated. The fact was neglected that it costs money and requires effective administration to create demand for fertilizer and to make its use profitable in practice. A second erroneous conclusion was that fertilizer should be imported and earmarked for cultivation of rice because this crop was "profitable"; yet it was evident that the use of fertilizer on other crops was even more profitable. The quota system devised—based on areas under wet-rice cultivation rather than on market or farmer demand—led to black markets, corruption, and a decline in farmers' confidence in government promises. Fortunately, this system of allocation has now come to an end.

With the evidence, on the one hand, that fertilizer is profitable from the standpoint of the national accounts, and, on the other, the ample evidence from black markets and bare warehouses that there is substantial demand for it, a clear policy implication can be drawn. Indonesia would benefit were it to import fertilizer up to the amount of effective demand at a price to the farmer pegged to bear the same ratio to the artificially low domestic price for rice as imported fertilizer bears to imported rice. The "subsidy" this would involve would be profitable from the national standpoint, the brake on rising rice prices would be maintained, and farmers would have economic incentive to use fertilizer but only up to the point where it ceased to be profitable from the national standpoint. How much fertilizer this might involve is not easy to estimate, but the limits of such a policy can be identified. The largest amount of fertilizer Indonesia ever imported was 472,000 tons in 1961. In 1966, only 90,000 tons were imported. On the other hand, the amount of money budgeted for rice imports in 1967 was enough to purchase approximately 700,000 tons of fer-

[2] Sie Kwat Soen, "The Use of Fertilizers in Indonesia," *EKI,* September 1954.

tilizer.[3] Hence, the policy prescription would be valid were the effective demand for fertilizer to lie somewhere between the low of 90,000 tons in 1966 and the high (limited by the value) of the projected 1967 rice imports. "Leaks" in the system caused by using fertilizer on other crops do not affect this analysis provided they do not drive total demand beyond the upper limit so defined.

A second example of how simple economic analysis can be used to point the direction to effective policy may be drawn from rubber cultivation in Sumatra. As long as a decade ago, policymakers were saying that rubber-tree replanting would not be profitable because of the cleverness of synthetic rubber producers. At the same time, rupiah prices were depressed relative to world (dollar) prices due to the government's exchange rate policy. It was therefore not surprising that estate managers concluded that new methods such as new tapping techniques—long proved worthwhile in Malaya—would be quite unprofitable. Such were the reasons that led policymakers to conclude that rubber was not profitable and would be even less profitable in the future. The same story is being told today, even though rubber remains a highly profitable crop for Indonesia. In 1958, the average full cost price for rubber on estates on the east coast of Sumatra was in the neighborhood of Rp. 12 per kilogram with a range of about Rp. 6 per kilogram. The domestic price for rubber at the time was about Rp. 20 per kilogram, so that the average gross margin was about 66 percent even in the absence of the higher yielding varieties and better cultivation techniques used across the Strait of Malacca in Malaya. Indeed, if the black market price for the rupiah had been used for the calculation, the price would have been about three times as high and the profit rate correspondingly higher. Today, a decade later, even though rubber prices on the world market have dropped by nearly half, rubber still remains extremely profitable in East Sumatra which has better soils, lower real wages, and higher labor productivity than Malaya. Yet the price policy of the nation is still structured in a manner which discourages rubber

[3] The government budgeted $70 million for rice imports in 1967, while the largest amount spent on fertilizer imports was $23.1 million (in 1961). In 1966, only $4.5 million was spent to import fertilizer.

production. In December 1966, the ratio between the world price for rubber and that of rice was about 3.3, while the rubber-rice price ratio in Indonesia was 1.2, even though the rupiah price of rice was 25 percent below the world price.

Agricultural economists through clearly stated, cogent analysis —which need not necessarily rely on complex or highly sophisticated techniques—have an opportunity to illustrate convincingly to policymakers such relationships as these and to outline policy implications which flow from them. Properly done, such analysis can serve as a guide for action in a variety of other fields. Careful farm management analysis, for instance, not only can point the way to increased agricultural productivity through better resource allocation on individual farms but can also serve as a very useful base for knowing more about farmers themselves, about social life in rural areas, and for learning about the interrelationships between agriculture and the other sectors of the economy. At this stage, the main contribution of economic analysis is to indicate the scope of the problem and to show what could be done to achieve certain economic goals. The "solution," the effort of will needed, depends on the national leadership and the people of Indonesia.

Economics in a Unique Cultural Environment

So much has been written about the impact of culture on the form taken by economic activity in Indonesia[4] that it may seem unnecessary to turn to this topic. Yet we contend it is quite important to see the cultural environment more clearly. What is needed is to see the application of economic tools and, more importantly, an economic way of thinking about Indonesian problems in a much broader context than is necessary in the well-understood cultural environment of the West.[5]

Agricultural development in Indonesia, as elsewhere, is a many-sided process. One of its core elements is economic. If what is done

[4] See, for example, Clifford Geertz, *Agricultural Involution,* University of California Press, Berkeley and Los Angeles, 1963.

[5] An early important contribution in this direction was Boeke's theory of dualism. J. H. Boeke, *Economics and Economic Policy of Dual Societies,* Tjeenk Willink & Zoon, Haarlem, 1953. [Cf. Professor Sadli's critique of Boeke's thesis in Chapter 3 of this volume.—Ed.]

is not "economic," then there will be no development. Economists have a responsibility to point to where the economic opportunities lie (and there are many more than is generally realized). Agricultural development in Indonesia is not possible without taking into account the economic aspects of introducing new technology and more scientific methods. Often new methods are suggested without proper consideration being given to profit and loss as seen by the peasant farmer. Economists must wrestle with the extent to which successful development depends on proper application of science and technology in a peasant farming environment, and, thus, must come to grips more realistically with the problem of creating incentive patterns that will lead to economic change and that will shape the "other factors" of importance in Indonesia. It is clear from the *bimas* program, and other instances of response to economic incentive, that one can realize economic improvement even though the land tenure system, the social structure in the village, the inefficient marketing structure, and the tools and equipment used all remain unchanged.

The social sciences and the physical and biological sciences and technologies each has a critical role to play in agricultural development. Even so, it is more the responsibility of the economists than of the anthropologists, sociologists, or physical and biological scientists to determine just what these roles should be. The problem of agricultural policy formulation in Indonesia is to work from the standpoint of "economics *and* . . . ," not "economics *in*. . . ." The responsibility lies with the economists—and through them the economic policymakers—to determine, based on what we already know in Indonesia and elsewhere about the economics of innovation in agriculture, what will best achieve a more rapid rate of development in Indonesia through the introduction of science and technology and through induced institutional changes. Coupled with this is a heavy responsibility for economists to outline what else we need to know about the economics of innovation and institutional change in Indonesia.

The importance of the cultural context in Indonesian economics lies in the usefulness of raising some unconventional economic questions which would be well worth studying. As an example, the government will doubtlessly put much more emphasis in the future on *gotong-rojong,* or mutual help, in order to accelerate progress in such areas as maintenance of irrigation systems. What are the economics of *gotong-rojong*? Initial assessment indicates it may be rather efficient in mobilizing labor, but more needs to be understood about the point at which *gotong-rojong* projects start to become less efficient than other institutional approaches. What are the economics of land reform in Indonesia? What are the economics of cooperatives versus privately owned and managed enterprises for the distribution of agricultural inputs? What are the economics of agricultural credit for the shopkeeper, the village moneylender, the government-sponsored program, and for the peasant farmer? What are the economics of interisland migration, and of induced settlement programs? What are the economics of the cost in terms of failure-to-succeed versus low outside investment for those settlers who do succeed in spontaneous settlement programs?

Yet another subject about which too little is known is that of house gardens. In 1961, a farm management study made in connection with the Tjiawi agricultural development seminar estimated the income in cash and perquisites from the house garden, dry land, and wet-rice land for a group of farms. The returns came out in that order. The seminar group, all senior civil servants, had estimated previously that it would be the reverse—that is, the wet-rice land would return more than the dry land and both would be more productive than the house plot. The figures for gross returns per unit of area indicated, moreover, that if the families studied had put all their rice land into house plots and dry land they could have bought more rice than they were raising. (No more investment would have been needed, either, since investment per acre is highest for wet-rice land). Paradoxically, the farmers of Java spend almost no time or thought on house gardens, even though these are more profitable than either wet-rice land or dry land sown to food crops. But the potential is great: there are over 1.5 million hectares of house gardens on Java.

One might even go a step further in applying conventional economics unconventionally. Farm management studies usually assume area as fixed and optimize by changing variables of labor and nonagricultural inputs. In contrast, in the tropical environment of Java farmers have over the years devised a cultivation system on house plots which takes advantage of the intense sunlight. They plant coconut trees which mature to heights of 15 to 20 meters; coffee, citrus, or other small trees which mature at heights of 5 to 7 meters; and herbs and vegetables which grow to heights of only half a meter; and there are other combinations as well. In this context, sunlight (and hence area) becomes a variable, and some very interesting problems of practical importance center on optimization of this use of sunlight.

Innovation Versus Subsistence-mindedness

A theory of Indonesian peasant behavior has been proposed which is summed up in the term "subsistence-mindedness." [6] Peasant farmers tend to pass up opportunities to increase their incomes even when it involves nothing more than rearranging their present capital, labor, and land inputs. Farm management analysis of village economies in Indonesia indicates that income in most could be increased merely by a change in resource use patterns. The incomes of farmers could be further increased if they were more willing to invest; many have capital but they prefer not to use it for productive investment. In the village of Suka Damai in North Sumatra, for example, a small transfer of labor from crop production to repair work on the irrigation system would increase total production considerably. Similarly, spending a little less money on fertilizer and more on animal vaccines would raise net income. In the Depok area of West Java, growing papaya and other fruits for the Djakarta market is much more profitable than growing food crops for sale, yet only a few farmers engage in the trade. In almost all parts of Indonesia there are one or more crops which if grown, or grown more widely, would yield higher incomes. All of these opportunities, and many more, could be grasped without farmers having to work harder or without making more than minimal demands on their capital resources.[7]

In many parts of Indonesia, moreover, farmers could afford to

[6] D. H. Penny, "The Transition from Subsistence to Commercial Family Farming in North Sumatra," Ph.D. thesis, Cornell University, Ithaca. N.Y., 1964.

[7] *Ibid.*

buy and use fertilizer, pesticides, improved seeds, vaccines, and the like, even though they rarely do. Many of these innovations will give very high returns, sometimes even 1,000 percent or more. One such is the use of selected rubber seed on rubber smallholdings.[8] Capital invested in any one of a number of new ways would yield much higher returns than it now earns, but few farmers are willing to take the plunge. As long as this situation persists, agricultural development will be limited.

Yet, given their context, these seemingly perverse activities are quite rational for the Indonesian farmer. The context involves subjective risk and uncertainty. It is this which lies at the heart of subsistence-mindedness, backward-bending supply curves, "agricultural involution," and a number of other seemingly obstinate, noneconomic responses. It strains conventional tools of economic analysis to tackle this problem, which is why this response pattern offers one of the greatest challenges to the agricultural economist interested in development.

Most peasant farmers in Indonesia attach extremely high discounts to risk and uncertainty, particularly the latter.[9] The risk discount may usefully be divided into a "real" or "objective" component and a "subjective" component. In the case of uncertainty, the distinction tends to disappear. Once the real or objective risk is determined, the firm that is not pressed for time and money need not apply any subjective risk discount at all; it can simply take the objective risk as its working base in much the same way a life insurance company does. But the Indonesian peasant strug-

[8] D. H. Penny, "Case Studies in Subsistence and Transition: North Sumatra, Indonesia," Agricultural Development Council Seminar on Subsistence and Peasant Economics, Honolulu, 1965.

[9] Economic jargon distinguishes between risk and uncertainty. In general, risk involves a collection of events which we can predict for a group even though we cannot predict the occurrence of one event for a particular individual. Risk, therefore, is something which can be insured against, and life insurance is the classroom example. Uncertainty applies to those events about which too little is known to predict their occurrence even for a group. Either these events have never occurred before or else they occur too infrequently to provide the basis for prediction. New technology is an example of the former; agricultural development theory based on historical example is an instance of the latter.

gling to support his family on half a hectare or less (and there are many of them) has a very different situation. He suffers from severe capital rationing and has a time horizon extending hardly to the next harvest (indeed, probably only to about the time of the next *patjeklik*[10] season). He has a very small risk base, indeed, yet it is this base which to a large extent determines how much of a chance the rational entrepreneur feels he can afford to take with some change in his farming practices—that is the size of his uncertainty discount. Furthermore, gains and losses are not equally weighted, since the possibility of a small loss, which means someone must go hungry, is more important than the equal possibility of a larger gain. Under these circumstances, it is hardly surprising to find peasants adopting large subjective discounts.

It is not only the peasants with small farms who are subsistence-minded and reluctant to adopt innovations that objective calculations have shown to be profitable. In many parts of Indonesia all farmers—including those with much land and cash—are subsistence-minded. The differences between subsistence-minded and development-minded farmers are most clearly seen in the new settlements on the east coast of Sumatra. In none of these new settlements are there landlords or moneylenders. In some of these settlements the farmers are willing to invest for the future. As a consequence, they have started to grow commercial crops, to use fertilizer, and so forth. In other settlements the farmers continue to believe that the most economic way to farm is for them to continue to use the tools and methods they are accustomed to in order to grow only food crops. The economic difference between the development-minded and the subsistence-minded farmer lies wholly and solely in the size of the subjective rate of discount each applies to his future income. For the development-minded this rate is low; for the subsistence-minded it is high.

The subsistence-minded farmer believes that the returns he might realize from new technology or from growing new crops, would be much lower than he would in fact receive if he were to adopt such innovations. He is deeply skeptical about the profitability of all innovation. In other words, the subjective rate of interest he uses to discount future income that would be gained

[10] Time of food scarcity just before harvest.

from new crops and new methods is very high. Even so, subsistence-minded farmers the world over generally are interested in new opportunities. It is not hard to generate interest in a conversation about new technology in an Indonesian village. If a new opportunity seems worthwhile, one or more men will try it experimentally on a small scale. If the experiments work, they and their neighbors will soon begin to accept the innovation. The trouble has been that new economic opportunities have often not turned out to be nearly as good as first anticipated. Farmers are keenly aware, as outside advisors may not be, of such things as market price fluctuations, the influence of rainfall variations on profitability of fertilizer applications, and cash liabilities in the face of in-kind income.

Most small peasant farmers with their narrow risk base value security highly. It is not surprising, therefore, that they define security in subsistence terms, for they measure their margin of safety according to the size of the marketable surplus of subsistence crops they can produce from their minute holdings with their labor intensive, low productivity—but low risk—technology.

In this context, it is clear why subsistence-minded farmers, whether poverty-stricken or more prosperous, are not economically irrational. In a basic sense, they, too, would like to get the same output for less effort, or a higher price for what they sell. Where most of them differ then from development-minded farmers is that they often do not perceive the opportunities inherent in their economic environment. In those cases where they do, they lack the resources or the organization to exploit opportunities, or they discount future income so heavily that they will not even try the new things, even though the prospective rate of profit is apparently very high. In short, they may be classed as acting in an economically irrational way only if their economic behavior is judged by standards other than their own.

A problem which arises in trying to deal explicitly with subjective uncertainty discounts is that the response of peasants to new opportunities tends to become automatic—hence, many observers insist that they are "tradition-bound." Subsistence-minded farmers who earn well above average incomes have such a high subjective rate of discount or else respond so automatically (no one can be certain which) that they act in a manner which is just as subsistence-minded as that of small peasants. The need to react to ceremonial occasions within the community conflicts with, and is stronger than, the "need" to respond to opportunities to innovate. Roekasah shows that on most occasions both rich and poor farmers in the Krawang region (an area on the coast of Java east of Djakarta) show a high preference for consumption, often conspicuous consumption, to investment.[11]

A high subjective discount for innovation may be characteristic of a group as well as of individuals, and when this happens the difficulties of introducing change are severely compounded. Geertz cites the instance of the progressive farmer who tried to introduce the use of a sickle only to find his fields burned by his neighbors who attached a much higher subjective uncertainty discount to the implications of labor-saving than would the individual.[12] But such is not strictly an Indonesian or even a developing nation phenomenon; after all, the Luddites were Europeans, and outmoded building codes are buttressed by craft union support in the United States.

The interrelationships of high discount rates with other influences show the complications which arise immediately if serious study is undertaken. But in the past, explicit understanding of the rational aspects of subjective uncertainty have too often been ignored and all resistance ascribed to tradition or culture. If such were the case, then innovation would be very hard to introduce indeed, for tradition and culture are clearly difficult to change. But to the extent that resistance to innovation can be ascribed to rational discounting—and it is our opinion that at least some significant fraction can be—then the problem of modernization of traditional agriculture is to that extent reduced. The result of the *bimas* program is only the latest in a series of incidents which indicate how high individual subjective discount

[11] Adiratma E. Roekasah, *The Rice Marketing Structure and the Price Received by Rice Farmers: A Case Study in Krawang, West Java,* Fakultas Pertanian, Universitas Indonesia, Bogor, 1963 (?).

[12] Geertz, *op. cit.*

rates can be quite rapidly lowered to a point where innovation can proceed. The problem, admittedly not easy, is how to lower the discount rates on a much broader scale.

A major contribution of agricultural economics to better policy formulation in Indonesia would be to begin to outline the dimensions of the influence of subjective risk and uncertainty discounts. At first, the need might be less for precise measurements than for orders of magnitude, and whether these differ significantly for various kinds of innovations or for various areas of the country. As the concept becomes more widely understood by policymakers, then new formulations of program approaches which permit farmers to reduce their subjective discounts can be proposed and gain support.

Closely related to the concept of uncertainty introduced by market fluctuations is the influence of price policies on economic incentive. The government of Indonesia has consistently depressed the prices of all agricultural products relative to the prices of goods bought by farmers. (DeVries argues this has been the case for 300 years.)[13] From mid-1960 to mid-1966, the ratio of rubber prices to rice prices on a per kilogram basis in the world market was between 4 and 5.5, while in Indonesia it rarely rose over 3 and sometimes fell to 0.5. As a result, far too few farmers turned to commercial crops, the first step to agricultural modernization in many instances. Artificially low prices for rice itself have also discouraged productivity improvements. The elasticity of marketable surplus of rice in Indonesia is admittedly low, but it is positive, as Mubyarto and Fletcher have shown.[14] Without more carefully designed agricultural price policies, however, no advantage can be taken of this. Transportation taxes and restrictions imposed on movement of rice between areas are other examples of disincentives in Indonesian agricultural policy. Agricultural economics can make a signal contribution if it can demonstrate the necessity for a more "economic" solution to these economic problems.

[13] Egbert deVries, "Rijstpolitiek op Java in Vroeger Jaren," *Landbouw*, Dertiende Jaargang, nos. 7, 8, 1937.

[14] Mubyarto and L. B. Fletcher, *The Marketable Surplus of Rice in Indonesia: A Study in Java-Madura*, Iowa State University Press, Ames, Iowa, 1966.

Seeing the Problem in the Proper Perspective

Agricultural economists in Indonesia will make their mark on the agricultural development of the nation as they contribute to a more widespread, more realistic view of the economic problems of innovation and adoption of science and technology by farmers. In doing this job they will probably find that the ideas and the theories developed in the West will need modification, and that new concepts and theories appropriate to the Indonesian situation will need to be developed. One way that the agricultural economists might do this is to identify the elements which have contributed to success in programs which have already led to favorable change, in order to draw from them the attributes which they bear in common. Indonesian peasant farmers can and will innovate, despite subsistence-mindedness and "shared poverty" concepts which seem to be such insuperable barriers to change at the present time.

A current example of a development activity enjoying at least modest success in the face of a very difficult situation is the *bimas* program. Under this approach, students studying the agricultural curricula in the universities take time out to live in a village during an entire rice-growing season. They devote their time to helping farmers adopt more productive cultivation techniques and to teaching them how to use modern inputs. The Direktorat Pertanian Rakjat is now trying to design a "systematized *bimas*" to extend this program and to establish it on a continuing basis. They have identified four elements of success in the *bimas* approach: (1) the *potensi* principle—that is, choosing to concentrate at first in those areas with water control, transportation, and similar favorable advantages; (2) adequate living allowances for the *bimas* workers so they can work without needing to resort to other sources of income; (3) a leverage on scarce stocks of fertilizer —although their supplies are limited, too; the point here is not so much quantity as it is an assurance that whatever does exist and is promised will in fact be available at the time needed; (4) a quality of "exhilaration" felt by the students participating in the programs.

To this list, some observers would add a fifth item: farmers feel that for once officials really are concerned with their problems so that the *bimas* program acts as a bridge between city and country.

Clearly, these "elements of success" cannot all be transferred without modification to an ongoing program. The fourth point, particularly—that of initial enthusiasm—cannot be reproduced as it presently exists. The objective of identifying success elements clearly is not merely to try to reproduce them. Rather, it is to recognize those elements so that programs can be designed in their light, and those which cannot be reproduced can be understood and accounted for. It is possible, for instance, that it will be decided that the enthusiasm of young college students is so critical to success and so impossible to replace that no ongoing program with permanent personnel can use the *bimas* approach; hence, additional resources allocated to this type of effort would be wasted. Or, it may be that some device of rotation or promotion of extension personnel can be devised to establish and maintain an atmosphere of enthusiasm over the next several years.

There are other instances of responsiveness and success in Indonesian agriculture which would bear broad-gauged economic and sociological analysis. One can cite the spread of vegetable crop production to supply the Singapore market, the persistence of a black market for government-distributed fertilizer when the ratios between rice prices and other agricultural commodity prices are not allowed to adjust, or a recent Bogor student's study in Tjipaku, (a village about 15 kilometers from Bogor) that found most farmers bought and used fertilizer even though no extension work had ever been done in the village and no local outlet sold fertilizer. The problem is that these instances of responsiveness are too few, too far between, and too slow in spreading. Economists, among others, must contribute to a better understanding of a mechanics of these success stories so that they can be duplicated elsewhere.

It would help, too, if it were more widely realized in Indonesia, that the country is not inherently "rich" and only some magic button need be pushed for a cornucopia to open up. Most of the soils remaining to be settled in Indonesia are not highly fertile; cultivating them will take skill and persistence. Indonesian farmers, like farmers everywhere, continue with good reason to regard nature as niggardly. It is the Europeans and the nonfarming people of Indonesia who talk of the untapped agricultural riches of the Indies. They do not understand the resource endowment picture very well, and until agricultural economists and others can convince them that development is problematical at best in Indonesia, requiring the most economic policies possible, then suitable development policies and programs cannot be expected.

Agricultural economists, among themselves, will have to develop more objective viewpoints. Many, but certainly not all, believe that farmers are so poor and exploited that only welfare policies are appropriate. Clearly, this is often not true—witness again the success of *bimas*. Indonesia is a complex country, and for most topics, research work must be undertaken in many places. Economists will have to examine much of what they will accept as given in their studies—e.g., the propensity to save, price elasticities of supply and demand, and subjective rates of discount. The magnitudes of all these parameters can be changed, perhaps in a short time, if vigorous, inventive policies are carried out. Economists must make themselves equal to the task of analyzing Indonesia's problems within the context of fewer "givens" without losing their grip on the realities of economics or losing sight of the valid elements among their economic tools. It is no small task.

Before better policy formulation can be expected, many of the government officials themselves must shake their own "subsistence-mindedness" and embark upon much more "economic" programs. The theoretical premises of many past agricultural productivity programs have been weak. For example, government officials note that farmers are poor, and draw the conclusion that they need cheaper credit. When farmers get this credit, they use it for consumption or to pay off old debts to storekeepers and moneylenders. They know the government is a lenient creditor. What the government has failed to take into account is that subsistence-minded farmers will not use production credit effectively until they feel more secure economically than they do now.

We have tried to indicate that there is much that agricultural economists can do through perceptive economic analysis, but without too elaborate use of complex new techniques. The *bimas* program is an example of success where economic elements are incorporated into a development activity. The report by Rangkuty on an extension and education project in North Sumatra discusses an example of an initial step which was highly pragmatic and very useful.[15] But if agricultural economists are to make their full impact on the development of Indonesia there are several steps—an agenda, if you will—which we feel they will need to undertake. The first is a better inventory of existing information, something which is already being undertaken through the Agro-Economic Survey. Another is to improve utilization of data already collected. There is a tendency to collect much and analyze little. Agricultural economists need to husband their resources. Research projects should be chosen carefully in full consultation with decision-makers and designed always from a policy-oriented standpoint, not a professionally oriented view. These projects must be continued long enough, and personnel maintained continuously enough, so that something like full fruition can be realized out of preliminary preparation and pilot projects. Such projects as are undertaken must be kept to a scale that can be coped with in present-day conditions. Nationwide surveys of ambitious scope should, for the most part, be reserved for later; smaller projects which can have a near-term impact on policy formulation will be a greater contribution to the economic advancement of the nation.

Happily, we can report that most of the points we have touched upon are drawn from our conversations with Indonesian agricultural economists and farmers themselves, so that we have reason to know that our comments and suggested directions of work are well-known to thoughtful economists in Indonesia. We hope, however, that by bringing them together in the context of improved policy-making that we can encourage Indonesian economists and decision-makers to see the role of agricultural economics in their national development effort more clearly, and, hence, to make better use of its potentials.

[15] R. Rangkuty, "Laporan Suatu Projek Penjuluhan di Kampung Kaju Laut, Tapanuli Selatan," Fakultas Pertanian, Universitas Sumatera Utara, Medan (mimeo.).

PART III

POPULATION AND MANPOWER

The two-sidedness of man as an economic agent—i.e., his role as consumer and his role as producer—creates a dualism of policy problems. Whereas rapid population growth and high population density create an abundant supply of a factor of production, the minimal costs of maintaining life could mean that, given low levels of labor productivity, the marginal impact of a net increase in population may be negative, as far as the welfare of the community is concerned. Demographers have relatively little to tell us about the kind of man-resources ratio which can be considered optimal, but they contend with fervor that the ratio is far surpassed on the island of Java, where two-thirds of Indonesia's population is located. Alex Hunter's summary and discussion in this section of recent demographic information offer nothing that would suggest that the concern is unjustified. Evidence is increasing that the growth rate of the Indonesian population is accelerating, making the near stagnation of total production in the 1960's more ominous month by month.

In view of this frightening neo-Malthusian prospect, the failure of the Sukarno government to undertake some sort of population control program adds weightily to its failure to induce significant growth of product. It also means that the incumbent government operates under a greater handicap than its predecessor governments. Fortunately the present government recognizes the demographic aspect of its problem. Thus, not until 1967 did the government of Indonesia adopt a policy of encouragement of birth control.

The limited experience of underdeveloped countries in dealing with high and rising natural population growth rates suggests that such programs take hold only very gradually. It would not be too conservative to anticipate that little, if any, effect of a new demographic policy can be hoped for within the next decade. This is not to say that allocation of resources in that direction would be uneconomic. The work of Stephen Enke,[1] among others, indicates that the long-term benefits of curbing population growth are likely to be very great indeed. However, the long lag in effecting programs of family planning, and the further lag in realizing their effect on the birth rate, require that hope for raising living standards for the near future rests almost entirely on raising productivity.

One of the most important aspects, but by no means the only aspect, of raising productivity, is investment in human capital. The Indonesian manpower pyramid has an extremely wide base composed of vast numbers of persons with limited and/or archaic skill and at the top a tiny group of persons with advanced training, skill, and experience. Thus, the quality of the labor force is, from the point of view of raising productivity, more important than its quantity. Indeed, it is necessary to improve its quality in order to make it possible to absorb the existing surplus and the inevitable increase in quantity. Peasants must learn to alter cultivation techniques in order to make use of nonconventional agricultural inputs, and the former peasants and villagers who migrate to the cities must acquaint themselves with the techniques of industrial production. The higher education system must contribute to the molding of a leadership group with not only expertise, but a conception of the economic world which is relevant to Indonesia's development problems.

As Everett Hawkins shows, Indonesian labor unions have contributed little or nothing to this process, having been predomi-

[1] See his "The Economics of Government Payments to Limit Population," in *Economic Development and Cultural Change,* July 1960, and "The Economic Aspects of Slowing Population Growth," *Economic Journal,* March 1966.

nantly concerned with the political struggle. And while the nation has done a remarkable job of expanding her education system since independence, little thought has been given to the rebuilding and reorienting of that system to meet the needs of a developing nation in the last half of the twentieth century.

In Indonesia, as in the rest of Southeast Asia, the ethnically Chinese minority plays a powerful economic role. Although overseas Chinese constitute only about 2.5 percent of the total population, they are very strategically located in business and finance in both the urban and rural sectors of the economy. Despite the fact that 30 percent of persons of Chinese descent residing in Indonesia have opted for Indonesian citizenship, the indigenous majority regard the power of the Chinese with suspicion, fear, and hostility. For in Javanese society, particularly, the prestige of business pursuits is by tradition extremely low, while the overseas Chinese have an equally strong affinity for such activity. Thus, the indigenous peoples typically regard the Chinese with derision for their devotion to trade, moneylending, banking, and manufacturing, while both resenting and envying the wealth and power which they enjoy.

Unfortunately for the economic policymakers in the Indonesian government, this dominance of Chinese entrepreneurship presents a major complication. Policies which attempt to revitalize the private sector benefit the Chinese ethnic group relatively more than the indigenous majority, so far as direct effects are concerned. Attempts to build an indigenous entrepreneur group through subsidy and protection have not been notably successful. One such attempt, the *benteng* policy of the 1950's, is described briefly in Chapter 2 of Part I. The failure of the *benteng* policy left many Indonesian leaders with the impression that only government dominance in economic activity offered a solution to the problem of the dearth of indigenous entrepreneurship. By the time the Sukarno government had fallen in 1966, however, the failure of the bureaucracy and government enterprises to produce satisfactorily had convinced President Suharto's economic advisors that only if the private sector could be revitalized, in a kind of "New Economic Policy," could they expect to give the economy a new start. The problem of the power of the ethnic Chinese is being met, in part, by the encouragement of foreign investment, but in doing so the challenge of the weakness of the indigenous entrepreneur remains. This challenge is fraught with serious political and economic implications which the new regime cannot avoid.

CHAPTER 6

Notes on Indonesian Population*

ALEX HUNTER

The Republic of Indonesia in 1961 undertook its first census. It revealed a population of 97,018,829 persons[1] including an estimated 700,000 residents in Western Irian. Therefore, since 1930 when the Netherlands East Indies census estimated a population of 60.7 million, there was an increase of the order of 60 percent. Further, it has been estimated (on the basis of the postenumeration survey of 1962) that, with a crude birth rate of 43.0 per 1,000 persons and a crude mortality rate of 21.4 per 1,000, the crude rate of growth is 21.6 per 1,000. This gives, near enough, a 2.2 percent per annum increase in population.[2] On this reckoning, by 1963 the population was about 101 million; by 1965, probably 106 million; and by 1970, it is likely to be 118 million. However, mortality rates could fall substantially. Before the departure of World Health Organisation antimalarial and advisory teams in

* These notes are designed to display the essential features of the 1961 census bearing on economic matters. Unless otherwise indicated all tabular data are extracted from Central Bureau of Statistics, *Sensus Penduduk 1961* (Population Census 1961), Serie S.P. I and S.P. II, Djakarta, 1963. Reprinted from the *Bulletin of Indonesian Economic Studies* (*BIES*), no. 4, June 1966, by permission of the author and the editors.

1 Note that only four countries are larger than Indonesia in the population sense—China, India, the U.S.S.R. and the U.S.A. Central Bureau of Statistics, *Sensus Pendukuk 1961,* Serie S.P. I and S.P. II, Djakarta, 1693.

2 Vaino N. Kannisto, *Population Increase in Indonesia,* Central Bureau of Statistics, Djakarta, 1963. Kannisto was a senior member of the United States team advising the Central Bureau of Statistics on census work.

1965, and before the beginning of the present period of civil disorder and scarcities of imported rice, there was every probability of a steady decline of the death rate. Therefore, some authorities have preferred to work on a 2.3 percent per annum increase—which doubles population every 30 years if kept up—and have estimated that there will be 125 million persons by 1970 and 250 million by the year 2,000. Others have worked on a 2.4 percent growth rate.[3] One demographer estimates a rate of growth of 3.0 percent per annum which would double the population every 23 years.[4]

As is well known, the main pressure of population growth is and will be exerted on Java. Almost 65 percent of Indonesia's 97.1 million reside on this island although it accounts for only 7 percent of the total area of the country. Some of the problem can be alleviated by interinsular transmigration. But experience suggests that this approach will yield little success. The densely forested areas and low-yield agriculture of the outer islands are scarcely attractive to the Javanese peasant accustomed to small plots and highly fertile wet-rice cultivation. In the colonial period, Dutch-sponsored migration never managed to organise as many as 60,000 persons to leave Java in any one year even during its best periods of the 1930's. After independence, the Transmigration Service, during the 1950's, moved less than this if one takes into account "spontaneous" migration in the opposite direction into Java. Indeed, spontaneous migration and company migration back to Java, between them, may operate to give a net migration inwards. But the evidence for this is somewhat thin. (In any case even a net migration of 100,000 persons per year—almost impossible to conceive as a practical occurrence—would remove only 7–8 per-

[3] The 2.4 percent rate has been used by K. Wirosvharojo, Director of Workshop on Population Issues, University of Indonesia; also cf. *Business News,* 1964 *passim,* and Central Bureau of Statistics, *Statistical Pocketbook of Indonesia, 1962* and *1963,* Djakarta, which assume a growth rate of 2.3 percent. The National Income Unit of the Central Bureau of Statistics appears to take an increase of 2.4 percent per annum for its calculations for 1960–1961 and 1961–1962 (see footnote 13).

[4] Nathan Keyfitz, "Population in Indonesia—The Short and the Long Run," *Workshop Masalah Penduduk,* Fakultas Ekonomi, Universitas Indonesia, Djakarta, 1964.

cent of Java's yearly increase in population.) Of the other major land areas, West Irian is at the opposite extreme with 22 percent of the land area but only 0.7 percent of the population. Kalimantan also is sparsely inhabited—4.0 percent of the population occupying 28 percent of the land area. Sumatra is somewhere between these extremes with 16 percent of the total population in 25 percent of the land area.[5]

Rather less than 15 percent of Indonesia's population is found in the cities (see Table 6.1). It is still predominantly a kampong

Table 6.1. Population distribution by rural and urban areas, 1961 (in percent)

Area	Urban	Rural	Urban and rural
Indonesia	14.8	85.2	100.0
Java	10.1	54.8	64.9
All other areas	4.7	30.4	35.1

Source: Sensus Penduduk 1961, Serie S.P. I, Table 1.

(village) economy despite the demographic density of Java. However, the cities are not inconsiderable and do play an increasingly important role in the economy. There is one city of nearly 3 million persons—Djakarta; two cities of about one million—Bandung and Surabaya; three cities with around half a million inhabitants—Semarang, Medan, and Palembang; and four with one-third of a million persons apiece—Macassar, Surakarta (Solo), Malang, and Jogjakarta. Of these ten largest cities in Indonesia seven—with a total population of 6.5 million—are located in Java. The pull of large-city areas and their apparent relative abundance of employment opportunities over the years, compared with the concealed underemployment problems of an overpopulated countryside, have exerted a strong attraction for young mobile workers. The proportion of persons aged 15 to 24 years is higher in urban than in rural areas (20.2 percent as against 15.3 percent; see Table 6.2). The inflow tended to be persistent over

[5] Persons per square kilometre are as follows: Java, 477.0; Bali and Nusa Tenggara, 76; Sulawesi, 37.0; Sumatra, 33.0; Maluku, 11.0; Kalimantan, 7.6; and West Irian, 1.8. The average number per square kilometre for Indonesia is 50 (*Statistical Pocketbook of Indonesia, 1963*).

a long period. Between 1930 and 1961, Djakarta and Bandung increased their population by 558 percent and 583 percent respectively; and the smaller cities of Java—Semarang, Surakarta, Jogjakarta, and Malang—from 230 to 344 percent.[6] We know the

Table 6.2. Population by age and sex groups, 1961

Age group	Males	Females	Both sexes	% of population
0–4	8,461,949	8,580,361	17,042,310	17.7
5–9	7,603,534	7,639,422	15,332,956	15.9
10–14	4,318,543	3,860,869	8,179,412	8.5
15–19	3,834,117	3,874,058	7,708,175	8.0
20–24	3,452,362	4,338,603	7,790,965	8.1
25–34	7,333,617	8,542,102	15,875,719	16.5
35–44	5,719,856	5,363,334	11,083,190	11.5
45–54	3,559,007	3,483,325	7,042,332	7.3
55–64	1,897,510	1,850,396	3,747,906	3.9
65–74	795,730	829,027	1,624,757	1.7
75+	377,747	406,609	784,356	0.8
Unknown	59,882	56,869	116,751	0.1
Total	47,493,854	48,824,975	96,318,829	100.0

Source: Sensus Penduduk 1961, Serie S.P. I, Table 2 (totals include the estimated population of West Irian).

Dutch discouraged movement to the cities, until 1942 presumably. And the inflow of young persons into Djakarta, many no doubt seeking government service, was accelerated markedly in the 1950's decade

Age and Sex Structure

Consider Table 6.3. The age and sex structure of the Indonesian population in 1961 reveals a relatively small 10-to-19 age group. This is the consequence of war occupation, malnutrition affecting the survival of young people, civil upsets, and forced separations and migrations increasing the death rate and possibly inhibiting births during the 1940–1950 decade. The impact on those born in that decade is clear. By contrast, the large population in the 0-to-9 age group reflects a resurgence in the birth rate

[6] *Ibid.*

and a decline in infant and child mortality because of better feeding; health services directed against the incidence of yaws, tuberculosis, etc.; and antimalarial campaigns sponsored by the World Health Organisation authorities.

The cohorts of the population born between 1940 and 1950

Table 6.3. Age groups distributed by urban and rural areas (in percent)

Area	0–14	15–24	25–44	45–64	65+	Unknown
Urban	40.1	20.2	27.7	9.7	2.2	0.1
Rural	42.5	15.3	28.1	11.5	2.5	0.1
Both areas	42.1	16.1	28.0	11.2	2.5	0.1

Source: Sensus Penduduk 1961, Serie S.P. II, Table 3.

have already in large part entered the working-age groups. They are therefore already decreasing the proportion of available working population. As they enter the reproductive stage they will also influence the number of births and the proportion of younger children in the 0-to-4 and 5-to-9 age groups being born from 1965 onward. On the other hand, when the 1950–1960 cohorts enter the working and reproductive stage of the life cycle they will, of course, have a reverse effect on the proportion of persons of working age and later on the reproductivity of the population. (Sixteen and seventeen year olds are already a substantial part of the work force.)

There are more females than males in Indonesia as Table 6.2 informs us. The masculinity ratio (males to 100 females) is 95. This low rate applies predominantly to Java; for Sumatra and Kalimantan it is slightly greater than 100. The sex ratio also is higher in cities (100.1) than in rural areas—a pointer to the movement of young male workers from the countryside to cities.

The large size of the age and sex groups (Table 6.3) is significant. If the working age is defined as 15 to 64 years than we have only 55.3 percent of the Indonesian population in this category, leaving 42.1 percent in the 0-to-14 age group and 2.0 percent in the over-65 and unknown groups. Expressed another way, it can be said that, for the population as a whole, the burden of dependency (the number of persons of dependent age per 100 persons of working age) is 81. For Java, where the percentage of the working population is larger, the figure is 77.

The Economic Activities of the Population

In classifying the economic activities of persons, the 1961 census bases itself implicitly on a work force concept. The work force is composed of all persons 10 years and over who were actually at work for at least two months during the six months preceding the date of census as well as those of this age who were not at work but were seeking employment.[7] Table 6.4 shows the results of this approach. We find that there are 34.5 million persons (or 54.1 percent of those 10 years of age and over) in the work force. Of these, the majority are men, 25 million, while women comprise 9.5 million or between one-third and one quarter of the work force.

Looking for a moment at the classifications under "other activities," it seems that most men outside the work force are students, 3.8 million or 12.2 percent of those 10 years and over. Among women, on the other hand, only 2.5 million are students. The vast majority, 18.5 million, are "home house-workers." This description should not be given the meaning it would have in Western countries. Since 85 percent of the population live in rural areas, a very large proportion of women, in practice, combine domestic duties with assistance in agricultural work of various kinds. Rice cultivation and rubber-tapping in small holdings are outstanding examples; and women are also occupied with tea, sugar, palm trees, and fisheries on a domestic basis. Consequently, the orthodox classifications understate, to a considerable degree, the real work force of Indonesia.

The formal census picture regarding unemployment can be summarized briefly (Table 6.4). Among men there were 1,203,106 unemployed according to the census definition—about 4.8 percent of the male work force. For women the corresponding figures were 666,514 or 7 percent; that is considerably higher than for males. The percentage unemployment figure for both men and women, as a proportion of the labour force, is 5.4 percent. It should be noted also that unemployment was greater in urban

[7] *Sensus Penduduk 1961,* Editorial Notes.

Table 6.4. Persons 10 years and older by economic activity, 1961 (with percentages in parentheses)

Sex	Work force			Other activities			Totals
	Employed	Unemployed	Total	Students	Home house-workers	Others and unknown	
Male	23,805,691	1,203,106	25,008,797	3,832,931	1,017,245	1,489,398	31,348,391
	(76.0)	(3.8)	(79.8)	(12.2)	(3.2)	(4.7)	(100.0)
Female	8,902,923	666,514	9,569,437	2,539,464	18,494,942	2,000,349	32,605,192
	(27.3)	(2.0)	(29.3)	(7.8)	(56.8)	(6.1)	(100.0)
Both sexes	32,708,614	1,869,620	34,578,234	6,372,395	19,512,187	3,490,747	63,953,563
	(51.2)	(2.9)	(54.1)	(9.9)	(30.5)	(5.5)	(100.0)

Source: Sensus Penduduk 1961, Serie S.P. I, Table 3.

Note: Of the 10–14 age group of the population, only 32.6 percent of men and 15.6 percent of women were part of the work force; and in the 15–19 age group, 66.7 percent of men and 30.6 percent of women were included on the basis of the census return. Further, the number within the 10–14 cohorts actually at work varied enormously between city and country. Mainly this difference is connected to the opportunity to attend school. In the cities, only 7.6 percent of boys and 6.8 percent of girls in the 0–14 age group worked, while in the countryside 25.5 percent of boys and 17.5 percent of girls were part of the work force.

areas than in rural areas.[8] It was 7.4 percent for men (as against 4.4 percent in rural areas); and 11.8 percent for women (as against 4.9 percent in rural areas). However, this discrepancy between city and country may be a statistical fiction. Unemployment is more apparent in cities than in the countryside. It is felt more immediately by the person who cannot fall back on rural part-time pursuits to earn a subsistence, and it is more readily registered by the authorities.

The general figure of 5.4 percent unemployment of the work force, men and women, probably is an unsatisfactory measure. For one thing, the census return does not differentiate between those persons permanently or temporarily employed during the six months previous to the census date. Two months' work in six months is a poor way of testing the incidence of employment. Probably it understates unemployment heavily. More important, the census cannot take into account the degree of underemployment, especially in rural areas where, frequently, families possess holdings of land so small as to make continuous agricultural employment quite untypical.

Of the 34.6 million persons ten years of age and over in the work force, 33.1 million are employed. Their distribution among the main industry groups—arranged by region and as between urban and rural areas—is displayed in Table 6.5.

Agriculture is the predominant industry for the country as a whole, absorbing almost 72 percent of the employed population. Manufacturing is a small component by comparison, only 6 percent. Most of the industrial sector, it should be noted, is concentrated on essential consumer goods such as food, drink, textiles, clothing, tobacco (which is the largest single industry), and furniture. The manufacture of chemicals, rubber products, and metal goods and engineering are all relatively small industries.[9] However, as many as one quarter of the persons who have indicated agriculture as their main occupation are also engaged in trading activities or in home industries such as textile weaving, batik wax-

[8] *Sensus Penduduk 1961,* Serie S.P. II, Tables 4.2 and 4.4.

[9] Douglas S. Paauw, "From Colonial to Guided Economy" in Ruth T. McVey, ed., *Indonesia,* Human Area Relations Files, New Haven, 1963.

ing, basketmaking, tile- and brickmaking and so on.[10] Consequently, the manufacturing and trades figures are understated; and correspondingly the agricultural figure overstated.

Services absorb what may seem a surprisingly high proportion

Table 6.5. Distribution of employed population by industry group, region, and urban and rural areas, 1961 (in percent)

Industry group	Java	Sumatra	Kalimantan	Sulawesi	Other islands	All Indonesia	Urban	Rural
Agriculture, forestry, and fishing	68.0	78.4	80.2	77.2	83.6	71.9	11.7	81.0
Mining and quarrying	0.1	1.0	0.2	0.2	0.1	0.3	0.5	0.2
Manufacturing	6.8	2.8	3.2	4.8	4.2	5.7	15.9	4.1
Construction	2.0	1.5	1.2	1.1	1.2	1.8	5.9	1.1
Electricity, water, and gas	0.1	0.3	0.1	0.1	0.1	0.1	0.8	0.1
Trade, banking, and insurance	7.8	5.4	4.9	4.3	3.2	6.7	20.5	4.6
Transport, storage, and communications	2.3	2.1	1.7	1.9	0.8	2.1	9.7	1.0
Services	11.0	6.7	6.4	8.1	4.7	9.5	33.1	5.9
Others and unknown	1.9	1.8	2.1	2.3	2.1	1.9	1.9	2.0

Source: Sensus Penduduk 1961, Serie S.P. I, Table 4.

of employment for a developing country, 9.5 percent. This category, which in 1950 probably was around 6.7 percent, expanded rapidly in the 1950–1961 period to accommodate the rapid growth of government administration in the new Republic of Indonesia and the even faster expansion of defence personnel.[11] Commercial activities—trade, banking, and insurance—account for 6.7 percent of employment. This seems not too high a figure for a country strongly oriented toward trade with the outside world. It could be considered to be on the low side.

Commercial activities and services apart, only 10 percent of persons are occupied in all other nonagricultural pursuits. It is a small proportion by any standard and helps to indicate how narrow is the base of "modern" industries on which Indonesia operates—manufacturing, mining, construction, and the infrastructure provided by electricity, gas, water, transport, and communication.

The regional picture as set out in Table 6.5 confirms that the

[10] E. D. Hawkins, "Labor in Transition," in McVey, *op. cit.*

[11] Paauw, *op. cit.*

strategic centre of economic activities clearly is Java. It has the lowest proportion of its employed population in agriculture (68.0 percent), and it has a higher proportion of its employed in the services and trade, banking and insurance sectors than any other island; similarly manufacturing, construction, public utilities, transport, and communication show higher proportions of the employed population in Java. Sumatra, the second largest economic region, surpasses Java only in the population percentage occupied in mining and electricity, approaches it in commerce and transport, but is substantially behind in the proportion of persons employed in services and manufacturing.

In the urban areas of Indonesia (Table 6.5), as is to be expected, manufacturing accounts for a reasonable proportion, 15.9 percent. But it is overshadowed by both services, 33.1 percent, and trade, 20.5 percent, which together make up well over half the employment of urban areas. In rural areas, on the other hand, agriculture has 81.0 percent of employment while services and trade between them have only 10.5 percent.

Table 6.6. Male and female employment by industry, 1961
(with percentages in parentheses)

Industry	Men	Women	Both sexes
Agriculture, forestry, and fishing	17,371,811 (72.9)	6,144,386 (67.6)	23,516,197 (71.9)
Mining and quarrying	76,959 (0.3)	10,435 (0.1)	87,394 (0.3)
Manufacturing	1,158,760 (4.9)	697,392 (7.7)	1,856,152 (5.7)
Construction	560,584 (2.3)	21,456 (2.4)	582,040 (1.8)
Electricity, water, and gas	48,104 (0.2)	2,625 (0.3)	50,729 (0.1)
Trade, banking, and insurance	1,510,566 (6.3)	693,412 (7.5)	2,193,978 (6.7)
Transport, storage, and communications	666,879 (2.8)	24,580 (2.7)	691,459 (2.1)
Services	2,038,531 (8.6)	1,056,708 (11.6)	3,095,239 (9.5)
Others and unknown	373,497 (1.6)	261,929 (2.9)	635,426 (1.9)
Total	23,805,691 (100.0)	8,902,923 (100.0)	32,708,614 (100.0)

Source: Sensus Penduduk 1961, Serie S.P. II, Table 9.

Finally, Table 6.6 shows the distribution of employment between men and women among industry groups. In absolute numbers men have the advantage, 23.8 million as against 8.9 million women in employment. And of those available for the work force, men have a higher concentration than women in the main industry, agriculture (i.e., 72.9 percent compared with 67.6 percent). This is so for mining and transport also. However, in every other industry group the female participation is the higher. Taking trade and services together, for example, there is a 19.1 percent concentration of available women in this sector as against 14.9 percent for men. And for manufacture the discrepancy is even greater: 7.7 percent of employed women are in manufacturing as compared with 4.9 percent of the men.

Every year the 2.2 percent or 2.3 percent demographic growth adds over two million to Indonesia's population (1.3 or 1.4 million of them to Java's already overcrowded agricultural areas). Unfortunately there is no evidence to indicate that the growth of national productivity is likely to offer increases which will materially improve per capita consumption. Up to 1958, the independent regime did experience perceptible improvement in per capita income. Some of this was probably recovery from the low levels of the postwar years and a return to the real income levels of 1938. But increases in the order of 2.5 percent per year did occur for most of the 1950's. From 1958 onward, however, various factors intervened to reduce the rate of growth—the rebellion of dissident groups in the outer islands, the consequent disruption of internal administration, and the assumption of Indonesian government control over former Dutch interests followed by the expulsion of Dutch managerial and technical personnel.[12]

The only recent reliable estimates[13] now indicate that for 1958–1962 national income computed at constant prices (Table 6.7, rows 2 and 7) moved at almost the same rate as population increases (rows 5 and 10). Consequently per capita income barely changed. There might even have been a slight decrease for the

[12] *Ibid.*, and the authorities quoted therein.

[13] Central Bureau of Statistics (National Income Unit), *Estimates of National Income of Indonesia by Industrial Origin, 1958–62* (provisional), Djakarta, April 1965.

period in question. Since 1962, the increasing economic vicissitudes associated with military adventures, inflation, and the withdrawal of foreign economic assistance suggests that, if anything, national product stagnation may have become retrogression.

Table 6.7. National income and per capita income of Indonesia, 1958–1962

Income	1958	1959	1960	1961	1962
1. National income at current prices (billion rupiah)	216.8	291.9	374.2	520.7	1,391.2
2. National income at 1960 prices (billion rupiah)	363.9	368.3	374.2	381.9	397.3
3. Per capita income at current prices (rupiah)	2,406.0	3,169.0	3,972.0	5,401.0	14,110.0
4. Per capita income at constant prices (rupiah)	4,039.0	3,999.0	3,972.0	3,962.0	4,092.0
5. Estimate of mid-year population (million)	90.1	92.1	94.2	96.4	98.6
Index numbers (1958 = 100) depicting growth rates					
6. National income at current prices	100.0	134.6	172.6	240.2	641.7
7. National income at constant prices	100.0	101.2	102.8	104.9	109.2
8. Per capita income at current prices	100.0	131.7	165.1	224.5	586.5
9. Per capita income at constant prices	100.0	99.0	98.3	98.1	99.8
10. Population	100.0	102.2	104.6	107.0	109.4

Source: Central Bureau of Statistics (National Income Unit), *Estimates of the National Income of Indonesia by Industrial Origin, 1958–62*, Djakarta, April 1965.

However, despite inadequate management of the economy, hunger and hardship are not too likely for Indonesians. Examination of the national income estimates reveals that most of the weak performances, or actual decreases in production, occur in manufacturing, public utilities, transport and communication, trade and banking—that is in those sectors where technical and management factors, also foreign assistance and capital, are most vital. Agricultural production, on the other hand, accounting for 54 percent of national product, increased between 1958 and 1962 at almost 4 percent per annum. Farm food crops in particular showed substantial increases, while estate crops, mainly rubber, coffee, and tea, fell off in productivity.[14]

The years since 1962 probably have not altered the trends implicit in the 1959–1962 period. Stagnant and diminishing national product means mainly a growing scarcity of locally manufactured or imported consumer goods—vehicles, radios, bicycles, electrical equipment, certain types of textiles, etc.—a scarcity made more acute for the consumer by the demands of the armed forces. The product of export industries, agricultural and mineral, seems to be decreasing also, and this could be dangerous since it diminishes the opportunity to purchase capital equipment for essential public utilities, transport, and shipping.

All this, however, does not imply outright scarcity of essential foods, and so long as civil disorder does not seriously interfere with the activities of the peasant a 2.3 percent population growth or better probably can be accommodated. The main reservation concerns population growth rates. So far there is no sign of any significant decrease in fertility rates. And mortality could fall substantially and give fresh impetus to population pressure in Java.[15]

[14] *Ibid.* The state sector of agriculture, deprived of foreign management, actually fell off in total production during the period 1958–1962 by 18 percent, while farm crops, food, and nonfood (comprising almost 80 percent of agricultural production) increased by 13 percent. It is generally thought that the peasant's relative freedom from intervention and his response to the high free market prices of rubber and rice are responsible for this phenomenon.

[15] Nathan Keyfitz, *op. cit.*

CHAPTER 7

Labor in Developing Countries: Indonesia*

E. D. HAWKINS

The Development of Labor Organizations

Since their birth in 1908, Indonesian trade unions have been influenced by nationalist aspirations for freedom. Political and ideological considerations have frequently been more important than economic demands. Leadership, whether Moslem, nationalist, socialist, or communist, still plays a more important role than the rank-and-file membership. Diversity in leadership has resulted in multiple unions in many plants and in twelve national federations, each with a known political orientation. Because of its role in agitating for freedom and actually fighting for independence, and because of the strength of the unions in key sectors of the economy, labor has been granted a significant role in the Republic of Indonesia. Unions are one of the functional groupings recognized as important in the attempts in 1958–1960 to reorganize the country's political life.

Trade union history in Indonesia can be divided into six major periods: (1) the early beginnings from about 1908 through World War I when the influence of the nationalist *Serikat Islam* was strong; (2) the 1920's, when communist leadership was most active; (3) the 1930's, when more moderate leadership was in control; (4) the period of suppression during the Japanese occupation,

* Excerpted from "Indonesia" in W. Galenson, ed., *Labor in Developing Economies* (Chapter 3), University of California Press, Berkeley and Los Angeles, 1962. Reprinted by permission of E. D. Hawkins, W. Galenson, and the Regents of the University of California.

1942–1945; (5) the growth of unions and the birth of the national federation SOBSI during the revolution, 1945–1949; and (6) the struggle among the various labor federations after gaining independence, 1950 to date.

Political Orientation and Ideological Leanings[1]

Just as the political parties can be divided along ideological lines into four categories—nationalist, religious, socialist, and communist—so the unions have been subject to the same forces. Because nationalism and freedom have been overriding considerations since the start of the trade union movement, almost all unions have been motivated by the drive for political and economic independence from Dutch colonialism. Only later did these ideological influences tend to be so strong as to divide labor's drive for national independence.

Until 1921, the most important organization which supported the struggling labor unions was the *Serikat Islam,* a nationalist religious movement, formed in 1912, which grew rapidly by including in its membership intellectuals, religious leaders, merchants, peasants, and laborers. As is frequently the case in colonial and underdeveloped areas, the first Indonesian unions were made up of government and railroad and other transportation workers. Only gradually did unions spread to some of the estates and industries. The first union in Indonesia, the Union of Railway and Tramway Personnel (*Vereeniging van Spoor en Tramweg*), was formed in Semarang, Java, in 1908.[2] Other unions which followed were those of customs officers and teachers in 1911, officials of the state pawnshops in 1913, employees of the state opium monopoly in 1916, and officials of the Treasury and Public Works Department in 1917. During the war period, several nongovernmental

1 See Iskandar Tedjasukmana, *Political Character of the Indonesian Trade Union Movement,* Cornell Modern Indonesia Project (monograph series), Cornell University, Ithaca, N.Y., 1959; J. Henry Richardson, "Indonesian Labor Relations in Their Political Setting," *Industrial and Labor Relations Review,* vol. 12, no. 2, October 1958, pp. 56–78.

2 An organization for Dutch workers, the National Arbeids Secretariat, dates back to 1890. For more details on the history of trade unions in Indonesia, see Sandra, "Gerakan Buruh Indonesia" ("Indonesian Labor Movement"), Ministry of Labor, Government of Indonesia, Djakarta, 1958, mimeo.

unions were started, the most important of which were the agricultural workers in 1915 and the Union of Factory Workers in 1917. "At the end of December 1919, the *Serikat Islam*'s central leadership managed to unite twenty-two Indonesian trade unions totalling 77,000 members, under one of its leaders, R. M. Soerjopranoto."[3] By August, 1920, the *Persatuan Pergerakan Kaum Buruh* (PPKB), the first Central Federation of Labor in Indonesia, could boast of 150,000 members. It elected Semaun, a railroad worker and a leader of the radical Semarang branch of *Serikat Islam,* as its first president; Soerjopranoto, a moderate, as its vice-president; and Hadji Agus Salim, who was to become the "elder statesman" of the Republic of Indonesia, as its secretary.

At this very first meeting the president, Semaun, who had helped Sneevliet, Bergsma, and other Dutch left-wingers to organize in 1917 a Social Democratic Federation of Indonesia, tried to wrest control of the new federation from *Serikat Islam* leaders. Being unsuccessful in this attempt, Semaun and Tan Malaka, following the lead of the Third International, took a group of fourteen unions out of the Central Federation of Labor and formed a new revolutionary trade union center. This left the Central Federation of Labor under the direction of moderate leaders who favored political representation of labor, social legislation, and adequate wage regulation. In 1922, Semaun was successful in forming a new all-embracing federation, the Union of Indian Labor Unions, or *Persatuan Vakbonden Hindia* (PVH). Thus the split between the socialists and the communists, which rocked European labor after the Russian Revolution and World War I, had its counterpart in the unions and labor parties of Indonesia.

During the 1920's, after splitting off the branches they controlled from *Serikat Islam,* the communists were active in organizing political parties and trade unions, in leading many strikes, and finally, in 1926, in trying to organize a revolt against the Dutch. The Dutch government gradually passed tighter antistrike measures and finally outlawed the Communist party of the Indies in 1927. Starting with Sneevliet in 1918 and Tan Malaka in 1922, most of the communist leaders were jailed, exiled, or expelled

[3] George McT. Kahin, *Nationalism and Revolution in Indonesia,* Cornell University Press, Ithaca, N.Y., 1952, p. 75.

from the country. Semaun himself had to leave in 1923 and went to Moscow, where he remained as a teacher of the Indonesian language until 1957. In 1959, Sukarno appointed him one of the five members of the new Supervisory Commission for Government Affairs.

During the 1930's Indonesian labor groups turned away from revolutionary communist leadership and looked to the evolutionary Social Democratic and Christian trade union movements of Europe. Hadji Agus Salim, after attending the International Labor Conference in 1929, organized a National Federation of Public Servants, or *Persatuan Vakbonden Pegawai Negeri* (PVPN), which was made up of fourteen unions and about 30,000 members. In 1931, the PVPN affiliated with the International Federation of Trade Unions. The depression of the 1930's and the arrest of many Indonesian leaders slowed up the drive for national independence.

During the period of suppression by the Japanese, many trade union leaders went underground and learned new techniques of organization. Others had opportunities to hold higher political offices than they had had under the Dutch. The Indonesian language was fostered by the Japanese, and in general the Indonesian leaders looked on this period as one of temporary occupation.[4]

The end of the war came sooner than had been anticipated, creating a problem as to what the next step should be. The Japanese had indicated that they would eventually give the Indonesians freedom. Some leaders felt, therefore, that they should wait and take no hasty action; on the other hand, a group of seventeen young medical students kidnapped Sukarno and Hatta and insisted that they sign an immediate declaration of independence on August 17, 1945.

Labor was one of the first groups to offer its services to the revolution. A revolutionary workers' army was organized, together with a women's corps. Instead of limiting labor, as had the colonial government, the new republic tended to encourage

[4] This belief was fostered by an old legend which said that there would be conquerors from the north for a short period of time, but that soon the Indonesians would be free. This was widely believed and was a factor which encouraged them to plan for eventual freedom.

trade unions. The government, however, was worried about workers' groups taking over Dutch plants in syndicalist fashion under the leadership of Tan Malaka, who was an anti-Stalinist communist. The government wanted the control in its own hands.[5] Iwa Kusuma Sumantri, later president of Padjadjaran University in Bandung, a left-wing labor leader who had been exiled by the Dutch, was appointed the first minister of social affairs, and tried unsuccessfully to organize in September 1945, one universal federation of labor, the Indonesian Labor Front or *Barisan Buruh Indonesia* (BBI).

Among the groups which were organized soon after the revolution, some out of prewar remnants, were the estate workers, the oil workers, the railroad workers, the gas and electricity workers, seamen, miners, teamsters, longshoremen, pawnshop employees, printers, and teachers. These groups formed several temporary organizations and in November 1946, the All-Indonesian Central Labor Organization or *Sentral Organisasi Buruh Seluruh Indonesia* (SOBSI) was organized along industrial lines, but with craft unions having full equality. For a short time SOBSI, the first permanent federation in the postwar period, was for all practical purposes the sole federation in Indonesia. Since 1946, SOBSI and its affiliated unions have been in the vanguard of the revolutionary movement in Indonesia and have led the protests against Dutch imperialism, capitalism, and management.

During the early days of the revolution there was a short period of cooperation among most leftist groups. The left-wing coalition, or *Sajap kiri,* was made up of the Socialists (PSI), the Indonesian Labor party (PBI), the Communists (PKI), the Socialist Youth Organization (PESINDO), the Indonesian Peasant Front (BTI), and SOBSI. In 1948, however, Premier Sjarifuddin split the *Sajap kiri* by organizing a left-wing People's Democratic Front (communist) to oppose the moderate socialist wing led by Sjahrir, a former premier. This new communist front refused to join in a new coalition cabinet of socialists and Moslims (Masjumi) led by Vice-President Hatta. This 1948 split in the party and in the un-

[5] Kahin, *op. cit.,* p. 474; Selo Soemardjan, "Bureaucratic Organization in a Time of Revolution," *Administrative Science Quarterly,* vol. 2, no. 2, September 1957, pp. 182–199.

ions has continued to the present time. Even the Trotskyites, led by Tan Malaka, supported the Hatta coalition as opposed to the communist group. In 1948, Tan Malaka established a rival federation called the Federation of Unions of the Revolutionary Workers of Indonesia, or *Gabungan Serikat Buruh Revolutioner Indonesia* (GASBRI).

SOBSI suffered a much more serious blow when many of its leaders took part with the communists in the abortive Madiun revolt in September 1948, against the Indonesian government. The nationalist government of Indonesia put this revolt down rapidly and firmly. Many of the SOBSI leaders were killed or fled the country. Since 1948, many rival federations have been formed and at times have seemed to be gathering real strength, but SOBSI remains the largest and most important labor federation.

In 1950, after the granting of sovereignty, SOBSI again began a strong organizing campaign and took the leadership in organizing strikes in the estates. Several regional groups opposed the growth of the SOBSI unions, but it was not until after many SOBSI and other left-wing leaders had been jailed in August 1951, because of a possible coup on Independence Day, that these groups gained much momentum. In 1953, with the foundation of the All-Indonesian Congress of Workers or *Kongres Buruh Seluruh Indonesia* (KBSI), it looked as if there would be a strong second federation. Actually, this organization had a very short honeymoon, because later in 1953 the president of the union, Mr. Kusnan, resigned and took the nationalist-oriented unions out of the federation. It is generally believed that this was done for political reasons, since SOBSI (communist-oriented) saw a possible threat in KBSI and therefore insisted that the Nationalist party, whose prime minister they were supporting, withdraw its unions from the new federation. Since that time other federations have been organized or have grown in power, so that at the present time there are twelve national federations of labor in Indonesia.

Most of these federations have a strong political orientation. In fact, many of the trade unions are the labor divisions of a political party. Each of the major political parties operates several branches or divisions: for example, a women's division, a veterans' division, a farmers' division, a youth division, and a labor division. This means that it is impossible to study the trade unions without considering the political parties.

Listed below are the national trade union federations in existence in 1959 and their political affiliation or orientation:*

SOBSI	Communist party	(PKI)
KBSI	Socialist party[a]	(PSI)
SBII	Masjumi party[a]	(Moslem)
KBKI	Nationalist party	(PNI)
HISSBI	Labor party	
SOBRI	Partai Murbah	(Independent Radical)
SARBUMUSI	Nadatul Ulamah	(Moslem Teachers' party)
GOBSII	PSII	(Orthodox Moslem)
GSBI	Nationalist party	(PNI)
KBIM	Masjumi[a]	(Moslem)
O.B. PANTJASILA	Catholic party	
SBKI	Christian party	(PARKINDO)

[a] Disbanded by government order, 1960.

As the first and leading federation in Indonesia, SOBSI includes many noncommunist members, but its leadership and politics are generally recognized to be communist-oriented. SOBSI has in recent years trained its own leadership apart from the leaders of the Communist party. Although it is easy to demonstrate[6] that many of the resolutions passed by the various SOBSI unions are politically in line with the views of the Communist party, it is also possible to show that its unions engage in genuine trade union activities. They are interested in and push for higher wages and better working conditions. In fact some employers feel that the communist unions are better organized and disciplined and, therefore, more responsible than other unions in Indonesia. Other employers, however, used to complain that many of the demands of the communist unions were so great that they could

* By 1970 these affiliations have become largely of historical interest, although those few unions which survived the Sukarno period have retained political connections.—Ed.

[6] In addition to many publications in Indonesian, SOBSI issues a mimeographed monthly in English, "Indonesian Trade Union News," which quotes speeches and resolutions and relates the activities of the Federation and its affiliates.

not possibly hope to win these requests, which were made to harass and disrupt production. Usually the communist unions have been more active in demanding large increases and in carrying out strikes when a government unfriendly to the Communist party was in office. Since 1957, SOBSI unions have strongly supported the government against the rebels and generally obeyed the no-strike ban for immediate political reasons, while stressing the right to strike as a basic trade union principle.

The KBSI claims that it is not a socialist trade union, but an independent trade union federation, because Dr. Kusna, the president, is a nonparty man. He also heads the large railroad union, PBKA, which prides itself on being an independent union with many officers who are not socialists. Mr. Silitonga, who heads a Sumatran union, PERBUPRI, of estate workers affiliated with the KBSI, also claims that his union is independent. In fact, although Mr. Silitonga himself is a socialist, he refused to allow the socialists to use his union in the national elections, with the result that two definitely socialist-oriented groups were split off from his union.

In 1959, the KBKI broke its formal connections with the Nationalist party[7] and moved into offices in separate buildings. Ideologically, however, the KBKI leans on the Nationalist party (PNI), which subscribes to a doctrine called Marhaenism, an indigenous philosophy opposed to the foreign ideologies of capitalism and Marxism. It favors group action by Indonesians and their government. Some would think of it as a sort of state socialism, or "Socialisme à la Indonesia." President Sukarno and other nationalist leaders talk a great deal about their five principles (*Pantjasila*): divine omnipotence, international humanitarianism, nationalism, democracy, and social justice. The first, belief in God, runs counter to Marxism, but this is not stressed by SOBSI.

It is no secret that the Masjumi party before it was ordered to disband fostered the SBII, even if there have been suggestions by SBII officials that the union should be separated from the party, since some of the Masjumi leaders supported the revolution in

[7] The GSBI also claimed to be independent, but most of its membership was made up of government workers, a large percentage of them oriented to the Nationalist party. It recently [about 1960–Ed.] affiliated with the KBKI.

Sumatra in 1958.[8] So far the Nadatul Ulamah has done relatively little with its new Moslem federation, but in a few centers SARBUMUSI is recognized by the employers. GOBSII, another Moslem federation, supported by the PSII party, seemed to be little more than a paper organization by 1960. SBII, however, became worried by this spate of new Moslem federations, including KBIM, which split off from SBII, feeling that by and large these new confederations would draw from the Moslem unions rather than struggle to take members away from SOBSI. For this reason the then secretary general of SBII proposed in 1956 that there be an agreement among Moslem unions not to proselytize from their own memberships but to concentrate on winning new members for their group. By 1959, a constitution was drawn up for a Moslem confederation to which all four Moslem unions would belong, while each would keep its own identity.

The difference in ideology between the communists, who stress the class struggle, and the Moslems, who talk about the principle of sharing the wealth with the poor,[9] is significant in labor relations in Indonesia. Since some of the Moslem unions tend to talk in terms of the Islamic faith instead of the class struggle, they sometimes refuse to join in certain strikes and are considered more "moderate." On the other hand, since they are in competition for members, they frequently must ask for and get the same things as the communist unions.[10]

These ideological differences have their counterparts in the international affiliations of various Indonesian unions. In 1947, at the Party Congress in Malang, SOBSI decided to affiliate with the World Federation of Trade Unions (WFTU). It sent its new president to the WFTU conference at Prague in June 1947, and since that time there has been a close affiliation between SOBSI and the WFTU. Because the WFTU helped support the revolution

[8] Wibisono, the president of SBII and a former Masjumi leader and minister of finance, was appointed as a labor representative in the 1960 parliament.

[9] Rich Moslems have a general responsibility toward their workers and a particular duty to make an annual contribution or bonus to them.

[10] Just as there was some tendency in the political field for the Masjumi and Socialist parties to work together before they were ordered to disband, so there has been a tendency among the Moslem and Socialist unions to join forces in opposing SOBSI.

against Dutch colonialism, workers have been willing to affiliate with this communist-oriented international group in spite of the so-called "independent" foreign policy of their government. After the death of Stalin, the small Trotskyite federation SOBRI also joined the WFTU. Several SOBSI unions are affiliated with the respective communist-oriented trade secretariats.

On the other hand, there was, until 1957, a great reluctance on the part of the noncommunist unions to affiliate with the International Confederation of Free Trade Unions (ICFTU). The WFTU and SOBSI have attacked this organization as procolonial in its outlook, since many of the unions and their leaders come from the so-called European colonial powers. Gradually in recent years there has been a tendency for some of the noncommunist unions to be interested in the ICFTU.[11]

In 1957, SBII applied for membership in the ICFTU and, after being investigated by a committee of unionists from other countries, was accepted and has subsequently participated in various international and regional meetings and congresses. Efforts were made at the second congress of the *Serikat Sekerdja PTT* (an independent union of postal, telephone, and telegraph employees) at Solo in 1958 to urge it to join the trade secretariat for this group of workers located in Berne, Switzerland. The railroad workers (PBKA) joined the international secretariat of the noncommunist Transport Workers Union. In spite of these growing relationships and the various training programs for labor leaders supported by the technical assistance program of the United States government, the Colombo Plan, and private foundations,[12] the links between the noncommunist unions in Indonesia and their counterparts in the rest of the world are less strong and less formal than those of the communists.

Undoubtedly Indonesian unions, or at least their leaders, have

[11] The ICFTU sent to Indonesia first a Swedish trade union leader for about a year and a half, 1955–1956, and second, a representative of the Malayan plantation union in 1959. For more information about their activities, see their monthly publication *Duniah Buruh Merdeka* or the ICFTU *Asian Bulletin*.

[12] For several years the Rockefeller Foundation gave fellowships for a few Indonesian trade unionists to study at the International Ladies' Garment Workers' Union's course for labor leaders in New York City.

been influenced by foreign ideologies. However, the beliefs of Islam and the nationalistic ideas of Marhaenism play a role in the labor movement. As long as many parties based on various ideologies and religions remain, and as long as they are active in supporting labor groups, it will be difficult to attain a single labor movement or even a few federations. On the other hand, President Sukarno has for several years been trying to reduce the role of the political parties, and he has also indicated that he wished to reduce the number of trade union federations.* A story was circulating in Djakarta at the end of 1959 that SOBSI wanted this number reduced to one, since it itself would undoubtedly be that one organization, while the nationalists wanted two organizations, one SOBSI and the other nationalist-oriented, including all the other federations. The Moslems were said to have wanted three federations, one communist-, one nationalist-, and one Moslem-oriented.

Leadership

Leadership is an especially important factor in trade unionism in Indonesia. Some leaders play a dominant role, setting the pattern for the workers to follow. Furthermore, the rank-and-file have less power than in some American and European unions. This reflects the scarcity of trained leaders and the low standard of education and living of the majority of the workers.

As has been indicated, leadership in Indonesia has frequently come from political groups; many of the union leaders are lawyers or politicians or both. In many cases men have served as both union and party leaders. The SOBSI unions since the early days of the revolution have had representatives in the appointed or elected parliaments. Although in former times functionaries of the Communist party served as key leaders of the SOBSI unions, an attempt was made recently to separate the party and the union leadership. This reflects the fact that the SOBSI unions have a much greater depth and strength in leadership than the noncommunist unions. The noncommunist unions may be fortunate enough to have one or possibly two paid union workers,[13] while the

* Professor Hawkins was writing in the early 1960's before the coup of 1965 which removed Sukarno from power.—Ed.

[13] Exceptions are unions with a check-off, such as PBKA, which has funds to pay many fulltimers.

SOBSI unions in the same field may have ten to twenty on a full-time regular payroll. This large number of trained leaders may account for the fact that SOBSI is by all odds the largest and strongest federation in Indonesia. Of course, its growth has been helped by the fact that it was the first permanent federation to be organized and that it took part in the revolution.

SOBSI has also been more successful in securing leadership from the ranks of the workers. As a result, the communist-oriented unions are apt to represent the manual workers (*buruh*) more completely than do the noncommunist unions, many of whose leaders are often white-collar (*pegawai*) or professional workers. This tendency toward stratification, where the SOBSI unions are reaching more of the workers at the lower levels and the noncommunist groups are attracting the more highly skilled and office workers, is particularly true among the railroad, oil, and estate workers.

Much of the time of union leaders is given over to handling grievances, either directly with the employer or through the ministry of labor and the Regional and National Disputes Committees. Political connections are helpful, and training in law is useful. Some union leaders also spend considerable time on more specific political activities, such as elections, demonstrations, and demands for labor legislation.

Other union leaders have become concerned with providing food and clothing and health facilities for their members at reasonable prices. SOBSI runs a clinic at its main headquarters in Djakarta. The leaders of the PBKA (railroad workers) are in the forefront of this movement; in fact, jointly with the railroad administration they operate the *Badan Sosial Pusat Buruh Kereta Api* (Social Welfare Department of the Railroad Workers). This organization operates as a cooperative entrepreneur, collecting small sums of savings from the workers; these have been invested in a rice mill, a *batik* plant, a soap mill, a clothing factory, and a shoe factory. Although the United States International Cooperation Administration has helped by supplying machinery from abroad, some technical experts, and training, the local capital comes from the savings of workers themselves, and the management comes from the union leaders. There is some talk that other government unionists may join in these projects to get necessities at low prices. In addition, this organization runs a housing department, a purchasing cooperative, a credit union, an insurance fund, and a clinic.[14]

When the government appoints labor representatives to the various disputes committees, it tends to choose labor leaders. Similarly, they are also tapped for the new Labor-Military Organization (BUMIL). Some of the same leaders were selected in 1959 and 1960 as functional representatives of labor in the National Planning Council, the Supreme Advisory Council, and the parliament. For example, Erning Pradja, the KBKI president, was elected to parliament in 1955, served as head of the Indonesian delegation to the ILO conference in 1956, was appointed by President Sukarno in 1958 as a labor representative to the National Advisory Council, and the following year was chosen by the president as minister of labor.

Because of the number of rival federations, each leader must push the claims of his union against all others. This makes it difficult to secure "moderate and responsible" leaders. Furthermore, as in many other countries, leadership rivalries must be recognized in studying the labor movement in general and the difficulties of trying to get the federations to work together.

Structure and Membership

The structure of the trade union movement is complicated by the large number of national federations, regional organizations, and independent unions. Although union organizational charts are popular in Indonesia, it is often difficult to learn how much is actually in operation and how much is a paper plan for the future. Furthermore, the real center of power may not be exactly as shown on the chart.

The organizational structure of SOBSI, the largest federation,

[14] PBKA, *Laporan Kerdja 3 Tahun, Nopember 1955 sampai achir, 1958 untuk Kongres KeV (Report of Work for Three Years, November 1955 to the End of 1958, for the Fifth Congress)*, Bandung, 1959. For stories on the dedication of the clothing and shoe factories, see *Times of Indonesia,* October 11, 1958, p. 3, and December 3, 1958, p. 3.

is not unlike that of the American Federation of Labor–Congress of Industrial Organizations. In fact, a SOBSI leader suggested that one of the reasons for the success of his organization and that of the AFL–CIO was the similarity of their structural form. SOBSI has two major lines of organization: one through the national unions, the other on a geographical base. SOBSI tends to give more weight to the national unions than the geographical representatives, as is the case in the AFL–CIO. Final authority is supposed to reside in the national congresses, the latest of which was held in 1959 after some delay on the part of the minister of defense. Actually, the executive committee and the elective officers make decisions between the congresses and are very influential in determining what is decided there.

Forty national unions are affiliated with the SOBSI organization. These include such workers as those on the railroads (SPKA), on the estates (SARBUPRI), in the textile plants (SBT), on the waterfront (SBPP), and in the oil industry (PERBUM). The national unions, with headquarters either in Djakarta or various other cities in Java, have their own officers, negotiate with employers, and carry their cases for arbitration to the Central Disputes Committee. An oil case coming from PERBUM in South Sumatra would be pushed by the PERBUM officials in Djakarta.

The national unions and their locals have considerable autonomy on trade union issues within their own industry. SOBSI stresses that each of the unions should finance its own activity. This independence of each of the national unions does not preclude sympathetic support of the activities of other SOBSI unions. At the local level, however, it is the responsibility of the local of a particular national union to handle its own strike situation with the support of the national union rather than aid from other local SOBSI unions. Each of the national unions has its own regional (*Daerah*) offices and local (*Tjabang*) branches, which coordinate with the geographic arm of SOBSI in carrying out general political objectives, holding demonstrations, celebrating May Day.

SOBSI itself has real power, although it grants certain autonomy over particular economic or trade union issues to its national unions. SOBSI sets for its unions political policies which do not deviate from those of the Communist party. It issues a number of journals and pamphlets, and supplies and helps train leaders. It holds many congresses and encourages affiliates to do likewise in order to indoctrinate their members and to spot potential leaders. Some claim it has to seek outside funds, since the dues of its member unions would not seem to be sufficient to finance all its activities. Although SOBSI and its affiliated unions are reported to have relatively good systems of communication, undoubtedly the great distances within Indonesia result in more local autonomy than is planned.

The structure of SOBSI is more fully developed than that of the other federations, because of its larger membership. In general, many of the other smaller federations follow the same model of national unions affiliated with the federation, plus the geographic pattern of local and regional offices. The real strength of KBSI seems to rest in a few of its large national unions such as PBKA (railroads) and PERBUPRI (estates), rather than in KBSI itself.* The treasury of the railroad workers, for example, is much larger than that of KBSI.

Another form of organization used in Indonesia is the one big union to which all members belong directly. The best example of this type is the Moslem federation SBII, and the nationalist-oriented organization KBKI follows essentially this same type of organizational structure. This may have some advantages in the initial stages, where the number of members is relatively limited in a given local district or region and where there is also a crying shortage of leadership. One leader in a district can serve workers in several different trades or industries. To the extent that these organizations are divisions of the political party, unity rather than separate national unions may be more desired by the parent organization.

The main organizational line of the SBII is from the national to the regional to the local level. On the other hand, the SBII already has recognized industry differences by establishing industrial departments to handle the special needs of the workers, for example, on the estates or in the oil industry. Whether or not these departments will eventually become separate national unions

* Note that the federations competed within industries. Thus more than one "national" union operated in railroads, estates, etc.—Ed.

is still undecided, and will probably depend on the growth of the organization. KBKI may also develop separate national unions and become a true federation. At the present time it is trying to secure the affiliation of a number of the independent unions.

An August 1955 report of the ministry of labor included seven regional and nine local federations, many of which are located in Sulawesi and the eastern islands. One of the largest covers seventeen locals of government workers employed by the local autonomous region of Jogjakarta. Not all regional government workers in Jogjakarta belong to one of the seventeen locals of this federation; in fact, a SOBSI affiliate (SEBDA) probably has a majority of the lower-paid workers.

The ministry of labor listed 67 independent (*non-voksentral*) national unions in 1955, compared to 84 unions affiliated with federations. By the end of 1958, 161 independent unions were registered, compared to 100 affiliated unions. A number of these unions have their headquarters away from Djakarta. One of the oldest and strongest of these independents, with members in all parts of Indonesia, is the Union of Pawnshop Workers (*Serikat Buruh Pegadaian*). There is no dual or multiple unionism among the pawnshop workers, and the union covers over 99 percent of them. Its officers come from various political groups. A careful system of accounting brings in sufficient funds for the union to own its own building and printing plant in Jogjakarta.[15]

The ministry of labor further listed, in 1955, 659 nonaffiliated local unions, many of them composed of workers in one firm only. There were then a total of 1,501 national, regional, and local unions, affiliated and nonaffiliated with federations.

The role of the union member is less developed in Indonesia than in Western countries. Meetings are held to rouse them to take part in strikes and demonstrations; membership cards are passed out to the workers. Much effort is made to collect dues from members, but here a serious problem frequently arises, because not only are the wages of Indonesian workers low in relation to the cost of living, but there is competition among several

[15] Profits from this plant are sufficient to enable it to publish its own monthly journal, *Suara Buruh Pegadaian*. The August 1959 issue presents financial statements for the union and the printing plant, pp. 235–237.

unions in the same field. One union will not put much pressure on a person to pay dues for fear that he will drop out and join another union which is less strict in its collection of dues.

Some workers may be considered members of two unions at the same time. This is particularly true because it is not necessary to pay union dues to be considered a regular member. In fact, many unions indicate quite freely that they collect dues from only 10 to 30 percent of their members each month. Some workers think it wise to belong to two unions to get protection from both, and because they have friends in both. Others may be encouraged to join another union so that the first union may have some control over its rival. The SBII has a special provision to test its membership. For a worker to be counted as a member of the SBII, he must have paid his initiation fee and the first month's dues. This is a better test of membership than just getting workers to raise their hands and receive cards from the union. However, although a careful check is made by SBII on dues from the field, there is no assurance that this system will record accurately at any time how many members are active in the union.

An exact way to find out the number of members in a union is through a check-off of dues, but there are few such cases in Indonesia, one of the most important being the PBKA (railroad workers) affiliated with the KBSI. The check-off has also been granted to the post, telegraph, and telephone workers. Other unions have tried to secure the check-off, but private management, Stanvac being an exception, has generally resisted such moves. Some unions have not wanted a check-off because it would disclose too accurately how few members actually belonged to their union.

With multiple unions, plural membership, and no exact test of membership, it is apparent that union figures in Indonesia must be scrutinized very carefully. The test of how many workers go out on strike is frequently used, but this may be faulty because a number of people who are not members of the union may decide to join the strike rather than stand out against their fellow workers. In fact, in some plants with multiple unions, if the number of members were counted in this way, the total number of those going out on different strikes would exceed the number of workers in the plant. Similarly, many estimates are made on the basis of the claims of the union leaders, which are apt to be exaggerated to try to stress the importance of their union in comparison with other groups. Many times the total claims of the union leaders in a given plant will exceed the number of workers, but this is not entirely impossible because of plural membership. On the basis of some field experience, it appears that the data become less accurate as one moves from the local union to the regional, to the national, and to the confederation, since there seems to be a compounding of the optimistic estimates the higher one goes. The desire for exact membership figures is greater on the part of some Western observers than of the Indonesian leaders themselves. Fairly general agreement among union leaders,[16] management officers, and government officials, however, exists about the relative importance of competing unions.

Recent estimates of union membership range from 1.5 to 5.5 million members. Although even the low figure is probably much too high for the number of workers who actually pay dues in any given month, probably some two million workers are effectively influenced by the unions in that they would take part in labor demonstrations or strikes and *consider themselves* union members. On the basis of data collected between July 1955, and July 1957, the ministry of labor reported that membership in registered trade unions, broken down not only by federation but by industry and geographical region, totaled 2,449,722 in 1957, as compared with 2,109,128 a year earlier. The increase of about 340,000 members is indicative of a more complete registration as well as an increase in total membership. There are still some indications that membership in some unions in certain industry classifications has been exaggerated. The largest group of union members was reported in agriculture, 1,009,962;[17] in industry, 596,115, and in the ser-

[16] Often this does not include the union leader's estimate of his own union's strength.

[17] By comparison, the Central Bureau of Statistics reported only 791,247 regular and temporary workers and employees on the nine major types of estates in June 1956 (*Wages Paid on Estates, 1956–57,* p. 7). In 1959, SARBUPRI, the largest national union in Indonesia, claimed 351,676 members out of an estimated 593,000 estate workers throughout the country.

vices, 275,047. Unfortunately, because of the unitary structure of some of the federations, 382,427 union members could not be classified.

From a cross-classification by federations and industries it is apparent that membership in SOBSI, KBSI, and the nonfederated unions is widely distributed in all occupations. The same may be true of SBII and KBKI, but unfortunately their membership has not been classified by industry. Although the figures indicate that SOBSI has substantially more members than all the other unions which are classified—in agriculture, mining, manufacturing, transportation, communication, and services—perhaps the most significant point to note is that it has about 530,000 members out of the total of 596,000 classified in manufacturing.

The heavy concentration of union membership is on Java, about three-fourths of the total, excluding those not classified by regions (406,043). The Medan area of North Sumatra also has a very large group of union members (366,472), a number in excess of those reported in Central Java. In all the rest of Indonesia, only about 140,000 members were reported in 1957.

A second method which the ministry of labor has used to gather trade union membership is to secure reports from each of the regions (*daerah*).[18] As of the end of December 1957, this total amounted to 2,295,066. The figures for most of the unions were considerably smaller than those included in the registered membership. On the other hand, the figures for SOBRI seem much too high, while those for KBKI and the nonaffiliated unions show a marked increase. The estimates for SBII may be too low.

The ministry of labor has published membership reports in a third way, based on claims made by the unions themselves without specific reference to location or industry. These range from 4,514,991 on June 30, 1956, to 5,693,898 on March 31, 1958. These figures represent the optimistic hopes of leaders rather than actual union membership. Almost all the figures are exaggerated, with the possible exception of the 180,000 in nonaffiliated unions on March 31, 1958.

[18] The ministry seems to favor this method and included these figures in *Two Year Report during the Karya Cabinet, April 1957–April 1959*, p. 8.

Whatever set of figures is used, however, SOBSI is the largest federation. KBKI, SBII, and KBSI are the next most important federations. A figure of about two million trade union members would seem correct, with possibly about half of these affiliated with SOBSI.

With what figure should the total trade union membership in Indonesia be compared? Probably not the total labor force of 33 to 40 million, because it includes such a large number of farmers and other self-employed workers. A better estimate for comparison purposes is about 8,000,000 people employed as wage or salary workers in industry and government service. (Government workers are included in this category because many of them are organized, perhaps more strongly than in private industry.) Of this total number of workers, 20 to 25 percent are trade union members.

If these percentage figures are used, there is still considerable room for trade union expansion of membership. If the optimistic claims of union leaders are used, however, there would seem to be less chance for union growth, except as there were additions to the labor force, particularly those in the industrialized sector. Since trade union membership is largely concentrated in the larger estates and plants, including government service, one further area for increase in membership is in the small plants, which are often managed by Chinese or perhaps Indonesians. Union leaders of both the Right and the Left, however, were conscious that if they pushed the small firms too hard they might put them out of business or keep them from expanding. If the unions could not secure higher wages for the workers in smaller plants, it might be difficult for them to organize such workers. In Singapore, however, some of the unions have made remarkable headway in organizing smaller shops and in securing benefits for workers in these industries. Many of these shops are owned and operated by Chinese. It is possible that the Indonesian unions may put pressure on the Chinese establishments, even if they are small in size, to provide better wages and working conditions for their employees. On the other hand, considering developments since 1958, the government may extend rules limiting Chinese ownership of undertakings.

This would involve more Indonesian management, which might not be strong enough at first to increase wages.

Influence in Social and Economic Life

Because the trade unions in the prewar period and after the Declaration of Independence on August 17, 1945, played such an important part in the movements for independence and nationalism, every Indonesian government has tended to be more pro-labor than pro-foreign-management. Certainly this contrast between government attitudes before and after the revolution is important. Trade unions have had some influence on the policy decisions of the ministry of labor. The fact that each of the major political parties is trying to form unions affiliated with it is a clear indication of the importance attached to the labor vote. In the general elections of 1955, several trade union officials were elected to parliament on various tickets. Every discussion of functional representation includes labor as one of the major groups, and labor is represented with twenty-five seats in the parliament appointed by President Sukarno in March 1960.

In some areas the unions have also been active in their local governments. For example, in Pakan Baru in Central Sumatra, the SOBSI trade unions in 1956 were playing a key role in the city government. A leader of the oil workers' union (PERBUM) spent most of his time on government affairs. Likewise in Surabaja, the trade unions connected with SOBSI have joined with the Communist party in winning a number of local elections. Several officials of the noncommunist unions also serve in important local and provincial offices. All these officeholders reflect the importance and influence of the unions in their community. One might speculate that, as in other countries, some men were becoming union leaders in order to gain political position.

Although some labor leaders are important members of the community, labor as a class does not have a high position in Indonesian society. As already pointed out, education is considered to be the important criterion for leadership and social standing, the professions and the white-collar workers (*pegawai*) standing higher on the social ladder than manual laborers (*buruh*).

Although relatively skilled workers do not have as high a social position as *pegawai,* in some cases they have enough economic power to command a considerable differential over unskilled workers. There are some who believe that the shortage of skilled workers and the surplus of unskilled workers causes a greater disparity of wages in an underdeveloped than in a developed country. The International Labor Organization reported that skilled workers in Djakarta in 1953 received Rp. 10–20, or two to four times the general level of wages for unskilled workers, Rp. 5–6.[19] Although wages in the building construction industry in Bandung have risen by over 60 percent from 1951 to 1958, there has been a constant differential system, with skilled workers paid twice as much, the most skilled three times as much, and the foremen (*mandurs*) four times as much as the unskilled. Female unskilled workers in a tea factory in West Java received early in 1959 Rp. 4.75 a day, and men Rp. 5.75. A skilled machinist, on the other hand, was paid about Rp. 20, or over four times the pay of unskilled women workers. Such a comparison of money wages is not accurate, however, since all the workers receive substantial wages in kind, especially rice, depending on the number of dependents in a family. The payments in kind on Javanese estates for a married man with two children were slightly higher in 1958 than his money wages. Adding about Rp. 5 to both the unskilled worker's and the machinist's money wages would mean that the latter received about 2.5 times as much as the unskilled worker with a family.[20]

A recent study of wages in Sukabumi, made with the assistance of N. K. Adyantaya, an ILO expert working with the Indonesian ministry of labor, indicated very narrow differentials for skilled over unskilled workers:

[19] *International Labour Review,* vol. 70, 1954, p. 39. Bakers and plumbers were paid Rp. 10; bricklayers and carpenters, Rp. 12.50; structural steel and electrical workers, Rp. 15; garage mechanics, Rp. 18; and motor freight truck drivers, Rp. 20.

[20] Length-of-service awards further complicate the comparison. The head of an office in a government ministry reported that he had working under him several people who received higher income because they had larger families and had [footnote incomplete in original.—Ed.]

Industry		*Average daily wages*
Plantations	Skilled	Rp. 5.36
	Unskilled	Rp. 4.15
Other establishments	Skilled	Rp. 7.90
	Unskilled	Rp. 5.22

This means a differential of about 30 percent on plantations, and just under 50 percent in other establishments.[21] Of course, the use of averages tends to reduce the differentials, since there are many degrees of skill in the skilled category. In some cases, however, the differentials for skilled workers may not be sufficient to induce workers to take the necessary training. Certainly the use of payments in kind and allowances for long service and size of family may tend to reduce substantially the apparent differentials.

Also there are considerable wage differences by industry. The cigarette industry is one of the lowest paid, and many of the workers in the *batik* industry also receive low incomes. Harbor workers are better paid, and oil workers are among the best paid. Wages in large cities tend to be higher for comparable positions than in small towns or rural areas. Further, the estates in North Sumatra tend to pay more than in other regions. In rice mills, woodworking shops, and rubber-remilling plants, wages in Sumatra are considerably higher than in Java.[22] Furthermore, on Sumatra and Kalimantan estates, more is given in wages in kind than in Java. See Table 7.1 for the monthly output of North Sumatra estates.[23]

The greater scarcity of all grades of labor in the outer islands tends to make for a rather large discrepancy in wages between the low levels of Java and the higher levels, for example, in Sumatra. The money differences, however, must be corrected to some extent for the higher cost of living in Sumatra than Java. As long as population tends to increase rapidly in Java without a corresponding increase in capital investment, severe pressure will remain on wages, and the bargaining position of unskilled labor will not be strong. The really low subsistence level of most wage earners in Indonesia keeps labor in its subordinate position. Not only are wages low, but the prices of nineteen basic foodstuffs in Djakarta

[21] *Tindjauan Masa'alah Perburuhan,* vol. 10, no. 6, October 1958, p. 10.
[22] *Ibid.,* pp. 19–20.
[23] *Ibid.,* p. 20; for other areas, see p. 21.

rose 77 percent from a base of 100 in 1953 to 177 in 1957, and then, even more rapidly, to 258 in 1958 and to 325 by the end of 1959.[24] None of the wages climbed as rapidly as prices. Payments

Table 7.1. Output of products per month, North Sumatra estates, 1958

Product	Worker	Wife/husband not working	Each child
Rice	18 kilos	12 kilos	9 kilos
Sugar	1 kilo	½ kilo	½ kilo
Salt	½ kilo	¼ kilo	¼ kilo
Dried fish	1½ kilos	1 kilo	½ kilo
Cooking oil	2½ bottles		½ bottle
Kerosene	4 bottles		
Soap	3 bars		½ bar (of 400 grams)
Peas	½ kilo		
Tea	½ kilo		
Textiles	2 meters	1 meter	1 meter (40% price by worker)
Canned milk			1 600 cc. can for each child under ten

in kind, of course, helped to hold up real wages, but the evidence seems clear that real wages have recently declined in most cases.[25]

[24] Central Bureau of Statistics, *Statistik Konjunktur* (*Monthly Survey*), Djakarta, December 1959, p. 76. There is no one satisfactory cost-of-living index in Indonesia. Prices continued to rise in 1960.

[25] Average earnings in Sukabumi rose in 1958 at a much faster rate on the estates than in manufacturing, but these increases were less than the rise in prices:

1958	*Average*	*Plantations*	*Manufacturing*
Mid-January	100	100	100
Mid-April	111.6	112.5	105.4
Mid-July	117.1	118.4	108.2
Mid-October	125.9	128.2	110.0

Source: Ministry of labor, "Note on the Compilation of Index Numbers of Earnings in the Plantation and Manufacturing Industries Sectors in Sukabumi," September 1959, mimeo. The ministry of labor has also reported substantial wage gains from the first quarter of 1957 to the fourth quarter of 1958 in a number of industries in the various provinces. In no case, however, were these gains commensurate with the price increases (*Two Year Report during the Karya Cabinet, April 1957–April 1959,* pp. 80–81).

The present trend toward multiple unions in a given industry is also a factor weakening the position of organized labor. Although management feels that competitive unions mean extravagant demands, labor believes that multiple unionism makes it possible for management to play off one group against the other. Government officials are not in favor of such a division, because it makes their decisions much more complex and difficult.

Some unions tend to join forces in a given area when they have to bargain with the employers. This cooperation perhaps is clearest in the estates on the east coast of Sumatra, where eleven unions cooperated in negotiation with the employers and in appealing to the Regional Disputes Committee, *Panitya Penjelesaian Perselisihan Perburuhan Daerah* (P4D), in Medan and the Central Disputes Committee, *Panitya Penjelesaian, Perselisihan Perburuhan Pusat* (P4P), in Djakarta. A regionwide decree resulted in an agreement for all estates and for all unions in that area. In the early months of 1959, the Government Estates Organization (PPN Baru) was negotiating with the various estate unions for three regional agreements. On March 1, 1958, the four large oil workers' unions signed a common contract with Standard Vacuum Oil Company which provided for no strikes or lockouts for the duration of the agreement.

As trade unions become older and more stable, it is likely that their real strength will increase in many communities even more rapidly than their membership. Conditions vary so much from section to section that generalization is difficult, but it seems likely that in the near future in most areas trade unions will have more political strength than economic power or social prestige. Certainly Indonesian unions today are larger, stronger, and more important than in the colonial period.

The Problems of Management

Just as there have been rapid changes in the labor organizations in Indonesia, so has the role of management also changed. In colonial times, management was largely foreign and, with the government, tended to control labor relations. With the revolution substituting an Indonesian government for a colonial regime, foreign management was put on the defensive politically. Furthermore, some managements found it hard to move rapidly enough from the older, feudalistic, authoritarian, paternalistic attitudes to a newer, constitutional basis. After the revolution, management was no longer in an absolutely dominant position; it was subject to checks by trade unions, public opinion, government legislation, and the ruling of the Central Disputes Committee. Many managements were worried about productivity, discipline, and profits; others were simply confused by changing work patterns, the complex wage payments in money and in kind, conflicting demands of multiple unions, and the uncertain political conditions.

With the take-over of Dutch estates and other businesses starting in December 1957, the role of foreign management was greatly reduced.[26] It has been replaced by Indonesian military and civilian management. Although the full effects of this change have not been experienced, this shift should mean that the antiforeign factor will be reduced, and that lack of experience may become the crucial problem. Because of this shift in management, the radical youth of the unions, and the rapidly changing labor relations picture, examples of organizations with democratic managements based on a community of interest with the unions still will be rare, although the government as manager of the former Dutch estates has tried since 1959 to introduce systems of consultation with the unions.

The Recruitment and Training of a Labor Force

Methods used by the Dutch in colonial times to hire a labor force and to control it by government regulation have had a marked effect on labor-management relations and the attitudes of many Indonesians toward work. Slavery, the "forced cultivation" system, compulsory labor service, and contracts with penal clauses have already been discussed. Traditional patterns of work developed under such systems of compulsion are apt to linger on in strange ways in a newly independent country. As already mentioned, the element of compulsion to work in the colonial period accounted for the feeling on the part of many Indonesians that *merdeka* or freedom meant freedom from work. Managements

[26] There is still some foreign management in Indonesia: European, American, Chinese, Indian, and Arab.

after the revolution complained in many cases about the lack of productivity of the Indonesian worker, the short work week, and the even shorter number of hours that most workers actually performed on a job. Foreign estate managers told of the carelessness of their workers and then regaled the listener with stories of how good it was in the prerevolutionary days. In those "good old days" it was possible for the manager to punish or fine the worker with little or no redress on the worker's part, while at the present time dismissal for cause often involves endless disputes.[27] Employers also pointed to the fact that Indonesia is a tropical country where many workers are not anxious to work long hours. The desire for leisure is strong in the cultural pattern and conflicts with the work standards of modern industry. On the other hand, Indonesian leaders have stressed the danger of this position and urged Indonesians to work harder in order to increase the wealth of the country.

Modern management still faces recruiting, committing, and training problems. By and large, in Sumatra and the other outer islands all the problems are serious, while in Java and Madura, with a large labor supply, the third problem is of primary importance. In all areas there is the task of finding people with specially needed skills, and, if there are not sufficient available, of supplying the necessary training.

The estates on the east coast of Sumatra prior to 1958 hired all their Javanese labor through AVROS, an association of estates in the region. They adopted a policy of not rehiring any estate worker who applied for long leave to go back to Java, since if all the legal conditions were fulfilled this required a considerable payment on the part of the estate. This required AVROS to hire new Javanese, some of whom would not be pleased with Sumatra and might later wish to leave. Furthermore, those who went on long leave might well be among the people who might recruit labor for the plantations. This policy tended to hold a number of Javanese in Sumatra somewhat against their will because they did not want to lose their jobs—a sort of forced commitment. However, there

[27] In the colonial period, corporal punishment was frequently used. A number of estate managers were disliked so intensely by their workers that after the revolution they were attacked, and some of them were killed.

are a number of second-generation Javanese working on the estates who are fully committed and want to remain. GAPPERSU, the Indonesian organization replacing AVROS, still faces a recruitment problem from Java, since many Sumatrans do not like to work on the plantations at what they consider to be "coolie" work.

The oil companies also have programs to recruit Javanese workers, especially through employees already on their payrolls. Such recruiting is frequently done when the worker goes from the oil fields back to Java on his long leave. The high wages in the oil industry, coupled with a variety of fringe benefits, seem to attract sufficient workers. To secure highly trained Indonesian staff employees, however, the companies have to offer good housing and educational facilities for the children. The latter is particularly difficult in some field operations where public schooling is still below the level of that in the major cities of Java. Where good facilities have been provided, the oil companies have been able to secure a permanently committed labor force, but in many of the smaller installations, particularly in Kalimantan (Borneo), the staff employees are apt to want to move after a short term of service.

Management has had to provide training for all types and skills of workers. Even though the number of graduates of commercial and vocational schools is increasing, these students often need some specialized training. Most of this has taken one form or another of on-the-job training. Some of the larger companies, however, have adopted major training programs. They have provided vocational training for those with only a primary education, and technical training for those who have had at least some high school training; at the present time they are offering fellowships to promising young students to complete a university course of studies.[28]

The drive for Indonesianization necessitates further training programs. Indonesians feel that with the coming of independence more of the higher staff positions should be open to them. One

[28] See Massachusetts Institute of Technology, Center for International Studies, Indonesia Project, *Stanvac in Indonesia,* National Planning Association, New York, 1957, esp. pp. 70–78. Shell also has a whole battery of schools and training courses, including an academy to train professional personnel.

way in which this was being accomplished was through the immigration authorities, who made it very difficult for foreigners to take jobs in Indonesia, even if they had worked in Indonesia for a great many years, unless it could be clearly demonstrated that there were no Indonesians available for the positions.[29] Because of such delays, some corporations decided to train Indonesian staff employees. Many Dutch employees prior to 1957 thought twice before applying for an exit permit because of all the difficulties of re-entry.

Some companies have openly publicized their Indonesianization programs, others have been going about it in a quieter fashion. Frequently it involves a period in which an Indonesian employee moves up from serving as an assistant to a foreigner to being a "responsible" officer with a foreign adviser. Until the adviser leaves, this new relationship involves many problems as to who is really in control. In one large oil company, some of the Indonesian staff employees refer to the program as Americanization rather than Indonesianization, because, although the Dutch staff has been greatly reduced, the Indonesian staff has not increased as rapidly as the American staff. Furthermore, many of the new American staff were unfamiliar with Indonesia and the Indonesian language and were so anxious to do a good job that they may inadvertently have taken over some of the functions which under the Dutch had already been passed to Indonesian staff employees. The company looked upon this as a transition phase and emphasized that it takes time to train more Indonesians for senior staff positions. In 1958 and 1959, Shell faced somewhat similar problems as it tried to "internationalize" its staff in a short period of time.

This problem is further complicated because to hire American staff it is necessary to pay salaries comparable to American salaries. This means that in some companies there is a wide discrepancy between those hired in America, those hired in the Commonwealth, those hired in Holland, and those hired in Indonesia. Some managements have done a great deal to reduce differences in local currency payments and perquisites for staff employees hired in Indonesia and abroad. Some of these new perquisites

[29] The Indonesian government, however, gave Stanvac the right to bring in specialists, subject only to a postaudit after they had arrived.

which have gone to Indonesians at the senior level are not widely publicized, since the firm is not in a position to give the same privileges to junior staff and lower-grade employees. Unions have mentioned this discrimination as one of the sources of friction in the oil companies and on the estates. The estate unions granted the fact that since independence a number of Indonesians have been made heads of certain plantation sections and been given homes and jeeps in the same manner as European managers. Basically this question of differences in pay and perquisites, however, is something which is bound to trouble Indonesian labor relations as long as foreigners are employed on foreign scales above Indonesian levels.

In the 1957–1958 take-over of Dutch estates, 2,300 managers were replaced, and Indonesians had to be trained to take their places on 400 estates. An urgent need was created for management training. The *Persatuan Pengusaha Perkebunan Besar Indonesia* or P3BI (formerly *Algemine Landbouw Syndicaat,* ALS) undertook the preparation of 130 correspondence lessons on thirteen subjects, including labor relations, agricultural law, techniques of marketing, insurance, statistics, and management. The universities are stepping up their courses in business management, and special seminars are being planned for Indonesian managers. Training-within-industry (TWI) courses are helpful not only to labor but to management. Certainly much more needs to be done in the training field as well as in the general field of improving labor productivity.

The key question now is whether management offers enough incentive to the workers to secure quality work and higher productivity. In the colonial period, employers could rely on force to secure industrial discipline. With force no longer possible, it is not surprising that many workers feel less compulsion to work hard, regularly, and carefully. Exhortation by the employers, or even by government leaders, has not been enough to improve plant morale, discipline, and productivity. Workers are afraid of, and resist, speed-up methods which they think might result in profits for the employers and more unemployment for labor. Some employers have thrown up their hands in despair, not knowing how to secure discipline without the old force.

Neither management nor labor is fully aware of the implications of the Indonesian revolution. New incentives and new methods must be devised to encourage worker discipline and productivity. Wages have usually been considered a basic incentive for all workers committed to an industrial way of life.[30] Piecework systems have been used in some cases where the work is repetitive and easily measured. But this may not result in a really high level of output, because workers fear working out of a job and because they may also be worried lest a speed-up result in a subsequent reduction in the piece rate. Here is a place where the unions might now provide an effective voice to assure workers that they would have some protection against the abuses of incentive systems.

Management Dealings with Trade Unions

Employer reactions to trade unions have generally been negative. Employers see their prerogatives threatened by these new organizations. The former colonial government generally offered management protection, while the Indonesian government tends to favor the Indonesian workers. Since excessive demands by SOBSI unions have often been exceeded by those of other unions, some managements say that all unions are alike. These employers further claim that none of the unions is realistic or realizes the importance of industrial discipline, increased productivity, or capital investment. Under such circumstances, collective bargaining and mutual concessions are hard to obtain. In fact, one manager said in 1956 that it was his position flatly to oppose all union demands because the union would appeal the case to the Central Disputes Committee which would tend to compromise the case on the basis of the last position of the employer and the union.

Even if management wants to get away from older, paternalistic practices, it is forced to continue many of them, especially on the estates and in the oil industry, where it has to provide housing, recreation, and health facilities for the workers, because none are available. Unions are including demands for more and better

[30] Some Balinese employers still complain that some of their workers are not fully committed to industrial life, since they prefer to have more time to dance than receive higher wages for longer hours of work.

perquisites, and many employers who would like to pay just money wages are required to continue a number of payments in kind.

Most managements realize that they must deal with the unions within the framework of the present labor laws. Some have tried to foster unions within their own plant, and a number of these exist in Indonesia, although they are not the common pattern as in Japan. Other firms have encouraged their own workers to form independent unions in opposition to trade unions belonging to national federations, thus adding to multiple unionism.

A few of the larger firms are spending a great deal of time trying to develop genuine collective bargaining with their employees and their unions. How successful this will be remains to be seen. For example, one firm which had spent months negotiating on the question of long leave with its union found that in another firm this same issue had been taken to arbitration. Obviously the decision of the government arbitration board in the case of the second company might undermine entirely the months of collective bargaining in the first firm. A pattern established either by arbitration or agreement may serve as a model for later decisions.

One of the unusual aspects of union-management relationships in Indonesia is the fact that unions draw their members much further up into management than in many other countries. Foremen and *mandur*s (supervisors) and even chief *mandur*s (chief supervisors) belong to the unions. A great many office workers also belong to the union and are able to supply labor with information concerning the finances of the company. In some plants, leadership for the unions comes from the junior staff and even some of the senior staff, although some companies try to insist that senior staff members should not join the union. Any supervisor who is a member of the union thinks of himself as part of the labor force and not of management. One of the basic problems facing many managements is the lack of a sufficient number of trained, loyal supervisors. This is undoubtedly an important factor in accounting for the low level of productivity. Furthermore, Indonesian managers as well as workers may need incentives to improve efficiency.

Labor relations have become so complicated since the revolution that firms have expanded their industrial relations departments. Some of the important functions to be handled are training, health services, housing, fringe benefits, wages in kind, and labor disputes. In a number of these fields, particularly in handling negotiations with the unions and the government arbitration boards, the large firms have developed Indonesian staff employees to act as spokesmen. Although this is helpful in many cases, sometimes the Indonesian company officials also find it difficult to get along with the Indonesian workers. At the Dolak Merangir plantation of Goodyear in August 1956, the unions struck against the allegedly arbitrary action of the first Indonesian (Batak) who had been made head of the labor department. The company supported its new manager, but later transferred him to other tasks.

The pressure of independence and of the new unions has also created management organizations that specialize in labor relations. From 1950 until 1958, AVROS became the central organization of the rubber producers on the east coast of Sumatra for handling labor recruiting and negotiating with the unions and governmental agencies. The individual estates felt that they were not large enough units to meet the new and growing unions. If they had no central organization, the unions might play off one estate against another. Even the large oil companies believe that the unions are in a position to try to gain an advantage first from one company and then another. For this reason there has been considerable circulation of information about labor relations among the oil companies. Suggestions have been made for a meeting of all the oil companies with the unions. Thus far, because of differences in company policies, this has not been the rule. Other firms have formed trade organizations, one function of which is to deal with the unions. In fact there is a rather sizable list of such employer organizations in Indonesia.[31]

Although many of these groups help their members with labor relations problems, they in turn have organized a special group to give their members advice on labor relations. This is known as

[31] The ministry of labor listed 37 such organizations in 1958—of which 29 had head offices in Djakarta plus several large estates and industrial federations. *Tindjauan Masa'alah Perburuhan,* vol. 10, no. 11–12, March–April, 1959, pp. 17–19.

the Central Consultative Bureau for Social Affairs of Employers, or *Jajasan Badan Permusjawaratan Urusan Sosial Pengusaha di Indonesia.* Its membership consists of sixteen associations made up of 1,463 estates or enterprises and 61 individual firms employing over 875,000 workers.[32] This organization has become Indonesianized and is now known simply as the Federation of Employers' Associations in Indonesia. It does not engage in collective bargaining, nor does it handle specific cases at the P4P, but it provides information to employers and discusses with government officials the employers' points of view on basic labor issues. It includes Indonesian, Chinese, and other foreign employers, and publishes special releases and a *Monthly Bulletin* in both Indonesian and English (formerly Dutch).

Management is now undoubtedly a short factor in Indonesian economic development.[33] It has the enormous task of recruiting and training a labor force, including more personnel in the management group itself. It has the even more crucial task, if Indonesia is to develop, of introducing new systems of incentives geared to the current situation in the country, to raise the level of productivity. This will undoubtedly require a less negative and a more cooperative attitude toward the unions. So far the clashes have largely been between foreign employers and Indonesian workers. Although the anticolonial issue is being buried, there is no certainty that there may not be clashes between Indonesian employers and Indonesian trade unions. Unless the workers through their own organizations believe the new incentives are mutually beneficial, they may resist them, just as scientific management was at first attacked in the United States.

The Role of Government

The government is a key factor in labor relations in Indonesia today. It hires a large number of workers, and the standards which

[32] In 1956, this organization reported 1,723 members and 836,288 workers (ILO, *Report of the Committee on Freedom of Employers' and Workers' Organizations,* Geneva, March 1956).

[33] See Frederick Harbison, "Entrepreneurial Organization as a Factor in Economic Development," *Quarterly Journal of Economics,* vol. 70, no. 3, August 1956, pp. 364–379.

it sets in governmental positions in turn affect local labor markets and local labor conditions. Although there are no general minimum wage laws, the minimum levels established for unskilled government workers in turn set local wage patterns, at least the lower level. Furthermore, the government tries to prevent price increases, especially in rice, to keep real wages from falling.

In the second place, it has instituted a certain amount of labor legislation which tends to protect the rights of the workers. Third, the government has established a system of disputes committees which results in almost universal compulsory arbitration rather than direct collective bargaining between management and labor to settle the terms of the labor contract. Fourth, starting in 1957 the military arm of the government has taken an increasing part in labor affairs. In March 1957, a State of War and Siege was declared, and in August 1957, a specific strike ban was issued for essential industries. Starting in December 1957, when a few unions began taking over Dutch properties, the government itself, as in 1945–1946, decided that the take-over must be in its hands, and military administrators were appointed by regional commanders to supervise the operations. In 1958, the government established four new organizations consisting of civilian officials and representatives of the army to take over and run the former Dutch properties.

Finally, the government of Indonesia, and particularly the parliament, is made up of people from a variety of political parties, each interested in promoting its own trade union. Furthermore, the minister of labor is a key figure, much more so than the secretary of labor in the United States. One former minister of labor became a prime minister and head of the Constituent Assembly. Several cabinet ministers and members of parliament have been associated with important trade union groups. The present minister of labor is the head of KBKI, the nationalist-oriented federation of labor.

The Government as Entrepreneur or Intitiator of Development

The government of Indonesia is a large employer of labor. The number of government workers was estimated in 1958 at about 1,800,000, including all national, provincial, and local government workers as well as those employed by government corporations, such as the railroads, public utilities, and government-owned estates—not including those businesses taken over from the Dutch. In spite of recommendations by some finance ministers to cut the number of bureaucrats in order to reduce government deficits, government employment has not declined, and in fact is apt to increase as the government takes over various business enterprises. As mentioned above, although the Five Year Plan, 1956–1960, called for a modest series of proposals rather than an overall program like the one in India, and although parts of the program were pushed aside because of political and security problems, a new National Planning Council was appointed in 1959 to work out a comprehensive plan. In the meantime the government has started a program of shops to distribute rice and cloth to the people. Whatever plan is proposed, one of the critical questions will be the foreign investments needed to supplement the meagre supply of domestic capital.

Since independence, the Indonesian government has followed a somewhat contradictory policy on foreign investment. On the one hand, it has been afraid that foreign investments might mean more, or new types of, imperialistic, colonial controls, and there has therefore been a tendency to avoid foreign capital. Old foreign investments, primarily Dutch, were supervised closely so that only a fraction of the profits might be repatriated. The take-over of Dutch properties starting in December 1957, of Kuomintang Chinese in 1958, and of mainland Chinese in rural trade in 1959, has not been encouraging to private foreign capital. On the other hand, a number of high government officials have recognized the necessity for foreign capital in a country where savings and investment are as low as in Indonesia. These officials have talked about encouraging foreign capital. President Sukarno himself made a statement favoring foreign capital while he was in the United States in 1956, and a bill to protect foreign investment was finally passed by the parliament late in 1958. Thus far, outside of the oil industry and one or two other exceptions, there has been little private foreign capital going to Indonesia since 1949.

Undoubtedly one of the factors which has made some foreign

concerns reluctant to make new investments in Indonesia has been the unsettled labor conditions. Labor conditions by themselves are not the only or even the most significant factor. Employers have cited other issues such as high taxation, difficulties in repatriation of profits, complex problems in foreign exchange controls, difficulties in importing essential capital goods and equipment at reasonable prices, and the long delays involved in securing entrance visas for foreign management experts. Unsettled financial conditions, inflation, and restriction on monetary movements have also played their part. In certain sections of the country, insecurity problems are serious, and in others the problems of squatters and land tenure make it difficult for estate managers to make long-term investments and commitments.

The current level of wages in Indonesia is not usually a serious problem for most foreign employers, if they could be assured of a reasonable level of output. The problem is not the seven-hour work day, but the fact that a number of people work less than a full day. Without any assurances on labor productivity, although money wage rates are low in relation to wages in other countries, the employer argues that labor costs are high. Labor disputes and strikes have been annoying, but their number and duration have declined substantially.

In judging whether there will be sufficient foreign investment in Indonesia, no one factor will be crucial. The general feeling of foreign investors is a great deal more significant. Labor problems may be a contributing factor to uncertainty, but by and large they are not the controlling factor. The reluctance of many foreign investors and the lack of a large, indigenous group of Indonesian employers, make the government turn to foreign government loans.

The United States, through the Export-Import Bank, has lent over $100 million to Indonesia, and has made grants since 1950 for technical assistance, and lent money to purchase rice and other agricultural surplus crops against repayments in rupiah. Indonesia has also received grants from other European countries, the Colombo Plan, and the United Nations, and more recently has signed loan agreements with China and the Soviet Union. Mr. Khrushchev, during his 1960 visit to Indonesia, agreed to loans of

$250 million in addition to the $100 million formerly agreed upon with the Indonesian government. The reparations agreement with Japan also provides for both development grants and loans.

The level of productivity is an important factor for all government development enterprises. One of the largest of these is the new cement plant at Gresik in East Java, near Surabaja, financed by the Bank Industri Negara and an Export-Import loan. The cement plant was constructed by an American engineering firm, Morris and Knudsen, which signed a contract with the Mineworkers' Union stating that it was hiring workers only for a temporary period of construction, and that when the construction was over the contract with the laborers would be terminated on payment of dismissal compensation. Already in 1956 there were signs that the union was anxious to continue to hold the same number of positions after the transfer of the finished plant to the operating agency of the Indonesian government. If this demand of the mineworkers were secured, the plans of the government to provide cement at lower costs and lower prices to the Indonesian economy would vanish. The manager of the cement plant was conscious of this problem, but union pressures on government plants are apt to be great. This problem of excess manpower was also an issue in the privately owned cement plant in Padang, Central Sumatra, which was taken over by the government. The government as an employer, therefore, faces the problem of the number of workers it will employ. Certainly the large number of employees attached to all government bureaus does not augur well for a low-cost, small work force in government enterprises. Here is an area of real conflict between the "job-conscious" unions and the government.

Another major conflict arises in the Indonesian government's attitude toward strikes. In general the government is prolabor, but believes it must prohibit strikes in time of emergencies, while the unions want to preserve the right to strike. Workers in plants taken over from the Dutch and in certain other establishments supervised by the government are subject to the general strike measures discussed in the next section, but in 1956 the government ruled against strikes of railroad workers, stressing their role as government workers. Labor disputes of government employees are not handled by the regular Central Disputes Committee, and government workers cannot engage in regular forms of collective bargaining, since their wages, hours, and working conditions are set by legislation. This, of course, does not keep the unions from agitating for improvements in the scale of government salaries. In 1956, the pay for government workers was raised, but many of the unions felt that this was inadequate to meet the rising cost of living. Some increases were given in 1957 to higher ranks, but in 1958 the pressure was strong for increased salaries for all government workers in the face of rising prices. The government will always find itself in a predicament as inflation caused by internal emergencies or by stepped-up development plans creates pressure for higher wages and salaries.

Since 1945, the government has done nothing to discourage unionization of government workers, and union membership is high among them. Each department may have its own union or group of competing unions. The railroad workers are divided into two major unions, and the workers on government estates belong to one of a dozen or more unions to which private estate employees belong. Although these government unions are limited in their bargaining and strike activities, they still play an important part in the Indonesian labor scene. Many of their members give leadership to other unions, and they exert pressure on cabinet officials and political parties to take prolabor stands.

Regulatory Policies

Indonesia is a country with relatively little labor legislation but a good deal of labor regulation. The most important labor laws in Indonesia are the Labor Code (Conditions of Employment), the Labor Disputes Acts of 1951 and 1957, the Workmen's Compensation Law, and the Collective Agreements Law. A number of specific bills have been proposed but not adopted because it was frequently difficult under the Provisional Constitution of 1950 to secure the necessary cabinet clearance, the parliamentary committee approval, and final passage by parliament. In the meantime, decrees or circular letters were frequently used by the ministry of labor to cover such subjects as the voluntary registration of unions, holidays, time off for election, and notification by employers of mass dismissals of ten or more workers. The decisions of the P4D and the P4P [34] are perhaps even more important in the labor relations field because these decisions cover a number of items not yet subject to specific laws. For example, the Central Disputes Committee has handed down binding decisions requiring employers to give one to four months' notice before dismissal, except for cause. Similar decisions have been made on almost all problems facing management and labor. In fact these decisions are generally a substitute for the system of free collective bargaining in the United States and Western European countries.

Although some Dutch colonial labor legislation dated back to the nineteenth century, it was not until after the institution of the Ethical Policy in 1901 that such protective measures were adopted as the appointment in 1904 of labor inspectors to supervise labor recruitment and labor contracts, the passage of the Factories Act of 1905 to prevent accidents, and the gradual cession to the Labor Bureau of greater responsibilities, such as the enforcement of regulations concerning child labor, the employment of women at night, safety standards in hazardous industries, and workmen's compensation. Although considerable new or improved legislation was passed in the 1930's, Indonesians felt that much of it applied to Dutch employees rather than to all labor. For example, special regulations were passed for estate assistants, most of whom were foreigners. In general the provisions of the Civil Code applied to European employees and to a few higher-paid Indonesians and other Asians who held jobs similar to those of Europeans. Only a very brief section applied to Indonesian workers. At the outbreak of World War II, several military ordinances tightened the provisions included in the penal code of 1923 against strikes or picketing which were against the public interest, and a tripartite Commission of Labor Affairs was formed to advise on labor problems and to issue binding decisions in labor-management disputes.

During the struggles with the Dutch, the Republic of Indonesia began to develop its own labor legislation. After the granting of

[34] P4D is the abbreviation used by Indonesians rather than PPPPD. The D stands for Regional. In P4P, the last P stands for Central. Both of these abbreviations are used widely in labor circles.

sovereignty and the formation of a unitary state, the government had to adopt labor legislation for the whole of Indonesia.

In Law no. 1 of 1951, parliament determined that the Labor Code of 1948 should become the law of the land for all of Indonesia.[35] This particular act is still in the process of development as the ministry of labor applies certain sections to more and more groups of workers. In general the law provides for a seven-hour day, a forty-hour week, with a weekly day of rest and holidays free.[36] It requires monthly days of rest and maternity leave of 3 months for women. It sets limits on the employment of children under 14, youths 14 to 18, and women. It provides for two weeks' vacation, and more recently the three-months'-long-leave sections have been applied to certain large corporations by the Central Disputes Committee. The law also requires that places of work and workers' living accommodations meet certain sanitary and hygienic standards to be established by the labor inspectors. Although penalties are provided for violations and the ministry of labor is charged with enforcement, it is impossible, with the present staff, to secure complete compliance. The unions insist, however, that the larger firms at least meet the standards provided by the Labor Code.

By all odds the most important of the 1951 labor regulations was Emergency Act no. 16, promulgated by the president on October 22, 1951, which established the basic pattern for handling labor disputes and which remained in operation until June 1958, when Law no. 22 of 1957 came into operation.[37] The act did not prohibit strikes but regulated carefully the handling of disputes with a view to minimizing the number of strikes.

[35] An English text for Law no. 1 of 1951 has been published by the ILO Legislative Series of Indonesia. The author also has had access to a compilation of *Labor Legislation of the Republic of Indonesia 1951–1959,* prepared by N. V. Standard Vacuum Petroleum Company, Djakarta, December 1957.

[36] Government Regulation no. 4, 1951, requires employers to secure permission from the Labor Inspection Service for longer working hours.

[37] This Act was preceded by an ordinance of the ministry of defense dated February 13, 1951, prohibiting strikes and lockouts in vital undertakings, because early in 1950 the number of strikes, especially on the estates, grew so rapidly that the cabinet became worried that they were disrupting the economy.

Basically the administration of labor disputes was handled at three levels, the local, the regional, and the national. In addition, there were special provisions for voluntary arbitration, which were not frequently used, and for *ad hoc* investigating committees which might be appointed to study particularly difficult cases. Although the act planned to have as much of the work as possible done at the local level where the disputes originated, in practice a great majority of the cases were appealed to the national level. The ministry of labor, in most of the key cities, had a chief of the industrial relations department whose obligation it was to be informed about all impending labor disputes and to offer his services as a mediator. If either of the parties was not satisfied at the local level, he had to file the dispute with the Regional Disputes Committee (P4D). For three weeks after filing the case, or longer if the P4D so ruled, no strikes or lockouts were legal. A ministry of labor official headed the P4D; the other six members were representatives of other ministries. They themselves, or their deputies, went to the scene of the dispute and tried to mediate it. They could also issue recommendations, but these were not binding on the parties. Unfortunately, most of the disputes were not settled by these recommendations, since one side or the other, more frequently labor, usually felt it to its advantage to appeal the case to the Central Disputes Committee (P4P) in Djakarta. The P4P from 1951 to 1958 handled 8,500 cases, or over one-third of the more than 22,000 disputes referred to the ministry of labor.[38]

When the case arrived at the P4P in Djakarta, it was generally turned over to one of the three major divisions: agriculture, manufacturing, or other industries. The case might be specifically referred to a representative from one of the seven ministries included on the P4P. Although each case was handled on its merits, there was a tendency for P4P, in the light of existing law, agreements, usage, equity and the interest of the state, to look to previ-

[38] There was considerable divergence between the number of cases settled at the local and regional levels in various areas of Indonesia. For example, the industrial relations officials in Jogjakarta were able to handle a number of cases at the local level before referring them to the regional headquarters at Semarang. On the other hand, the Medan regional office in North Sumatra referred about 95 percent of their cases to Djakarta for solution.

ous cases and to establish certain rules which became widely accepted practices. Furthermore, P4P tended to lump together cases of a similar character and hand down one general ruling. For example, rulings were handed down for all the estates and all the unions on the east coast of Sumatra. In East Java, although separate decisions were made for each of the estate unions, the decisions were based on the same principles.

Individual discharge cases received a great deal of attention from the local officers, regional boards and even the P4P. This resulted in delays in handling the major disputes, which often involved a variety of issues. In such complicated cases the P4P might make a ruling on certain of the issues and then, to study other complex points, would appoint an *ad hoc* investigating committee made up of representatives of the various ministries particularly concerned in this dispute. This investigating committee reported to the full P4P before a final decision was made. For example, the P4P established a study committee on pensions in the 1956 estates dispute on the east coast of Sumatra. A second board was set up to study the issue of yearly bonuses. In some cases, therefore, before one dispute was settled in its entirety another might have begun. Labor relations were in a state of constant flux, with no real periods of quiet.

The decisions of the P4P might be in the form of a simple recommendation, but since it was known in advance, because of the long preliminary stages, that one side or the other would not accept a mere recommendation, most of the decisions of the P4P were binding in character. This meant that most labor disputes in Indonesia were really settled by compulsory arbitration rather than by collective bargaining. The P4P could appeal to the courts for enforcement of its decisions. There was a tendency prior to 1957 not to take illegal strike cases to the public prosecutor.

Although cases were handled individually and conditions changed, these decisions developed into a system of industrial jurisprudence which in many respects supplements the Labor Code. One cannot understand labor legislation in Indonesia without a knowledge of the major P4P decisions.[39]

[39] The Board sends its decisions to the management and labor perticipants, while important cases are reported in the newspapers. The ministry of labor

In the light of the above machinery, what has been the record on (a) disputes not resulting in loss of work, and on (b) strikes or work stoppages? These results should be studied in two parts, from 1950 to 1956, and then from 1957 on, after the emergency strike ban was in effect. The number of disputes rose from 180 in 1950, to 3,891 cases officially filed with the ministry of labor in 1956.[40] Strikes also tended to increase from 1950 to 1956 (1953 actually being the highest year), but the number of workers involved has decreased and the number of working hours lost by strikes has declined markedly from 54 million hours in 1950 to less than 7 million in 1956. These trends reflect the greater experience of unions and management in labor relations, the use of shorter strike techniques, and the increasing effectiveness of the mediation and arbitration machinery. Furthermore, although over 3,100,000 workers were involved in labor disputes in 1956, the number of workers actually on strike was less than 11 percent of those involved in disputes. The three largest causes for disputes and strikes were wages, discharge, and special allowances.

In comparison with 1956, the figures show a rise in 1957 in both the number of disputes and the number of workers involved. The strike figures, however, indicate a very marked decrease in 1957, if the million workers who lost over seven million manhours of work in the short protest strikes against the Dutch position in West Irian are excluded. The 1958 figures show a further decline to a negligible amount of 98,000 hours of work lost through strikes. On the other hand, there were 3,350 disputes involving about three million workers.

Ever since the Emergency Act no. 16 of 1951 was promulgated, plans had been under way to amend the law or to put it on a permanent basis. A number of proposals were made, including a

---

issues mimeographed books containing the cases in serial order, but these are not for general circulation. They do, however, index the disputes by the contestants and in terms of the major question involved, such as individual discharge cases, mass dismissals, wages, bonuses, vacation pay, and other topics.

[40] The 1953 change in the definition of disputes, to include only those which were submitted to the ministry of labor, may account in part for the decrease in number of disputes from 1952 to 1953.

specific bill which was discussed by the parliamentary section of labor in 1956 after receiving cabinet approval. Some specific provisions were disliked by organized labor, some by management, and some by certain legislators. At that time several general criticisms about the 1951 act and the proposed amendments were also voiced. A few labor leaders, management spokesmen, government officials, and foreign advisers suggested that the system should be completely changed to get away from compulsory arbitration. One labor leader conceded that this would not reduce disputes in the first year or two but argued that, after a period of trial and error, unions would be forced to take more responsible positions, to carry through collective negotiations, and to reach amicable decisions. One representative of a large estate group had a similar idea, although he recognized that many of the smaller estates would fear such a decision because during the first year or two conditions might became so intolerable that they would have to go out of business. Similarly, some of the smaller unions did not like this proposal because only the stronger unions could withstand the strikes which might develop. Furthermore, the smaller unions might not be able to secure recognition by the employers. Some labor advisers suggested that to avoid multiple unionization, P4P, like the NLRB in the United States, should have the power to hold elections and to determine who represented the majority of the workers, the group which secured the majority being given exclusive bargaining power. Such a suggestion has been attacked in Indonesia as undemocratic, since it would eliminate the smaller unions. Furthermore, some of the noncommunist unions have opposed such a measure on the ground that it would play directly into the hands of the largest labor group, SOBSI. No such radical change was politically feasible, since the initial disruption to the economy might be so great that the cabinet in office would fall. It was much safer for the government to continue to use its power of compulsory arbitration, even its right to forbid certain strikes, to preserve a quasipeace in industrial relations and to allow production to continue.

Parliament finally passed a new law, the Settlement of Labor Disputes Act no. 22 of 1957, which was promulgated on April 8, 1957, and came into effect in June 1958. The present law includes most of the features of the 1951 act, with three major changes: an attempt to have more cases settled at the local and regional level, a plan to include worker and management representatives on the committees, and the right of the minister of labor to veto the decisions of the P4P.

The first change provides that all possible steps must be taken by the union and the employer to settle a dispute themselves before referring it to the Labor Relations Office of the minister of labor for mediation. Moreover, if either labor or management wants to take action against the other it must give written notice to the Regional Disputes Committee (P4D) specifying that negotiations have been attempted through a government mediator, or that the other party has refused to negotiate, or that twice in the last two weeks the requesting party has tried in vain to induce the other party to negotiate. Such action may be taken only after official confirmation from the chairman of the P4D, which shall be given within seven days after receipt of the notice. In addition to the right to make recommendations in the 1951 act, the P4D is given the right to make binding decisions at the regional level in certain cases involving local issues and individual discharge cases. This has relieved the national P4P of a great many time-consuming disputes which have only local significance.

The second new provision involves functional representation of labor and management as well as the government at both the regional and national levels. The original proposal of five government, three labor, and three management representatives was modified to five, five, and five, with the further provision that five deputies be appointed to represent each group. This has made it possible to have a wide representation of both trade unions and employer organizations, which might have been politically difficult if a smaller number had to be chosen. In Djakarta, the Central Disputes Committee has been divided into two subcommittees: one handles cases arising in agriculture, in commerce and on the docks; and the other takes industry and other cases. Each committee includes some regular members and some deputies, so that for all practical purposes the deputies have as much voice as the regular members. All the appointments were made by the president on the basis of slates prepared by the ministry of labor on recommendations from labor and employer organizations. Once sworn in, all members and deputies are supposed to consider the public interest, not to grant special favors, and not to represent their own particular organization.[41]

In the third place, the minister of labor may within fourteen days of a P4P decision suspend or reverse it, "in case he considers such necessary to ensure public order and to protect the State's interest." As finally provided in Article 17, this veto power of the minister of labor can be exercised only after consulting the ministers having representatives on the P4P. Although up until January, 1960, this veto had not been exercised, there is the possibility that important cases might be appealed to the minister of labor, thus introducing another layer in public mediation and arbitration of labor disputes.

During the period just before the dispute goes to the government and while it is being mediated or handled by the P4D, a special inquiry committee, or the minister of labor, or while it is being submitted to outside arbitration, neither labor nor management may change the labor conditions or take any retaliatory action such as a strike or lockout. Although the new law encourages more decisions at the local and regional levels and prescribes relatively short periods for normal consideration, in important cases strikes may be postponed for a long time until a final decision is reached.

Experience with the new machinery indicates a great reduction in the load of the Central Disputes Committee (P4P), because the regional committee (P4D) can issue binding decisions which cannot be appealed unless the issue involves more than one region or industry. The case load has also been reduced because of the emergency situation in the country, with workers knowing that they have no right to strike. Of the 102 cases before the P4P from January to July 1959, about half (52) dealt with wages, other important topics being dismissals, labor relations, and housing.

[41] Government Regulation no. 51 of 1957 covers the appointment and discharge of the chairman, members, and deputy members of the Central Settlement Committee. See also Government Regulation no. 50 of 1957 and Regulations of the Ministry of Labor, nos. 6 and 7 of 1958, which provide for various procedural rules governing P4P, P4D, and their secretariats.

The new tripartite boards seemed to be working together quite harmoniously. More than 90 percent of the cases heard by P4P the first year were decided unanimously. In general the new law was preferred to the old one, but some observers were skeptical about how much the change in labor relations could be attributed to the administration of the new law and how much to military and political conditions within the country.

One of the most important of these conditions is the strike ban instituted in 1957 as part of the emergency security measures which gave military commanders broad authority in their respective territories. In order to implement the joint statement of the war administrator and minister of labor of October 10, 1957, stating that workers as a functional group should assist and cooperate with the government in its efforts to solve national problems, the Chief of Staff, General Nasution, issued orders on November 6, 1957, establishing a Central Labor-Military Organization, *Badan Kerdja Sama Buruh dan Militer* (BKS *Bumil*). On December 12, 1957, after the break with the Dutch in Indonesia, representatives of fourteen labor organizations, consisting of eleven of the federations of labor and three special groups of bank employees, civil servants, and workers of foreign-owned concerns, signed a charter of cooperation with the military administrator. Because of the importance of the struggle for West Irian, the working program dated January 13, 1958, gave top priority to coordination with the West Irian Liberation Front. *Bumil* was to see that in the firms taken over from the Dutch the workers did their duty, that no sabotage took place, and that the plants were kept in good running condition. *Bumil* was also to make suggestions as to how to absorb workers who had lost their employment as a result of the West Irian struggle. Each of the fourteen labor groups appointed a permanent and an alternate member to the labor consultative council which was to advise the military commander on matters in the labor field. The chairman, vice-chairman, and heads of financial administration and information bureaus were military men, but the security, the economic, and the social affairs divisions were each headed by three union representatives. In addition to the central organization, *Bumil* established regional (*Daerah*) offices in such cities as Semarang and Medan, and sub-regional offices in cities like Jogjakarta and Balikpapan. In each place a military man was in charge of *Bumil* with representatives from all the labor organizations in the region. Its charter provided that *Bumil* should not enter into the internal affairs of the unions, and that all expenses would be charged to the military organization.

Since one of the purposes of this organization was to provide industrial peace, some of the unions began to appeal their labor disputes to *Bumil.* This brought *Bumil* into conflict with the regular arbitration machinery of the government. The issue was resolved by maintaining the jurisdiction of P4P and P4D over regular dispute cases. Though P4P itself has no direct representation at *Bumil,* the ministry of labor maintains a liaison officer. There is no question that the military commanders have been active in preventing strikes and political demonstrations.[42]

Labor has tried to gain concessions from *Bumil,* and the latter has kept strong unions in line. Some of the smaller unions have used their positions in *Bumil* to try to secure more prestige. One union official was frank enough to admit that he appointed one of his officers to *Bumil* so he could draw a salary, since it was hard for the union to collect dues because there could be no strikes.

Some of the top military leaders, however, had hoped their organization might lead to a united labor movement. On certain broad labor issues like higher wages, all the union groups were united, but on political issues, groupings tended to follow along ideological lines. Although a number of informal meetings have been held among noncommunist trade unions with a view to securing greater unity, most of these efforts have resulted in *ad hoc* working cooperation rather than unity.

President Sukarno and his followers are interested in forming a new National Front which would include the military and all political and functional organizations. In July 1960, the minister of labor held a conference of all the leading labor unions and numerous government bodies to discuss a draft regulation for the estab-

[42] In 1960, at Palembang a PERBUM leader was jailed for an illegal strike of wax-workers (*Times of Indonesia,* February 16, 1960, p. 4). SOBSI was barred from demonstrating against the explosion of the French atom bomb in the Sahara (*Ibid.,* February 25, 1960, p. 4).

lishment of an all-embracing Labor Front (*Organisasi Persatuan Pekerdja Indonesia,* OPPI). SOSBI refused to approve the plan, while a number of specific modifications were proposed by other labor leaders.[43] Despite the backing of the President and his minister of labor, it appears that voluntary unity among all labor groups is not to be realized in the immediate future.

The government is ubiquitous in the field of labor relations. It is a large employer of civil servants, it manages a great variety of business, it provides for tripartite labor disputes and arbitration machinery. Through the military it has established the Labor-Military Organization. The President, with the assistance of his minister of labor, who is head of one of the largest federations of labor, is trying to establish an all-embracing Labor Front. Labor representatives have been appointed to the new parliament and major councils of the country. In a labor dispute today a union may deal with a government organization such as the estate organization PPN *Baru,* which is composed of both civilian and military officials, and then appeal the case to a tripartite body on which the unions, the employers, and the government have an equal voice. The employer group may be able to appeal to the military commander, as may the representatives of the union. The union may also seek help from the labor members of parliament or the National Planning Council. The extent to which collective bargaining between management and labor can be carried on in this atmosphere is difficult to judge. It is likely that some collective bargining will continue, with frequent appeals to government agencies. As long as a state of emergency exists in Indonesia the military will play an important part in labor relations. As long as President Sukarno pushes for a "Guided Economy," the civilian government will continue to become more actively enmeshed in labor problems.

Conclusions

Industrial relations in Indonesia reflect a transition from a colonial to a nationalist economy, in which older autocratic and pa-

43 Department of Labor Affairs, Government of Indonesia, "Conference on Presidential Draft Regulation on the Establishment of the Indonesian Workers' Association Organization, July, 1960," Djakarta, 1960, mimeo.

ternalistic attitudes and policies still linger on. The country is trying to move from an agricultural economy with raw material exports to a more commercialized and industrial base, but as yet no plan of rapid economic development has been implemented. The labor force of 35 to 40 million persons out of a population of about 90 million is made up largely of farmers and other self-employed individuals. Only about eight million people are employed by others, including the government, for wages or salaries. Population densities vary so much that there is surplus labor in Java, Madura, and Bali, while there is a relative scarcity of labor in Sumatra, Sulawesi, and some of the other islands. In all areas the number of skilled professional and managerial personnel is very small indeed.

Trade unions were born with the rise of nationalism; they were part of the active phase of the revolution against the Dutch from 1945 to 1949; and they still are one of the major protest forces in the country. These relatively new organizations, with the vigor and enthusiasm of youth, have risen in importance since 1945. They face a series of problems, including multiple unionism with various political and ideological ties, a shortage of experienced and trained leaders, lack of an active and educated dues-paying rank-and-file, and an insufficient appreciation of the necessity of productivity and economic development.

Management is no longer predominantly foreign, as it was in colonial times and even up to 1957. The remaining foreign managers face real difficulties in adjusting to their new political and social position and in adapting their labor relations practices to current conditions. More and more, management is becoming Indonesianized. Whatever the nationality, whether private or government, management faces the key problems of eliminating older practices based on force, of training more supervisors, and of finding incentives which will tend to stimulate workers to higher levels of productivity. The scarcity of sufficient trained managers is a real bottleneck to industrialization and economic development.

The government is an ever-present factor in labor relations in Indonesia, as in many other newly nationalistic economies that have overthrown colonial control. The government has its own labor problems as a large employer, both in its regular departments and in various types of enterprises. It has formed new organizations to run the estates and other enterprises taken over from the Dutch. It has organized a ministry of labor, and some labor legislation has been adopted, the most important providing for tripartite arbitration of labor disputes. This system has tended to be a substitute for free union-management negotiations, although there is some evidence of increasing use of collective bargaining, subject always to appeal to arbitration. It is unlikely in the near future that the government will take its hands off labor relations or give up its power to arbitrate disputes or to declare strikes illegal in times of emergency. Nor will the military give up its power in the labor relations field as long as a state of emergency exists.

The future of labor relations in Indonesia is dependent upon the economic, social, and political developments of the country. Indonesia is passing through the long, second stage of its revolution, the more difficult phase because, unlike the active phase where almost all the people rallied against the colonial power, there is no great positive area of agreement. Sukarno is trying to have a "guided democracy" with an increasing number of national controls over all phases of life. There are indications that not all of the federations of labor are willing voluntarily to join his proposed Labor Front.

The great danger in Indonesia is drift, in which there will be some attempts at political stability and some measures for economic development, but no concerted and coordinated effort to achieve these twin objectives. Such a drift may lead to more and more regional revolts, military coups, serious shortages, and further economic deterioration.

If, as many people hope, political problems can be resolved and a good deal of effort is put forth in the field of economic development, the government, the unions, and management may be able to replace older policies such as low subsistence wages, low output, and employment of extra workers, with new industrial relations practices geared toward increasing the level of production and the standard of living of the people. During this period of concentrated effort to secure economic development, however, some checks on wage-price policy may have to be introduced by the government, as in other developing countries. In the long run, the gains from political stability and economic development would seem to hold out the most hope for an increase in the standard of living of labor, farmers, and the rest of the people of Indonesia.

Addendum: Recent Developments in Organized Labor[44]

Indonesian unions in the last half of the 1960's and the start of the 1970's continue to be fragmented and greatly influenced by internal political events. SOBSI, the largest and strongest trade union in the Sukarno period, was outlawed along with the Communist party and its other functional organizations after the abortive coup of 1965. Most of its leaders and activists were arrested and some of them executed in the violent aftermath, while its ordinary members were ruled ineligible to join other unions.

Since then, in spite of several attempts to unify the labor movement, the noncommunist unions have remained fragmented with a number of splits having taken place. Probably the four largest unions, in alphabetical order, are: GASBIINDO, an independent Moslem union, which has some leadership ties to the new Moslem party of Indonesia (PMI); KBM, which is tied to the Nationalist party of Indonesia (PNI); KONGKARBU SOKSI, which was organized by the military during the Sukarno regime especially for government firms and estates; and SARBUMUSI, which has always been identified with the conservative Moslem party, *Nahdatul Ulama.* None of these organizations yet approaches the old strength of SOBSI.

The Joint Secretariat of Trade Union Federations (SEKBUR), with 10 organizations affiliated, weathered the various political storms of the 1960's with the guidance of the ministers of labor, and (later) ministers of manpower. A larger, more inclusive, group was formed at the end of the 1960's, the Workers' Consultative Council, *Madjelis Permusjawaratan Buruh Indonesia* (MPBI). This group comprises twenty-five member organizations, including all ten unions in SEKBUR—but each keeps its own organization and identity. There is some talk of GASBIINDO, SARBUMUSI,

[44] The following summary of recent developments was written for publication in the present volume in April 1970.

and KBM getting together, but it seems that plural unionism is still entrenched in Indonesia.

The political power of the unions is not great because the party system was weakened by Sukarno, and the New Order (*Orde Baru*), dominated by the military since 1965, has not encouraged political parties nor their labor unions. The PNI has been watched very closely because of earlier connections with Sukarno. As the time approaches for the elections of 1971, however, the PNI seems to be gathering strength and government favor. It is hard to predict how much strength the parties will gain during and after the elections. To the extent that some gain power, their affiliated unions will also gain strength.

In other countries, independent trade unions have not tended to flourish under regimes where the predominant power is military. Frequently the military have tried to channel labor organizations. *Bumil* has faded away and KABI, which was formed as a joint labor action group along with KAMI and KAPPI (the student organizations which played such an active part in the overthrow of Sukarno) never played a strong role and seemed to be declining rapidly early in 1970.

The labor supply is so great relative to demand that wages are low and the unions have little economic bargaining power. To the extent that government policy provides for more economic growth through the Five Year Plan for 1969–1974 (and through other economic policy measures), and especially as the domestic and foreign private sectors grow, some unions may gain strength.

The change of the name of the ministry of labor to the ministry of manpower (*Tenaga Kerdja*) involves a real shift in emphasis, indicating the Suharto government's interest in manpower planning as part of the Five Year Plan. Rationalization of the Civil Service comes under this ministry as do the more traditional fields of industrial relations and administration of labor legislation.

A large body of manpower data was collected in the 1960's by the Census of 1961 and the Social Economic Surveys I, II, and III of 1963–1964, 1964–1965, and 1967. The Census of 1961 showed about 35 million in the labor force out of a total population of 97 million. In 1970 the estimated population is 120 million, with approximately 45 million in the labor force. Agriculture, forestry, and fishing still account for about 70 percent of the labor force with services, commerce, and manufacturing following in that order. Self-employed or independent workers still exceed wage and salary workers, while unpaid family workers have declined relative to the other two groups.

Labor legislation did not substantially change in the 1960's. Labor has the right to organize, except under the Communist-SOBSI banner. Labor disputes in the private sector are still handled by conciliation and arbitration at the local, regional, and national levels under Law no. 22 of 1957, so that few disputes resulting in strikes were reported during the 1960's. Strikes in essential industries are still prohibited. At the time of this writing, the parliament is working on new labor legislation. The prospects of labor in Indonesia in the 1970's, therefore, depend to a large extent on future, somewhat uncertain, political and economic developments.

PART IV

INDUSTRY

Manufacturing industry in Indonesia remains, in the late 1960's, predominantly very small scale and dominated by hand labor rather than machinery. Total employment in manufacturing constitutes only 6 percent of the employed labor force, and total output of the manufacturing sector is barely one-tenth of net national product.[1] The oil industry is not included in manufacturing industry in official Indonesian statistics, being regarded for such purposes as part of the mining industry. However, it is the most modern and dynamic sector in the Indonesian economy. It contrasts strikingly with the textile industry. The one is the hope and the other the despair of the current Indonesian development effort. Early estimates indicate that production and export of crude oil expanded by 17 percent in 1967,[2] and the interest of foreign investors in the industry continues to be enthusiastic. Five new exploration contracts were signed between PERMINA (the Indonesian state company responsible for exploration) and foreign enterprises in 1966–1967.

By contrast, the Indonesian textile industry operated in 1967 at less than one-third of capacity.[3] The elimination of controlled pricing in the industry in 1966 and the subsequent exposure to

[1] The former figure is from Nugroho, *Indonesia Facts and Figures*, Djakarta, 1967, p. 112; the latter from the same source, p. 537.

[2] *Far Eastern Economic Review, 1968 Yearbook*, p. 203.

[3] J. Panglaykim, D. H. Penny, and Dahlan Thalib, "Survey of Recent Developments," *Bulletin of Indonesian Economic Studies* (*BIES*), no. 9, February 1968.

international competition have revealed the inefficiency of many firms, and the structural imbalance between spinning, weaving, and finishing hampers even the most efficient firms. To some extent the malaise of the textile industry may be laid to bad handling of imports of finished textiles and raw materials. In particular, the careless flooding of the market in 1966, in anticipation of the *Lebaran* holiday is often cited. However, most observers agree that the basic problem is one of bad planning and overprotection in the past.

Solution of this sort of structural problem and the finding of new means for expanding nonagricultural employment is basic to the problem of planning Indonesia's economic development program. At least two million people are already overtly unemployed, most of them in the cities. Another million persons, roughly, are added to the labor force annually. Both the agricultural sector and the public sector suffer from labor redundancy and disguised unemployment. Hence manufacturing, mining, and trade must bear a heavy burden in any successful labor absorption effort.

At the same time, the failure of Indonesia's manufacturing sector to grow has made her dependent on imports of manufactures of virtually everything except petroleum products. Any improvement of her balance-of-payments position will thus very probably depend, in the long run, as much on her ability to produce things now imported as it will on her expansion of exports.

Finally, raising of the general level of productivity of the Indonesian labor force requires capital-deepening in addition to the investments in human capital referred to in the introduction to the previous section. Capital-deepening is a normal concomitant of industrial development, whereas such possibilities are much harder to devise and implement in traditionalistic and labor-saturated agriculture. These comments are not to be regarded as contradictory to the comments offered in the introduction to Part II. Agricultural and industrial growth must grow complementarily, in the view of most development economists.[4]

[4] See, for example, G. Ranis and J. Fei, *Development of the Labor Surplus Economy,* Richard D. Irwin, Homewood, Ill., 1964; and B. Johnston and J. Mellor, "The Role of Agriculture in Economic Development," *American Economic Review,* September 1961.

While the petroleum industry presents the most optimistic growth picture in the industrial sector, and the textile industry is the largest employer of industrial labor, other industrial activities are also of importance in terms of those criteria. The small pharmaceutical industry is growing rapidly in response to a widening market. Milling of rice and rubber are major employers of labor—though probably of low employment growth potential by comparison with the textile industry. Modern plants now exist in the country producing tires, cement, and urea and assembling automobiles. All can be expected to grow as the domestic market expands. The nation is large enough to offer scope for achieving full-scale economies in much modern industry, excepting such inherently vast-scale activities as automobile production, and the building of large ships. The domestic market readily absorbs all the output of the Gresik cement plant and the Palembang urea plant—both modern plants designed by Western engineers.

Nevertheless, industrialization will very likely be accomplished only very slowly, limited on the one hand by the need for the rebuilding and expansion of the native's infrastructure in transport, communications and power, as well as the growth in quantity and quality of their labor force and entrepreneurs.

CHAPTER 8

The Indonesian Oil Industry*

ALEX HUNTER

Historically the Indonesian oil industry was an important segment of the world oil scene, and with about 24,000,000 metric tons per annum, or 1.6 percent of total world production, remains a considerable producer of crude oil. For Australia, Indonesia is a large and strategic element in the oil situation, since it supplies one quarter of this country's crude imports; certain radical alterations in the structure and performance of the oil industry which are at present taking place could have a special impact on oil policies in Australia. For the student of economics, these same changes are of a more general interest. Recent Indonesian developments bring out the prime importance for newly independent countries of preserving the effectiveness of their inherited investments in export industries such as oil. There is a warning, for private enterprise and governments, in the ambivalent attitude of new nations to foreign investment no matter how essential or productive. The effect of *Socialisme à la Indonesia* (to use President Sukarno's label for the particular brand of state control) on the operations of Western-type enterprise is worth

* Although the writer is indebted to people connected with or employed in the Indonesian oil industry for facts and advice, it is generally impossible, for reasons relating to company affairs or Indonesian politics to acknowledge these sources of information. This paper was published initially in the *Australian Economic Papers*, June 1966. It is reprinted here with the permission of the author and of the editors of the journal. Six statistical tables of considerable historical interest have been deleted for this reprinting. Scholars interested in the detailed data are referred to the original.

noting. Finally, there is the reaction, surely unique, of international oil companies large enough and resourceful enough to hold off encroaching nationalism while making dispositions of their affairs which will leave their total situation unchanged and possibly improved.

Developments to the 1960's

Indonesia is one of the oldest centres of world oil production. As early as 1871, Dutchmen were drilling in seepage areas in an attempt to secure petroleum for refining into illuminating oil. In 1883, a tobacco planter, A. J. Zylker, took out a concession to drill in North Sumatra which did yield, at the shallow depth of 400 feet, commercial production. This first productive concession, when he sold it to financial interests, led to the foundation of the Royal Dutch Company for the Working of Petroleum Wells in the Netherlands Indies, which later became the Royal Dutch Company. Formed in 1890, it took over the Zylker concession. Many other entrepreneurs were opening up the sedimentary basins of South Sumatra, East Java, and East and Northeast Borneo. Altogether there were eighteen companies active during the period. But the Royal Dutch Company, by virtue of exploration work and financial penetration of these companies, quickly dominated the industry. In 1907, it amalgamated with the Shell Transport and Trading Company, which operated in eastern Borneo. Thus the second largest international oil company, the Royal Dutch-Shell group, had its beginnings in the Indonesian archipelago.[1]

The operating company of the Royal Dutch-Shell group, in what was then the Netherlands East Indies (NEI), was the Bataffsche Petroleum Maatschappij (the BPM). By 1911, it was the only operating company in the NEI, with altogether 44 concessions (19 in Sumatra, 18 in Java, and 7 in Borneo). Total production in this year was 1,700,000 metric tons, with North Sumatra

[1] See I. Swemle, "Indonesia, British Borneo, and Burma," Chap. 12 of W. E. Pratt and D. Good, eds., *World Geography of Petroleum,* Princeton University Press, Princeton, N.J., 1950 for a brief historical picture and the general structure of the industry prior to 1940. For a very extensive analysis of the early years in the Netherlands East Indies see F. C. Gerretson, *History of the Royal Dutch,* E. J. Brill, Leiden, 1957.

producing 22 percent, East Java 10 percent, Borneo 34 percent, and the island of Tarakan 14 percent. In those days, this was 3.7 percent of world production. Competition began in 1912, when the American company, Standard-Vacuum Oil, a subsidiary of Standard Oil (New Jersey) and the Vacuum Oil Company, secured concessions to prospect (as Nederlandsche Koloniale Petroleum Mij.) in Sumatra, Java, Borneo, and elsewhere. Its main strike was in South Sumatra in the high-yielding Talang Akdar-Pendopo area. By 1925, this company accounted for 5 percent of NEI production; BPM had the remaining 95 percent.

Until 1928, all concessions were granted for 75 years, few obligations to drill were imposed; and entire areas and therefore complete oil structures were exploited within each concession. Thus there was no possibility of competitive high-density drilling over favourable ground with the attendant dangers, common in the United States, of high-cost, low-productivity wells. This practice of providing large concession or contracting areas persists to the present day and helps maintain Indonesia as one of the relatively high-productivity areas of world petroleum in terms of either annual tonnage per well or unit costs of production. In 1928, the concession terms became more onerous. The concession period was reduced to 40 years; there was an obligation to drill (although the prospecting company could give up segments of its concession if the results of exploration were regarded as unfavourable) and the state, in addition to the royalties due from each concession's production, received a progressive profit share typically as high as 20 percent of the net profits of the operating company. A further significant intervention of the government in this period was the formation of NIAM (Nederlandsche Indische Ardalie Maatschappij). The government and legislature considered that the concession system in general operated too much in favour of the oil companies and sought to redress the balance by creating, in the early 1930's, the NIAM as an enterprise shared on a 50:50 basis between it and BPM. This was to exploit the rich oil province of Djambi in Sumatra which, since 1906, had been held in reserve. As is usual in these mixed enterprises, the private partner, BPM, provided the operational management and disposed of the production.

In 1931, Caltex, a subsidiary of Standard Oil of California and the Texas Company, secured extensive exploration concessions (as the Nederlandsche Pacific Petroleum Mij.) in Central Sumatra and West Java and shortly before the war was about to commence commercial production in the Central Sumatran field of Duri. Then, in 1935, the NNGPM (Nederlandsche Nieuw Guinea Petroleum Mij.) was formed to exploit western New Guinea. In this company, Royal Dutch-Shell and Standard-Vacuum each had a 40 percent interest and Caltex a 20 percent interest. Discoveries were made but production did not begin until 1948.

Thus, by 1938, production of crude oil totalled 7,398,000 metric tons per annum in the area that was to become Indonesia. Of this, the BPM (Royal Dutch-Shell) share was 72 percent, including NIAM output, and that of Nederlandsche Koloniale (Standard-Vacuum) 28 percent. East Borneo was no longer the most prolific area. This position had been taken over by South Sumatra, with most of the production centering on Djambi and Palembang provinces. At this date, all crude oil production went into the seven refineries of the NEI. Four of these refineries were small and served mainly local markets (three in Java and one in North Sumatra). The remaining three were large export refineries: the Nederlandsche Koloniale plant at Sungei Gerong (South Sumatra) and the BPM refineries at Pladju (South Sumatra) and Balikpapan (East Borneo). Of the 8,065,000 metric tons of petroleum products manufactured in 1938, 6,015,000 tons went abroad to Southeast Asian markets; and only 1,401,000 tons, or 19 percent, were used to satisfy domestic demand.

World War II provided a depressing episode for the Indonesian oil industry following the Japanese invasion in 1942. The "scorched-earth" policy of the Dutch colonial government was carried out conscientiously by military personnel;[2] it severely damaged fields, pipelines, pumping equipment, and refineries, and succeeded in limiting Japanese production. It is estimated that the Japanese extracted 3,250,000 metric tons in 1942, 6,500,000 tons in 1943, 3,750,000 tons in 1944, but only 850,000 tons in 1945

[2] Massachusetts Institute of Technology, Center for International Studies, Indonesia Project, *Stanvac in Indonesia,* National Planning Association, New York, 1957, pp. 25–26; hereafter cited as MIT CENIS, *op. cit.*

when South Sumatran installations in particular were subject to Allied bombardment. Even these totals included the production from British wells in North Borneo.[3] Japanese wartime disregard for proper maintenance of oil field and refinery equipment or for sound engineering practice in extracting oil added to the total damage caused by "denial" policies and military operations.

The period 1945–1950 also offered frustration. The Japanese usually handed over installations to Indonesian deputies; and frequently *de facto* management organisations stemming from this action had to be persuaded to relinquish the equipment, which they used incompetently, or be forced to surrender it to its legal owners. Political instability made its contribution also; first in the "police" action of the Dutch in Java and Sumatra in 1947, then in the settling-in processes of the new Indonesian legislative assembly, many members of which were eager to deny the foreign companies any role in the new Indonesia. BPM managed to resume production at Tarakan in 1945 and in Borneo in 1946, and partially reactivated its Balikpapan refinery in the same year. In South Sumatra, the experience was less happy. In October 1946, the Pladju refinery was returned to BPM, and the Sungei Gerong refinery to Nederlandsche Koloniale Mij. (Stanvac) for reconstruction. But neither company had access to its oil fields until 1947, and neither could show much production before 1948. In Central Java, BPM did not secure access to its Kawenga fields near the Tjepu refinery. Initially this area was taken over by an oil-workers' cooperative and, in the course of time, came to be controlled by the state enterprise PERMIGAN. Similarly in North Sumatra, BPM fields were rendered inaccessible, first by local oil workers and later, in 1952–1953, by the unwillingness of the new Indonesian legislature (as distinct from the government) to sanction the return of the wells. The refinery at Pankalan Brandan also remained in local Indonesian hands despite the small quantities and poor qualities of the products produced. Eventually this area came to be controlled by the *de facto* company North Sumatran Oil Industries (which later became the state enterprise PERMINA) after the Indonesian government conceded to a militant

[3] Swemle, *op. cit.*

legislature, in October 1956, that the fields and partially crippled refinery should not be returned to BPM.[4]

Production of crude oil in these circumstances moved up slowly from 302,000 metric tons in 1946 to 1,113,000 in 1947, 4,326,000 tons in 1948, and 5,930,000 tons in 1949. Only by 1950 was it approaching 1938 figures. The throughput of refinery products was greater than this figure would suggest; and a considerable volume of export products began quite soon to move out of Indonesia to local markets.[5] But this was possible only because imports of crude oil by 1949–1950, mainly from Sarawak, amounted to over one quarter of the total oil processed in Indonesia. The two refining companies, being international, were, to a large degree, independent of local Indonesian conditions.

Subsequent to the Indonesian government coming into power in 1949, the three foreign oil companies—all ostentatiously active in an economically disrupted Indonesia, and their expatriate staff very affluent by local standards—had to endure severe criticisms despite the admittedly great value of the industry to the country both in terms of export earnings and the development of many otherwise desolate areas in Sumatra and Kalimantan. In particular, the so-called "let alone" agreements, initially negotiated by the companies with the Dutch colonial government in 1948, attracted a barrage of nationalistic censure in the legislature. Thus, the new Indonesian government, which chose to uphold the "let alone" agreements mainly for their promise of rapid reconstruction of the industry, had a difficult time damping down extremist legislative opinions and, later, the demands of the militant trade unions which developed to disconcert the oil companies.[6]

[4] John O. Sutter, *Indonesianisasi, Politics in a Changing Economy, 1940–1955,* Data Paper no. 36. Department of Far Eastern Studies, Southeast Asia Program, Cornell University, Ithaca, N.Y., 1959, pp. 374–375, 814–846; The Java Bank, *Report of the President and of the Board of Directors,* 1949–1950 and 1950–1951 (annual), Djakarta (cited hereafter as *Java Bank Report*); and G. C. Allen and A. Donnithorne, *Western Enterprise in Indonesia and Malaya,* Macmillan, New York, 1957, pp. 176–180.

[5] In 1948, there were 3,850,000 metric tons of products exported; in 1949, 5,692,000 tons and, in 1950, 6,091,000 tons (*Java Bank Report,* 1950–1951).

[6] Sutter, *op. cit.,* pp. 820–830.

The term "let alone" is scarcely appropriate. It suggests preferential treatment such as wholesale freedom from taxation. This was not so. The agreements referred exclusively to the disposition of foreign exchange earnings from the export of petroleum products and, later, crude oil. It was early recognized that, if the existing companies withdrew, fresh investment would not easily be forthcoming. (In those days, proved reserves were not extensive, especially when compared with the fabulous new Middle East areas; and the rise of Japan as a major consumer of crude oil in the Far East was as yet over the horizon.) It was also clear that the rehabilitation of war-damaged fields and refineries would be exceedingly expensive in terms of foreign exchange. Therefore the "let alone" agreements were negotiated. They permitted the companies to retain the foreign exchange they received from their sales abroad of products and crude, for an agreed number of years, on condition that they made no demands on the government's foreign exchange fund for the purpose of rebuilding the industry or in any way extending crude production.[7] This arrangement did not release the companies from any of the usual obligations to meet taxation. It merely meant that their exchange earnings did not pass through the normal channels of the Foreign Exchange Institute. Thus the companies covered their obligations in Indonesia in the following way. Their local earnings on the sale of products they used to meet local wages, materials, supplies, and services. They also paid royalties on oil production, various import duties, and wage taxes; and their net earnings attracted a profits or income tax. The excess of these rupiah obligations over local rupiah earnings were then met from a conversion of part of their foreign exchange earnings. The rest they retained. The *quid pro quo* for this freedom was that the foreign companies rebuilt the Indonesian oil and refinery industry from their own overseas financial resources.

The "let alone" agreements eventually came to an end. Stanvac's

[7] Compare this arrangement with the severe regulations which the Indonesian government applied to foreign enterprise in rubber in respect of dividend remittances. Overseas remittances attracted a 66 percent levy and, even so, were frequently delayed for several years. Rubber also attracted a large export tax. Allen and Donnithorne, *op. cit.*, p.135.

arrangements ran to the end of 1951, when the government took over control of this company's foreign exchange proceeds (the difference between proceeds from petroleum exports and the sum of all payments for imports of crude oil, lubricating stock, and the hard currency content of operating costs). For two years this company undertook tedious negotiations with the government to discover a reasonable reconciliation on this critical question of foreign exchange disposition. In March 1964, a four-year agreement was signed. The company obtained a general permit to spend foreign currency on imports of equipment and services necessary to maintain and develop petroleum operations in Indonesia. The agreement also provided for a monthly transfer of dividends and a monthly settlement of outstanding taxes. In return, the company agreed to undertake a three-year development programme estimated to cost U.S. $70–80 million in foreign currency, the money to be found from sources outside Indonesia (hence the necessity to reach agreement and establish a procedure for future transfer claims involving foreign exchange). Another *quid pro quo* was that Stanvac was granted a ten-year exemption from import duties on its supplies of capital goods and materials from abroad—a substantial advantage in a country where the negotiation of dutiable goods through a rapacious and corrupt customs service assumed the proportions of a major campaign for senior management.

The other two companies came into line with Stanvac. At the end of 1953, the Caltex "let alone" agreement expired; and in 1954 this company signed a new five-year agreement for foreign exchange matters on the Stanvac models including freedom from import duties, etc. There was one difference: Caltex agreed to turn over U.S. $60 million worth of "acceptable" foreign exchange to the Foreign Exchange Fund over the five-year period. It was not made clear for what consideration this cash was paid. But a reasonable guess is that Caltex agreed to turn over this money in lieu of building the Caltex refinery in Indonesia which had been the subject of discussions and half-promises since before World War II. The third company, BPM, had its "let alone" agreement expire at the end of 1955 and, although no precise information exists concerning its agreements with the government, it is usually assumed that the arrangements adopted were the same as for the two American companies.[8]

It should be noted that there was no marked change between the "let alone" agreements and the financial arrangements which succeeded them, except that foreign exchange transactions were recorded by passing through the Foreign Exchange Institute. The oil companies continued to have a degree of freedom on foreign exchange matters not accorded to any other foreign-owned industry in Indonesia—in respect to import duties, expenditure on new equipment and exploration services, and in remittances of dividends to the parent companies overseas. So long as the rehabilitation of the industry continued and so long as exports could continue to earn substantial foreign exchange for Indonesia, the large petroleum companies retained this strong position *vis-à-vis* the government. However, there was one addition to the new agreement. The government negotiated a new profit division at the same time; that is, the royalty and tax position was re-examined and re-assessed. Unfortunately the details of these reportedly complicated settlements remained secret. But it is generally presumed in petroleum circles that the net result of the various royalties, income tax, export taxes, levies on foreign exchange, pay roll tax, etc. for which the companies were liable amounted to something around a 50:50 division of net revenue (profits) between the companies and the Indonesian government.[9] These arrangements lasted until the 1963 agreements redefined the ground.

[8] Bank Indonesia, *Report of the Governor,* 1954–1955, Djakarta, pp. 141–142; Sutter, *op. cit.,* pp. 826–830; and MIT CENIS, *op. cit.,* pp. 43–45.

[9] The pre-World War II taxation system for oil companies which persisted substantially into the 1950's was made up of the following: a 4 percent royalty on the well-head value of crude oil produced, a 20 percent profit tax on the "5A-contract-areas" concessions (*i.e.,* concessions given subsequent to 1928) based on profits, and the application of a general corporate profits tax of 20 percent. Thus, a company such as Stanvac which received the majority of its more prolific concessions subsequent to 1928 would be paying at least a 40 percent profits tax; and, with the various additional taxes which grew up in exporting and marketing, it claimed that it was, in the early 1950's, paying more than the 50 percent profit share which was normal in most oil-producing countries at the time (MIT CENIS, *op. cit.,* pp. 40–42). This point is con-

While these difficult negotiations were taking place, the three companies adopted protective colouration in an attempt to divert nationalist ill-humour. One apparently superficial, but probably important, move was to drop company names which recalled the colonial past. Around 1955, the Nederlandsche Koloniale Petroleum Mij. and the Nederlandsche Pacific Petroleum Mij. re-entitled their Indonesian operating companies by their American titles, Stanvac Petroleum and Caltex Pacific. And the Bataafische Petroleum Maatschappij (the BPM) became Shell Petroleum, tactfully ignoring in the selection of name its 60 percent Dutch ancestry. A more substantial and important move in the same direction was the Indonesianisation of oil company personnel. The number and relative affluence of Dutch, American, and British personnel in this important industry was, and is, greatly resented by Indonesians. And, starting in 1950, the oil companies put considerable efforts into the task of replacing them by local employees at all levels. In some types of work this was not too difficult. Stanvac reports that it was easy enough to replace the ordinary refinery manufacturing personnel—from 100 percent foreign before the war to 100 percent Indonesian by 1953. Powerhouse operators, drillers, and pipeline technicians also offered no special problems. But an extreme scarcity of Indonesians trained in higher technical and maintenance work could not be so easily overcome. Stanvac and BPM established in South Sumatra, in both refinery and producing areas, technical training schools for welding, laboratory work, pipe-fitting techniques, petroleum analysis, etc. Undertaking this training also meant in many cases undertaking the secondary education of those employees selected for technical training. At higher levels again, scholarships were granted to attend the Technical and Science Faculties in Bandung, the best of the local universities. And a growing number of promising

---

firmed in the *Java Bank Report* for 1951–1952, which indicated that, in 1952, company taxes were increased from 40 percent to 52½ percent, and export duties of 8 percent had another 15 percent added. "It would seem that the burdens which are placed on the petroleum companies are heavier in this country than in any other" was the Bank's comment; and it added speculation on the willingness of oil companies to invest in these circumstances.

employees were sent abroad for university training in business administration and accounting as well as technical subjects such as geology and petroleum technology.[10]

Throughout the postwar period up to 1963, exploration for petroleum—or rather the lack of exploration—played a crucial role. In 1941, the Dutch colonial government restricted exploration rights, and the independent Indonesian government upheld this decision whilst the affairs of the oil industry were under legislative examination. By a resolution of 1951, a State Commission on Mining Affairs was appointed to report on the desirable operation of all mineral rights in the new Indonesia and on the related affairs of the extracting industries. Unfortunately, a subsidiary Part II of the resolution setting up the commission asked the government "to postpone all granting of concessions and exploitation permits or extending expired permits" pending the report of the commission. The commission took eight years to report, and it was not until 1960 that a law regulating exploration and development of petroleum was passed.[11]

Meanwhile the three foreign companies were confined to existing concessions. It is typical of Indonesia that oil reservoirs, although found at shallow depths, are contained in relatively small structures quite unlike, for example, the large oil pools of the Middle East. Most important fields are in the 300,000-to-1,500-000-metric-tons-per-annum class; and there are many much smaller fields. Only one field, Minas in Central Sumatra, operated by Caltex, is in the over-10,000,000-tons-per-annum category (whereas Iran, Iraq, Kuwait, and Arabia would each have two or more fields with production of twice or three times this quantity). Another indicator is the number of wells and the proportion on artificial lift. Even the Minas field requires 145 wells to extract its oil

[10] In 1939, the three main companies employed between them just over 2,000 American and European staff members (many of the latter Dutchmen in supervisory, clerical, and technical posts). By the 1960's—although output was up 3½ times and another company, Pan American, was exploring—this figure was down to around 400, mainly employed in exploration and development and in refinery management. The declared aim of the authorities (1965) was to reduce the number to 50 (Swemle, *op. cit.*, p. 294 and private reports).

[11] Sutter, *op. cit.*, pp. 820–825. Also, see section below entitled "The 1963 Oil Agreements."

(compared with 60 wells in a larger Arabian field), and 130 of these are on pump. The output of Shell comes from about 18 fields, mostly small, using more than 1,000 wells, and Stanvac obtains its crude from 500 wells in South and Central Sumatra, two-thirds of them on artificial lift. Thus, without continuous exploration to enlarge the area of production, the output of an oil territory such as Indonesia inevitably stagnates and sooner or later declines.[12]

Stanvac, in particular, was seriously affected by the halt to new exploration. It had available to it for development 1.8 million acres of long-term concessions dating from prewar days—about 10 percent of all long-term petroleum concession areas in Indonesia. Most of this was located in the already well-exploited South Sumatran basin. Its output from here, and later in 1958 from the new Lirik field in Central Sumatra, was expected to be sufficient for the throughput of the Sungei Gerong refinery in the 1950's. But the company had to look forward to the probability that, in the 1960's, there would be insufficient crude from its own fields to employ the refinery to capacity. Indeed, Stanvac's crude output, after reaching a peak of 4,602,000 metric tons in 1959, fell off to 2,637,000 tons—just enough, with 807,000 tons supplied by other companies, to keep the refinery at capacity and leave a small margin of crude for export. Shell Petroleum had a larger concession area, but part of its acreage was shared with NIAM, and therefore fell into the hands of PERMINDO, the Indonesian state enterprise which took over from NIAM in 1959. (This company was later to become the PERTAMIN state enterprise.) Also, many of Shell's concession areas, in East Kalimantan, Tarakan, and East Java for example, were almost exhausted of their accessible oil. And the company, since 1945, had no access to its Central Java fields or to the still productive North Sumatran concessions in the hands first of Indonesian oil workers, then the army, then the state enterprise PERMINA. For some time in the early 1950's, the two large Shell refineries imported considerable quantities of Sarawak crude. Since then, the rehabilitation of the South Sumatran production areas, and even the completion by 1955 of the 250-kilometre pipeline from the new Tandjung field in South

[12] See *Oil and Gas Journal,* December 28, 1964 (supplement on world oil statistics) for comparisons of various national outputs.

Kalimantan to the Balikpapan refinery, seem not to have made the company self-sufficient in the Indonesian crude. It continued to import about one and a half million metric tons per annum, or almost 20 percent of its refinery throughout.

Caltex, by contrast, was very fortunate. Most of its concession acreage was in the Central Sumatran basin. Its important discoveries, the fields of Duri and Minas, were made just before the war, and indeed only Duri had initiated production by 1941. Therefore when the company finally regained access to its concession in 1950 it still had the best years of development and exploitation to come. The company made the most of its opportunities in the area by undertaking extensive geophysical and seismic exploration early in the 1950's. Pipelines were constructed to terminals on the River Siak to take the output of the Minas field to the sea; and later, pipelines were constructed from both Duri and Minas to Dumai where an ocean terminal sufficient to accommodate 80,000-ton tankers was constructed by 1958. By 1963, these two fields accounted for over 50 percent (11,534,000 tons) of Indonesian output. It seems likely that by 1965 they will produce between them 13½ million tons or more. Caltex is now easily the foremost producer of crude, and has, in these two fields, the most productive strikes in Indonesian oil history.[13]

The 1963 Oil Agreements

The 1963 oil agreements marked a new phase in the development of the Indonesian oil industry. Shell and Stanvac, throughout the 1950's, had negotiated for additional exploration and development areas adjacent to their main producing fields in order to maintain and raise their crude output. They received no satisfaction from these endeavours. On the other hand, starting in 1959,

[13] The changing shares of crude production over the years can be seen from the following percentages taken from Swemle, *op. cit.*, and *Bank Indonesia Reports*. (By 1963, PERMINA had 5 percent of total production.)

Company	*1925*	*1938*	*1957*	*1963*
Shell	95	72	23	26
NIAM			10	3
Stanvac	5	28	20	11
Caltex			47	55

the Indonesian government undertook a number of *ad hoc* contracts and long-term agreements with foreign oil companies other than Shell, Stanvac, and Caltex. It is generally thought that these arrangements were designed to demonstrate the independence of the Indonesian government in oil matters, and at the same time condition the "majors" into a frame of mind more amenable to Indonesian demands. They included a technical and financial assistance contract in 1960 between PERMINA and a Japanese group, the North Sumatra Oil Development Co-operation Company, to rehabilitate the former Shell fields in North Sumatra in return for deliveries of crude (one of the first "production-sharing" arrangements between Indonesia and foreign enterprises). By 1964, over 600,000 tons per annum were being exported to the Japanese group. PERMINA also had drilling contracts in North Sumatra with Canadian and American companies; PERTAMIN in South Sumatra took some technical advice on exploratory drilling from Shell during 1959 and 1962 and later employed a French geophysical contractor; and PERMIGAN in 1962 contracted with another Japanese group to rehabilitate the old Shell Kawengan fields in Java and other deposits in certain of the eastern islands.[14]

However, the most significant of these arrangements was the agreement undertaken in 1962 between Pan American International, a subsidiary of Standard Oil of Indiana, and PERTAMIN. It is an agreement which must be seen against the background of Law no. 44 concerning Petroleum and Natural Gas Mining of 1960. This law changed the legal status of foreign companies in Indonesia by stipulating that, for the future, all foreign companies could only act as contractors and could no longer have concession rights.[15] Hence Pan American did not get to own a concession: it could only make a contract to work for and supply the state enterprise PERTAMIN. It was this 1960 law which initiated the protracted two and a half years of negotiation with the three major companies which ended in the Tokyo agreements. Thus the Pan American contract is of special interest because it created the

[14] See Alex Hunter, "The 1963 Oil Agreements and After," *Bulletin of Indonesian Economic Studies* (*BIES*), no. 2, September 1965, for further details of these contracts.

[15] *Ibid.*

prototype of the agreements negotiated in 1963 with the three major oil companies. In addition, it constituted the first substantial oil exploration "concession" in new territory given in Indonesia to any company, foreign or otherwise, since pre-World War II days. The arrangement gave Pan American a thirty-year oil exploration and development contract in a desirable prospecting area of Sumatra. The area covers a total of 816 million acres, including a small offshore sector of 8,436 acres, the whole adjacent to and partly surrounding Caltex's fruitful holdings in Central Sumatra. Pan American contracted to pay a U.S. $10 million bonus for its right to explore and develop: $5 million at the time of ratification of the contract and another $5 million to be paid after the end of the first year in which oil exports averaged 15,000 barrels per day (or 750,000 metric tons per annum). The exploration period was arranged for six years, with provision for two-year extensions, and carried an exploration investment expenditure minimum of $28.5 million. A 25 percent proportion of the total acreage was to be relinquished after the first five years of commercial production, and another 25 percent after ten years. These acreages would then become available for exploration and development contracts with other companies or state enterprises. The contracting company had to employ at least 75 percent Indonesians —100 percent after fifteen years. Finally the contract was based on a 60:40 profit division in favour of the Indonesian state enterprise PERTAMIN (after current operating expenses were met and exploration costs written off at 10 percent per annum). These profits were to be calculated on realised rather than posted prices.

Against this background of *ad hoc* production-sharing contracts and agreements, the three international majors went to Tokyo in May 1963 for the final phase of their two one-half years of attempts to find an understanding with the Indonesian government on the basis of the 1960 petroleum law. (The occasion was an official visit by President Sukarno to Japan.) The companies entered the final phase of negotiations reconciled to tax increases but determined to have a definite understanding of their future in Indonesia, particularly in respect to exploration and development. The companies reportedly shocked the Indonesian negotiators by the statement that they intended to quit operations in Indonesia if understanding could not be secured. The Indonesians also employed some brinkmanship by asserting that the companies must leave if, by June 1963, there was no agreement. A special emissary despatched by President Kennedy from the United States, accompanied by a team of petroleum consultants, entered the negotiations seeking a compromise which would keep both sides in the ring. The United States' view was that a poorly-managed oil industry, by aggravating the country's economic ills, would push Indonesia further into the communist sphere.[16] In the event, the mediation attempt was successful, at least for a time.

The area of understanding between the parties was crystallised in Heads of Agreement reached in Tokyo. These became Indonesian law in June 1963, and were embodied in working contracts which, after lengthy negotiations in detail with each company, were concluded in Djakarta by September 25, 1963—between PERTAMIN and Caltex, PERMINA and Stanvac, and PERMIGAN and Shell. There are five substantive elements in the agreements:

(i) Each of the three foreign enterprises gave up its concession ownership rights granted under the old colonial government and agreed instead to act as contractor to one of the three state oil companies.

(ii) In exchange they were awarded twenty-year contracts to continue the exploitation of the old concession areas. More important, they were permitted to make application for thirty-year contracts to explore and develop new areas adjacent to existing concessions. The new area contracts required immediate payment of cash bonuses of $5 million, and continued tenure was subject to the expenditure of $15 million over eight years for each area, relinquishment of unused areas after certain periods, a further $5 million payment when commercial production was established, Indonesianisation of the operating company's staff, etc.

(iii) The marketing and distribution facilities were to be

[16] See *Petroleum Press Service,* London, June–December issues, recent years, for various comments on these negotiations, and the Economist Intelligence Unit, *Three Monthly Economic Review,* Indonesia, no. 45, 1963.

handed over to the contracting state companies within five years at prices based on agreed formulae which depreciated the original "acquisition costs" of the assets. The foreign companies agreed to supply products to the state distribution organisation at cost plus a fee of ten cents per barrel for as long as required. Pending transfer, distribution would be performed by the companies for an additional fee of ten cents a barrel.

(iv) Refinery assets would be transferred to Indonesia within ten to fifteen years again according to agreed formulae for ascertaining their value. Subsequently the international companies would be prepared to supply crude oil to the Indonesian state enterprise refineries at cost plus a fee of 20 cents per barrel for as long as required, and in quantity, up to 25 percent of their output of crude from Indonesian fields.

(v) The operating profits of the international companies would be divided, as from June 1963, in the ratio of 60:40 between government and company. But in any event the government would receive a minimum payment equal to 20 percent of the gross value of the crude oil produced in any one year by a foreign company.[17]

The substance of these agreements, at least in respect of the crucial contracts to explore and develop and the equally crucial matter of profit division, was foreshadowed in the 1962 Pan American contract. Therefore the international companies, although perhaps relieved, should not have been surprised at the outcome. In addition, certain elements of the contracts gave them reason for satisfaction. First, the principal problem concerning the future of these companies in Indonesia appeared to have been settled. A twenty-year contract to exploit old areas, a ten-year contract to continue operating old, well-established refineries and eventually to transfer them at agreed values, and thirty-year contracts to prospect new areas of crude oil production, all gave reassurance enough. Second, the 60:40 division of profits was severe but less severe than was being currently negotiated for new (al-

[17] See Hunter, *op. cit.*, for a detailed analysis of the financial and technical provisions of the Tokyo agreements; and, for a version of the working agreements, the Commercial Advisory Foundation in Indonesia (CAFI), *Legal Section Circular no. H466,* December 10, 1963.

though superior) concessions in the Middle East and Venezuela.[18] Third, the companies probably regarded as an unmixed blessing the gradual transfer of marketing and distribution facilities, very soon after the signing of the agreements. Price control has operated in petroleum products since 1945, and the course of inflation had rendered the fixed price completely unrealistic.[19] Until 1963, the losses involved in this trade, which also included diesel and fuel oil for state transport and generating facilities, were carried by Shell and Stanvac and subsidized from their profitable trade in the export of products to Southeast Asian countries. Fourth, even the impending loss of the refineries was not without its compensations. So long as the export products dominate, they do provide a remunerative set of outlets. But there was already, in 1963, much evidence to indicate that most refinery output, especially the more profitable gasoline and kerosene trade, would be absorbed by a swiftly rising domestic demand. And the margins arranged in the agreement, 20 cents per barrel for crude and 10 cents for refinery processing, were not especially attractive by comparison with earnings in international trade. Finally, the companies concerned, Shell and Stanvac, may well have reasoned that refineries are, in an underdeveloped country, ostentatious objects which can only attract numerous demands for Indonesianisation of personnel leading eventually to reduced efficiency or outright nationalisation.[20]

[18] J. F. Hartshorn, *Oil Companies and Governments,* Faber, London, 1962, pp. 274, 287.

[19] The operation of price control is discussed more fully in the section below entitled "Production, Refining, and Distribution."

[20] The companies also had various minor victories in the Tokyo negotiations which simplified the administration of the agreements. The 60 percent share of profits going to the Indonesian government as income tax was arranged to include *all* forms of tax applicable to oil operations—export and import taxes, dividend taxes, levies on foreign exchange, etc.—and therefore left the companies free of any obligations to contribute "fringe benefits" to the fiscal authorities. Realised prices of oil rather than posted prices were taken as the datum for calculating profits—thus relieving the companies of a burden which, in their Middle Eastern and Venezuelan operations, they would rather be without in this era of discounts from posted prices. And, on the foreign exchange issue, they successfully resisted an attempt by the

Altogether the prospects for the international companies in Indonesia during 1964 looked more promising than for the past two decades. The 1963 agreements appeared to provide that *modus vivendi* which the majors sought, giving the assurance of considerable freedom of action, particularly within the exploration and development field, where the future of the oil industry could be made or marred. At the same time, Indonesia was provided with a solution acceptable to any government primarily concerned for the economic welfare of the country: a soundly constructed and operated refinery system to be handed over at agreed prices after a period in which the Indonesianisation of the operating personnel was completed; a guarantee that domestic product needs would be met from the crude petroleum resources of the country; and a period of growth in crude production for the subsequent 20–30 years to be supported by foreign technique and finance. In view of Indonesia's nationalist aspirations and backward technology, it was a rational and reasonable solution. The companies themselves lost no time in demonstrating their confidence in the arrangements. Shell chose two areas in South Sumatra and one area adjacent to its Tandjung field in Kalimantan; Caltex obtained two sections east and west of its Duri field; and Stanvac selected a block around its Lirik field in the same area of Central Sumatra. Each of the three paid the necessary $5 million bonus before beginning its survey work,[21] and each spent money freely in attempts to discover the possibilities of its new areas. Stanvac, for example, reports that it spent $3 million in the first year of its work contract as against an obligation to spend only $1 million.

The reasons for satisfaction on the part of the companies did

---

Indonesian negotiators to have all of the 60 percent income tax on profits paid in sterling or dollars. Instead, they secured an agremeent that some part of taxation, depending on the extent of their domestic operations in Indonesia, could be paid in rupiah (see Hunter, *op. cit.,* for additional comment on the fiscal problems).

[21] So-called "bonus" payments are fees paid to national governments merely for access to prospecting land likely to hold out good returns. These substantial payments are now normal practice in all countries known to have productive oil territories—Venezuela, Libya, Arabia, Iran, Iraq, Kuwait, etc. The OPEC (Organization of Petroleum Exporting Countries) have had considerable influence in establishing this system of bonus payments.

not long survive. Late in 1964 and early in 1965, political pressure was brought to bear by various left-wing elements in the legislature and the trade union movement. The large oil companies, with their antecedents placed firmly in the colonial period and their parentage tainted in Indonesian eyes as being simultaneously prime examples of 'monopoly capital' and creatures of imperialistic governments, made ideal instruments for any extremist party which wished to make the political running in opposition to the more moderate, pragmatic influences in the government concerned to alleviate the economic distress of the country. The appeal to nationalist sentiment was difficult to resist. After all, by late 1964, petroleum was the one substantial surviving bastion of foreign enterprise in Indonesia.[22] Also, private individual greed was an important component in the desire to be quit of the oil companies. The removal of foreign managements always means more well-paid appointments with, in Indonesian practice, the ancillary houses, cars, and servants. It also means, unfortunately, greater opportunities for corruption in both the acquisition of petroleum equipment and the disposition of petroleum supplies.[23] A crisis in the mounting campaign of criticism was reached on March 18, 1965, when trade unions demonstrated in Sumatra at the Palembang refinery installations and at Pendopo on the oil fields, demanding that company property be handed over to the government and that foreign personnel be compelled to relinquish their jobs. Although no actual take-overs occurred, the minister then responsible for the industry, Dr. Chairul Saleh, was forced to make an announcement that:

> for the purpose of securing the oil companies as well as for continuing to recognise the property rights of the foreign oil companies, upon guidance of the President, the Government immediately places all foreign oil companies under the control/supervision of the Republic of Indonesian Government.

At the same time it was stated that the measures taken were temporary and without prejudice to the companies' property rights.[24]

[22] See L. Castles, "Socialism and Private Business: The Latest Phase," *BIES* no. 1, June 1965.

[23] *Ibid.*

[24] A statement not necessarily reassuring to the companies since similar

The control and supervision teams were named and included representatives of the state oil enterprises, the Direktorat Minjak dan Gas Bumi (Oil and Gas Directorate), senior Indonesian oil company employees, and trade union representatives. They were instructed to check into and keep abreast of all company affairs, including mail, the export of oil, the safeguarding of domestic supplies, and the Indonesianisation of the oil companies' management personnel. However, according to the oil companies themselves, these teams did not interfere in the normal operations and procedures of the companies; nor was there, in general, any overt hostility to the foreign employees of the companies. Further pressure on the government came in June 1965, when the PKI leader, D. N. Aidit, urged the congress of PERBUM, the oil workers' union, to drop the facade of the control-supervision teams and completely expropriate the companies.[25]

In retrospect, 1965 can now be seen as a year of retreat from the Tokyo agreements. (Only partly was this in response to extremist pressures: it is detectable that certain elements within the government—notably the minister for oil affairs and the directorate of oil and gas—had begun to think more determinedly in terms of a national oil industry.) First, there was an acceleration in the handing over of Indonesian marketing facilities. Originally the wording of the working contracts appeared to contemplate a 20 percent per annum sale of distribution and retailing facilities over five years. In fact, the official report by PERTAMIN of its program of take-over indicates that between July 1964 and July 1965 it had signed for, taken control of, and paid for the marketing facilities of Shell, Stanvac, and Caltex in various parts of Indo-

---

formulae were used when taking over the management and physical and financial control of various British, American, and Australian enterprises. It would seem that the formulae of "control/supervision," and "without prejudice to property rights of the companies" are devices to enable the *de facto* nationalisation of foreign enterprises while avoiding, or delaying interminably, the *de jure* consequences of this action, *i.e.,* the liability to pay compensation. At any rate, such well-known companies as Bata (shoes) Goodyear (rubber tyres), Naspro (pharmaceuticals), and Frazer & Neave (soft drinks) have passed completely into Indonesian hands without negotiations on compensation having advanced far.

[25] *Financial and Economic News,* Djakarta, June 8, 1965.

nesia.[26] This rapid take-over was completed with the full consent of the companies. Possibly there was some financial advantage under the 1963 agreements in transferring the facilities earlier than later. But it is more likely that the companies preferred to remove their names from port terminals, bulk storage depots, road tankers, and retail outlets as soon as possible in order not to attract undue political attention. Second—and a more surprising change in the programme of transfer—there commenced negotiations on the refineries. These had been scheduled to remain with the foreign companies for ten years at least. However, negotiations for their transfer began in August 1965—a full seven and a half years ahead of schedule. Apparently discussions went forward with the consent of the two companies concerned, Shell and Stanvac, although it appeared that the initiative came from the Indonesian authorities. On the last day of 1965, the Shell management formally handed over all Shell property in Indonesia to the minister for oil affairs.

Production, Refining, and Distribution

Indonesian oil territory is moderately productive and profitable by world standards. Most *production* comes from relatively shallow depths—less than 3,000 feet for most wells and with many small fields producing in the 1,000–2,000 feet range. The advantages of exploring and developing at these depths are offset, however, by the expensiveness of transporting equipment and accommodating personnel in the isolated, equatorial forest conditions of most oil-bearing sedimentary basins. Moreover, the oil structures are typically small and scattered. Many of them are old and have declining outputs. For example, in South Sumatra, responsible for nearly one-fifth of Indonesian crude production, there are in operation twenty fields using almost 1,000 wells (over 700 of them on pump, so low are the reserves for most of this area) scattered over an area of 16,000 square miles. Yet there is a sufficiently productive group of newish fields to give Indonesia some

[26] P.N. PERTAMIN, *Pengoperan Marketing Dan Distribution Assets,* Djakarta, July 1963. PERTAMIN's organization of distribution and marketing will be considered in this chapter under "Production, Refining, and Distribution."

standing in world production stakes. The average productivity per well per annum (a useful measure since it takes into account both the natural fertility of the oil structure and most of the capital input component required) is 10,000 tons, not very impressive perhaps besides Venezuela (16,000 tons), the Sahara (33,000 tons), or Libya (97,000); and still less compared with the fabulous Middle Eastern areas of Iraq, Iran, Arabia, and Kuwait (168,000 tons per annum per well): but it is much higher than that of two large producers, the U.S.S.R. (2,300 tons per annum) and the United States (only 600 tons per annum per well). More significantly, it is well above the world average of 2,000 tons per annum per well. Most of the high-productivity output (amounting to 82 percent of the total) is located in six fields; the remaining 18 percent is distributed among almost fifty small, low-productivity fields mainly in older concession areas.[27]

The quality of the crude oils is, on average, good. There are a few heavy asphaltic types of a low API gravity reading of 18–28 degrees, mainly found in the smaller fields of Java, East Kalimantan, certain eastern islands such as Ceram, and in Tarakan. The yield of such crudes is mainly fuel oil and asphalt. There are a few crudes of light paraffinic quality with high API gravity readings of 44–52 degrees. The gasoline yield of such crudes is good —as high as 65 percent for one North Sumatran crude—which is a favourable factor in Southeast Asian markets, and one reason why Indonesian crude travels as far as the Pacific coast refineries of the United States. But over two-thirds of Indonesian crudes are paraffinic or heavy paraffinic oils with an API gravity of 35–38 degrees; for example, the output of the large Minas field in Central Sumatra and Tandjung in Kalimantan. Such crudes compare well enough with the main competitive crudes of the Middle East. They have a high gasoline content and are "sweeter" (sulphur free).[28] On the other hand, they all have a high paraffin content

[27] See *World Oil*, no. 10, August 15, 1964, and *Oil and Gas Journal*, December 28, 1964 for data on reserves, number of wells, production, etc. Also British Petroleum Co., *Statistical Review of the World Oil Industry, 1963* and *1964*.

[28] The value of crude oil varies with its specific gravity (traditionally $.02 per degree calculated on American Petroleum Institute or API ratings). The higher the gravity reading, the greater the yield of gasolines and kerosenes,

and are therefore waxy. Not only do these waxy crudes offer problems at the refinery stage; often they also are difficult to transport from the well head. For example, Stanvac, in its Lirik field, is compelled to steam-heat the pipelines carrying the crude to the river terminal to about 40 degrees centigrade and to construct specially heated river tankers in order to move the crude to the refinery. Shell, for the same problem affecting its Tandjung crude, used a different technique. Through the 250-kilometre pipeline to the refinery at Balikpapan the waxy crude is pumped suspended in water. At the refinery, the oil is then separated for processing. Such techniques add to transport and manufacturing costs, but no more than would be caused by, for example, the high sulphur content of many Middle Eastern crudes.

The output of crude rose substantially in the postwar years, demonstrating some of the potential of Indonesian oil territory. After the late 1940's period of resuscitation in the old South Sumatran and Kalimantan fields, crude oil production rose from the 1950 figure of 6,816,000 metric tons to 22,860,000 in 1963. At first, during 1950–1954, Shell with its subsidiary NIAM was the most substantial producer, providing about 5,000,000 tons per annum. Later, in 1959, NIAM became an independent state

---

which are the more remunerative petroleum products. Impurities, such as sulphur compounds, are also important. They must be reduced in the refining process to below a certain value in order not to damage combustion engines. And the paraffin content (showing itself in a high wax element and a high pour point) also involves extra refinery processing which adds to cost and lowers somewhat the value of the crude. However, this traditional method of valuing crudes is not more than a rule of thumb suitable for ordinary distillation processes and on the assumption that the end products are destined for markets dominated by the demand for gasolines. Two developments have altered matters. First, catalytic and thermal cracking, although expensive, enables refiners to break down middle and heavy distillate fractions to obtain larger yields of gasoline (and also feed stock for chemical production). Thus middle-range and heavy crudes are again more acceptable. In practice, the international majors, who account for 75 percent of refining capacity outside the U.S.A. and the Soviet bloc, adjust their refining techniques, on the one hand, to the regional market demand and, on the other, to the nearest available and reasonably suitable crude, usually obtained from their own concessions at intracompany prices. In these circumstances, it becomes rather difficult to give a market value to any given crude.

enterprise. Shell, operating by itself, suffered a decline in output in 1955–1956, and, after 1960, could not rise far above 5,000,000 tons even with the help of the newly developed field at Tandjung. Stanvac produced just over 3,000,000 tons by 1951. But production fell for a few years because of the partial expiry of the South Sumatran fields; and it was 1955 before it touched this level again. Thereafter, the development of the Lirik field, which reached full production by 1958, helped out, but by 1960 the company was producing only about 3,300,000 tons and by 1963 output had not risen above this figure. Caltex, the concessionaire for the recently discovered fields, Duri and Minas, was much more fortunate. These areas were at the beginning of their development period. Minas started production in 1952, adding to a small output from Duri. By 1958, when Caltex had completed its ocean terminal at Dumai, the company was producing 7,318,000 metric tons per annum, or 45 percent of Indonesian output, from these two fields. By 1963, the Caltex figure was 11,534,000 metric tons or 52 percent of total Indonesian output. Thus the older fields of Indonesia provided little long-term expansion, and most increases came from the newly exploited fields discovered just prior to the war.

Since 1963, new exploration and development has not had much time in which to change this pattern of stagnation in one part of the industry and growth in another. In 1964, for example, Shell drilled eight wells, mainly at deep levels, in South Sumatra and Kalimantan. Three were dry. Stanvac drilled fourteen in Central and South Sumatra, and three of these also were dry. PERMINA—through its contractor Asamera—also was active: thirteen wells were drilled, six of them dry and two yielding gas. Pan American in Central Sumatra drilled eight dry wells. By 1965, it was reported that Asamera had made three very promising strikes in North Sumatra—outside the old BPM development areas—and a pipeline to the coast is proposed. Shell had made two discoveries, one in South Sumatra and one in Kalimantan. However, Pan American, having spent fruitlessly over $24 million between 1962 and 1965, has had no good fortune and may therefore withdraw from all prospecting in Indonesia. Meanwhile, Caltex in 1964, drilled three development wells and two exploratory wells (making a new field discovery)—the smallest drilling effort of all the active companies. Yet its output from the Duri and Minas fields rose 23 percent and 15 percent respectively in 1964 and 1965. These Caltex increases were largely offset by the marked decline in production of the other companies; consequently total Indonesian output during 1964 and 1965 rose only in the region of 2 or 3 percent per annum.[29] Hence, although by 1964–1965 the annual output of Indonesian crude was running close to 24,000,000 metric tons—three and a half times the 1950 figure—the immediate outlook was not promising. Even the Caltex fields are expected to reach the beginning of their period of decline within the next few years.

In retrospect it is now clear that had the three international majors, especially Shell and Stanvac, been permitted to explore and develop new areas during the course of 1950–1963, instead of being restricted to prewar concessions, the present crude oil outputs would have been much greater. It seems reasonable to hypothesise that Shell and Stanvac would easily have doubled their production and Caltex could have added to its present output significantly. Total Indonesian output could have been 33,000,000 metric tons at least. The price paid for revolutionary vigilance truly was a severe one in the case of Indonesian oil.

The cost of production of crude oil in Indonesia, at least in the newer fields, is almost certainly low by international standards. Two-thirds of the costs of crude lie in the exploration and development of fields required before oil begins to flow from the ground. The remainder are the variable or "lifting" costs of extracting the crude and conveying it to the field terminal.[30] From calculations made by the petroleum department of the Chase Manhattan Bank, we know that the unit costs of *maintaining and expanding crude production* (over 1952–1961) by means of exploration and development were $.78 per barrel for the Far East, of which Indonesia was the most substantial producer (86 percent). From 1958 onwards, the unit cost figure dropped rapidly until it was $.51 by

[29] See *World Oil,* August 15, 1965, pp. 211–212 (International Outlook Issue). Shell's output fell by 14 percent between 1963 and 1964, Stanvac's by 19 percent, PERMINA's by 8 percent, PERTAMIN's by 14 percent, and PERMIGAN's by 11 percent.

[30] See M. De Chazeau and A. E. Kahn, *Integration and Competition in the Petroleum Industry,* Yale University Press, New Haven 1959, pp. 67–68.

1961[31]—a reflection of the expanding production of Caltex in its Duri and Minas fields and of Shell in its Tandjung field. Judging from output figures, we can expect that for the period 1958 and 1965 unit costs for exploration and development will be significantly lower than $.78—probably in the region of $.60 per barrel. This would imply total f.o.b. costs of production in the region of $.90 per barrel in the 1960's. The international price for Indonesian crude (discounted) is around $1.77; thus the margin of profit on crude oil exports, from newer fields at least, is handsome enough.[32]

Altogether, in the physical output sense, Indonesian oil production remains a good prospect, although exploration obviously carries at least its share of uncertainty and disappointment. In the economic sense, it is quite attractive. Apart from the profit margin on crude, there is no shortage of markets for Indonesian oil provided satisfactory contracts can be made with refiners. The country's oil resources do not have the same importance as in the 1930's when its 7,500,000 tons per annum represented 12 percent of eastern hemisphere output. Nowadays, with a production approaching 24,000,000 tons, it has only 3 percent of eastern hemisphere output on account of new production coming from the Persian Gulf countries, now the chief suppliers of crude east of Suez. However, Indonesian crudes and export products refined in Indonesia do retain a substantial advantage in their strategic location. They are 2,000–3,500 miles nearer than Middle Eastern

[31] See Chase Manhattan Bank, *Capital Investments by the World Petroleum Industry,* New York, 1961).

[32] *Petroleum Intelligence Weekly,* New York, November 30, 1964. These discounts normally go to independent refiners such as Ampol in Brisbane or one of the Japanese companies. A 100 percent subsidiary in, say, Australia or the Philippines until a few years ago was liable to pay a "posted" price such as $1.96 for Minas. This differential pricing has been reduced in incidence as taxation authorities have insisted on "arm's length" contract prices to increase refinery profits and taxes.

These are aggregate figures based on the expenditures of the three large companies. But Caltex by virtue of its production on a relatively large scale from its two recent fields, Minas and Duri, will of course have rather low costs of production. In the trade, it has been suggested to the writer that Caltex' total cost of production is one-sixth of the posted price, *i.e.,* about $.33 per barrel for Minas Crude.

oil fields to the refineries and markets of Southeast Asia and to the rapidly growing consumption areas of Japan (where demand increases by 20 percent per annum) and Australasia (8½ percent per annum); and, because the relatively small outputs of crude from Indonesia must adjust their landed prices to the same levels (allowing for quality) as for the dominant supplies from the Persian Gulf, they are made more valuable to an extent which can be represented in tanker freight rates. In 1965, this nearness to main markets gave Indonesia a margin of $.20–.30 per barrel in freight charges—a handsome geographical advantage.[33]

In the prewar, *refining of crude into petroleum products* Indonesia was one of the main centres for the Far Eastern areas (including Japan and China). In 1938, of 7,416,000 metric tons produced, 81 percent was exported within the Far Eastern area, leaving a relatively small proportion for domestic consumption. After 1945, this role in Far Eastern markets was taken up again by the two companies mainly involved, Shell and Stanvac. Refinery throughput rose rapidly from zero to 7,552,000 tons by 1950. The recovery to prewar output was markedly more rapid than that for crude production, which did not level until 1953–1954. This refinery resuscitation required imports of foreign crude, mainly from Sarawak in the earlier years and later from Brunei and the Middle East. Shell still imported more than a million tons per annum up to 1963 to keep refineries employed. The refinery-yield pattern reflects Indonesian and, to some extent, Southeast Asian product markets which are still heavily influenced by the demand for kerosene. Hence Indonesian refineries produce much higher proportions of kerosene than is typical elsewhere. The moderate proportion of gasoline produced is of a low-octane rating.[34] Consequently the refineries are not technically sophisticated. A higher proportion of equipment than is common in, say, Australia or the newer refinery centres of Southeast Asia or Japan, is devoted to straight distillation; and a smaller proportion to catalytic or thermal cracking or reforming (techniques designed to break up the molecular structure of certain distillates and residual oils in

[33] Freight advantage is calculated at AFRA rates (average freight rate assessment—London Brokers Panel) for large tankers.

[34] The following table shows some percentage refinery yields in 1963 as

order to provide larger proportions of valuable and useful products, for example, gasoline, diesel fuel, and chemical by-products).

However, the Indonesian refinery industry, still of a substantial size, is undergoing a transformation away from its traditional role as an exporter to the Far Eastern market area. There are various reasons for this change.

The first main factor affecting the position of the refinery industry is a rapid increase in domestic demand for petroleum products. Since 1950, it has shown, on average, a yearly increase of about 12 percent. There are elsewhere higher rates of annual increase—Japan 26 percent and Western Europe 14½ percent per annum. But this Indonesian rise is greater than, for example, the 7½ percent for the rest of Asia, Australia's 8½ percent, or the average for the world of 7½ percent per annum.[35] The reasons for this better-than-average increase are not straightforward. The population of Indonesia is rising steadily—at about 2.2 percent per annum. On the other hand, the more reliable estimates indicate that Indonesian national income is rising at much the same speed—perhaps a little more slowly. Consequently per capita income is not changing and is possibly falling slightly. Therefore, affluence cannot be said to account for the rapid rise in domestic demand for petroleum products.[36] It seems (apart from some

---

given in Bureau of Mines, U.S. Department of the Interior, *International Petroleum Quarterly, Annual 1963,* Washington, D.C.

Country	*Gasolines*	*Kerosenes*	*Middle distillates*	*Residual oils*	*Other refined products*
Indonesia	22	25	23	17	13
U.S.A.	42	8	22	14	14
Australia	41	5	15	22	17
Western Europe	17	3	27	36	17
Japan	15	9	11	47	18

[35] British Petroleum Co., *Statistical Review of the World Oil Industry, 1963* and *1964.* Within the 14 percent per annum increase, kerosene accounted for a 20 percent increase and petrol a 10 percent increase up to 1960.

[36] Central Bureau of Statistics (National Income Unit), *Estimates of National Income of Indonesia by Industrial Origin, 1958–62,* Djakarta, April 1965. There is no evidence that national growth showed much better progress before 1958.

normal growth in the demand for petroleum products such as is caused by the wider use of motor vehicles and industrial diesel engines) that most of the increase in demand is the consequence of certain structural changes in the Indonesian economy and, to a large degree, the failure of the Indonesian government to maintain realistic fiscal, monetary, and public utility pricing policies.

Consider some changes which have taken place. Coal production once was important in Indonesia for electricity generating, industrial use, and rail transport. Despite strong efforts by the government, production during the 1950's never rose above half of the 1,781,000 metric tons of 1939, and by 1962 it had fallen to 471,836 tons, because of transport problems, labour difficulties, and lack of spare parts.[37] Public electricity supplies for thermal stations have therefore never been sufficient to provide the increasing power needs of manufacturing in addition to transport and domestic consumption. Indeed, industry now takes only 10 percent or less of public electricity supplies and relies instead for most of its power and electricity on its own engines and generators. Of the total electricity and power thus supplied by manufacturing for itself in 1962, just over one-tenth was steam-generated (some of this on oil). The remainder came from combustion engines. Expenditures by manufacturing industry on fuel for power and electricity are significant; 24 percent of that expenditure goes on coal, gas, and coke; 36 percent on fuel oil; and 40 percent on petrol. The use of coal by the railway system (except in Sumatra, where the main deposits lie) had declined also. For Indonesia as a whole the proportion of oil-burning or diesel locomotives rose from 5 percent in 1952 to 30 percent by 1962. Road transport has made a major contribution to demand. The registration of vehicles (excluding motorcycles and three-wheelers), rose from 60,000 in 1950 to over 180,000 by 1959, a majority of them being trucks and buses.[38] These figures do not include the sizable fleet of military and naval vehicles brought into Indonesia for the armed forces

[37] Central Bureau of Statistics, *Statistical Pocketbook of Indonesia, 1963*, Djakarta.

[38] De Leuw, Cather, and Coy (consulting engineers), *Land Transportation Survey for Indonesia*, U.S. International Cooperation Administration, Chicago, 1961.

and which, on appearances, seem to constitute about a third of the vehicle population of the larger cities. Finally, there is the increase in the demand for kerosene which is the most substantial of all. Demand, from 1950 to around 1960, rose by over 20 percent per annum. The tonnage of kerosene, as a proportion of total domestic demand, moved from 16 percent in 1938 to 20 percent in 1954, and 25 percent in 1963. The increase per annum slowed down in 1960 on account of sheer inability of the refinery industry to process more of this commodity. The secular increase in demand for kerosene was due partly to its substitution for charcoal and firewood in cooking (especially in Java, where these fuels are becoming very scarce). It is also due to the more widespread employment of kerosene as an illuminant in the countryside. In addition, this abnormal increase was further supported by the failure of the Indonesian authorities to develop any significant rural electricity supply or even a reliable urban electricity supply. Kerosene is still widely used by poorer people as an illuminant in major and minor Indonesian cities. (Wealthy citizens do their best —emulating manufacturing industry and business—to have a standby diesel-electric generating set to supply their own electricity.)

Pricing policy was a second factor drastically affecting the refinery industry. All product prices have been the subject of controls since 1945. Whereas the cost-of-living index constructed officially by the Biro Pusat Statistik (Central Bureau of Statistics) rose to 15,482 by February 1965 (1953 = 100), prices of petrol, kerosene, and other petroleum products barely moved from their 1950 level. Normally the price elasticity of demand for the lighter petroleum products—petrol, diesel oil, kerosene, and lubricants—is low, at least in the short run. Even substantial shifts in price will not cause large changes in the quantities demanded, which are determined by technical factors and by the general level of economic activity. The heavier distillates and fuel oils, on the other hand, may have low price levels in terms of their thermal and labour inputs relative to the prices of older, more established fuels. (This is true of heating and furnace oils which have shown in industrialised countries a substantial elasticity of demand over secular periods on account of their greater thermal value and convenience.) But in Indonesia, prices have been held to such a low level as to encourage considerable substitution in both groups of products: from one set of heating fuels (charcoal, firewood, and coal) to another set (kerosene, heating oil, and furnace fuels; and from one set of transport media using little or no fuel (bicycles, trishaws, motorcycles, and three-wheelers) to another set (cars, buses, and heavy road vehicles) using large quantities of petrol and diesel fuel. In general, absurdly low prices have permitted an increase in the consumption of all petroleum products not restrained in any very significant manner by demands for income to be expended on alternative sources of satisfaction. Petroleum products almost moved into the category of free goods over the period 1950–1965.[39]

Thirdly, there is the position of export markets for petroleum products. Traditional export markets for the refined products of Indonesia have been progressively closed off by developments in various countries. Japan, which in 1940 took half a million tons of Indonesian products, now manufactures nearly all of its needs in over thirty domestic refineries. China, formerly a customer, imports nothing and is busily engaged in developing her own refinery industry based on indigenous crudes. Hong Kong, which as recently as 1961 imported half a million tons of Indonesian products, now secures its supplies predominantly from the Middle East, Singapore, and Japan. Singapore itself is the most serious loss to the Indonesian refinery industry. As an entrepôt centre for Malaya and the largest bunkering port in Southeast Asia, it was the biggest single market outlet, prewar and postwar. In 1958, 4,131,500 metric tons were taken through this port from Indonesia, of which almost 2,000,000 tons were diesel and fuel oil for ships—heavier petroleum products not easily disposed of in world markets. Even before confrontation terminated exports to Singapore, this outlet had diminished to 3,329,000 tons in 1962 as Singapore and Malaya obtained supplies from the Shell refinery built (1961) on Pulau Bukom, an island offshore Singapore. Then the Shell and Esso

[39] Petroleum products did not quite reach the status of free goods, principally because the distribution system could not accommodate the quantities involved and black marketeering arose to take advantage of the resulting scarcity.

refineries were built at Port Dickson on the mainland of Malaya (1963). In all, these three refineries provided 75,000 barrels per day (BPD) throughout, or 3,750,000 tons per annum. As confrontation developed into a specific policy, the British Petroleum Company took over a new 15,000 BPD refinery in Malaya (1964) while the Mobil Company, a former parent of Stanvac,[40] has an 18,000 BPD refinery under construction in Singapore. Finally in 1966, Shell announced plans to build another 60,000 BPD refinery on Pulau Bukom. In the nearby Philippines, the picture has changed also. Shell has a 25,000 BPD refinery there (completed in 1962); the Bataan Refinery Corporation, an independent company operating since 1961, provides 36,000 BPD; and Caltex as early as 1955 opened up a 30,000 BPD installation. Thailand and South Vietnam have refining capacities of respectively 57,000 BPD and 24,000 BPD, constructed or in the making.[41] Altogether the refining capacity of Indonesia, about half of which could be available for highly remunerative exports, has been more than replaced[42] by developments in these nearby areas.

These trends in refinery production are reflected in the figures

[40] Stanvac was a subsidiary of Standard New Jersey and the Mobil (formerly Vacuum) Oil Co. of the United States. Subsequent to an antitrust suit in 1962, these companies agreed no longer to combine as Stanvac in Southeast Asian and Pacific markets and to divide Stanvac assets and interests between the two parent companies. Eastern Standard Esso (a Standard N.J. subsidiary) is now the operating company for the Stanvac installations in Indonesia.

[41] *Statistical Pocketbook of Indonesia, 1963,* Table 34; *Oil and Gas Journal,* December 28, 1964, p. 130; and *Petroleum Times,* London, January 8, 1965, p. 19.

[42] The development of refinery capacity in the Southeast Asian area has been accelerated by the reduction in construction costs of building refineries of 20–30 thousand BPD. It is estimated that, in the past 8–9 years, relatively simple techniques which make full use of local materials, services, etc., have caused costs to fall by 30–40 percent (United Nations Economic Commission for Asia and the Far East [UNECAFE], *Economic Survey of Asia and the Far East 1963* [annual], Bangkok, pp. 140–141). Another factor is the substantial savings to be secured by transporting large single cargoes of crude in tankers ranging from 25–80 thousand DWT from the crude oil producing centres to the consuming countries as against the unfavourable transport economics involved in carrying a variety of small cargoes of products from the same centres in tankers rarely greater than 2,000 DWT.

for the export of Indonesian petroleum products. They quickly reached 6,091,000 metric tons in 1950 in response to the acute scarcity in the Far East in 1945–1950. Oddly enough, this figure was again at the prewar 81 percent of total Indonesian refinery throughput. Exports reached a peak of 7,689,000 tons in 1953—but were now only 71 percent of throughput. Another peak of 7,969,000 tons occurred in 1959 (the highest point ever reached by refinery exports from Indonesia); but this was only 60 percent of refinery throughput, leaving 40 percent for domestic demand. From 1959 onward, total throughput of Indonesian refineries failed to rise significantly, and exports began to decline absolutely as well as relatively. The 1964 figure dropped to almost half that of the peak year of 1959. This is in marked contrast to the general experience of the Southeast Asian area, where refinery capacity and consumption steadily increased at an average of 11 percent per annum.[43]

It is clear that the Indonesian refinery industry missed, or was denied, an opportunity to increase its export of products substantially during 1955–1963. Now the effects of *confrontasi* are upon Indonesia. Internationally collated figures show a drastic decrease in tonnages exported in the order of 39 percent between 1962 and 1964. For 1965, it was reliably reported that the Shell export refineries at Balikpapan and Pladju operated at less than two-thirds of their capacity. But the precise extent of the drop in exports for 1965 and 1966 remains unconfirmed.

The fourth factor re-orientating the Indonesian refinery industry away from its traditional reliance on exports of products is the changed attitude of the three international companies since the highly nationalistic Indonesian government began interesting itself in oil industry affairs. These companies could have expanded their refining activities to satisfy domestic demand *and* develop export markets. But they chose not to do so. Shell and Stanvac had their unfortunate experiences in the domestic market. Apart from all the vicissitudes involved in taxation and supervision of the industry by the government, both companies suffered severe losses due to price control and inflation before 1963. After 1963, a

[43] British Petroleum Co., *Statistical Review of the World Oil Industry, 1963*; and *International Petroleum Quarterly, Annual 1963* and *Annual 1964*.

refining margin of 10 cents per barrel was guaranteed by the agreements. But this margin is subject to the same 60:40 percent profit division as for all Indonesian oil activities, to say nothing of the negotiations required to satisfy the Indonesian government of what is, in fact, the true level of refinery operating costs. Furthermore, the Shell and Stanvac companies could be expected to be subject to continual pressure to satisfy the internal domestic market in preference to export markets. By 1964–1965, this obligation had reached the stage that scarcely any kerosene and petrol were exported. Most exports of refined products consisted of the relatively low-profit residual oils and marine diesel oils. In these circumstances the obvious policy of international companies is to refine (using Indonesian crude or Middle Eastern crudes, whichever can conveniently be supplied) in the consumer countries outside Indonesia, where their refining will be subject only to ordinary corporation tax and will, on international prices, earn a higher refining margin anyway.[44] Caltex displays this inclination most clearly of the three companies. Since prewar days the proposal to build a Caltex refinery in Indonesia has been discussed off and on. But this company has successfully avoided crystallising discussion to the point of action; and indeed, in the 1950's (after compensating the Indonesian government), pointedly undertook the construction of a refinery in the nearby Philippines to be supplied by crude from its Minas field. For their part, Shell and Stanvac after the first postwar rehabilitation simply have avoided refinery expansion in Indonesia. And it is significant that most of

[44] Posted prices at Singapore (Shell) and Sungei Gerong, Sumatra (Stanvac) for international trade are consistently stable and can be held above Middle Eastern prices for all products because of the protection given by geographical location and the fact that the same international companies are the main marketeers in both areas. (Gasoline and kerosene are usually $.05 to $.07 per gallon higher than Persian Gulf prices at Abadan or Ras Tanura; industrial diesel oil higher by $.25–.35 per barrel; and marine diesel oil $.40 per barrel more expensive.) Despite probably higher costs of crude in the Far East, these arrangements guaranteed a refinery margin comparable with Middle Eastern refinery margins—"among the highest of the major oil centres of the world" ("Representative Market Quotations" in *Petroleum Press Service,* any issue; and C. Issawi and M. Yegenah, *The Economics of Middle Eastern Oil,* Faber, London, 1962, p. 69).

the new refineries constructed in Southeast Asian market areas have been established by parents of the original foreign companies in Indonesia (Shell, Standard, Mobil, and Caltex). Evidently the major oil companies are looking for locations more profitable and, equally important, conditions more stable than they believe can be offered in Indonesia.

The *distribution of refined products* throughout Indonesia, because of the archipelagian character of the country (3,000 miles long, composed of four large island areas and many lesser island groups) and the location of the large refineries away from the main marketing centres, is necessarily a maritime operation in its first phase. For this interisland trade in products, tankers operate from the refineries to the main receiving ports and marketing centres for inland distribution: Djakarta (for West Java), Medan (for North Sumatra), Surabaya (East Java and some eastern islands), Semarang (Central Java), and Macassar (Sulawesi and the Moluccas). In addition, small tankers, 1,000 DWT or less, distribute around the coasts of the archipelago and up rivers to numerous smaller ports which serve the locality immediately surrounding them: Benoa in Bali for example; also Tjirebon in West Java, Tjilijap in South Java, Benkulan and Padang on the west coast of Sumatra, Pontianak and Bandjarmasin in Kalimantan, Ambon in the Moluccas, Kupang in Timor, etc. This interisland distribution is to be transferred progressively to the state enterprise PERMINA, which before 1965 already had about nine or ten small tankers carrying crude oil in international trade. By the end of 1965, it is hoped that PERMINA will have taken over the Shell operations in interisland distribution and then go on to assimilate the Stanvac facilities. (Caltex has no interisland tankers.)*

There are problems. Some of the receiving ports for inland distribution have, through neglect, become silted-up to the extent that the 1,000 DWT tankers find their use hazardous and are compelled to tranship their cargoes to lighters—an expensive and lengthly process. This situation is reported for the harbours of Pontianak, Tjirebon, and Semarang, the last two serving large

* While the former did occur, the latter has not. See Addendum, below.—Ed.

inland market areas. The transfer of ships itself is hindered by a shortage of suitable tankers. Shell had only a limited number available for sale—the remainder of its fleet is chartered from Norway and Britain. Chartering of foreign ships is not regarded as desirable by the Indonesian authorities but the alternatives—building new ships in Japan and buying on the second-hand market where small tankers are scarce—are initially very expensive in foreign exchange. Consequently the transfer of marine operations may take longer than is programmed. In addition to the shipping problems, there is a shortage of qualified officers and engineers to operate coastal tankers. It is reported that the present PERMINA interisland fleet has only 50 percent of the effectiveness (volume per annum moved per 1,000 DWT) of a comparable chartered fleet manned by Norwegian or British officers and Singapore seamen and surveyed and serviced in Singapore. Low effectiveness is a problem experienced in interisland trade generally.[45] Part of it may, of course, be due not so much to incompetent operation of the tankers as to a failure to coordinate supplies and shipping. A committee, representing PERMINA, Caltex, Shell, and Stanvac was set up during September 1965 to attempt to iron out this difficulty. There are also problems for PERMINA in estimating demand. Some inland distribution areas find difficulty in moving their products according to schedule; and military and naval authorities frequently pose supply problems which are unpredictable in their incidence on tanker capacity.

Inland distribution and marketing operations were taken over by the state enterprise PERTAMIN by July 1965,[46] and are now organized in five marketing areas—Sumatra, West Java and Kalimantan, Central Java, East Java and the lesser islands, and Sulawesi and the Moluccas. (West Irian continues to be supplied, for the present, by Shell from its Philippine refinery.)

[45] See Shamsher Ali, "Inter-Insular Shipping," *BIES,* no. 3, March 1966.

[46] The total paid for the assets involved—bulk storage depots, road tankers, rail tankers, marine terminals, blending plants for lubricants, etc.—was $12.496 million (P.N. PERTAMIN, *Pengoperan Marketing Dan Distribution Assets,* Djakarta, July 1965). Shell's assets accounted for $8.024 million; Stanvac's cost $4.605 million; and Caltex's $317 million, giving an accurate indication of the relative involvement of the three companies in distribution and marketing.

The majority of the problems in inland distribution and marketing stem from the unfortunate price policy of the Indonesian government for petroleum products. In 1945, in a period of extreme scarcity, the Dutch colonial government set up a petroleum board to supervise supplies and their allocation to the three marketing companies and to control the prices of all products. The Indonesian government abolished the physical control of distribution in 1953, but retained price control on all products.[47] Thus, during the period 1950 to November 1965 prices, so far as the companies were concerned, were permitted to move only twice. At first, during 1950–1954, petrol and kerosene were priced (bulk price at terminal, including excise duty and sales tax collected by the companies for the government) around Rp. 1.37 and Rp. .53 per litre respectively. This period did not cause very great losses; and they were in any case compensated by the profits to be obtained from export sales. From 1955 to the end of 1961, the controlled prices were Rp. 1.69 and Rp. 1.12 for petrol and kerosene. As early as 1958, all companies were suffering severe losses in their sale of products to the domestic market. Memoranda were submitted applying for price increases. The Stanvac memorandum, for example, displayed a breakdown of its costs of manufacture—sea freight, administration and storage costs, excise and sales taxes, etc.—which demonstrated that costs on petrol and kerosene were respectively Rp. .56 and Rp. .55 per litre greater than the controlled prices the company was permitted to charge. Total losses in 1958 for this company, on all products, were shown as Rp. 529 million (piquantly enough nearly three times what the company collected for the government in excise and sales tax). At the rate of exchange available to oil companies, these losses were about $17 million for Stanvac.

From 1962 to 1965, the consumer prices in Djakarta, Medan, Surabaya, etc. were Rp. 4 and Rp. 1.5 for petrol and kerosene. However, this was also a period of the most catastrophic inflation, and there grew up many local arrangements for "pump operators' allowances," "compensation for transport," and the like, which established themselves in the retail price structure. Thus by mid-1965, a typical, semiofficial retail price (Djakarta and Surabaya)

[47] MIT CENIS, *op. cit.*, pp. 34–36.

for petrol was Rp. 10; and for kerosene Rp. 6. But these local fringe adjustments were nominal compared with what had happened elsewhere in the economy. The total money supply (bolstered by large budgetary deficits and implemented by the printing press) rose from Rp. 7.486 billion in 1953 to Rp. 625 billion by the beginning of 1965. The official cost-of-living index of the Biro Pusat Statistik (1953 = 100) moved to 15,482 by the end of the first quarter of 1965, and the free market price of rice rose from Rp. 2.25 a kilo in 1953 to Rp. 375 a kilo in mid-1965 (Djakarta prices).[48] The wages of oil workers, transport costs, and distribution costs all rose correspondingly. After the 1963 agreements, when the oil companies did not sell on their own account but supplied the state enterprises with refined products or distributed on their behalf, the burden of supporting controlled prices fell on the state. Dr. Saleh Siregar, president-director of PERTAMIN, admitted that the controlled prices of petrol and other products were "far below production costs"; and Major General Ibnu Soetowo, president-director of PERMINA and minister for oil affairs, divulged that the petrol subsidy alone was running at Rp. 35 billion annually by 1965.[49] The total subsidy for all products, according to the Direktorat Minjak Dan Gas Bumi, was expected to be in the region of Rp. 60 billion for 1965.[50]

Price control had the most deleterious effects on distribution. Inflated money demand could not possibly be equated to supply at such nominal prices as Rp. 4 and Rp. 1.5 for petrol and kerosene. To fill the vacuum, there emerged a large class of "middlemen" or black marketeers who provided largely unnecessary, indeed undesirable, services and pushed up retail prices to something approximating an equilibrating level. Some of these individuals

[48] *Statistical Pocketbook of Indonesia, 1963,* and *Business News,* Djakarta, various issues.

[49] *Financial and Economic News,* Djakarta, December 31, 1965, p. 10; and November 10, 1965, p. 10.

[50] This is a mere 4½ percent of the Rp. 1365 billion expenditure originally contemplated in the 1965 state budget. Of this sum, approximately Rp. 444 billion, or nearly 40 percent was not covered by revenue (Commercial Advisory Foundation in Indonesia, *Circulars* H.497, H.498, and H.499, commenting on the state budget).

were substantial operators who bought whole or part loads of petrol and kerosene from road tanker agents or drivers as they moved from the ports or bulk depots toward the retail outlets. They paid prices better than the official bulk prices (which the tanker agent had to remit to the supplying company); the petrol and kerosene were stored in drums; then, when the commodity failed to materialise at the petrol stations and retail outlets, the black marketeers offered it to the general public (and transport companies) in 20-litre jerricans sold from roadside booths or backyard garages. Less ambitious operators merely arranged to buy substantial quantities of petrol at the official retail price from the pumps; waited until the pump ran out of petrol for the day, then set up to sell this now scarce commodity to the public at high prices a mere 20 to 50 yards from the empty service station. In these "free market" conditions, prices varied from district to district depending on local scarcities and the state of the distributive organisation. A 20-litre jerrican of petrol could sell for Rp. 800 to Rp. 2,000 (Rp. 40 to Rp. 100 per litre). Kerosene prices were higher relative to the controlled price because of its greater physical scarcity by 1965. The prices of fuel oil and industrial diesel oil, on the other hand, could not be so easily manipulated since they normally are delivered, on invoice, to business premises. But scarcities created by disrupted distribution facilities did lead to some middleman manipulation and the payment of "premiums" on the prices of such industrial petroleum products.

Naturally there was general resentment concerning this state of affairs. Transport organisations and the general public complained bitterly. Incidents concerning high prices, long queues of vehicles waiting at petrol-less stations, the viciousness of black marketeers, etc., were daily fare in newspapers. Ministers made declamatory pronouncements condemning "manipulators"; prosecutions and confiscations of supplies occurred frequently; and occasionally President Sukarno himself went the rounds of port terminals, road tanker agents, and petrol stations to admonish the distributive trades for their antisocial behaviour in allowing petroleum products to escape into the black market. But all to little effect. The proliferation of middleman activity in petroleum distribution progressed steadily with the pace of inflation.[51] Whereas in 1958, black market prices were from two to three times the controlled price, by 1965, such was the pace of inflation and the spread of the black marketeering that they were from ten to twenty-five times the controlled price. The take-over by PERTAMIN from Shell, Stanvac, and Caltex in 1965 made no noticeable difference, except that inexperience caused rather more dislocation of distribution for a time in the large cities of Djakarta and Bandung—to the advantage of the "manipulators."

Behind the more obvious anomalies of the black market, there were other severely damaging effects of price control. The international companies, as they informed the government frequently in memoranda, were unwilling to invest in distributive facilities. There was little prospect of anything but losses at controlled prices. Therefore there was an insufficient increase in road tankers, rail tankers, bulk storage tanks, and even port terminal equipment to deal with rising domestic demands. All of these facilities became congested and, by 1965, were causing serious obstacles to the movement of products. Service stations, substantially unchanged in number since 1955 and many taken over for military purposes, were too few to handle the increasing number of vehicles. And insufficient maintenance or renewal expenditure was given to old equipment. When PERTAMIN took over these distributive problems in 1965 there was little prospect that it would receive permission to spend scarce foreign currency in building new facilities.[52] On the other hand, a more effective

[51] For examples of prices, complaints, confiscation, etc., see *Financial and Economic News,* Djakarta, March 6, 1965, p. 8, and June 15, 1965, p. 4.

[52] Some of the more significant general misallocations of resources resulting from controlled petroleum prices in the face of catastrophic inflation should be indicated. Coal extraction was discouraged by low fuel oil and diesel oil prices (Rp. 0.8 and Rp. 1 per litre). Charcoal and firewood industries declined and created concealed rural unemployment on account of cheap kerosene. Industrial planning went forward on the basis of prices of fuels which did not reflect their true opportunity costs to the community. For example, sugar mills turned to fuel oil and abandoned firewood, coal, and desaccharinated sugar cane; textile factories generated power for machinery on very low, almost zero, fuel costs; and public utilities (electric power, railways, airways, buses, and road transport), partly because of low

remedy was to hand at all times. Without doubt, many and probably most of the shortages of equipment in distribution could have been eliminated simply by raising prices.

In mid-November 1965, the government of Indonesia at last made the obvious moves to end this farcical situation. As part of a wide-ranging attempt to bring inflation under control, and to introduce some economic realism into the prices of public goods and services, the price structure for all petroleum products was lifted radically. Petrol, for example, went up 6,000 percent and kerosene 10,000 percent. Then, in January 1966, prices were raised again fourfold, although some were reduced again three weeks later. Petroleum products had become indispensable commodities by 1965 and therefore were selected as one of the main vehicles for anti-inflationary policies.[53]

Through its *export* performance, the petroleum industry has made an important contribution to the Indonesian economy. It is one of the few industries which (despite the hazards of official policies and the uncertainties offered by nationalism) caused substantial new investment to take place and which continuously and consistently has demonstrated an increasing ability to earn the foreign exchange so urgently required for ambitious industrialisation and national defence programmes. In an economy where both export volumes and values have shown a declining trend, it

---

fuel costs, could not force authorities to permit them to raise tariffs. Consequently, low fares and prices encouraged a demand for their services which they could not meet and the results were power failures, two-day queues for airway and rail tickets, hopelessly congested railway and bus accommodations, breakdowns, poor maintenance, and a general loss of morale on the part of the public services.

[53] At various dates the official controlled prices (in old rupiah) of petroleum products (consumer prices at main ports of Djakarta, Medan, Surabaya etc.) were, according to *Business News,* October, 12, 1965, p. 12a; and *Monitoring Warta Berita,* Djakarta, January, 22, 1966:

Dates	*Petrol*	*Kerosene*	*Automotive diesel oil*	*Industrial diesel*	*Fuel oil*
1962–1965	4.0	1.5	1.0	1.0	1.0
Nov. 1965	250.0	150.0	150.0	100.0	100.0
Jan. 1966	1000.0	600.0	600.0	400.0	400.0
Jan. 21, 1966	500.0	300.0			

is unique in having maintained until 1964 a steady increase in both. Total exports (crude and products) moved threefold from 6,099,000 metric tons in 1950 to 19,167,000 in 1963. Foreign exchange earnings rose also, but by rather less, from the 1950 figure of $147 million to $269 million by 1963, the smaller proportional increase in value being due to the high proportion of residual oils and crudes exported in later years instead of the more remunerative gasolines and kerosenes.[54]

The improved performance over the years is significant and promising, but it is easy to exaggerate the earning ability of petroleum and its products by looking solely at gross foreign exchange receipts. If we examine instead *net* export earnings we find that rubber is still a much superior performer. This result arises because, unlike rubber growing (where most of the value added is in respect of inputs indigenous to Indonesia), the oil industry operates with a very substantial import component among its inputs. These include exploration and drilling equipment, production, pipeline and marine terminal equipment, refinery plant, and certain raw material inputs (catalysts, blending stock, etc.). Moreover, Shell and Stanvac refineries never ceased to import some foreign crudes during all of 1950–1963; and lubricants

[54] Agricultural export production, by contrast, declined from 14.9 percent of net domestic product to 6.8 percent in 1958. Among plantation export crops, tea, coffee, sugar, tobacco, palm oil, and kernels have declined and in all cases show production below prewar. (There is a substantial shift towards smallholders' production for the domestic market.) Mineral production has gone down in coal, tin, and iron ore; only bauxite and petroleum have gone up. The only export commodity other than petroleum and its products to show a respectable performance is rubber (from $200 million exported in 1951 to $368 million in 1960, or 43 percent of Indonesian merchandise exports, although the 1960's show some decline from this position). Even so, two-thirds of this increase is derived from smallholders' rubber, where large-scale investment is not a factor. A slump in prewar years and high prices in postwar years did the rest. Estate rubber, on the other hand, because of inadequate management and failure to invest in new plantings after the expropriation of Dutch, then British and American companies, has shown a steady decline in output from 1952 (see Douglas S. Paauw, "From Colonial to Guided Economy," in Ruth T. McVey, ed., *Indonesia,* Human Relations Area Files, New Haven, 1963, pp. 182–189; and *Statistical Pocketbook of Indonesia, 1963*).

are an imported commodity. Besides the payment for these items, there are the salaries of expatriate exploration and development teams and management personnel. In addition, the whole investment in Indonesia of the oil companies requires periodical remittance of dividends. Consequently the foreign exchange available for financing imports into Indonesia (other than oil industry requirements) is much less than gross earnings suggest.

In 1958, the gross earnings of $315 million were 39 percent of merchandise exports. But deduction for the imports of the industry in respect of consumption goods, raw materials, and capital goods totalling $113 million left only $202 million or 26 percent of merchandise exports in 1958. The deduction of profit remittances of $67.5 million takes the real contribution of the oil industry's capacity to earn foreign exchange to only $134.5 million. Both 1958 and 1959 were unusually good years (on account of relatively high values received for both products and crude). Over the more recent period, partly because of declining prices for crude and the export of lower-value products, exports have declined and the real net earnings, for 1960–1962 inclusive, are nearer an average of $90 million per annum. This still makes a substantial contribution, but much less than the figure popularly ascribed to petroleum outside and inside Indonesia and decidedly less than the $300 million per annum brought in by the rubber-growing industry in the same period. Here as elsewhere the benefits as well as the disadvantages of foreign investment are over-emphasized.

The Future

It would not be disputed that the future of the oil industry is important to Indonesia. Its efficient operation is necessary to exploit the country's most valuable mineral resource. It is one of the few technologically advanced industries in Indonesia likely to be in a position to add significantly to the corpus of modern skills so urgently required. The industry, since most of its exploration and extraction of oil takes place in sedimentary basins covered by virgin jungle or along desolate coastlines, is one of the main developers of sparsely settled areas in Indonesia; and, incidentally its main tasks, a notable provider of social capital in the form of roads, airfields, navigable river channels and harbours.[55] Over the years since World War II, the increase in domestic consumption has reached the point where petroleum products are an essential component of living standards in both urban and rural areas. Most significant of all perhaps, petroleum is one of the few industries which, despite the obstacles offered by official policies, has continued to perform adequately as an exporter of Indonesian products to the outside world. One must then ask: What is the future of Indonesian oil? At this point in time it is venturesome to undertake an answer when so many established features are undergoing change. But it seems necessary.

Consider first distribution. The price increases of mid-November 1965 and January 1966 were radical economic reforms. They should convert a scarcity of some petroleum products on the domestic market into a surplus, and thus release them for export to Southeast Asia in order to realise international prices and earn useful foreign exchange. It is certain that they will eliminate many of the worst distribution problems of PERTAMIN by offsetting its shortage of facilities. The black market—at those prices—should dissolve overnight. There is one other objective, of course: a reallocation of fuel resources away from uneconomic uses which can then be satisfied with smaller inputs of petroleum products and/or by a reversion to other fuels. However, it seems likely that even an approximation to the opportunity costs of petroleum products is not the intention of this exercise. Take petrol for example. At the mid-November price increase, to Rp. 250, the consumer was paying over five times the supply price received by PERTAMIN (Rp. 50) for delivery at main ports. Almost all the remainder of the consumer price went in taxation of various kinds to the government (including a 10 percent sales tax, a special government tax, an excise tax, contributions for war veterans, and payments to provincial governments). The same applied in lesser degree to the other products.[56] Thus it was cal-

[55] See MIT CENIS, *op. cit.,* Chap. 8. The population densities of Sumatra and Kalimantan are 33.0 and 7.6 persons per square kilometre, as compared with 477.0 persons for Java.

[56] *Business News,* October 12, 1965, p. 12a. For kerosene, the retail price was over 2.7 times the bulk supply price received by PERTAMIN; for auto-

culated that the mid-November increases raised the petrol or diesel fuel cost of operating a road transport vehicle in January from ½ percent of unit operating costs to approximately 30 percent, which of course would increase the cost of transport of certain commodities and eventually their end price. These changes seemed reasonable in the circumstances.[57] Many countries have employed severe petroleum taxes as the simplest way to solve fiscal problems.[58] But after the fourfold increases of January 1966, which pushed up petrol to Rp. 1,000 and kerosene and diesel to Rp. 600, the price policy looked to be of a thoroughly different character. The retail petrol price then became ten times the bulk supply price earned by PERTAMIN; automotive diesel oil became fifteen times the supply price, industrial diesel oil ten times, and fuel oil eleven times. The taxation per litre to be collected on petrol became Rp. 945.

Clearly, long-term criteria of resource allocation for fuel within the Indonesian economy were abandoned in favour of other policies. The president-director of PERTAMIN, on the occasion of the January 1966 price changes, said as much. He is reported to have stated that, whereas in 1965, 90 percent of his company's expenditures on distributing petroleum products were covered by government subsidy, at the new price PERTAMIN "would be able to provide 50 percent of the States expenditure budget for 1966." [59] Possibly this was an overoptimistic evaluation of the lowness of demand elasticities for petroleum products and of the corresponding buoyancy in the direct revenue to be expected, but it did indicate the authorities' line of thought. Domestic demand, including industrial demand, was severely to be curbed by high

---

motive diesel oil, over 3.7 times; for industrial diesel oil, 215 times; and for fuel oil, 2.8 times.

[57] *Business News, op. cit.*

[58] *International Petroleum Quarterly, Annual 1963,* November 1964, p. 29. which indicates that, of the retail price of petrol, the French tax component is 70 percent, the Italian 72 percent, the German 55 percent, the Norwegian 62 percent, the Netherlands 55 percent, the Indian 62 percent, Israel's 50 percent, and Britain's 57 percent.

[59] Actually, on the 1966 expenditure budget, petroleum products were reported as yielding $3 billion out of a total revenue of $7,232 million (new rupiah). See *Far Eastern Economic Review,* no. 160, January 20, 1966.

prices in order to provide a smaller, better balanced, and more remunerative refinery output (in the tax sense primarily and only incidentally at company level), and a larger share of the throughput was to be made available for exports. Whether this policy of constraining consumption by means of high prices is politically viable is another matter, of course. Petroleum products in lavish supply at almost zero prices have become something of a necessity to consumers and certain industries. It is fairly certain that the authorities will be compelled to retreat[60] on this issue.* But without doubt, if the policy initiated on January 1966 continues with cost-price relationships of this order, it will change fundamentally the place of petroleum products in Indonesia. They will become mainly instruments of budgetary policy with industrial performance and consumer welfare taking second place to problems of inflation and the balance of payments. Eventually, petroleum products will sink to the role of tax-gatherer, such is the facility with which they perform this task and their relative freedom from corruption.

For the refinery industry the new price structure is a welcome relief. But it also throws up problems. The restriction on quantities demanded of kerosene and petrol will permit a better balanced refinery output; and there should be substantial quantities of these two remunerative products available for export to Southeast Asia. However, it is far from certain that they can be sold in traditional markets. Southeast Asian countries such as Thailand, South Vietnam, Malaya, Cambodia, Singapore, Sarawak, and the Philippines will rely increasingly on refineries recently constructed within their territories.[61] The refineries were of course constructed mainly by the international oil companies to ensure that their local markets would be supplied fairly exclusively from their own installa-

[60] By January 21, 1966, the government in fact was compelled to halve petroleum prices. Petrol then became 50 sen a litre (500 old rupiah) and kerosene 30 sen.

* No overt retreat has occurred, but rapid inflation in 1966 reduced the real significance of the new prices quickly.—Ed.

[61] See section above on "Production, Distribution, and Refining." The exception perhaps is Thailand, where the ministry of defence is the principal operator.

tions. It seems most improbable that Indonesian state enterprises will be able successfully to compete with the established international refiners and marketers in these areas. Probably they will not attempt to do so. This leaves Indonesian refineries with the prospect of finding new sales in such countries as North Vietnam, perhaps Laos and Cambodia, and possibly Burma—collectively a very small market area. Otherwise it will be able to sell only the less remunerative products—fuel oil, furnace oil, marine diesel oil—in very competitive markets such as Japan and Hong Kong. It seems that both export and domestic markets for refined products will be smaller.

PERMIGAN, the state enterprise which probably will operate the refinery industry in future, may well welcome this prospect in view of some of the technical problems looming on its horizons. Under Indonesian management PERMIGAN cannot expect to maintain the throughputs of the British–Dutch and American companies. There have been persistent reports that the progressive Indonesianisation at the management level in refineries has given rise to serious difficulty. Maintenance of pumps, valves, instrumentation, pipelines, etc., is not as conscientiously performed as before. Absenteeism is a growing problem.[62] Even more serious for petroleum refining is the fact that Indonesian management appears unable to prevent persistent pilfering of vital stores and spare parts or even working components of the refinery. Finally, to judge from the experience of other Indonesian manufacturing industry, it appears most probable that a state enterprise will experience great difficulty in securing from the authorities the foreign exchange required to import spares, new equipment, and quantities of crude oil or blending stock on the lavish scale demanded of an international refining industry. The independence of the inter-

[62] Indonesians typically work a shorter week than Europeans, Australians, Chinese, or Japanese. From 34 to 37 hours per week in industry is common, especially where the workers are effectively organised by a strong trade union as is the case for oil refining. Few Indonesians have the same strict approach to punctuality, attendance, and the completion of assignments which is characteristic of European races or Chinese and Japanese. The introduction of Indonesian management usually is attended by a relaxation of Western-type discipline on such matters.

national oil companies in these matters has been of great assistance in the past in maintaining an efficient refining industry and will be sadly missed in the future by Indonesian managers.

Altogether, the Indonesian refinery industry can be expected to produce less. No new construction of a major sort is under way and, after purchasing the Shell and Stanvac installations, it is not likely that a government so short of foreign exchange will contemplate the building of a new one.[63] Therefore, for all these various reasons—domestic price policies and taxation, the failure to retain expanding export markets, lack of equipment and inexperienced management—refining in Indonesia will decline absolutely and relatively, and turn in on itself to become a mainly domestic supplier of uncertain efficiency. Certainly it will not be the dominant force in Southeast Asian and Far Eastern products' markets that it once was.

The production of crude oil in Indonesia presents a happier prospect. Whatever happens, it is likely that total output will increase. However, it may do so by two different routes, each having quite different political and economical consequences. First, the Indonesian government may rely on a development of the *status quo*. With distribution and refining transferred to Indonesia, it may leave the international majors to exploit crude oil resources along with Pan American and the state enterprises assisted by foreign contractors. Currently, the outputs of Shell, Stanvac, and the three state enterprises are all in the decline; only the 15 to 20 percent increases of Caltex production keeps total output moving up by a small percentage per annum. Exploration activity, which was considerable until quite recently,[64] could alter this rate of

[63] There have been reports that the national Italian company ENI was interested in building a 40,000 BPD refinery in Sumatra on a 50:50 sharing basis with Indonesia (*Petroleum Times,* November 1963, p. 559). For some years negotiations have taken place with the Rumanian government to advance a $50 million credit to rebuild the old Shell Tjepu refinery in Central Java to a 30,000 BPD size—a most unfortunate location to propose since the main proved sources of oil are now all outside Java, but no doubt the local trade unions have pressed this project (*Petroleum Press Service,* November 1962 and August 1964). Very little has been heard of these projects recently.

[64] Total exploration and development activity in 1964 for the Far Eastern region totalled $225 million. Indonesia accounts for 85 percent of pro-

growth substantially. Not much more can be expected from the twenty-year development contracts held by Shell and Stanvac over their old concession areas, which are all markedly on the decline (although this is not so for Caltex). The thirty-year contracts in the new areas offer a different, although much less certain, outlook. They are all promising prospecting areas selected by the three major companies which had had considerable experience with Indonesian conditions. All three companies possess good records for exploration in Indonesia and elsewhere and sooner or later should show substantial strikes. In addition, there is the exploration work of Pan American, also an experienced company, and the Canadian and Japanese contractors to PERMINA and PERMIGAN.

From all of this activity, it is not too optimistic to forecast that a new surge of production could take place in the next decade. It would be remunerative for Indonesia. Indonesia's crudes are of good quality and are favourably located relative to growing consumption areas in Japan, Southeast Asia, and Australia. Of the operating profits, 60 percent would go to the Indonesian government under the 1963 agreements. Up to one quarter of the production of each company can be designed for supply to Indonesia at cost plus 20 cents for home consumption; and, if the government so desires, the Indonesian state enterprises may take, as part of its profit division, up to 20 percent of the crude oil production of each company in kind in order to set up as international traders in crude petroleum on their own account. Whatever good fortunes the international oil companies encounter, the Indonesian government therefore would share in them in a flexible manner domestically and in foreign trade. It would not be called upon to find the capital to develop the companies' large contract areas. Moreover, it is open meanwhile to the three state enterprises, PER-

duction in this region, which seems to indicate an expenditure of $190 million only $15 million of which is bonus payments, the remainder being expended on geological and geophysical searches, wildcat drilling, and development drilling (Chase Manhattan Bank, Petroleum Division, *1964 Capital Investments of the World Petroleum Industry,* New York, 1965). Incidentally, $190 million is a large sum to expend on exploration and development in a relatively small producing area like Indonesia (1.7 percent of world production); in Venezuela (12.2 percent), 165 millions were spent in 1964; and in the whole Middle East (26.0 percent), $205 millions.

MINA, PERTAMIN, and PERMIGAN, to undertake their own exploration in any area they choose, thus helping sustain Indonesian oil production through the medium of national companies using indigenous enterprise. These arrangements seem comprehensively to protect Indonesian interests and guarantee oil production as reasonably as can be done given the hazards of this industry.

Nevertheless, nationalism may prevail and the other alternative may be chosen—total expropriation (with or without compensation) of the three major oil companies and the transfer of their operations in crude oil production to the Indonesian state enterprises.

At first blush this seems a not-too-difficult task for indigenous companies to undertake. After the take-over of the more complicated problems of refining, the extraction of crude from established fields appears a relatively simple operation. And, so far as it goes, this is an accurate assessment. But in Indonesia established fields quickly decline; consequently the key to effective expansion or even maintenance of oil production, as the history of Shell and Stanvac over the past fifteen years testifies, lies in exploration. However, exploration calls for technological competence of a high order, lengthy field experience, and, most important, extraordinary financial staying power. Except for some little work done by PERTAMIN in South Sumatra with the assistance of Shell and a French company, the Indonesian enterprises have little direct experience in exploration. They have relied mainly on Canadian, American, and Japanese contractors in their North Sumatran developments and on Japanese contracts in Java and the eastern islands. On the technological side, therefore, they can be assessed as beginners. On the foreign exchange side, it is unlikely that the government of Indonesia would choose to sustain the effort required for a large and decisively commercial strike of oil. It has too many expensive development projects and military expenditures in hand. Some examples of the kind of expenditure and experience required in exploration should be considered. In Egypt, for example, after World War II one company spent, fruitlessly, $35 million exploring in the Western Desert. In Libya, altogether $350 million was spent before two companies succeeded in discovering oil and getting their strikes to the point of commercial production. In Australia, between 1946 and 1964, private enterprise and government between them spent $240 million to realise, by 1964, only a tiny commercial flow (300,000 tons per annum).[65] Nearer home to Indonesia, the NNGPM Company started work in Netherlands New Guinea in 1935, supported financially by the three large international companies; it spent tens of millions of dollars on air survey work, geophysical work, and drilling; but by 1940, it had discovered no appreciable reserves to justify the expenditures, and the small fields in that area today produce only about 120,000 tons per annum. Caltex began exploration in 1931 in widely dispersed areas of West Java and Central Sumatra and took nine years before settling down to commercial production on its Duri and Minas fields just prior to World War II. Finally, Pan American, during three years of intensive exploration of a favourable area in Central Sumatra, and the expenditure of $24 million, has achieved no commercial production. Truly, exploration is an uncertain affair yielding highly random results.

If, despite these prospective difficulties, expropriation of the crude oil production of Indonesia were carried through, there would remain the problem of disposal of the oil at reasonable commercial prices. It would not be easy to find buyers for total exports of 11 or 12 million metric tons per annum of Indonesian crudes. They are generally waxy crudes and, to be economically processed, should go to refineries adapted for this purpose. The refineries presently using these crudes tend to be tied to this particular quality of crude. But, naturally, the same applies vice versa. The position is rendered more delicate by the fact that, at present, there is only one substantial exporter of Indonesian crude, Caltex, responsible for over nine-tenths of the 12 to 13 million tons exported. The majority of the Caltex exports, about 40 percent, go to Japan, where this company has half shares in a number of refineries which can take altogether about 10,000,000 metric tons per annum; 30 percent goes to Australia to refineries owned or partly shared by Caltex, which can absorb over 4,000,000 tons per annum; and a further 18 percent goes to the west coast

[65] Issawi and Yegenah, *op. cit.*, pp. 85–86; and Petroleum Information Bureau, *Oil and Australia,* 1965.

of the United States, where the parent companies of Caltex (Standard Oil of California and Texaco, Inc.) have refinery runs of well over 15,000,000 tons per annum. Caltex also has refineries in the Philippines, Hawaii, and India which take Indonesian crude. In all, this company has more than ample refinery capacity to absorb its total Indonesian production; and, indeed, practically all of its crude goes to subsidiaries or affiliates or to refining companies such as AMPOL in Australia with which it has had long-standing market connections. The only other exporter of significance is PERMINA which sends a mere 600 to 700 thousand tons per annum to Japan and 350,000 tons to the United States, mainly to independent refineries.

It is clear from this situation that most Indonesian crude exports have ties with a particular refinery group. It is equally clear that, if Indonesia were to undertake complete expropriation of the crude oil industry, there would be relatively few independent refiners available to take up this considerable tonnage. As we have already noted, most refineries in the immediate neighbourhood in Southeast Asia are owned by Shell, Standard of New Jersey, Mobil, Caltex, and British Petroleum. Apart from company "ethics," which may be pleaded to resist the purchase of crude from Indonesian companies which have expropriated a fellow member of the international oil club, each of these companies has its own sources of crude in the Middle East and Borneo which it could reasonably prefer to use and for which, indeed, its refineries were designed and built. Japan has a number of independent refiners and therefore offers a more promising outlet; even so, three quarters of Japanese refinery capacity has American or British international companies as half or one-third owners and is mainly tied to Middle Eastern crudes.[66] Moreover, Japanese independents rely largely on heavy Middle Eastern crudes and some Russian crude from the Black Sea area, none of which demands specialist equipment for removing wax. India, where the government can dictate to the international companies to some extent concerning the source and price of their crudes, is another possibility, but here again there is no special reason or

[66] See "Annual Survey of Refinery Capacity," *Petroleum Times,* January 8, 1965; and *Skinners Oil and Petroleum Year Book,* London, 1964.

advantage in buying Indonesian crude. The majors are already importing from their ample Middle Eastern fields at substantially discounted prices. China, yet another potential market, appears devoted to a policy of self-sufficiency in crude oil.[67]

Finally, there is an important background factor to the crude oil situation which Indonesia cannot ignore. Total available world productive capacity of crude oil in 1965 was more than 50 percent greater than world consumption. There is a glut of oil which will remain for at least five years; and the largest component of this excess capacity (firmly under the control of the international majors) resides in the Middle Eastern countries which are the main competitors of Indonesia in the eastern hemisphere.[68] One principal result of this excess of crude available on world markets is that all independent refiners, tough-minded national refining companies, or interested governments can secure substantial discounts from posted prices when purchasing crude. It is therefore almost inconceivable that Indonesian oil could secure, in open competition with other crudes, prices superior to those presently provided by the "tied" refiners of the Caltex group.

Without doubt, complete expropriation is studded with hazards for Indonesia. Only too probably it would result in an unfortunate combination of factors: poor management of petroleum reserves; exploration of an episodic character with uncertain results; and the dumping of a diminishing supply of Indonesian crude into difficult, unfriendly markets. Little that is rational can be said in its support.

There is an inbetween course which has advantages but requires considerable tactical skill in handling not only external market forces but also internal political pressures. Caltex could be preserved in its present status (which would suit this company), and Shell and Stanvac could be bought out, reasonable compensation being paid for oil field equipment, pipelines, drilling rigs, etc., as well as for the refineries. The Indonesian government could well reason that while Caltex is in its present productive

[67] B. Heenan, "China's Petroleum Industry," *Far Eastern Economic Review,* September 23, 1965.

[68] J. McAfee and W. B. Davis, "Is There Enough Oil?", *Institute of Petroleum Review,* London, June 1964.

stage, both as regards quantities and the prices it can secure from its wide array of subsidiaries, there is little point in killing off the goose which is so competently and consistently laying the golden eggs—not yet, at any rate. Shell and Stanvac, on the other hand, are both in a phase of discovery and exploitation which has so far little to show for their efforts and therefore have interests divergent from Caltex. There may be little economic loss or gain by being quit of them, while the political kudos for removing two such prestigious symbols of neocolonialism would be considerable. (But they should not be antagonised too greatly since some day they could be important purchasers of crude oil from Indonesia—hence the reasonable compensation.) To replace them, the three state enterprises could employ a judicious mixture of foreign contracting companies—Japanese, Rumanian, French, small American, and Canadian companies—on the same basis as Pan American presently operates to discover new fields, also foreign geophysical and drilling specialist companies to assist the state enterprises in their exploration operations and to help them acquire much-needed experience. Such an organisation of the crude oil end of industry could well induce a degree of competitiveness among fairly numerous contractors of different nationalities which would compensate for the loss of experience caused by the departure of Shell and Stanvac and could well result in a set of useful strikes.

There are executives among the Indonesian state enterprises who are prepared to think about the future in this way. But they may not be permitted to do so. The quality of Indonesian nationalism is not such that authorities are likely to be attracted to this kind of cooly calculated balance of economic advantage against patriotic preference. Unfortunately, precedent seems to indicate that, despite the delicacy of the oil situation for Indonesia, emotion will win the day and Indonesia will insist on taking the entire complement of the oil industry under its direct control and supervision.[69]

[69] Shell assets in Indonesia (the refineries, oilfield equipment, pipelines, etc.) were handed over on December 31, 1965 to the ministry of oil and gas affairs for a sum of $110 million. Payment is to be in cash and kind: a down payment of ten percent in cash and crude oil, the remainder to be paid over

Addendum: Recent Developments in Indonesia's Oil Industry[70]

After the abortive coup of September 1965, uncertainty dominated the affairs of the Indonesian oil industry. The Royal Dutch-Shell group continued with its settled plan to withdraw from Indonesia and, in the event, did transfer all of its assets to the republic on December 31, 1965.* But the movement to transfer Stanvac assets progressed only in a desultory manner. And investment in the industry, including even that of the prolific Caltex leases in Central Sumatra, moved very hesitantly. Output in 1966 reflected the indecision of these months and fell slightly from the 1965 figure of 24.1 million to 23.8 million metric tons—the first drop in output since general resumption of production in 1949. However, as the determination of the Suharto regime to correct the economic ineptitude of its predecessors became clear, the tide of confidence reversed. Stanvac quietly forgot the negotiations to transfer its assets to one of the state companies; and Caltex, in any case never willing to contemplate such a course of action, went ahead with far-reaching development plans for its Central Sumatran fields and associated, onshore and offshore, areas. Simultaneously, a new outlook on foreign participation in the oil industry of Indonesia appeared. While difficult to pinpoint the source exactly, it did seem to be one more by-product of an

---

a period of five years in crude only. (This would amount to about 1.7 million metric tons per annum.) At the time of transfer, the minister of oil and gas affairs stated that the Indonesian government was actively negotiating with the two remaining international companies to end their existing contracts and arrangements. So far no agreement on price has been reached, he added, with the implication that this was the sole remaining obstacle to complete Indonesianisation of the industry (*Indonesian Herald,* Djakarta, January 5, 1966; and *Far Eastern Economic Review,* February 3, 1966; and *Petroleum Press Service,* February 1966).

[70] A more detailed account of the developments in Indonesian oil between 1965 and 1968 can be followed in various notes in *BIES* nos. 2, 6, 7, 8, and 10, September 1965 to June 1968. See especially "Indonesian Oil: A New Generation of Explorers," no. 8, October 1967; and "The Future of Indonesian Oil," no. 10, June 1968.

* Having departed from Indonesia, presumably forever, in December 1965, Shell, in late 1969, was negotiating with PERTAMINA to return as a contractor-explorer on offshore concessions and in Kalimantan.—Ed.

infiltration of hardheaded economists' ideas into the Suharto regime. In 1966, an Oil Committee was formed for the examination, mainly, of foreign proposals to explore for and produce oil and natural gas. It operated under the chairmanship and effective control of Major General Ibnu Sutowo, manager-director of PERMINA; but the committee also included among its members the influential chairman of the Technical Committee on Foreign Investment.[71] Some twenty foreign firms initiated negotiations during 1966—a forerunner of eventful changes for 1967 and 1968.

Exploration developments provide most of the new elements in the oil industry situation. Although Indonesia is one of the world's oldest oil-producing areas, much of its archipelagian area remains unexplored. No one can examine the large continental shelf area of Indonesia without being struck by the probability that potentially immense, oil-bearing strata lie beneath its shallow water areas. These offshore possibilities have not had the attention they deserved in Indonesia because of the long interregnum in large-scale exploration activity since 1940. Thus, bearing in mind the advances in offshore seismic survey and drilling technique since those years, one is not surprised to find that most foreign companies are interested primarily in offshore rather than onshore exploration.

A second characteristic of the new wave of exploration is that the international "majors" are not well represented. Mobil Oil Corporation (one of the parents of Stanvac in Indonesia) has acquired rights from other groups to explore over 1,860 square miles in North Sumatra. Also, Cie. Française des Pétroles (CFP) has contracted to explore 8,000 square miles on land and 2,000 square miles offshore in the Djambi area of Sumatra. But these are relatively recent arrangements made in June and July of 1968, and come after the main spate of agreements in 1966 and 1967 opening up the main offshore prospects of Indonesia to a number of

[71] A committee, set up at the instigation of the more economics-minded members and advisors of the Suharto regime and influenced strongly by a youngish, foreign-trained generation of geologists, mining engineers, and economists, determined to initiate a systematic exploitation of Indonesia's underground wealth. See Alex Hunter, "Minerals in Indonesia," *BIES,* no. 11, October 1968.

smaller companies. Some are American (Union Oil, Continental Oil, Ashland, Cities Service, Sinclair-Phillips, Southeast Asia Petroleum, etc.); one or two are small Australian companies; and two Japanese companies (Japex and Kyushu), have taken out immense acreages. The single most important area covered by the new contracts are the shores of the Java Sea and the Straits of Makassar. Thus, all the north coast of Java and Madura, offshore and onshore, is contracted out to two groups of American companies with some Australian participation, IIAPCO (the Independent Indonesian American Petroleum Company) and Australian Drilling; Kyushu will operate offshore South Kalimantan—at 50,000 square miles the largest of the contract areas around the Java Sea; IIAPCO will take in the shores of Southeast Sumatra and Northwest Java; and another American group, Continental Oil, is committed to onshore South Kalimantan around Bandjarmasin. The east coast of Kalimantan is taken up by Japex (Bunju Island and Mahakam areas), and by Kyushu (Southeast Kalimantan). These are enormous tracts taking in altogether some 250,000 square miles of seas around the Java Sea and Makassar Straits; and perhaps about 40,000 square miles onshore. Along the north coast of West Irian, the Phillips-Superior group has contracted to explore over 100,000 square miles of offshore territory. An Australian company, International Oils N.L. (No Liability) is undertaking exploration over all of Indonesian Timor and adjacent islands. (And Timor Oil, another Australian enterprise, is operating in Portuguese Timor.) The Indonesian Texas Petroleum Corporation (Indotex) similarly will explore around Halmahera. Union Oil of California has a very large section offshore and onshore of the northwest coast of Sumatra to Bukittinggi including some islands. Finally, onshore, two American companies will jointly drill to depths hitherto unknown in Indonesia—in Kalimantan and in South Sumatra. Other negotiations on oil leases take place continuously (1968) as company representatives come and go in Djakarta.

The terms on which foreign oil companies become contractors to the state company PERTAMINA[72] are fairly standard. They

[72] The two state companies, PERMINA and PERTAMIN, were merged in August 1968 as part of a general centralisation programme for all the industries coming under the ministry of mining (see Hunter, *op. cit.*).

are, in some degree, production-sharing agreements—although export sales probably would take place through the foreign company. To cover exploration and production costs, 40 percent of the production of crude oil from a given contractual area is at the disposal of the foreign contractor. Of the remaining 60 percent, the contractor retains 35 percent, and 65 percent goes to the state company. In most agreements when production rises above 75,000 barrels per day, these latter shares become 32.5 percent and 67.5 percent respectively. Certain contractors agreed to pay a bonus "for geological information" thirty days after signing a contract; and another after reaching a designated production of 75,000 BPD or 100,000 BPD. These bonus payments can be as low as $100,000 or as high as $2.0 million. One American group has agreed to build a petro-chemical plant in South Sumatra presumably using natural gas by-products of oil production in that area. All installations put in by the contractor become the property of PERTAMINA. Maximum periods of exploration and exploitation are, generally, ten and twenty years respectively (although in some remote areas such as West Irian and Timor, thirty years for exploitation is written into the contract). All contracts are conditional on active exploration and a corresponding expenditure of foreign capital. The foreign company carries all the risk but the full costs of exploration and development are recoverable, subject to the 40 percent maximum if and when a commercial show of oil is made. Relinquishment is at 25 percent of the area after three years, another 25 percent after six years. When ten years of exploration have passed, a company could be left with less than 10 percent of the original area.

Production will increase substantially in the next few years even without assistance from the new exploration areas. But the increase will stem mainly from one company—Caltex. In 1967, total crude production was just over 26 million metric tons or 500,000 BPD. Of this output, Stanvac provided some 55,000 BPD from its old established fields in Southeast Sumatra and the Lirik field in Central Sumatra. PERMINA produced around 65,000 BPD from the former Shell fields in Kalimantan, South Sumatra, and Java. PERMINA also had some production from the Djambi field—a reversion to the state from the old BPM company. But, at 65,000 BPD, PERMINA evidently has made little contribution over the past five years to an increase in Indonesian production. The one new field discovery made by PERMINA, at Tutupan, 19 miles east of the Tandjung field in Kalimantan, in collaboration with a German geophysical exploration company, is as yet unknown in size. And the North Sumatran areas coming under PERMINA control (although operated by the Japanese NSODCC, North Sumatra Oil Development Corporation Company, and a Canadian–U.S. company ASAMERA Oil, Indonesia) also have had little increase in their outputs.

The Caltex contribution in 1967 was 360,000 BPD or 70 percent of total production. Minas, the most productive field, gave 250,000 BPD; Duri and Beksap fields gave each 30,000 to 40,000 BPD; and the remainder came from Pematung and Pungut which started production in 1966. From January 1968, as a consequence of successful negotiations with the Indonesian government, the f.o.b. (ex-Dumai) price of Caltex crude (Minas with a blending of Pematung for most markets) was reduced from $1.77 to $1.62 per barrel. This reduction kept the Indonesian crude prices in line with the decline in realised prices for Middle Eastern crudes. Subsequently, as a result of this price move, and because of increasing confidence in the political and economic stability of Indonesia, Caltex announced substantial new investment in Sumatra —development drilling, construction of gathering lines, storage facilities, and jetties—which by the end of 1969 will permit it to ship 600,000 BPD from Dumai. This is an increase of 66 percent over its 1967 figure. And it will add 48 percent to Indonesian total production.

Refinery output also, by one route or another, will receive a substantial uplift. Since 1947, Caltex has declined more than one proposal to build a refinery in Indonesia. But a Japanese group agreed with PERTAMINA (late 1968) to construct a 100,000 BPD refinery at Dumai. The group is composed of the refiner Sumitomo Shoji Kaisha and the Far East Oil Trading Company, set up in Japan in 1966 by NSODCC and PERMINA to dispose of the 20 percent of Caltex crude which, by the 1963 agreements, PERMINA may take in kind instead of in profit shares. Presumably this refinery will process most of the 20 percent Caltex production from Minas, Duri, and associated fields (120,000 BPD by 1970). It will add 35 percent to Indonesia's refinery capacity when constructed and will become the property of Indonesia after five years operation. There is provision to increase capacity to some 220,000 BPD at some unspecified time in the future. Payment to the Japanese group will be in kind—3 million kilolitres of fuel oil per annum (50,000 BPD). The lighter products, gasolines, kerosenes, and diesels will most likely find their main markets in Indonesian domestic consumption and in export to nearby Southeast Asian markets.

Two more refinery projects are in what may be termed a hypothetical state. IIAPCO, which has contracted to explore two areas, one on the North Java coast, Djakarta to Semarang, and the other off Southeast Sumatra, has agreed to build a refinery once its Sumatran production exceeds 100,000 BPD. The indications are that PERTAMINA would prefer to have this refinery located on Java. And INDOTEX, the company under contract to explore onshore and offshore Halmahera, has also agreed to build a refinery location—in this case if production reaches 200,000 BPD or more.

In relatively underdeveloped countries, crude oil production, more than most industries, requires very large injections of foreign capital and technology. Consequently, the Suharto regime's new approach to foreign participation opens up the opportunity for a remarkable transformation of the prospects of the Indonesian oil industry.

CHAPTER 9

The Textile Industry*

INGRID PALMER and
LANCE CASTLES

As the commercial economy penetrated the Indonesian archipelago in the nineteenth century, the cheap cotton textiles from which most Indonesian clothes were made became its staple import. The Indonesian slogan, *sandang-pangan,* gives clothing (*sandang*) pride of place with food (*pangan*) among the basic necessities of life. The unavailability of textiles at reasonable prices is keenly felt by the normally long-suffering Indonesian consumer, and postindependence governments have continuously desired, and sporadically achieved, the maintenance of supplies at appropriate levels. At the same time the textile industry was chosen as one of the obvious vehicles of industrialization and import-replacement, and the expansion of productive capacity during the 1950's was one of the comparatively successful economic ventures of the government. But the installation of capacity was accompanied by neglect of the financial strength of the industry and by the inability of the government to protect the domestic industry from the effects of the blunt-edged instruments of corrective monetary and foreign trade policies. These factors account for the chronic insecurity experienced by textile manufacturers, and the often-noted poor record of capacity utilization.

* This article is a revised version of an article of the same title originally published in the *Bulletin of Indonesian Economic Studies* (*BIES*) no. 2, September 1965; published here by permission of the authors and editors.

Productive Capacity

Indonesia now has enough looms to weave 744.5 million metres and to knit 225 million metres of cloth per annum (see Table 9.1).[1] This amounts to 8.1 metres per capita which is as much as the country would consume even in her prosperous years. About 55 percent of this quantity can be produced by power looms and knitting machines and can hence be considered the capacity of the "modern" textile industry. There is an imbalance between spinning and weaving capacities with the spinning industry able to provide only 24 percent of total domestic yarn requirements, but 46 percent of yarn requirements of the modern sector alone. The modern finishing factories can handle 217 million metres of cloth a year, which means that the remainder of domestic production is finished by primitive backyard washtub methods. In general, this industry produces materials of inferior quality, and there is therefore a marked preference for foreign textiles in the consumer market. All other things constant, these shortcomings have the derived effect of lowering the profitability of establishing a modern weaving industry.[2]

The chronic underutilization of weaving capacity referred to above cannot be attributed to inadequate spinning capacity, because the country is and has been free to import yarn if it wished. Indeed, the periodic underutilization of the spinning industry[3] indicates that it was not able to supply the weaving and knitting industries with its capacity output, despite yarn shortages. The idle capacity of the weaving sector has been mainly the result of inadequate protection from foreign competition and (when do-

[1] The findings of the Team Sandang KOTOE (described later in this chapter) suggest that statistics based on reported capacity are too high.

[2] The profitability of the individual weaver rests on the final effect of protection measures, as foreign competition plays a dominant role.

[3] The much higher rates of capacity utilization in the spinning industry might be considered to approximate full economic capacity rather than full engineering capacity, although in view of continuous and serious inflation as well as arbitrary multiple exchange rates for cotton, yarn, and cloth, it is fruitless to attempt a definition of "economic capacity." Moreover, expansion of the spinning industry, unlike the modern weaving industry, came as the result of large, indivisible capital investments in the state sector.

Table 9.1. Full capacity input and output of the textile industry at dates of latest available information

Industry division	Annual input	Annual output
*Spinning**		
480,000 spindles working three shifts, 260 days a year†	46,210 tons raw cotton	41,590 tons yarn
*Weaving**		
223,905 handlooms‡ working one shift, 240 days a year	80,606 tons yarn	429.8 million metres
29,000 power looms working two shifts, 240 days a year	56,140 tons yarn	314.7 million metres
Total, weaving	136,746 tons yarn	744.5 million metres
*Knitting**		
6,100 hand machines		
3,300 power machines	33,530 tons yarn	225.0 million metres
Finishing§		
Three shifts, 260 days a year.	216.6 million metres‖	

Source: Data on spinning, weaving, and knitting capacities were taken from "Cotton Textiles and the Prospects for Synthetic Fibres in Indonesia," in *Far East Trade and Development*, vol. 24, no. 12, December 1969. Finishing capacity data were taken from Department of People's Industry, *Pembangunan Industri Rakjat*, Djakarta, 1962, pp. 11, 17–27.

* The figures given are as of November 1969.

† The production coefficients and capacity definitions of 260 days a year are those used and described extensively in Ingrid Palmer's "The Indonesian Cotton Textile Industry During Inflation, 1950–1964," Ph.D. thesis, Australian National University, Canberra, April 1968, p. 319.

‡ Official statistics indicate that 280,000 handlooms were "available" in 1969. But since the raw material situation in 1969 was no better than in 1964, the handloom figure for the latter year is used to indicate capacity of the handweaving section. The rundown condition of these looms and their long idleness have prompted W. Boucherie ("The Textile Industry," *Bulletin of Indonesian Economic Studies* [*BIES*], vol. 5, no. 3, November 1969, p. 61) to suggest a *minimum* of 100,000 to 125,000 looms as the potential handloom capacity.

§ The figures given are as of April 1962; a small, but unknown capacity has been installed since.

‖ W. Boucherie gives a figure of 230 million metres as capacity for the finishing industry, but states that part of this capacity was used in 1969 on unfinished cloth imports of high quality. The Five Year Plan, 1969–1974, is aiming at a target capacity (undefined) in 1974 of 250 million metres. Together with the data in this table, this suggests little new capacity has been installed since 1962. However, in view of the publicity given to finishing in the mid-1960's, this is difficult to believe; thus finishing capacity estimates must be treated with caution.

mestic production and imported cloth did not add up to the corresponding domestic capacity output) to shortages of foreign exchange.

Before World War I, only *gedogans* (primitive handlooms) were used by domestic weavers.[4] Some weaving factories were set up during the War, but failed afterward. During the 1920's there was a slow expansion of the cottage (handloom) industry, but only one Western-style weaving shed was erected.[5] The development by the Textile Institute at Bandung of an improved, locally made handloom, five times as productive as the *gedogan* loom, provided a great impetus to the industry. Shortly afterward, the first power-driven looms (ATM), with seven times the capacity of the improved handloom (ATBM), were installed.[6] A rapid expansion of weaving capacity followed these two innovations.

The impressive growth of the weaving industry in the last few years of Dutch rule (yarn imports rose 500 percent from 1930 to 1940) was largely the result of the policy of the colonial government, which fostered small industry to counter the decline in indigenous incomes, and was extended by the government of independent Indonesia. Although the numbers of both kinds of looms increased greatly before and after independence, the expansion of the power-loom sector occurred more particularly before independence, and of the handloom sector after independence. From 1935 to 1950 (in effect, 1935–1941 and 1946–1949, as little new capacity was installed during the Japanese occupation), the number of power looms rose nearly twenty-eight times, that of handlooms less than nineteen times. But from 1950 to 1969, the trend was reversed; the number of power looms increased by 238 percent while handlooms increased by 289 percent. The weaving industry

[4] J. O. M. Broek, *Economic Development of the Netherlands Indies,* Institute of Pacific Relations, New York, 1942, p. 83.

[5] A. G. C. Allen and A. G. Donnithorne, *Western Enterprise in Indonesia and Malaya,* Allen and Unwin, London, 1957, p. 257.

[6] Undated department Memorandum of the Department of People's Industry prepared by Hirawan, Djakarta mimeo., pp. 10, 12. The new handloom was originally called the TIB loom after the Textielinriching te Bandoeng, where it was developed, and subsequently the ATBM (*alat tenun bukan mesin*). The ATBM is now sometimes called the ATKT (*alat tenun keradjinan tangan*). ATM stands for *alat tenun mesin.*

in Indonesia is thus unusual in that its less efficient and (as now appears) largely redundant section is not a legacy from an earlier technological phase but has been created quite recently and with government assistance. (See Table 9.2).

Table 9.2. Weaving looms, registered totals from selected dates, 1930 to 1969

Year	Handlooms (ATBM)	Power looms (ATM)
1930	257	44
1935	3,915	414
1940	44,000	8,000
1950	71,997	11,390
1955	78,857	12,697
1957	111,522	15,301
1960	150,000	16,896
1962	223,905	22,171
1967	n.a.	26,536
1969	280,000	27,000

Sources: Undated departmental memorandum of the Department of People's Industry prepared by Hirawan, Djakarta, mimeo., p. 12; M. R. Adisendjaja, "Industri Tekstil di Indonesia," *Madjalah Industri Rakjat*, no. 6, June 1963, p. 31; Report from Department of People's Industry, April 1962; number of ATM's in 1967: *Asian Textile Survey 1967–1968, Far Eastern Economic Review*, p. 101, and "Cotton Textiles and the Prospects for Synthetic Fibres in Indonesia," *op. cit.*

Until 1962 it could be shown that the majority of power looms installed dated from the earlier, pre-independence phase of the industry and that the larger (and probably more efficient) units are those dating from before the War.[7] A surprisingly small percentage of the power looms installed in the 1950's are in large mills.

The spinning sector has developed more recently than the weaving sector; its first unit was opened only in 1939. Its main expansion has taken place after independence. Capacity rose from 15,000 spindles in 1940,[8] to 59,000 in 1957,[9] and to 480,000 in 1969.[10]

[7] M. Zen Rahman, *Report of Sampling Survey of Weaving Factories Which Use ATM's*, Ministry of People's Industry, Djakarta, November 15, 1962, p. 6.

[8] Broek, *op. cit.*, p. 83.

[9] Letter to the author from Platt Bros., Oldham, U.K., February 21, 1964.

[10] *Far East Trade and Development*, vol. 24, no. 12, December 1969.

Until the late 1950's, finishing had been mainly a cottage industry, whose production capacity was flexible.[11] On a commission in order to supplement their income, Javanese households have willingly taken unfinished cloth from the weavers to wash and dry and sometimes to print. But the facilities have not been good and the quality of the finishing poor. Alongside the cottage industry there is a small number of large sheds each with several large tubs. The eight modern finishing factories in Indonesia are comparatively new.

Location and Structure

The textile industry is highly concentrated in Java and, except for spinning, the greatest development has been in West Java, above all in the Bandung region. In 1967, West Java accounted for 32 percent of the handlooms, Central Java for 30 percent, and East Java for 9 percent.[12] The remainder were located in the outer provinces. In 1960, East Java had 17 percent of these handlooms,[13] indicating that East Java has lost ground to other parts of Java in the rapidly expanding handloom industry. Her position in the modern weaving sector was much weaker, taking a share of only about 16 percent, against West Java's 65 percent and Central Java's 12 percent.

Most of the large spinning mills in whose establishment the government has played a significant role are in Central Java as part of a programme to redistribute employment and income within Java. During the government's financial crisis in 1964 there were attempts to sell spinning factories to private enterprise but the response was poor because the future of the textile industry was extremely uncertain. Today the central government owns three mills, and regional governments another three.

The employment capacity of the textile industry can only be guessed. If we assume one job for every handloom and two jobs for

[11] *Batik* printing, an important indigenous type of cloth finishing, is not considered in this chapter, following the usual custom of treating it as a separate industry.

[12] Surjo Sediono, "Indonesia," in *Asian Textile Survey 1967–1968, Far Eastern Economic Review,* p. 99.

[13] M. R. Adisendjaja, "Industri Tekstil di Indonesia," *Madjalah Industri Rakjat,* no. 6, June 1963, p. 36.

every power loom and knitting machine, the jobs created by handlooms, power looms and power knitting machines would total 224,000, 54,000 and 6,600, respectively. A spinning industry consisting of 480,000 spindles can employ around 11,740 persons.[14] (These figures do not include jobs of management employees.) Finishing establishments are believed to be able to provide work for about 6,400 workers. Thus the "modern" textile industry, operating at full capacity, can employ at least 69,160 persons with an additional 224,000 workers using handlooms.

No statistics are available for actual total employment in the industry, and rates of capacity utilization provide only a rough guide since manufacturers are urged by legislation to retain workers for as long as possible in periods of low activity. Official sources exclude the activities of very small units which do not make statistical returns. In 1961, a reasonably "normal" year for production, the textile industry officially accounted for 19.4 percent of total manufacturing employment, or 92,806 jobs.[15]

The expansion of the textile industry in the late colonial period was the work of businessmen of four ethnic groups: Chinese, European, Arab, and Indonesian. On the eve of World War II, European weaving mills were the largest and best-equipped, and included 39.5 percent of the power looms and 2.0 percent of the handlooms.[16] Indonesian mills, though most numerous, were small and had few mechanized looms, accommodating 7.0 percent of power looms and 35.0 percent of handlooms; while the Chinese and Arabs were in an intermediate position.

During the last years before World War II indigenous entrepreneurs in the weaving industry appeared to be losing ground to the Chinese; an investigation of 94 sales of weaving enterprises

[14] Based on coefficients in I. Palmer, "The Indonesian Cotton Textile Industry During Inflation, 1950–1965," Ph.D. thesis, Australian National University, Canberra, April 1968. Data on equipment taken from "Cotton Textiles and the Prospects for Synthetic Fibres in Indonesia," *Far East Trade and Development,* vol. 24, no. 12, December 1969.

[15] Central Bureau of Statistics, *Statistical Pocketbook of Indonesia 1963,* Djakarta, p. 112–113.

[16] John O. Sutter, *Indonesianisasi, Politics in a Changing Economy, 1940–1955,* Data Paper no. 36, Department of Far Eastern Studies, Southeast Asia Program, Cornell University, Ithaca, N.Y., 1959, p. 42.

by Indonesians revealed that 52 were bought by Chinese, 15 by Arabs, and only 27 by other Indonesians.[17] This trend probably continued for a few years after the War when many Chinese-owned factories were built in and near Bandung, sometimes incorporating the equipment of Indonesian enterprises. Since independence, many, though not all, Chinese and Arab textile manufacturers have become Indonesian citizens and, though the political distinction between indigenous and nonindigenous remained important, no precise information is available on the present ethnic composition of ownership in the textile industry.[18] As a general rule the larger, better equipped, and better financed factories are owned by ethnic Chinese. However, there are many exceptions. Two of the largest textile firms (Pardede and Ratatex) are owned by indigenous businessmen. Moreover, the government now owns a considerable part of the industry. Some large weaving mills of Dutch or British ownership have been nationalized, and most of the spinning sector is government-owned. In 1964, the government owned four spinning mills, five weaving factories, and three finishing plants.[19]

Raw Materials Shortage

Textile manufacturers complain of several factors which limit production, including the shortage of spare parts, of electricity, and of skilled labour; but the main reason for the inactivity of so much of the industry in recent years has been the limited supply of raw material. Though cotton has long been grown in Indonesia (in eastern Java and the lesser Sunda Islands), yields are low

[17] *Ibid.*, p. 44.

[18] The reports of the Team Sandang KOTOE give an impression of "foreign" (Chinese) domination of the industry, but the objectivity of their remarks on this subject may be doubted. Nevertheless, during interviews in 1965 strong impressions were gained that the Chinese manufacturers were the financing contractors to a large share of the indigenous textile industry. Cf. KOTOE Team Chusus Penertiban Bahan Baku Untuk Produksi Sandang (Special KOTOE Control Team for Textile Production Raw Materials), *Progress Report II*, Djakarta, February 1965, pp. 7–8.

[19] Commercial Advisory Foundation of Indonesia (CAFI), no. 45/HM/64, July 2, 1964.

and production is small. In 1958, the last year for which data are available, smallholders produced 401 metric tons ot cotton from 1,653 hectares.[20] State cotton plantations produced only 91 tons in 1960–1961 and 38 tons in 1962–1963.[21] The Eight Year Overall Development Plan (1960–1968) envisaged a great expansion of cotton acreage in Indonesia, and investigation teams have reported such an expansion to be feasible. But it is unlikely that enough domestically produced cotton will be available in the next few years to ease the raw material problem. Inadequate insect control and unfamiliarity of farmers with the technical requirements of the crop appear to be major obstacles.

Consequently the textile industry must continue to import its raw materials, either as raw cotton or (since spinning capacity remains so limited) as yarn (see Table 9.3). As a result of the general decline in Indonesia's exports, and the mounting burden of debt service, foreign exchange available for imports has contracted sharply in recent years. If the existing productive capacity of the spinning, weaving, and knitting sections were to be fully utilized, $165 million would have to be allocated for imports of raw cotton and yarn.[22] This is much more than is likely to be available for this purpose in the near future.

As noted earlier, spinning capacity is sufficient to supply only 24 percent of yarn requirements for the total weaving and knitting capacity (46 percent excluding handloom capacity), while less than 29 percent of potential weaving production can be finished properly. But the proportion of weaving capacity used in past years has sometimes been less than this 29 percent. Capacity utilization rates have fluctuated a great deal because of the indirect effects of disturbances in other sectors of the economy. The levels of activity in the modern spinning industry have been

[20] Deperindra staff working paper (unpublished), Department of People's Industry, Djakarta.

[21] Interview at P. P. Serat (State Fibre Plantations Office), November 1964.

[22] I.e., $14 million for 20,241 tons of raw cotton and $120 million for 150,000 tons of yarn. The calculations are based on the costs of raw cotton and yarn noted by Henry N. Bresette, U.S. industry advisor, in his report to Deperindra, June 8, 1964.

Table 9.3. Capacity, utilization rates, and imports of competitive textile materials, 1950–1968

Year	Imports of raw cotton (tons)	Spinning capacity output (tons of yarn)	Utilization rate (percent)	Imports of yarn (tons)	Weaving capacity output (million metres)	Utilization rate of weaving industry (percent)	Imports of bleached and unbleached cotton piece goods; dyed, printed, woven, coloured cotton piece goods; and textile materials—clothing and underwear (million metres)
1950	2,860			15,317	269	36	286
1951	4,042			5,812	275	16	331
1952	4,071	5,506	71	8,228	272	22	311
1953	5,078	5,810	82	12,959	280	34	428
1954	5,684	8,540	63	14,374	287	37	340
1955	7,116	8,540	77	17,957	298	40	299
1956	7,841	10,439	69	20,465	295	45	363
1957	9,327	10,439	82	10,554	374	22	318
1958	8,124	10,579	69	16,868	419	30	176
1959	6,493	10,683	55	20,486	n.a.		110
1960	11,117	10,716	94	49,342	483	57	185
1961	12,157	n.a.		50,263	n.a.		339
1962	10,591	14,053	68	29,542	664	22	206
1963	n.a.	17,780		23,000	n.a.	n.a.	83
1964	n.a.	19,340		26,000	n.a.	n.a.	0
1965	n.a.	20,960		n.a.	n.a.	n.a.	n.a.
1966	n.a.	32,670	26	n.a.	n.a.	n.a.	n.a.
1967	28,630	35,820		7,680	875.9	n.a.	n.a.
1968	n.a.	n.a.		47,470	n.a.	n.a.	n.a.

Sources: I. Palmer, *op. cit.*, pp. 82, 197, 293; *Asian Textile Survey 1967–1968*, *op cit.*; Bank Indonesia, *Report of the Governor*, 1959–1965, Djakarta; H. W. Arndt, "Survey of Recent Developments," *BIES*, vol. 5, no. 3, November 1969.

higher and more stable than in the weaving industry, partly because spinning is largely in the public sector, and partly because productivity is more uniform and the industry therefore presents fewer problems of overall protection.

As the country's foreign exchange crisis became more serious in the late 1950's, the Department of People's Industry assumed responsibility for acquiring foreign exchange for the textile industry's raw material requirements.[23] It applied to the exchange-allocating authority for foreign exchange, which it then distributed among producers on the basis of their reported capacity. The size of the total application was determined on the basis of domestic capacity and the estimated cloth requirements of the people. Until 1961, the exchange-allocating authority was the Department of Trade and thereafter the minister co-ordinator for development; in September 1964, foreign exchange allocation became the responsibility of the Supreme Command of Economic Operations (KOTOE). As the foreign exchange shortage became more acute, the gap between the industry's need, as represented by the Deperindra application, and the funds finally allocated tended to grow. In the second half of 1962, only 5 percent of nonmechanized looms were in operation, and it was estimated that the West Javan weaving industry was receiving only enough yarn to utilize about 11 percent of its capacity.[24] By late 1964, it was rumored (though the evidence is inadequate) that all handlooms were idle and that only about 5 percent of power looms were operating. The last yarn to arrive before Christmas 1964 was a shipment of 2,200 tons in July.[25] Toward the end of 1964, 10,000 tons of raw cotton were received from Mexico.[26] The only yarn or raw cotton which is known to have arrived in 1965 was

[23] In May 1965, a Department of Textile Industry (Deperindteks) was set up under the supervision of the previous minister of people's industry, now elevated to the rank of a co-ordinating minister. Deperindra itself was created by the subdivision of the Department of Industry which dates from the Djuanda cabinet of 1957. Before that the ministry of economic affairs was responsible for the industry.

[24] Economist Intelligence Unit, *Three Monthly Economic Review,* no. 44, Indonesia, May 1963.

[25] *Warta CAFI,* no. 45/HM/64, July 2, 1964.

[26] *Warta CAFI,* no. 44/HM/64, February 2, 1964.

a consignment of 15,600 tons of yarn, worth about $20 million, from China on a two-year credit.[27]

The political troubles and foreign exchange crisis of 1965 and 1966 were felt in the textile industry as much as in any other economic field. The first main relief came at the end of 1966 with 90,000 bales of raw cotton and 50,000 bales of yarn (equivalent to approximately 190 million metres) under a P.L. 480 agreement.[28] Another 69,462 bales of raw cotton were supplied in mid-1967 for a further six months; and this, together with a consignment of spare parts, was intended to put the spinning industry at full capacity production by the end of 1967. Unfortunately, at the same time the October 1966 monetary reform had led to a liquidity shortage in the production sector and the large stocks of raw cotton were held in godowns while only half of spinning capacity was being utilized.[29] For the whole of 1966, the eight established spinning mills produced 46,530 bales of yarn, or 40 percent of their potential.[30] This crisis lasted through most of 1967. Other problems faced by the spinning industry at this time included inadequate spare parts (partly overcome by "cannibalizing" more broken-down equipment), administrative bottlenecks, and transport and storage difficulties.

It was reported that large weaving plants were operating at 75 percent of capacity, medium-sized plants at 40 percent, and small-sized plants at 5 to 10 percent in 1966. The overall average utilization rate was said to be 30 percent.[31] This comparatively high rate was due to a lack of imported finished textiles and, bebefore October 1966, to what was a sellers' market in Indonesia with a favourable foreign exchange rate for importers of yarn and cotton. But by mid-1967 the weaving and knitting sections had suffered a slump. Total yarn imports in 1967 amounted to 42,190

[27] Komando Tertinggi Operasi Ekonomi (KOTOE), Decision no. KPTS 39/WPB—KOTOE/1964. Also late news from Deperindra, June 1965.

[28] H. W. Arndt, "Survey of Recent Developments," *BIES*, no. 11, October 1968, p. 22.

[29] Sediono, *op. cit.*

[30] *Ibid.*

[31] *Ibid.*, p. 103. This figure seems very high in view of our capacity estimates, and therefore ought to be treated with caution.

bales.[32] Imports of cloth increased, as a result of credit being made available for that purpose, and raw material imports jumped in price. The Indonesian textile market became a buyer's market and domestic producers faced a hopeless situation. Unemployment increased and some mills closed down.

In April 1967, it was reported that textile factories were operating at 15 percent of their capacity,[33] and at the beginning of 1968 at 10–25 percent.[34]

The complaints from textile manufacturers during 1967 were successful, for supplies of yarn imports rose more than five times to 260,700 bales (equivalent to 380 million metres) in 1968, and in the first half of 1969, 88,940 bales (equivalent to 130 million metres) were imported (twice as many as for the whole of 1967).

It is likely that weaving activity has become increasingly concentrated in the large, more efficient enterprises due both to the prolonged financial crisis of the smaller establishments and to changes in methods of distributing the raw material.

Raw material imported with the foreign exchange allocated to Deperindra was channelled to producers through the officially supervised cooperatives and Organizations of Homogeneous Enterprises (OPS) to which they belonged.[35]

This raw material was imported at an exchange rate which, though changed from time to time, was always far below the free market rate. The price of imported yarn was fixed, until May 1963, at landed cost plus 25 percent. From May until November 1963, this control was removed in an attempt to allow prices to find their equilibrium level, but in November 1963, KOTOE, the newly established price-fixing authority, restored the landed cost plus 25 percent pricing practice. The margin of markup over landed cost was raised to 95 percent in January 1964, but

32 Arndt, *op. cit.,* vol. 5, no. 3, November 1969, p. 7.

33 Arndt, *op. cit.,* no. 7, June 1967, p. 6.

34 Arndt, *op. cit.,* no. 9, February 1968, p. 25.

35 There are several such organizations linked in a Federation of Homogeneous Enterprises (GPS) for the entire industry. Their main functions, apart from the allocation of raw materials, are advice to members, financial help to weaker members, collection of statistics, and liaison between producers and Deperindra.

reduced to 45 percent in April 1964. The purpose of this system of low exchange rates and controlled prices was to make raw materials available at reasonable cost to manufacturers and to keep down the price of textiles for mass consumption. But as the quantity of yarn available was much less than required, a black market developed with the "black" price as high as nine times the official price.

There were two main sources of black market yarn. In theory, yarn was imported by the State Trading Corporations and distributed by the cooperatives according to the absorption capacity of their individual members. The cooperatives were obliged to circulate lists of factories' quotas to members to enable each to check that he had received the correct amount. There should, therefore, have been no leakage. In fact, however, the State Trading Corporations began to sell part of the yarn on the free market with the compliance of, and for the benefit of, the cooperatives. Though Deperindra officials were aware of this, they winked at it, apparently accepting the argument that without it the State Trading Corporations could not have continued importing and the cooperatives could no longer have provided financial assistance to their members. In 1964, about a quarter of all yarn imports seems to have entered the black market in this way.

The other source of black market yarn arose from the wide differences in technical and financial position among the manufacturers themselves, all of whom were receiving yarn at official prices according to their capacities. Most of the smaller producers did not have enough funds to purchase their quotas, which had to be indented for an advance, and they found bank credit hard to obtain. Consequently they either processed the yarn on a commission basis for a middleman who financed the purchase of the raw material; or paid part of the quota to a moneylender as interest; or sold the entire quota to the middleman who financed the purchase. In this way, the greater part of the yarn allocations of small- and medium-sized producers was channelled to the larger and more efficient factories. In 1964, some factories obtained as much as 80 percent of their supplies from the black market. Some yarn was also imported under the Export Exchange Certificate System (the SPP), that is, at a free exchange rate, though the black market price of yarn has usually been below that of yarn imported under this system.

It appears that the demand for textiles was usually sufficient to enable the more efficient producers (generally the larger mills with power looms) to use profitably the yarn bought on the black market or through the SPP system. As these free prices rose, most of the smaller producers, who are weaker both technically and financially, suspended production and lived from the sale of their yarn quotas to their more efficient domestic competitors. The system of yarn allocation at fixed prices according to reported capacity, therefore, came to represent a subsidy to compensate the less efficient manufacturers for not producing, thus permitting the more efficient mills to process the limited yarn available. This arrangement, in addition to benefitting the less efficient manufacturers and the officials connected with yarn distribution, was acceptable enough to the strong (mostly Chinese) manufacturers. The sufferers (apart from the government budget)[36] were the workers in the more labour-intensive, small- and medium-sized enterprises who were left idle.

Late in 1964, a team of officials under the Supreme Command of Economic Operations (Team Sandang KOTOE) was given the task of cleaning up the yarn distribution system. Its investigations revealed that manufacturers were overstating their capacities in order to receive larger allocations; that some who had not produced anything for three years were still receiving allocations; that some factories had unreported stocks of yarn; and that bribery of officials of Deperindra, the cooperatives, and the Organizations of Homogeneous Enterprises was rife.[37] This led to many arrests and, for a time, to an easier supply situation.

However, the activities of the Team Sandang did not solve the basic problem of the yarn shortage, and some of its actions (for instance the freezing of large sums of money deposited by manu-

[36] The government has foregone the rupiah revenue which it would have obtained if it had sold foreign exchange used for yarn imports at a higher exchange rate.

[37] KOTOE Team Chusus Penertiban Bahan Baku Untuk Produksi Sandang, *Progress Report I*, October 1964 [and] *II*, February 1965.

facturers for future yarn allocations) created much opposition. One of the leading members of the team has himself been charged with large-scale corruption.[38] In September 1965, a further reorganization of the system of raw material allocation was under way, centering around a National Clothing Conference (*Mubesan*). A new-style Organization of Homogeneous Enterprises for the textile industry was set up, together with a National Clothing Council (*Dewan Sandang Nasional*) and an executive body (*Badan Pelaksana Sandang Nasional*) into which the Team Sandang KOTOE was absorbed.[39]

The keynotes of the new policy foreshadowed by the National Clothing Conference were "logistics" and "guided integrated planning." As in the fields of banking and foreign trade, the government had been moving in the direction of stricter control up to 1966.[40] The government wished to allot yarn according to a production plan, instruct manufacturers as to what to produce, and control distribution. Another decision of the Conference was to stimulate the production of raw cotton in line with the prevailing emphasis on self-reliance (*berdikari*).

In 1965, a special department was created for the textile industry under the auspices of a director general, and in 1966 it was announced that no new licences for weaving and spinning were to be issued except for mechanizing existing units. One reason, no doubt, was to put an end to the claiming of larger-than-justified raw material allocations through forgery. Finally, the allocation system was abolished in January 1967[41] so that former black market practices were no longer necessary. Since licences were no longer of significance, data on the number of handlooms and power looms which might be brought into use without much delay is not now available. The advantage of the

[38] *Harian Ekonomi Nasional* (newspaper), Djakarta, September 15, 16, 22, 1965. The (then) current attack on Team Sandang KOTOE was by leftist organizations.

[39] *Ibid.,* September 14, 18, 20, 22, 23, 1965.

[40] Arndt, *op. cit.,* no. 2, September 1965, p. 11.

[41] W. Boucherie, "The Textile Industry," *BIES,* vol. 5, no. 3, November 1969, p. 56.

abolition of allocations is that the distribution of landed raw materials should be considerably faster.

Competition from Imports of Textiles

While the domestic textile industry has periodically suffered very low rates of utilization of capacity, large amounts of competitive textile imports have been permitted. It is unquestionably true that Indonesian textile manufacturing is less efficient than most overseas manufacturing[42] and, therefore, if the policy goal were that of free international trade, it would deserve to be ignored. But all governments in Indonesia have approved the prominent position of textiles in the overall industrialization and employment-creating programme, and it is in this light that the neglect of the industry and the importation of cloth while foreign exchange was scarce must be judged.

The data in Table 9.3 indicate not only capacity output and actual utilization rates of the spinning and weaving industries, but the magnitude of competitive yarn and cloth imports. Where both domestic and foreign supplies were low this can be explained in terms of overall foreign exchange shortage (although there is no established good reason why a larger proportion of the available foreign exchange should not have been devoted to raw materials for the industry). But spinning utilization was low and yarn imports were high in the years 1954, 1956, 1958, and 1959, and in most years later. In the case of the weaving industry this situation occurred most markedly in 1951 and 1957. The fact that the spinning and weaving industries did not experience it in the same years suggests that the level of effective protection at any time was not the same for both sections—reasonable assumption to make, since the output of one becomes the input of the other.

The chief causes of this erratic protection policy were inadequate initial tariff protection, the erosive effect of inflation on any initial level of protection, and the periodic liquidity crises in the industry. Lesser causes include the existence of separate groups of lobbyists for the spinning and weaving industries, and the

42 See Palmer, *op. cit.*; and Boucherie, *op. cit.*

variable and disappointing quality of domestic output in the smaller establishments. ("Initial tariff protection" is that level of tariff which is set just after an exchange rate adjustment has been made to offset a spell of inflation.)

Tariff protection on the different forms of textile materials varied from zero percent to 200 percent. But there was not a strong correlation between the level of the tariff and the amount of value added in the commodity. For instance, in August 1952 there was no tariff on yarn and the simpler textiles which would be a close substitute for domestic production, while in September 1955 yarn imports remained tariff free but cloth imports faced tariffs of 50 percent and more.[43]

Between August 1952 and June 1957 the basic exchange rate was not altered in spite of a general price rise of approximately 90 percent. Devaluations of the effective rates were invariably marked by a crisis in working capital during which supplies of most consumer goods declined. The improved position of domestic weaving, as reflected in Table 9.3 must be attributed to import quotas in 1954 and to higher tariff protection in 1955.

Inflation varied from 6 percent to 46 percent per annum during the 1950's and reached a peak of more than 600 percent in 1966. This meant that two years of inflation uninterrupted by exchange rate adjustment could bring the domestic industry to a standstill without the interference of other measures, such as import quotas or prepayments on import orders. The liquidity crises in the production sector have been caused either by monetary or exchange rate reform, or by a movement of money from specific production activities to speculation in a less risky variety of goods.

The final column of figures in Table 9.3, competitive imports, reflects all combinations of these factors. The fluctuations in imports have been considerable, and have induced instability in domestic production. There is no suggestion of a deliberate conspiracy to thwart the textile industry, even though it might seem a natural political target, being dominated by the Chinese. The

[43] W. M. Corden and J. A. C. Mackie, "Development of the Indonesian Exchange Rate System," *Malayan Economic Review*, vol. 7, no. 1, April 1962, p. 45.

dismal production record is due to an inability to isolate the progress of the industry from general economic problems and from corrective measures. In the constant flux of economic forces in Indonesia it would have been difficult for the most experienced planners to evaluate tariff levels appropriate to a prescribed level of profitability in different parts of the textile industry. In the event, government economists were not sufficiently conscientious about the welfare of individual sectors and have placed too much reliance on orthodox aggregative economic policies.

Against this general background there might well have been times when importers who found finished goods more profitable and simpler to handle than cotton and yarn lobbied the exchange-allocating body successfully. This was certainly true of the years prior to 1965 when the Department of Trade was responsible for the allocation of foreign exchange to the Department of People's Industry, to itself, and to other departments. During this period cloth imports were more profitable to the State Trading Corporations than yarn imports, partly because of the price controls designed (ironically) to protect the weaving industry by keeping down its raw material costs. The fact that the directors of these Corporations were appointed by the minister of trade encouraged personal relationships and mutual support between them. In an earlier period, the politically influential, private "national" importers had similarly favored easy imports of finished textiles to the detriment of the domestic industry.

The 1965 National Clothing Conference decided to limit or, if necessary, stop altogether the import of finished textiles, thus reserving the limited foreign exchange available for raw materials and spare parts. This repeated a decision of KOTOE eight months earlier that there would be no official imports of finished textiles and that yarn imports would be 300 percent greater than in 1964.[44]

The Textile Industry under the Suharto Government

The new (post-1965) government has repeated the mistake of permitting competitive imports. One aspect of recent policy which has left manufacturers demoralised has been the use of foreign

[44] Interview with the author at Department of Trade, March 2, 1965.

credits (as in 1966 and 1967) to import huge amounts of finished textiles. In 1967, out of a total of $15.9 million of credits spent on all textile materials purchased from the U.S. and Japan, $12.7 million were spent on finished textiles.[45] Even after allowing for Japan's desire to sell the finished product, it is hard to believe that competent economists with the courage of their convictions would have had to settle for such an outrageous bargain. During a prolonged period of stagnation of domestic production, large imports of textiles on these credits were permitted because of the government's desire to demonstrate price stability as soon as possible after the monetary reform of the previous September. The result of this short-sighted policy was that during the 1966–1967 Christmas, *Lebaran* (Muslim feast), and Chinese New Year purchases of textiles, prices fell 25 percent aggravating the slump in the domestic industry. Monetary reform, overseas competition, and lower profitabilities combined to produce the first policy on textiles of the new pragmatic government.

Although the Indonesian textile industry can theoretically produce most of the country's textile requirements, imports provide more variety and better qualities. Because of interruptions of supplies and transport difficulties, it often happens that textiles of the right kinds at the desired time are more easily available from imports than from domestic production. In such situations the authorities responsible for trade policy might prefer to make foreign exchange available for textile imports, knowing full well that this wastes dollars and discourages the domestic industry.

After the change of government in 1965–1966, there was no clear indication that textile manufacturers would fare better under the new pragmatic economic policies. Indeed, it appeared for two years that the fresh team of Western-trained economists were even less mindful of the need for qualitative safeguards during monetary reforms than their predecessors. In 1966 and 1967 precious supplies of P.L. 480 raw materials were held in godowns at factories and ports due to the shortage of working capital following the October 1966 reforms and the uncertainty surrounding profitability of manufacturing cloth while large shipments of imported cloth were in the offing.

[45] "Statistical Section," *BIES*, no. 11, October 1968, p. 118.

Since the traumatic experience of 1967 there has been great concern over the industry. The measure to abolish yarn allocations has the advantages of a revenue potential for the government and the speeding up of the flow of yarn to its processors; although it is likely to cause localized economic distress. The government must still guard against corrupt personal relationships in the allocation of foreign exchange between producing and importing interests. There is no good reason for supposing that this will be less likely to occur in the future than in the past, especially in view of the fact that textile producing interests are predominantly Chinese and importing interests are Indonesian. When the current economic vigilance weakens, these political considerations are likely to re-emerge.

Far more encouraging have been the signs of a long-term rationalization of the industry: the realistic assessment of viable handweaving capacity; the intention to reduce the imbalance between the different sections of the industry; and the priority given to expansion of the finishing industry rather than the spinning industry. The new Five Year Plan (1969–1974) has the modest target of increasing domestic production from (about) 300 million metres to 900 million metres of cloth. An addition of 750,000 spindles to the present 480,000 would be necessary to equate spinning and weaving capacities,[46] but only another 360,000 spindles have been planned.[47] In view of the technical problems arising from intricate spinning machinery and various output qualities this is a promising concession to reality. Furthermore, the private sector is being encouraged to expand finishing facilities and is responding well. Additional finance for finishing capacity is being made available under the Plan. This process is less intricate than spinning and the quality of output more easily standardized. Its importance lies in the justification of the large weaving capacity and the future respect of local consumers for the domestically produced cloth.

The hope has been expressed by the government that foreign enterprise will enter the field of cotton production, and 500,000

[46] Boucherie, *op. cit.*, p. 69.

[47] "Cotton Textiles and the Prospects for Synthetic Fibres in Indonesia," *Far East Trade and Development*, vol. 24, no. 12, December 1969.

acres of land are reputed to be available for its cultivation. In view of the constraints imposed by foreign exchange reserves this is a sensible "residual" policy since there is no urgency over development of domestic cotton production. It also carries the advantage that foreign capital usually brings with it skilled personnel to deal with technical problems which are bound to occur.

It must be pointed out, however, that the long-term rationalization of capital investments in the modern textile industry does not automatically provide a programme for maintaining high levels of activity in the industry: it merely reduces the number of anomalies and contradictions in policies. There remains concern for the textile industry when substantial debt repayments commence in 1973. Net available foreign exchange will then very likely be considerably less than it has been in the late 1960's. Approximately $165 million must be allocated annually for imported inputs if full capacity utilization is to be attained—or the equivalent of 8.1 metres per capita. Despite a good showing in growth of export earnings since 1966, an allocation of that order of magnitude in the absence of continued large net inflows of foreign assistance will be a difficult goal to meet.

PART V

MONEY AND FINANCE

The role of monetary, fiscal, and foreign exchange institutions and policies in a developing economy is a crucial one. Internal price relations, price levels, and capital accumulation are profoundly influenced by the wisdom and effectiveness of a nation's bankers and financial officials—in particular those who run the central bank; and the extent to which the government must rely on credit expansion in financing public-sector activities may enhance the efforts of the bankers—or frustrate them completely. Also, the government's ability to marshal resources in increasing quantity, as the demand for public-sector goods and services grows, depends on effective integration of fiscal policy, bank-lending policy, and interest rates.

The pricing and allocation of foreign exchange are closely linked with these other aspects of money and finance. Imported goods can be crucial to the development effort—in the form of food for employment of domestic labor, fertilizer for domestic agriculture, or equipment and spare parts for the textile industry. If there is domestic inflation, the temptation to prevent a rise in the prices of vital imports is very great, and many low-income countries, including Indonesia until recently, have chosen to do this by fixing the price of foreign exchange and substituting rationing devices for markets in determining the pattern of use. The complex of problems which emerges with this effort to substitute government for market often leads to comparable complexity in the devices developed to cope with them. Recent alterations of this system are discussed in the editor's article in this Part.

CHAPTER 10

The Indonesian Banking System: The Central Bank*

ALI WARDHANA

The Java Bank under the Dutch Regime

In 1818, when English merchants dominated the entire Indonesian market and monopolized the various trade activities, the Netherlands' government supported Dutch enterprises with capital and profit guarantees in the hope that this would enable them to compete with the English entrepreneurs. This plan failed completely since, as a British economist puts it, "the Dutch preferred an easy-going, unadventurous life of petty retail trade at home." [1] In its place, a new policy was introduced and a bank, the Java Bank, was created with the object "to colonize Java with capital rather than with men." [2] The apparent intent of its creator was to establish the Bank as a private corporation, but as the public showed little interest in the offer of its shares,[3] practically all the capital was provided by the government and a large Dutch business enterprise, De Nederlandsche Handel Maatschappy (the Neth-

* Reprinted from "Monetary Problems of an Underdeveloped Economy; With Special Reference to Indonesia," Ph.D. thesis, University of California, Berkeley, 1964. By permission of University Microfilms, Inc., Ann Arbor, Michigan.

1 Cf. J. S. Furnivall, *Colonial Policy and Practice, A Comparative Study of Burma and Netherlands India,* Cambridge University Press, London, 1948, p. 220.

2 *Ibid.*, p. 221.

3 Benjamin H. Higgins and William C. Hollinger, "Central Banking in Indonesia," in G. Davis, ed., *Central Banking in South and East Asia,* 1st ed., Hong Kong University Press, Hong Kong, 1960, p. 53.

erlands Trading Company), the latter of which the king of the Netherlands was the principal shareholder.

Since the beginning, the Java Bank's field of activity was primarily the financing of private enterprises and, to a limited extent also, the issue of banknotes. During the later decades of its existence, it gradually became engaged in various forms of commercial banking activities and concentrated to an increasing extent on its note-issuing function. It was not until the institution of the Java Bank Act in 1922, that it was formally granted the right to become the only bank of circulation for Indonesia.[4]

This action, however, placed the Bank, originally founded as a private corporation, under close control of the government. It was subject, for instance, to the supervision of a commissioner appointed by the government (Article 24, par. 1), who also had the right to nominate the Bank's president (Article 23, par. 1). In addition to many restrictions in the sphere of its activities, the approval of the governor-general had to be secured before a branch could be established or an agent appointed (Article 4, par. 5).

As has been noted, the Bank's responsibility with respect to the formation of monetary policy, was, to a greater or lesser degree, dependent on directives outlined by the government in the Netherlands. As such, it was closely intertwined with their general economic policies. Its primary objective was that of unifying the Indonesian currency system with the monetary system of the Netherlands by maintaining the official rate of exchange between

[4] The text of Article 2 of the Act reads as follows: "(1) De Bank blijft onder de volgende bepalingen en voor een tijdperk van fijftien jaren, ingaande den lsten April 1922 en dus eidigind den 31sten Maart 1937, gerechtigd om als circulatiebank in Nederlandsch Indie werkzaam te zijn. [The Bank, shall, under the following regulation and for a period of fifteen years commencing April 1, 1922 and terminating March 31, 1937, have the right to function as a bank of circulation for Netherlands India.] (2) Dat tijdperk wordt geacht telkins opniew met een jaar verlengd te zijn, tenzij door den Gouverneur-Generaal, ingevolge onze machtiging, of door de Bank door opzegging van ongeneigdheid tot die verlenging blijk zij gegeven. [The period is considered renewable for one year unless the Governor General or the Bank expresses their unwillingness to do so.]" See the Java Bank, *Report of the President and of the Board of Directors,* 1921–1922, Djakarta, p. 26.

them at a one-to-one parity.[5] Throughout its career, the Bank clung to this principle as the core of its monetary policy. This responsibility was interrupted twice only—by the financial crisis of the 1930's and by World War II; conversion of the Netherlands Indies guilder into gold was suspended, and thus the link with the Dutch guilder snapped.

Another reason that the Java Bank could not fully develop an independent monetary policy for Indonesia was the fact that the money market for Indonesian funds was in the Netherlands. Practically all Dutch enterprises in Indonesia had their domicile in the Netherlands, and it was customary to transfer any excess funds to their head offices; this was even brought about automatically as earnings from Indonesian exports were, for a large part, received in the Netherlands.[6] Furthermore, the abundance of profitable government bonds or other high-yielding securities, many of which could by law be issued only in the Netherlands,[7] provided a very attractive object of investment for the transferred excess liquidity as well as the personal savings of the Dutch in Indonesia.

On the other hand, when the need arose to bridge liquidity tensions in Indonesia, many enterprises exhibited an unwilling attitude to depend on the sources of the Java Bank as a "lender of last resort," but would simply rely on the money market in the

[5] See C. F. Scheffer, *Het Bankwezen in Indonesia, Sedert het uitbreken van de Tweede Wereldoorlog,* Noordhoff-Kolff, Djakarta, 1951, pp. 22–23. Also Higgins and Hollinger, *op. cit.,* p. 53.

[6] The Java Bank, in its annual issue, reported: "Ware het wereldgeldverkeer normaal geweest, dan zou men ongetwijfeld het overtollige geld in Nederlandsch Indie . . . zeker niet hebben gehouden en meer gebruik gemaakt hebben van de gelegenheid om dien gelden elders in soliede en hoge rentegevende obligaties to beleggen [If it were not for the abnormal financial situation in the world, the excess liquidity would have never been kept in Netherlands India, but would undoubtedly have been invested elsewhere in high-yielding bonds or securities]" (*Java Bank Report,* 1921–1922, p. 27). See also Scheffer, *op. cit.,* pp. 22–23.

[7] This was, for instance, the case with the 7 percent Nederlandsch-Indische Leening (7 percent Netherlands-India's Bonds). It was reported by the Java Bank (1921–1922) that rate differences rendered impossible the issuance of government securities in Indonesia and in the Netherlands on the same basis (p. 27).

Netherlands through its main office. Resort to the Bank was limited to emergency or unavoidable situations only.

Here, from the viewpoint of monetary policy, lies the major difference between the powers of the Java Bank and those of a full-fledged central bank. The latter, by virtue of its powers to create as well as to contract credit, thus being the ultimate source of money supply, could exert a tight control on the country's liquidity needs; in Indonesia, on the contrary, the financial and business world would fall back on the Netherlands' money market, thus reducing the activities of the Java Bank to a mere intermediary.

The reluctance of the colonial government to fully develop an autonomous monetary policy for Indonesia has also been interpreted in terms of the sensitivity of the Indonesian economy to external cyclical fluctuations. As has been explained above, a decline in foreign exchange earnings through a recession in foreign demand for Indonesian export products is likely to cause violent disturbances in the balance of payments. Moreover, the disturbances tend to be even more pronounced if there is a lag between the decline in exports and the consequent fall in imports. In Indonesia, it was estimated that, following a drop in export prices, a lag exists of six months to one year before imports start to decline, thereby accentuating the balance-of-payments disequilibrium by more than the decline in exports taken alone.[8] To protect the domestic economy from such violent fluctuations the Java Bank, in the implementation of its monetary policy, could call not only on its own exchange reserves, but also, as a secondary line of defense, on reserves in the form of credits extended by the Netherlands' government. In this way, equilibrium in the balance of payments could be maintained for relatively longer periods while drastic limitations on the use of foreign exchange, as well as other short-term measures interfering with the free import-export trade, could be avoided.

Finally, the limited competence of the Java Bank to develop a strong monetary policy was further impeded, although to a lesser

[8] Cf. Benjamin H. Higgins, "Central Bank Reserve Systems and Indonesia's Foreign Exchange Problem," *Ekonomi dan Keuangan Indonesia* (*EKI*), November 1954, pp. 747–748.

degree, by its carrying on of ordinary commercial banking business. Despite the many suggestions and persuasions that the Bank confine itself to functions proper to a central bank,[9] it continued, to the great annoyance of its competitors, to undertake direct business with the public.

It is generally observed, however, that such operations were, and still are, common among many note-issuing banks,[10] for it is exactly in this way that banknotes come into circulation. But in the case of the Java Bank, its particularity has been explained in terms of its direct interference with the business sector in the form of providing working capital. Quantitatively, in terms of the volume of credit, competition with other commercial banks was not exceptionally noticeable; qualitatively, however, the effect was relatively more severe.[11] The lower rates of interest the Bank offered on its loans and discounts attracted the larger European and Chinese firms, of which, by discrimination, only the most preferred were selected.

Although to some extent this is true, it is not quite relevant from the point of view of monetary policy. A more serious problem than its overemphasis of the commercial interest, at least in the case of the Java Bank, was its failure to develop its powers and prerogatives as a central bank, as well as its failure to train a truly central-bank-minded staff. "Among the Dutch experts working with the Bank there were apparently none with central bank experience. The higher ranks had gone through the archipelago, collecting enviable experience in commercial banking, but none whatsoever in central banking." [12]

Following World War II, and also after the transfer of sovereignty, several efforts were made by the Java Bank to continue its policy of monetary dependence on the Netherlands. On the other hand, with respect to its relation with the new Indonesian government, it was considered of vital importance that the Bank should

[9] See, for instance, Scheffer, *op. cit.*, p. 18.

[10] Cf. M. H. DeKock, *Central Banking*, Stapless Press Limited, London, 1954, pp. 13–17.

[11] Ting Ham Djie, *De Algemeene Banken in Nederlandsch Indië*, W. P. van Stockum, Den Haag, 1926, p. 41, as cited by Scheffer, *op. cit.*, p. 18.

[12] Philip Stephani, "Indonesia, Banking Under Guidance," *Far Eastern Economic Review*, April 6, 1961, p. 45.

be developed on an independent basis, and that government interference should be strictly limited.[13] Furthermore, the president of the Java Bank insisted that, within the framework of the monetary system in Indonesia, existing banks which were predominantly Dutch should not be controlled but should "be left free in their extension of credit." [14] With respect to Indonesian enterprises entering the field of banking or foreign trade, however, he proposed limitations through stringent requirements.[15] This has led Schmitt to conclude that apparently "a new aim of central banking was being developed: that of effectively neutralizing a national government in favor of foreign interest by interposing the Bank between them . . . ," [16] for "in effect a Dutch private institution had control over a vital aspect of Indonesian Government policy." [17]

The government, however, primarily motivated by the fact that a bank of circulation could not work fully in the national interest as a private institution, became increasingly intent upon pursuing an autonomous monetary policy. Such ideas were not compatible with a policy of monetary dependence on the Netherlands. This situation, then, culminated on June 19, 1951, when a committee was called into being by the government to take the necessary steps for the nationalization of the Java Bank. After two years of preparations and parliamentary discussions, a statute to govern the central bank's operations came into effect, while a new name, "Bank Indonesia," was chosen.

The Bank Indonesia

In the statute of the Bank Indonesia, established on July 1, 1953, it is stated, among other points, that within the framework of monetary policy, the Bank Indonesia shall be the central bank of Indonesia. Many observers claimed that the Bank Indonesia Act, however, did not bring principal changes, and that the basis

[13] *Java Bank Report,* 1949–1950, p. 11.

[14] *Ibid.,* p. 45.

[15] Higgins and Hollinger, *op. cit.,* pp. 54–55.

[16] Hans O. Schmitt, "Some Monetary and Fiscal Consequences of Social Conflict in Indonesia, 1950–1958," Ph.D. thesis, University of California, Berkeley, 1959, p. 30.

[17] Higgins and Hollinger, *op. cit.,* p. 54.

of central-banking policy as laid down in the statutes represents in part only a reorganization of the former Java Bank. In support of this opinion, I shall first describe the functions generally recognized as those of a central bank, and then I will attempt to apply the main uniformities and differences to the Bank Indonesia as well as the Java Bank. For this purpose, the most simple but elaborate concept of central-bank functions seems to be the one worked out by DeKock.[18] He acknowledges that the methods of central banking vary in kind and in degree between one period and another, in accordance with the need and the structure of the economy as well as in the trend of political and social actions; but that, at present, a clearly defined concept and a well-established technique have been evolved in many countries. He therefore considers the following activities to be widely accepted as constituting the apex of the monetary and banking structure of a country.[19]

a) The regulation of currency in accordance with the requirements of business and the general public, for which purpose it is granted either the sole right of note issue or at least a partial monopoly thereof.

This obligation is carried out by the Bank Indonesia as the only bank of circulation in Indonesia (Article 8, par. 1), and for that matter, was by the Java Bank also (Article 9, par. 1).

b) The performance of general banking and agency services of the State.

The Bank Indonesia Act stipulates that the Bank shall take custody of the Treasury fund, undertakes the transfer of funds on behalf of the government, and render its assistance for the issue of government bonds (Article 18, par. 1–4). The same provision can be found for the Java Bank under its own statute (Article 12).

c) The custody of the cash reserves of the commercial banks.

This requirement was not fully met by the Java Bank. It was customary for commercial banks to deposit their excess balances

[18] DeKock, *op. cit.*

[19] *Ibid.*, p. 22. For similar analysis with respect to the Java Bank, see also Scheffer, *op. cit.*, pp. 22–23.

with the Bank, but we have seen that these were, under normal conditions, transferred to the Netherlands.

For some time, commercial banks in Indonesia have followed this practice and voluntarily maintained certain balances with the Bank Indonesia. It became compulsory when, in 1957, a statutory provision required that banks maintain certain minimum credit balances with the Bank in relationship between their cash assets and the amount of current liabilities plus deposits. In addition to cash, Treasury notes and bills were included among the reserve-eligible assets.[20] From the viewpoint of monetary control, this definitely represents a major step toward central-banking development.

d) The custody and management of the nation's reserves of international currency.

Gold and foreign exchange were always under control of the Java Bank and now are with respect to the Bank Indonesia. Following World War II, the movement and holding of gold and international currency was further restricted by the introduction of a bureau of foreign exchange which concentrated the earnings from foreign trade.

e) The granting of accommodation, in the form of rediscounts or collateral advances, to commercial banks, bill brokers and dealers, or other financial institutions and the general acceptance of the responsibility of lender of last resort.

Rediscounts with the Java Bank were indeed possible. The banks restricted opportunity, however, only to situations when the support of the money market in the Netherlands could not be relied upon, or when all other available resources were exhausted. The Bank's function as a "lender of last resort" could therefore not be effectively employed, as the importance of this function emerged only through the Bank's rediscount activities.

With respect to this problem, Higgins contended that the Bank Indonesia is not actually, but *potentially* a lender of last resort, on the basis that "the liquidity position of the commercial banks has so far been so good that they have not been obliged to fall

[20] Decree of the Monetary Board, no. 28, May 28, 1957.

back on the Bank Indonesia as a lender of last resort," and that "only once, during the second period of required prepayments for imports, have the commercial banks experienced liquidity difficulties." [21]

It is open to debate, however, whether the high liquidity position of the banking system since independence had caused rediscounting to be ineffective, or whether the great uncertainty that prevailed as to the willingness of the Bank to provide these facilities had compelled commercial banks to maintain higher reserves. Higgins recognized that the lack of an efficient clearing system and the undeveloped capital market restricted shiftability, and hence solvency as well, but admitted that the banking system would institute rather strong measures to avoid a drop in liquidity "unless the central bank was willing to come to their aid with newly created credit as the lender of last resort." [22]

f) The settlement of clearance balances between the banks.

Since 1909, daily clearing activities took place, but were limited to certain large cities and between prominent banks only, with the Java Bank acting as the clearing house.[23] The Bank Indonesia took over this responsibility and, so far, the development in this sector, although far from being efficient, seems to be not entirely discouraging.[24]

g) The control of credit in accordance with the needs of business and with a view to carrying out the broad monetary policy adopted by the State.

Today this is accepted by most economists as the main objective of a central bank policy. Although considerable differences still exist as to its implementation, it is generally recognized that there is some relationship between changes in the volume of credit and the general level of economic activity and employment. That disturbances in this relationship might engender severe fluctuations in the purchasing power of money has led many to conclude the

[21] Higgins and Hollinger, *op. cit.,* p. 61.
[22] *Ibid.*
[23] Scheffer, *op. cit.,* p. 21.
[24] *Report of the Governor,* 1958–1959, Djakarta, pp. 257–258.

necessity of subjecting the creation and distribution of credit to some other form of control.

This is admitted in Article 7 of the Bank Indonesia Act which requires that the Bank promote a sound development of the banking and credit system and bear full responsibility for the supervision of it. This responsibility had been denied the Java Bank, either in its statutes or in its daily policy matters.

h) It should not, to any great extent, perform such banking transactions as accepting deposits from the general public and accommodating regular commercial customers with discounts or advances.

In reaction to this philosophy, Sjaffrudin Prawiranegara, the first governor of the Bank Indonesia (also a former minister of finance and prime minister), stated that it is not advisable to insist upon the principle that a central bank ought to be a "banker's bank" only.[25] The absence of a money and capital market of any significance, he argued, in addition to the inadequate capital of the Indonesian banking system to satisfy all applications for credit facilities, are sufficient reasons for the Bank to consider it premature to surrender its commercial banking business. He cited that in countries like Belgium and France, where banking development is well in advance of Indonesia, the central banks conduct general banking business even up to the present time.

This statement became a much debated issue. Just before the draft bill, constituting the new charter of the Bank Indonesia, had been submitted to parliament for approval, the minister of finance took the view that the Bank should not continue its commercial banking operations on the grounds that such might come into direct conflict with its functions as a "banker's bank."[26] He considers that the success of a central bank depends largely upon the support and cooperation of the commercial banks, and that such can be obtained only if the central bank refrains from competing with the lesser banks in the field of commercial banking.

Many times the central bank must appear unfair to its own banking department. Unfortunately, the charge of discrimination

[25] *Java Bank Report,* 1951–1952, pp. 19–21.

[26] Sumitro Djojohadikusumo, "The Central Bank of Indonesia," *EKI,* February–March 1953, p. 98.

has been made against the Bank Indonesia because its banking department, unlike the state and other private commercial banks, has been excluded from the regulation to maintain reserve requirements.[27] Furthermore, the Bank Indonesia Act specified that all activities granted to the Bank to perform normal banking operations (Article 13), insofar as they do not refer to the sphere of activities as a central bank, should be delegated in the shortest possible time (by December 31, 1953, at the latest) to other banks. This has never been realized.

Summarizing the result of my survey, I have observed that the Bank Indonesia, to some extent, remained what the Java Bank had been: a bank of circulation with a considerable interest in its commercial banking department. The new act "did not expressly give the Bank Indonesia any more powers as a central bank than those which were exercised by the Java Bank, namely, the right to issure currency, to manage and administer gold and foreign currencies, to engage in open market operations and to advance funds to the central government." [28]

Entirely new, however, are the duties specified in Article 7 of the Bank Indonesia Act, containing modern conceptions of the monetary system, the inclusion of which also reflects the new trend in central banking objectives in many underdeveloped countries today: (1) It shall be the Bank's duty to regulate the value of the Indonesian currency in a way that will be most expedient to the welfare of the state, and in so doing, to aim toward the utmost stability of the currency; (2) the Bank shall attend to the internal money circulation in Indonesia as far as bank notes are concerned; it shall facilitate transfers inside Indonesia and promote the facilities for payments to and from foreign nations; (3) the Bank shall further promote a sound development of the banking and credit system in Indonesia in general, and of the national banking and credit system in particular; (4) the Bank shall undertake supervision of the credit system in Indonesia; (5) pending legal provisions, the government shall issue by decree regulations for the supervision of the credit system by the Bank, more

[27] Harold K. Charlesworth, *A Banking System in Transition,* New Nusantara, Djakarta, 1959, p. 92.

[28] *Ibid.,* pp. 29–30.

particularly in the interests of the solvency and liquidity of the credit institutions and of a healthy credit system, based upon the principles of good banking.

In this regard, however, Harold Charlesworth rightly remarks that "it was not until May 1957 that reserve requirements were imposed on the banking system, and the Bank Indonesia began to exercise more of the central bank functions which is its right and duty as implied in Article 7. Since that date the Bank has adopted various selective credit controls, and has begun to perform all the central bank functions discussed above." [29]

The Bank Indonesia and the Government

In the evolution of central banking in many countries, it became increasingly apparent that a central bank had to occupy an important place in the monetary structure of a nation. Its power to influence and its responsibility to control the currency and credit system constitute one of the prominent safeguards for the proper function and stability of the nation's economy. These essential functions distinguish the central bank from an ordinary commercial bank.

On the other hand, it has been observed that the central bank's particular position was established by law or other government guarantees. This presupposes, to some extent, a certain relationship between the bank and the government. As the state granted the bank certain rights through statutory enactment, the bank is obligated to reserve certain of these rights and privileges. Several central bank acts, among them the Indonesian, even recognize the powers of the government with respect to the management as well as the policy to be pursued by the central bank.

It is equally important, from the bank's standpoint, that its operations be coordinated with the general economic policy of the government, and that the Treasury keep the bank fully informed of its policy and counsels on that matter. That the relationship of the government and its central bank, in this and other related areas, does not always give rise to a smooth cooperation and interchange of information between them, but to conflicts and opposite policies as well, is not difficult to understand.

[29] Cf. Charlesworth, *op. cit.*, p. 31.

Consequently, the fundamental question is how far the government should be allowed to interfere with, or have some influence over, the central bank's policy; for that matter, to what extent the bank should be given independence in determining its own strategy in the monetary field.

Before World War I, the independence of central banks was never a problem; its policy toward serving the public was never questioned, while its attitude toward liquidity and solvency was very much like that of a private enterprise or business firm.[30]

Today, the intense efforts to uphold this philosophy are motivated by the desire to protect monetary policy from being influenced by any political expediency or financial exigency of the government. This fact, in conjunction with the tendency of governments to change often, and with them policies, is considered to increase the susceptibility of monetary policy to any political bias.

In the United States, for example, stress has been placed on the desirability for the independence of the Federal Reserve System. In a struggle to free monetary policy from the Treasury's inveterate tendency to support the interest-rate structure of the federal debt, the Douglas Committee, reaffirming the primary responsibility of the Federal Reserve System with respect to monetary managment, came out with the proposal that: "It is the will of Congress that the primary power and responsibility for regulating the supply, availability, and cost of credit in general be vested in the duly constituted authorities of the Federal Reserve System, and that the Treasury action relative to money, credit, and transaction of the Federal debt shall be made consistent with the policies of the Federal Reserve." [31]

In the course of the years, as government intervention with banking affairs became stronger, central banks came to be looked

[30] Henry C. Wallich, *Monetary Problems of an Export Economy,* Harvard University Press, Cambridge, 1950, p. 279.

[31] Eighty-first Congress, 2nd session, Senate Document no, 129, *Monetary, Credit, and Fiscal Policies,* Report of the Subcommittee on Monetary, Credit, and Fiscal Policies of the Joint Committee on the Economic Report, *U.S. Government Printing Office,* Washington, D.C., 1950. See also Howard S. Ellis, "The Rediscovery of Money," *Money, Trade, and Economic Growth,* Macmillan, New York, 1951, pp. 263–268.

upon as agencies occupying a subordinate position within the hierarchy of government apparatus. Particularly since the depression of the 1930's, the trend toward state control became more and more general, accentuated by the belief that a direct and stringent interference with the banking and credit policy by the government might have prevented the large-scale bank failures.[32]

After World War II, especially in the underdeveloped countries, government participation in all sectors of the economy was generally accepted on socioeconomic grounds, namely, to achieve a higher income per capita for its population and a more rapid rate of economic development.

In an attempt to diminish the tendency of governments to exercise complete authority over the central bank, or conversely, to give the central bank more powers to determine the monetary policy of the country, there has been an increasing tendency to establish monetary boards where officials of both agencies are members.[33] It is interesting to note, however, that within the framework of such coordinating bodies, in many cases it is always the central bank's representative that would have to yield in case of conflict.

During discussions on the new statute for the central bank, the governor of the Bank asked, with respect to the principles required for a proper relationship between the Bank and the government, the following question:

> Should the management of the Central Bank be subordinated to the Government, so that the Bank is nothing more than its tool and cashier, or should the bank of issue be granted a measure of autonomy, so that it is not only a Government implement and cashier, but also its financier, in which expression there is the implication that the Bank can, when necessary, give the Government the benefit of its advice and also, should the occasion arise, reject applications from the latter for credit facilities on the ground of the Bank's responsibility for maintaining the value of the money? [34]

[32] Wallich, *op. cit.*, p. 279.

[33] Arthur I. Bloomfield, "Monetary Policy in Underdeveloped Countries," in C. J. Friederich and S. E. Harris, eds., *Public Policy*, Harvard University Press, Cambridge, 1956, pp. 38–39.

[34] *Java Bank Report*, 1951–1952, p. 13.

Acknowledging that the Bank is obliged to cooperate and, in many cases even, align its policy with the government, he emphatically urged that the Bank be given some degree of freedom to determine its own policy. Popular confidence in the monetary system, the governor continued, can be insured and maintained in the best possible manner only when operations in so delicate a medium as money be entrusted to the central bank. If the Bank enjoys the advantages of a state management free from any political influences, it has more freedom to develop long-term policies than would an everchanging government agency. All the government needs is the authority to ensure that the activities of the Bank do not deviate from the function established by the government and embodied in its statutes.

In this connection, the minister of finance, representing the government on financial matters, cogently replied that in an underdeveloped economy such as Indonesia's higher levels of production can be achieved, and monetary equilibrium and economic stability maintained, only if all instruments of control, including monetary policy, are concentrated in the hands of the government. In such countries then, he argued, "monetary policy, just as budgetary and fiscal policy, has become an instrument of public policy. If this is recognized, it only stands to reason that monetary policy must be the responsibility of the government," and as such, "it is the government that should be the guardian of public interest and no one else." [35] In short, this statement implicitly assumed the incompetence of the central bank as "the guardian of public interest" in the economic field.

That in this dispute the Bank Indonesia came off second best was to be expected. The formulation of general monetary policy, as stipulated in the Bank Indonesia Act, is entrusted to a *Dewan Moneter* (Monetary Board) consisting of five voting members—the minister of finance as chairman, and, as members, the governor of the Bank Indonesia, the minister of distribution, the minister of production, and the minister of development and construction.

Should a disagreement arise between the government and the Bank Indonesia, Article 24 of the Act provides that the governor

[35] Djojohadikusumo, *op. cit.*, p. 96.

of the Bank not only has the right to request that the dispute be submitted for decision to the cabinet but also to publish his opinion in the "Berita Negara" (Government Gazette), unless the cabinet decides this to be incompatible with the interests of the country.[36] In other words, the cabinet is the highest monetary authority in Indonesia while the Monetary Board is the policy-making body. The Bank Indonesia, through the Board of Managing Directors, is to execute the monetary policy laid down by the Monetary Board.

In conclusion, to illustrate the historical development of government interference in banking affairs in Indonesia since the establishment of the Bank Indonesia, I draw attention to the two following statements. At the beginning of the period, one individual glorified the absence of government interference: "It is an interesting fact that Indonesia has not followed this (state interference in the banking field) general trend. Up to now the banks in this country are not curbed in any way by the Government. . . ."[37]

Eight years thereafter, when the Bank Indonesia had become more and more "another Government agency," another lamented that "the Government has reduced the Central Bank to a lending office from which the State can borrow unlimited funds."[38]

The Bank Indonesia and Its International Reserves

Like any other underdeveloped country with great sensitivity to foreign trade fluctuations, Indonesia is concerned with the problem of seeing that it accumulates and holds adequate international reserves to meet, at any time, adverse balance-of-payments situations.

To avoid any persisting drains on a country's foreign exchange reserves many central banks in underdeveloped countries have provided a criterion or warning signal by imposing central bank

[36] Article 24, sub 4 and 5 of the Bank Indonesia Act.

[37] C. F. Scheffer, "Some Aspects of the Relation between the State and General Banking," a speech delivered on entering upon the Professorship in Monetary Economy in the Economic Faculty of the University of Indonesia, Djakarta, January 1953, *EKI,* June 1953, p. 317.

[38] Philip Stephani, *op. cit.,* p. 45.

reserve requirements of various types.[39] In Indonesia, the central bank is required by law to maintain a minimum reserve against its note issue and other demand liabilities. The ratio of the Bank Indonesia's total gold and foreign convertible currency to the total amount of bank notes and the current demand liabilities should be maintained at a minimum of 20 percent.[40]

Twice during its existence, the Bank failed to prevent a fall in its obligatory ratio and was compelled to suspend temporarily its reserve requirement. The first occurred during the aftermath of the Korean War boom in raw materials when Indonesia suffered substantial losses in its international reserves. The second, in 1959, was primarily brought about by large increases in the money supply through budget deficits as domestic social security conditions reached catastrophic dimensions. In such extraordinary circumstances, the statutes of the Bank Indonesia provide a clause under which the Bank may "escape" from its responsibility to maintain its required reserve for a period of three months. (Article 16, par. 3) Should the Bank, however, fail to restore the legal ratio within the specified period, the government must present the case to the parliament and obtain its permission to extend the period for another three months. (Article 16, par. 5) If at the end of this period the reserve ratio is still below 20 percent, the government may be compelled to consider revision of the statute.[41]

The Bank Indonesia Act does not specifically mention the purposes the minimum reserve requirements are supposed to serve. But it has been argued by central bank and other official authorities that a drop below the legal reserve would endanger public confidence in the value of the Indonesian currency.[42] A fall in the ratio might occur as a result of a drain in foreign exchange because

[39] Bloomfield, *op. cit.,* p. 22.

[40] Article 16, par. 1 of the Act reads: "The total amount of banknotes, balances on current account, and other demand liabilities of the Bank shall be covered for one-fifth either by gold, gold coin or bullion, or by the reserves consisting of foreign currency which are generally convertible; or by the right to draw on the International Monetary Fund and the World Bank, which has been or shall be endorsed to the Bank by virtue of law."

[41] Higgins, *op. cit.,* p. 737.

[42] *Ibid.,* p. 739.

of unfavorable balance of payments, or through an increase in the money supply in Indonesia mainly due to budget deficits, or both. Consequently, policy measures to prevent a drop in the reserve ratio have been concentrated primarily on maintaining adequate international reserves and restricting central bank advances to the government. With respect to the latter, the desirability of the reserve requirement has even been explained as an automatic check on any overexpansion of credit to the government.

The problem of maintaining "adequate" foreign exchange reserves seems to result from the difficulty in defining the concept properly. So far, no formulas have been discovered to provide the "warning signal" or to indicate the "critical level" for the monetary authorities. To a large extent, the staff of the International Monetary Fund argued, the "critical level" depends on "the prospective problems that confront a country and, therefore, will differ from country to country and from problem to problem. No amount of reserves can be adequate to finance a chronic or continuing imbalance in a country's payments." [43] As such, the criterion for "adequacy" of reserves is a relative one. Implicitly, it is assumed also that the countries concerned are willing to take the necessary steps to straighten out any imbalances in their foreign-payments position over the entire business cycle.

More specifically the Fund suggested the following criteria for the adequacy of monetary reserves: (1) Enough to enable a country in bad years, by resort to restrictions, to maintain its external debt payments and to purchase the goods and services necessary to avoid hardships to its population or dislocation to its economy and the possible emergence of an exchange crisis, i.e., to permit a reasonable distribution over time of the payments which it can afford to make over the entire cycle; (2) Enough to maintain currency convertibility, barring a severe depression, but with occasional necessity to resort to trade and exchange restrictions for balance-of-payments purposes; (3) Enough to maintain currency convertibility, barring a severe depression, but without the necessity for occasional resort to trade and exchange restrictions; (4)

[43] International Monetary Fund, "The Adequacy of Monetary Reserves," *Staff Papers,* vol. 3, no. 2, October 1953, p. 185.

Enough to maintain currency convertibility, even through severe depressions (but not through prolonged periods of international deflation such as occurred in the 1930's), without either the necessity for occasional resort to trade and exchange restrictions or the necessity for resorting to domestic deflationary policies for the purpose of restraining imports, even if this involves a substantial drain on reserves.[44]

Furthermore, the principal factors that determine the "adequacy" of reserves in a certain country would be, first, the normal seasonal variation in the country's imports and exports; second, the extent to which the balance-of-payments position is subject to extraordinary variation; third, the variability in the prices of its imports and exports; and fourth, the extent to which the country is dependent on imported raw materials and foodstuffs.[45]

Before as well as after the war, Indonesia has been faced with sudden decreases in export earnings from 25 to 30 percent. It is not difficult to understand that in view of such fluctuations a country like Indonesia needs a larger amount of reserves. Benjamin Higgins estimated that under such conditions Indonesia should hold reserves amounting to about 20 percent of the yearly export proceeds.[46]

I may further add that the necessity to hold larger reserves of gold and foreign exchange is substantiated by the almost permanent character of the budgetary deficits. These deficits may arise from seasonal fluctuations in government expenditures and receipts, as well as because of a deliberate policy to finance a development program.[47] In Indonesia, the first is considered to have some importance since such fluctuations can bring about a maximum drain on reserves amounting to between 10 and 20 percent of the current budget receipts.[48] With respect to the latter, the utilization of foreign exchange depends on the extent to which the inflationary effects of the deficits are being offset by an increase in imports.

[44] International Monetary Fund, *op. cit.,* p. 188.
[45] *Ibid.,* pp. 188–189.
[46] Higgins, *op. cit.,* pp. 747–748.
[47] *Ibid.,* p. 747.
[48] *Ibid.,* p. 748.

No drain on foreign exchange resources would occur if the development program were entirely financed by foreign aid.

Precisely, the same can be argued for inflationary effects financed by an expansion of credit in the private sector. In Indonesia, however, the degree of its absorption is comparatively less than that caused by budgetary deficits.

The foregoing arguments support the desirability of maintaining adequate reserves of gold and foreign exchange. The need for a legal minimum reserve seems to have been associated with the idea of providing an automatic limit to any overexpansion of money and credit.

In Indonesia, as continuous government deficits provided the source for monetary expansion, the statutory limit could not have prevented the ratio from falling below the legal minimum. Twice during its short life, the Bank Indonesia was compelled to resort to the "escape clause." Despite its objections, there is nothing the central bank can do but yield to the government's insistence on pursuing inflationary financial policies to accelerate economic development. There is little possibility that the government can manage to produce any surplus or balanced budget in the near future. "The question is, therefore, whether the mere existence of a statutory reserve requirement will ever really prevent a government from undertaking budget deficits, or running a balance-of-payments deficit, if the general economic and political situation makes it difficult for the government to take the actions necessary to achieve budgetary and balance-of-payments equilibrium." [49]

It must immediately be admitted, however, that on various occasions the strict enforcement of the minimum reserve did have deflationary effects on the economy. In this respect, Grove says, "Statutory reserve requirements should not be regarded as establishing a minimum level below which reserves must not be permitted to fall under any circumstances. It seems preferable to regard them as standards which can be suspended or reduced by appropriate authority if extreme circumstances make this desirable. As many economists have noted, the rigid observance of minimum reserve requirements in periods of exchange crisis would defeat the

[49] Cf. Higgins, *op. cit.,* p. 739.

very purpose of reserves, since it would have the effect of locking up a substantial portion of the central bank's holdings of gold and foreign exchange." [50]

Establishment of a minimum reserve requirement has usually been related also to preventing the consequences of any overexpansion of credit, viz., price inflation, excessive speculation, and balance-of-payments disequilibrium. In other words, reserves are held to assure internal stability as well as external convertibility of the currency.

This does not imply that currencies without the direct backing of gold and international reserves are subject, or are vulnerable, to frequent economic disturbances. Today, many countries, among them the Philippines, Ceylon, and Thailand in Asia, no longer require obligatory reserves against their note issue, but still enjoy the confidence of the public and even manage to stabilize their currencies at official rates. Many factors—among them the productive capacity of the country, a relatively stable government, and a strong balance-of-payments position—have contributed to this development. Statutory reserves alone are not a sufficient economic index to watch for.

[50] David L. Grove, "The Function of Central Bank Reserves and Reserve Requirements," as quoted in Higgins, *op. cit.*, p. 742.

CHAPTER 11

Banking in Hyperinflation and Stabilization*

H. W. ARNDT

This chapter falls into two parts. The first describes the condition of the Indonesian banking system in 1966, after several years of accelerating inflation. The second outlines more briefly developments since the fall of Sukarno and especially the new government's approach to banking reform.[1]

The Banking Structure

Indonesia inherited from the Dutch a characteristically colonial banking structure.[2] The main prewar institutions were eight for-

* Reprinted by permission of the author and by S. Gethyn Davies, editor of *Central Banking in South and East Asia.* This volume, originally published in 1960 (Hong Kong University Press) is under revision, and will include Professor Arndt's chapter when the new edition appears.

[1] The first part is based on an article on "Banking in Hyperinflation" published in the *Bulletin of Indonesian Economic Studies* (*BIES*), no. 5, October 1966; the second part draws on the survey articles in nos. 5–8 of the *Bulletin* and on information collected in Djakarta in March 1968. The author is greatly indebted to Indonesian bankers and economists for their kind help. The responsibility for errors and opinions is his alone.

[2] For accounts of the Indonesian banking system, see especially the annual reports of the Bank Indonesia until 1959–1960; H. K. Charlesworth, *A Banking System in Transition,* New Nusantara, Djakarta, 1959; Douglas S. Paauw, *Financing Economic Development,* The Free Press, Glencoe, Ill., 1960; B. H. Higgins and W. C. Hollinger, "Central Banking in Indonesia," in S. G. Davies, ed., *Central Banking in South and East Asia,* 1st ed., Hong Kong Uni-

eign exchange and commercial banks—four Dutch, two British, and two Chinese. One of these, the old-established, semipublic Java Bank, had a monopoly of note issue but few other central banking functions. The main concern of the foreign exchange banks was short-term finance of exports and imports and of the foreign-owned estates and other enterprises. Through their credit to the great Dutch commerical houses, which in turn financed the Chinese middlemen, the foreign exchange banks also formed the apex of a credit pyramid whose base was the trade credit extended to villagers by the small traders and collectors of export produce. Three Japanese banks had branches in Indonesia and there were, in 1939, three small domestic banks, one each in Batavia, Medan, and Semarang. A public credit institution, the Allgemeene Volkscredietbank, had been set up to provide small-scale credit to village and rice banks and other small borrowers. Some direct financial assistance had also begun to be provided by the government to indigenous manufacturers. But domestic industry and trade depended for credit mainly on the unorganised market of more or less informal moneylenders. So, for money loans, did peasant agriculture.

After World War II, during the struggle for independence, two state banks emerged in republican territory. The Bank Negara Indonesia was established to provide general banking facilities but intended also to serve as the Republic's central bank; and the Allgemeene Volkscredietbank was transformed into a state bank, under the name Bank Rakjat Indonesia, to provide rural and other small-scale credit. In 1952, a third state bank was added to operate as an industrial development bank, the Bank Industri Negara. In the following year, the Java Bank which the Republic, in the negotiations for the transfer of sovereignty, had reluctantly agreed to retain as the bank of issue despite continued Dutch private ownership and management, was nationalised. Renamed Bank Indonesia, it became the country's central bank but through its large banking department retained the status and functions of a commercial and foreign exchange bank. In 1957–1958, the

versity Press, Hong Kong, 1960; J. A. C. Mackie, "The Indonesian Economy: 1950–1963," *Schriften des Instituts fur Asienkunde,* vol. 16, Frankfurt, 1964, pp. 115–155.

three remaining Dutch foreign exchange banks were nationalised, along with other Dutch enterprises. The other foreign banks continued to operate for some years as foreign exchange banks, except for the Japanese banks whose Indonesian branches did not survive the war.

Under official encouragement, inspired by the belief that Indonesia needed national banks adapted to the needs of national economic development, a swarm of private national banks came into existence in the early 1950's, mostly established by Chinese business groups. Three of the more substantial of these were accorded foreign exchange bank status, and a number of others operated as viable though small commercial banks. But the great majority of the hundred or so private national banks supposedly in existence by the end of the decade did not carry on any significant public banking business. Much more important as sources of finance were the specialised credit agencies through which numerous government departments disbursed government funds as credit for purposes under their jurisdiction.[3] While the major state banks had nationwide networks of branches, the private national banks were mostly unit banks, concentrated in Djakarta, with at most one or two branches in other cities.

Thus, by 1959–1960, the last year for which the Bank Indonesia published an annual report, the Indonesian banking structure consisted mainly of:

(1) the central bank (Bank Indonesia);
(2) thirteen exchange banks, including
    (a) six state banks: Bank Indonesia Banking Department, Bank Negara Indonesia, Bank Rakjat Indonesia, and the successors to the three nationalised Dutch banks (Bank Umum Negara, Bank Dagang Negara, and Bank Koperasi, Tani dan Nelajan);
    (b) four foreign banks (2 British, 2 Chinese);
    (c) three private national banks;
(3) 90–100 private, nonforeign-exchange banks; and
(4) various specialised credit agencies of government departments.

[3] Cf. Paauw, *op. cit.*, pp. 136f.

In addition, there were the postal savings banks and state pawnshops inherited from the colonial period, a stock exchange opened in Djakarta in 1952,[4] a variety of small credit cooperatives (village and rice banks in rural areas and the traditional *arisan* credit unions in towns), and the large and important unorganised market of moneylenders and trade credit.

The statute of July 1953 which established the Bank Indonesia aimed to make it a modern central bank on the accepted Western pattern. It was assigned the tasks of regulating the currency and supervising the banking and credit system with the aim of maintaining the "utmost stability of the currency" and promoting national economic development.[5] It was given a monopoly of the note issue, subject to a 20 percent reserve requirement, authority to make advances to the Treasury limited to 30 percent of Treasury revenue in the preceding year, and control over foreign exchange transactions and reserves. While authorised to carry on commercial banking, it was enjoined to delegate these functions as soon as possible to other banks—an injunction it never carried out. The man who had largely inspired the design of the new central bank, Sjafruddin Prawiranegara, was appointed governor, but the formulation of monetary policy was entrusted to a Monetary Board in which he was in a minority, with two cabinet ministers (the minister of finance and the minister of economic affairs) as the other two members and the minister of finance as chairman. The government of the day, therefore, was in direct control of policy.

In the following years, the powers of the central bank were elaborated in various decrees of the Monetary Board. In 1955, an attempt was made to regulate the proliferation of small private banks by excluding banks from trading, requiring them to obtain licences from the central bank, and laying down conditions for minimum capital funds. In 1957, the central bank was given powers to impose on all private banks minimum-cash and liquid-asset reserve requirements (later extended to the state banks), to exercise selective control over bank credit, and to fix maximum

[4] Cf. on this, *Ibid.*, pp. 137f.

[5] Higgins and Hollinger, *op. cit.*, p. 58.

interest rates.[6] But monetary policy was a continuous struggle with inflation and balance-of-payments difficulties.

The central bank was in no position to resist government pressure to finance ever-growing budget deficits, even its legal safeguards being swept away in 1957 and 1958 by the suspension of the limit on advances to the Treasury and the abolition of the note-issue reserve requirements. It had little effective control over the state banks often allied with powerful ministries. The main instrument of domestic monetary policy became the device of import prepayments, reinforced by credit ceilings on bank finance of these prepayments. A complex system of multiple exchange rates was devised (and incessantly revised) to cope with the balance-of-payments problem without open devaluation.[7] The role of the central bank as guardian of financial stability was further weakened after the resignation of Governor Sjafruddin to head the rebel "government" in Sumatra in February 1958 and the appointment of two more cabinet ministers to the Monetary Board. In 1961, Jusuf Muda Dalam, a former PNI member of parliament, became minister of central bank affairs and governor of the Bank Indonesia.

Between 1960 and 1965, the structure of the Indonesian banking system underwent a number of further minor changes. The Bank Industri Negara was transformed into a state development bank, Bank Pembangunan Negara. In 1960, an attempt was made to create a private development bank, the capital to be compulsorily supplied by the private owners of deposits frozen in the monetary purge of the year before plus 5 percent of the profits of state-owned enterprises; but the scheme was not enforced and the bank never effectively operated. Another scheme, for regional development banks to be owned by local authorities in the regions and to finance regional industrial development, was also largely stillborn. Of the nine banks for which the central government supplied the initial capital, only the bank at Palembang, which obtained considerable support from local rubber merchants, got

[6] Charlesworth, *op. cit.*, p. 58.

[7] See W. M. Corden and J. A. C. Mackie, "The Development of the Indonesian Exchange Rate System," *Malayan Economic Review*, April 1962.

well under way. In 1964, the remaining foreign banks, increasingly confined by restrictive government regulations, ceased to operate in Indonesia.

Finally, in 1965, Jusuf Muda Dalam determined on a complete reorganisation to bring the whole banking system under his own control. Already in the previous year an order had gone out to the five state banks to specialise: Bank Indonesia on finance of extra-budgetary and other "vital" projects, and each of the other four on credit for industries or activities within the jurisdiction of more or less related government departments.[8] A May 1965 regulation transformed the whole group of state banks into a single monster institution to be called Bank Negara Indonesia and to consist of five "Units." Bank Indonesia became "BNI (Bank Negara Indonesia) Unit I"; Bank Koperasi, Tani dan Nelajan "BNI Unit II"; the former Bank Negara Indonesia "BNI Unit III"; Bank Umum Negara "BNI Unit IV"; and the state savings banks and pawnshops collectively "BNI Unit V." One state bank, Bank Dagang Negara (the former Dutch Escompto Bank), thanks to the political skill of its director, a former minister for private banks, escaped integration and in the remaining months of the old regime operated with some independence as a "little central bank" with its own foreign exchange funds. Plans were announced to incorporate the private banks into the integrated system but nothing more was heard of them. Integration, in fact, never went beyond the change of names which was energetically carried through from buildings and stationery to the ambulances owned by "BNI Unit I" and official documents.

Inflation: The Statistical Picture

Tables 11.1–11.4 summarise the available statistics of the expansion of money supply and bank credit.

Between 1948 and 1960, total money supply rose at an average

[8] The departmental jurisidictions were somewhat oddly allocated as follows: *Bank Negara Indonesia*—basic industries (except mining), information, land transport, post and tourism, public works, basic education and culture; *Bank Koperasi, Tani dan Nelajan*—agriculture, fisheries, cooperatives, community development, forestry; *Bank Dagang Negara*—people's industries, sports; *Bank Umum Negara*—estates and health.

annual rate of 26 percent. The year-to-year changes reflected both external influences, chiefly export prices and the balance of payments generally, and policy influences, chiefly the alternation of years of large budget deficits and spurts of credit expansion with periodic efforts at stabilisation. Although the annual figures to some extent blur the picture, it is not difficult to trace the main phases in Table 11.1: the Korean export boom and subsequent balance-of-payments crisis of 1950–1952; the large budget deficits of 1953 and 1954, followed by the temporary stability achieved in 1955 by the "Sumitro reforms"; the even larger budget deficits of 1957 and 1958 called forth by the military effort to deal with the Sumatran rebellion; the 1959 monetary purge, soon to be undone by emergency credits to alleviate the liquidity crisis it had caused; and the final phase which began in 1961 with exuberant spending associated mainly with the initiation of the Eight Year Plan and the preparations for the West Irian campaign.[9] From an average annual increase of about 25 percent up to 1960, the money supply increased by nearly 50 percent in 1961, approximately doubled in 1962 and 1963, rose by more than 150 percent in 1964 and more than quadrupled in 1965.

More significant even than the acceleration in the expansion of money supply after 1961 was the dramatic change that year in the relative growth of money supply and prices exhibited in Graph 11.1. The steep rise in food prices in 1961 partly reflected the severe drought of that year. But except for 1964, prices continued to run ahead of the expansion of money supply. The evidence strongly suggests that confidence in the currency, which had until then been well maintained, began to give way. People became anxious to hedge against expected further inflation by getting out of money into goods. In quantity-theory terms, the upward pressure exerted on prices by the expansion of money supply was reinforced by rising velocity of circulation of money.[10] The inflation had entered the stage of runaway or hyperinflation.

[9] Mackie, *op. cit.*, p. 148.

[10] The climacteric of 1961 has been noted before: see K. D. Thomas and P. Drysdale, "Indonesian Inflation 1951–60," *Economic Record*, December 1964, p. 548.

Table 11.1. Money supply (Rp. [new] million)

Date	Currency* (1)	Deposits† (2)	Total‡ (3)	Currency as % of total (4)	Annual increase (%) Currency* (5)	Deposits† (6)	Total‡ (7)
Mar. 1938§	0.24	0.18	0.42	57.1			
Dec. 1947	1.27	1.23	2.50	51.0			
1948	1.64	1.37	3.01	54.5	29	11	20
1949	1.75	1.56	3.31	52.9	7	14	10
1950	2.58	1.73	4.31	59.9	47	11	30
1951	3.33	1.71	5.04	66.1	29	−1	17
1952	4.35	2.25	6.60	65.9	31	32	31
1953	5.21	2.27	7.48	69.7	20	1	13
1954	7.47	3.64	11.10	67.3	43	60	48
1955	8.65	3.59	12.20	70.9	16	−1	10
1956	9.35	4.02	13.40	69.8	8	12	10
1957	14.10	4.82	18.90	74.5	51	20	41
1958	19.90	9.49	29.40	67.7	41	97	56
1959	26.40	8.50	34.90	75.6	33	−10	19
1960	34.10	13.80	47.90	71.1	29	62	37
1961	48.50	19.10	67.60	71.8	42	38	41
1962	102.90	33.00	135.90	75.7	112	73	101
1963	175.50	87.90	263.40	66.7	71	166	94
1964	452.70	222.40	675.10	67.0	158	153	156
1965	1,966.60	615.40	2,582.00	76.0	333	176	282
Mar. 1966	4,261.20	1,332.20	5,593.40	76.2	2,118‖	2,077‖	2,108‖

Sources: 1938–59: Bank Indonesia, *Report of the Governor*, 1959–1960, Djakarta, p. 53; 1960–63: BNI Unit I (Bank Indonesia), *Weekly Return*, June 1966; 1964–66: BNI Unit I (Bank Indonesia), *Weekly Return*, January 1968. Both issues of the *Weekly Return* were kindly made available to the author by the central bank.

* Currency: The data represent the central bank's liabilities on account of notes in circulation *net* of notes held by the foreign exchange banks but without deduction for notes held by nonforeign-exchange banks.

† Deposits: The data represent nongovernment demand deposits with the foreign exchange banks (including Bank Indonesia) but do not include the deposits of nonforeign-exchange banks.

‡ Total: Total money supply is therefore understated by the amount of nonforeign-exchange banks' deposits and overstated by their holdings of cash. The net understatement was probably about Rp. 25 million in December 1964 and Rp. 80 million in December 1965.

§ Estimated.

‖ Annual rate.

Table 11.2 brings out the dominant role of deficit finance in the expansion of money supply throughout the whole period. In every year from 1955 until 1963 (with the exception of 1960 when revaluation of the gold and foreign exchange reserve fol-

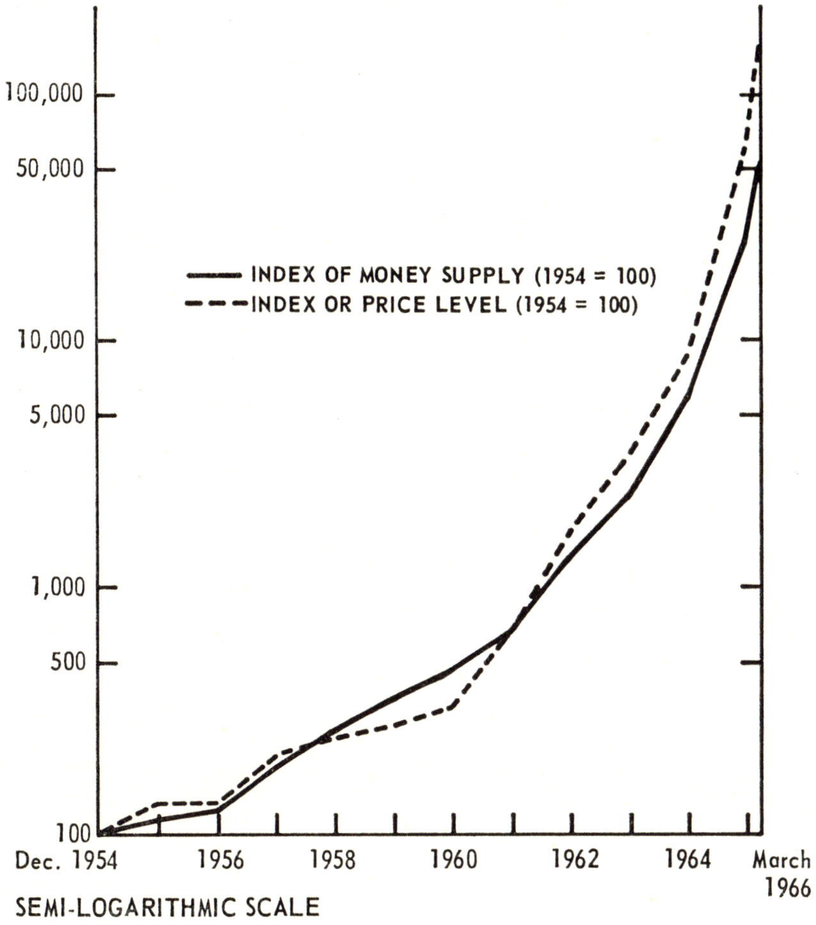

Graph 11.1. Money supply and price level, 1954–1966

lowing the 1959 devaluation yielded a large accounting profit), the contribution of "government"—budget deficits financed by the central bank—almost equalled or exceeded the total increase in money supply. The contribution made by bank credit to public and private enterprises was, in most years up to 1963, only about one-third of that made by government deficit finance. It became much more substantial in the last three years. But then, as Table 11.3 partially reveals, the distinction between the two categories became blurred: bank credit increasingly became cen-

Table 11.2. Causes of changes in money supply (Rp. [new] million)

Date	Government	Enterprises		Foreign	Other	Total money supply
		Public	Private			
1955	+1.6	+0.2	−1.3	+1.0	−0.4	+1.1
1956	+2.5	−0.2	+1.0	−1.8	−0.3	+1.2
1957	+5.8	+0.1	+2.2	−1.0	−1.5	+5.5
1958	+9.5	+1.3	−0.9	+0.6	−0.1	+10.5
1959	+3.4	+5.3	+1.1	+14.0	−18.2	+5.5
1960	−0.8	+3.3	−1.2	+4.5	+7.2	+13.0
1961	+23.4	+3.1	+7.1	−6.8	−7.0	+19.8
1962	+53.6	+12.8	+5.1	−9.4	+6.1	+68.3
1963	+122.8	+23.6	+10.0	−11.0	−17.9	+127.5
1964	+345.6	+81.9	+32.4	−10.2	−38.0	+411.7
1965	+1418.5	+395.2	+237.4	−3.6	−140.6	+1906.9
1966 (Jan.–Mar.)	+1292.2	+627.6	+200.2	+5.5	+885.9	+3011.4

Sources: 1955–59: *Bank Indonesia Reports*, 1956–1957, 1957–1958, 1959–1960; 1960–63: BNI Unit I (Bank Indonesia), *Weekly Return*, June 1966; 1964–66: BNI Unit I (Bank Indonesia), *Weekly Return*, January 1968.

tral bank finance at one remove (Table 11.3, column 9) and went increasingly to finance government enterprises and extra-budgetary expenditures.

Little useful statistical information is available on the distribution of bank credit among sectors or industries. For the years between 1955 and 1959, the central bank published a classification of advances granted by the major banks which is summarised in Table 11.4. But the corresponding data for subsequent years are, for various reasons, not comparable and of doubtful value. We shall return to this question later on.

Much more interesting is the information provided in Table 11.1 on the distribution of total money supply between currency and deposits (column 4). As in other less developed countries, currency has been and remains much the more important form of money in Indonesia, representing about two-thirds of total money supply, as contrasted with one-fifth to one quarter in countries with highly developed monetary systems. Indeed, what is surprising is the large share of deposits in 1938, probably a reflection of the low degree of monetisation of the colonial economy out-

Table 11.3. Bank credit granted (increase in advances outstanding) (Rp. [new] million)

Date	To government by			To public by					To banks by	Totals		
					FE†							
	BI* (1)	FE† (2)	Total (3)	BI* (4)	State (5)	Private (6)	Non-FE‡ (7)	Total (8)	BI* (9)	BI* (10)	FE† (11)	Non-FE‡ (12)
1955	1.8	−0.3	1.5		1.2		n.a.	1.2		1.8	1.2	n.a.
1956	2.3		2.3		0.7		0.3	1.0	0.2	2.5	0.7	0.3
1957	5.4	−0.2	5.2		−0.4		0.3	−0.1	−0.1	5.3	−0.4	0.3
1958	8.8	0.4	9.2		2.1		0.5	2.6		8.8	2.1	0.5
1959	3.3	−0.1	3.2		6.5		0.2	6.7	0.2	3.5	6.5	0.2
1960	(−0.8)§	n.a.	(−0.8)	−0.9	8.6	−1.7	0.6	6.6	5.4	(3.7)	(6.9)	0.6
1961	(23.4)§	n.a.	(23.4)	0.1	9.6	−0.1	1.1	10.7	2.6	(25.1)	(9.5)	1.1
1962	59.6	−0.9	58.7	−0.5	16.3	0.5	3.2	19.5	6.6	65.7	15.9	3.2
1963	167.0	−23.0	124.0	1.9	30.6	1.4	6.8	40.7	9.8	178.7	9.0	6.8
1964	355.8		355.8	13.3	104.4		13.9	131.6	50.3	419.4	104.9	13.9
1965	1,580.4		1,580.4	216.6‖	485.7	6.9	87.8	797.2	194.6	1,991.6	492.6	87.8
1966 (Jan.–Mar.)	1,555.9		1,555.9	320.4‖	(76.5)#	(6.4)	(70.8)	n.a.	512.3	2,388.6	(82.9)	(70.8)

Sources: *Bank Indonesia Reports*, 1956–1957, 1957–1958, 1959–1960; BNI Unit I (Bank Indonesia), *Weekly Return*, June 1966.
* BI = Bank Indonesia.
† FE = Foreign-exchange banks.
‡ Non-Fe = Nonforeign-exchange banks.
§ "Government" contribution to increase in money supply (from Table 11.2).
‖ The annual balance sheet data for Bank Indonesia given in the June 1966 *Weekly Return* show unexplained large increases in "other" assets in 1965 and January–March 1966 (Rp. 310 million in 1965 and Rp. 148 million in January–March 1966) which are not included in these figures.
January and February only.

Table 11.4. Classification of bank credit (advances outstanding for foreign-exchange banks) (Rp. [new] million)*

	By sectors				By industries					
Date	Public (1)		Private (2)		Exports (3)		Production (4)		Other (5)	
Dec. 1955	0.61	(17.9)	2.79	(82.1)	0.94	(33.7)	0.30	(10.8)	1.55	(55.6)
1956	0.46	(11.7)	3.47	(88.3)	0.94	(27.1)	0.35	(10.1)	2.18	(62.8)
1957	0.53	(15.0)	3.01	(85.0)	0.78	(25.9)	0.38	(12.6)	1.85	(61.5)
1958	1.47	(28.7)	3.65	(71.3)	1.16	(31.8)	0.37	(10.1)	2.12	(58.1)
1959	5.89	(56.9)	4.46	(43.1)	1.54	(34.6)	0.60	(13.5)	2.32	(52.0)
[Data for 1960-1962 are of doubtful value.]										
1963		(41.1)		(58.9)		(29.5)		(43.3)		(27.2)
1964		(40.8)		(59.2)		(32.2)		(45.2)		(22.6)
1965		(27.5)		(72.5)		(30.0)		(44.9)		(25.1)
Feb. 1966		(50.3)		(49.7)		(24.1)		(61.3)		(14.6)

Sources: 1955–59: *Bank Indonesia Report,* 1959–1960, p. 87; 1963–66: BNI Unit I (Bank Indonesia), *Weekly Return,* June 1966.

Note: For 1955–59, "export" includes exporters, sugar estates, and agricultural estates; "production" includes only "industries"; "other" includes all other categories with importers, transport, finance, private, and miscellaneous as the main groups.

No information is available about the grouping for 1963–66. The data for 1963–66 relate to government foreign-exchange banks only, and for them only to credits granted "from their own liquidity."

Other reasons for doubting the comparability of the two sets of data are (a) changes in the relative size of the public and private sectors between the two periods, and (b) the likelihood that the figures in columns (3)–(5) in the latter period were influenced by a desire to demonstrate compliance with central bank selective controls.

* Percentages in parentheses.

side the foreign enclave sector. In the postwar years, the share of currency rose rapidly from 51 percent in 1947 to 70 percent in 1955. During the next ten years, contrary to what one might have expected, it did not rise further, fluctuating around this level.

Since central bank finance of budget deficits generated currency while credit expansion by the commercial banks generated deposits in the first instance, it is tempting to explain the movements in the currency-deposits ratio in terms of the relative contributions of these two sources of change in the total money supply. As Table 11.5 shows, there was indeed a fairly close conformity, if not in any given year, between the "government" contribution and the increase in currency in circulation, on the one hand, and between the "enterprises" contribution and the increase in deposits, on the other. But this explanation is clearly inadequate. If bank customers had been unwilling to hold on to the volume of deposits created by the banks, the latter would have no option but to convert these deposits into currency, relying on the central bank to bail them out of their liquidity difficulties. It remains to be explained, therefore, why holders of money balances in Indonesia chose to hold currency and deposits in the proportions they did in any year.

Table 11.5. Government and enterprise credit related to Indonesian currency and deposits (Rp. [new] million)

Date	"Government" contribution (1)	Increase in currency (2)	"Enterprise" contribution (3)	Increase in deposits (4)
1955	1.6	1.2	−1.1	−0.1
1956	2.5	0.7	0.8	0.4
1957	5.8	4.7	2.3	0.8
1958	9.5	5.8	0.4	4.7
1959	3.4	6.5	6.4	−1.0
1960	−0.8	7.7	2.1	5.3
1955–1960	22.0	26.6	10.9	10.1
1961	23.4	14.4	10.2	5.3
1962	53.6	54.4	17.9	13.9
1963	122.8	72.6	33.6	54.9
1964	345.6	277.2	114.3	134.5
1965	1,418.5	1,513.9	632.6	393.0
1961–1965	1,963.9	1,932.5	808.6	601.6

Sources: Columns (1) and (3): Table 11.2; Columns (2) and (4): Table 11.1.

Viewed in this light, the rise in the share of currency during the years 1947–1955 is much more easily accounted for than the failure of this share to rise further in the next ten years. Changes in the structure of the Indonesian economy could readily explain a shift away from deposits toward currency roughly in step with the rates at which the two kinds of money were generated by deficit finance and commercial bank credit respectively. These structural changes involved both the extension of the use of money into rural and other sectors where currency was more likely to be used than deposits and the relative contraction of the foreign enterprise sector, which is accustomed to using deposits. (This latter tendency was perhaps reinforced by reluctance to have more or less dubiously obtained funds recorded in bank ledgers.) What needs to be explained is the extent to which deposits have held their own in the last ten years when the arguments against keeping money in the bank must have weighed even more heavily with increasing numbers of private individuals and firms.

"Shortage of Money"

The outstanding feature of the monetary situation in Indonesia in the last three years of the Sukarno regime was the paradoxical characteristic of all hyperinflations: shortage of money.[11] The basic reason for the paradox is simple enough. As prices run ahead of expansion of money supply with increasing loss of confidence in the currency, the "real" value or purchasing power of the money supply shrinks. In Table 11.6. this phenomenon is illustrated by deflating the series for the volume of money and for bank credit to the government and to enterprises by the index of consumer prices. It suggests that the "real" volume of money (at 1954 prices) reached a peak in 1960 at Rp. (new) 14.5 million and then declined steeply to Rp. 3.7 million by March 1966. The volume of central bank credit obtained by the government more than held its own in real terms until 1964 but then also shrank in 1965. The "real" value of credit to enterprises fell from Rp. (new) 2.4 million in 1959 to Rp. 1.1 million in 1963; its apparent recovery in the last two years probably reflects mainly the inclusion

[11] Cf., e.g., Costantino Bresciani-Turroni, *The Economics of Inflation: A Study of Currency Depreciation in Post-War Germany,* Allen & Unwin, London, 1937; K. N. Chang, *The Inflationary Spiral: The Experience of China, 1939–50,* Wiley, New York, 1958; C. D. Campbell and G. C. Tullock, "Hyperinflation in China, 1937–49," *Journal of Political Economy,* June 1954; F. F. Winkle, "Some Aspects of the Recent Inflation and Stabilisation of the Hungarian Currency," *South African Journal of Economics,* September 1947; R. Nurske, *The Course and Control of Inflation,* League of Nations, Geneva, 1946; A. J. Brown, *The Great Inflation, 1939–1951,* Oxford University Press, Cambridge, 1955.

Table 11.6. Money supply and bank credit at 1954 prices (Rp. [new] million)

		Money supply		Bank credit			
				To government		To enterprises	
Date	Consumer price index (1954 = 100) (1)	Current prices (2)	1954 prices (3)	Current prices (4)	1954 prices (5)	Current prices (6)	1954 prices (7)
1947		2.50					
1948	44	3.01					
1949	42	3.31	7.9				
1950	51	4.31	8.5				
1951	84	5.04	6.0				
1952	89	6.60	7.4				
1953	94	7.48	8.0				
1954	100	11.10	11.1				
1955	135	12.20	9.0	1.5	1.1	1.2	0.9
1956	133	13.40	10.1	2.3	1.7	1.0	0.8
1957	206	18.90	9.2	5.2	2.5	−0.1	
1958	243	29.40	12.1	9.2	3.8	2.6	1.1
1959	275	34.90	12.7	3.2	1.2	6.7	2.4
1960	330	47.90	14.5	−0.8		6.6	2.0
1961	644	67.60	10.5	23.4	3.6	10.7	1.7
1962	1,648	135.90	8.2	58.7	3.6	19.5	1.2
1963	3,770	263.40	7.0	124.0	3.3	40.7	1.1
1964	8,870	675.10	7.6	355.8	4.0	131.6	1.5
1965	61,400	2,582.00	4.2	1,580.4	2.6	797.2	1.3
1966 (Mar.)	152,200	5,593.40	3.7				

Sources: Column (1), 1948–50: 12-foodstuffs (Djakarta) index, quoted in R. McVey, ed., *Indonesia*, Human Relations Area Files, New Haven, 1963, p. 204; 1951–60: 19-foodstuffs (Djakarta) index, from Central Bureau of Statistics, *Statistik Konjunktur*, January–April 1963, p. 74; 1961–66: Cost-of-living, 62-items (Djakarta) index, from *Bulletin of Indonesian Economic Studies* (*BIES*), no. 4, June 1966, p. 21; Column (2): Table 11.1; Columns (4) and (6): Table 11.3.

of much government extra-budgetary finance under this heading.

We need of course to be careful in interpreting these facts. There cannot have been any *overall* shortage of money in the sense that the total supply of money became insufficient to finance the overall volume of transactions at current prices. For the cause of rising prices was rising effective demand, rising money expenditure financed by rising velocity of circulation, as well as rising money supply. But while the increasing reluctance of some to hold money balances, by increasing the velocity of circulation, helped to push up prices, each rise in the general level of prices, in turn, by reducing the real value of existing stocks of money, gave rise to demand by others for additional supplies of money.

To the central government, with open access to central bank credit, the ever-growing volume of money needed to finance expenditure at rising prices presented no great problem. The only limit was the capacity of the printing press at Kebajoran, the Djakarta suburb.[12] This did indeed become strained in the last months of 1965. It was the sheer incapacity of the press to meet the huge additional demand for banknotes, implied in the government's decision in December to grant a large New Year bonus to government employees, which occasioned the "currency reform" of that month. The introduction of the new rupiah, equal to 1,000 old rupiahs, made it possible to draw on large unused stocks of Rp. 50 and Rp. 100 notes printed five years earlier but overtaken by the inflation, and thus gave the printing press a brief breathing space.[13]

Physical shortage of banknotes also troubled banks and business enterprises at various times during 1965. Banks found it necessary to ration the cashing of cheques. Knowledge that cheques might prove difficult to cash, in turn, made people reluctant to accept cheques in payment. There is some evidence that cheques went to a discount, as compared with notes, either directly or by quotation of differential prices. While no attempts seem to have been made by anyone to produce the unofficial or semiofficial "emergency money" which became a feature in the German hyperinflation of 1923,[14] private traders in Djakarta and elsewhere resorted to issuing their own promissory notes which even achieved a limited circulation as a substitute means of payment.

Far more important, however, than physical shortage of currency were the liquidity problems which beset most enterprises in varying degrees. In conditions of hyperinflation, with market rates of interest running at 10 percent per month or more, credit

[12] Or to have notes printed abroad. This alternative was apparently again considered but rejected in December 1965.

[13] See *BIES,* no. 4, June 1966, pp. 2f.

[14] Cf. Bresciani-Turroni, *op. cit.,* p. 80.

tends to be increasingly diverted to financing "speculation," that is to say, transactions which consist wholly or in part of buying now for later resale at higher prices. Any other economic activity tends to get priced out of the market for credit, unless it has access to credit at subsidised (below-free-market) rates from official or other institutional lenders. This does not mean that it necessarily becomes impossible to finance productive activity, such as manufacturing; for the manufacture should, in principle, be able to reap the capital gain (in money terms) on his work in progress. But the very fact that a manufacturer's products are specific while the trader is freer to adjust his activities gives an inherent bias in the distribution of credit towards trading ("speculation") and among traders against exporters and others whose selling prices lag behind the inflationary process.

Conditions in Indonesia in the last two or three years of the Sukarno government exhibited all the features of credit under conditions of severe inflation. But to the distortions resulting from inflation were added others produced by increasingly arbitrary monetary controls and management. Not the least victims of the liquidity squeeze were the banks themselves. Despite strenuous and not unsuccessful efforts to hold on to their deposits they became increasingly mere channels for the infusion of central bank credit into the economy. As credit rationing and, despite official controls, ever higher interest charges choked off nonpriority borrowers, the organised banking system lost ground to the unorganised market. The distribution of credit came to be determined by more or less illegal market processes, which tended to channel most of it to speculative trading, and by more or less arbitrary exercise of official authority and political or personal influence.

Bank Deposits and Liquidity

We noted before that, at least until the end of 1965, the Indonesian banks appear, on the evidence of the available statistics, to have been surprisingly successful in holding on to their demand deposits in the face of accelerating inflation.[15]

[15] The foreign exchange banks' time deposits were throughout a negligible fraction of their total deposits; their share fell from 4.7 percent in 1961 to

Part of the explanation is that the banks themselves, with the backing of the authorities, did what they could to encourage deposits. A major and somewhat specious contribution towards sustaining the statistical volume of deposits was made by the widespread use of the American device known as the "compensating balance," whereby borrowers were required to hold on deposit up to 40 percent of the amount lent.[16] Another practice which more or less compelled private firms to retain current accounts was that all government payments to them were, on principle, made by cheque. During 1964 and 1965, also, most of the banks offered interest on current accounts at rates of 1 to 2 percent per month.

A quite distinct, and possibly more important, explanation is that government departments and enterprises were required by regulation to hold funds on deposit with the state banks. The only published information on ownership of deposits in those years relates to one of the state banks, Bank Negara Indonesia, which reported that, at the end of 1963, 17 percent of its deposits were held by government departments, 46 percent by public enterprises, and only 37 percent privately.[17] The share of the private sector probably declined further during 1964 and 1965 as more and more money in private hands came to consist of "grey" or "black" money, best not recorded in the books of government banks. By the time the December 1965 monetary "reform" imposed a 10 percent tax on deposits (which some months later was annulled and the money laboriously returned to depositors), few private firms are thought to have held more than minimum working balances on deposit with state banks.[18]

0.6 percent in 1965 (Bank Indonesia, *Weekly Return,* Djakarta, June 1966, Table 2a).

[16] The statistical effect of such compensating balances is exactly the opposite of unused limits under the overdaft system; while the latter constitute a component of money supply not recorded in the statistics, the former are a component of the statistical money supply which does not really constitute purchasing power.

[17] *Bank Indonesia Report,* 1963, p. 36.

[18] According to the June 1966 *Weekly Return,* the foreign exchange banks' demand liabilities declined from Rp. 698 million at the end of December 1965 to Rp. 381 million in the third week of January 1966 but rose again to Rp. 783 million by the third week of February. The movement may have had something to do with the tax on deposits.

Table 11.7. Liquidity position of foreign exchange banks (Rp. [new] million)

Date (end of period)	Liquid assets (1)	Demand liabilities (2)	Liquid asset ratio (1) ÷ (2) (3)	Prescribed minimum 30% (4)	Excess liquid assets† (1) − (4) (5)
1959	4.0	6.4	63.0	1.9	2.1
1960	4.7	10.5	43.2	3.1	1.6
1961	8.3	19.0	43.5	3.7	4.6
1962	15.0	31.3	47.9	9.4	5.6
1963	45.8	81.3	56.3	24.4	21.4
1964					
Mar.	38.6	81.7	47.2	24.2	14.4
June	41.6	100.1	41.5	30.0	11.6
Sept.	51.0	126.1	40.4	37.8	13.2
Dec.	66.1	190.8	34.7	57.2	8.9
1965					
Jan.	43.6	193.5	22.5	58.0	−14.4
Feb.	54.6	176.7	19.6	53.0	1.6
Mar.	38.4	182.5	21.1	54.7	−16.3
April	42.7	216.8	19.7	65.0	−22.3
May	59.3	232.1	25.5	60.5	−1.2
June	74.7	270.8	27.8	81.2	−6.5
July	112.1	322.9	34.7	96.9	15.2
Aug.	117.7	383.7	30.7	115.1	2.6
Sept.	151.6	478.0	31.7	143.4	8.2
Oct.	160.1	567.4	28.2	170.2	−10.1
Nov.	217.2	627.4	34.6	188.1	29.1
Dec.	411.3	698.5	58.9	209.6	201.7
1966					
Jan.	363.0	543.4	66.8	163.0	200.0
Feb.*	291.0	783.4	37.1	235.0	56.0

Source: BNI Unit I (Bank Indonesia), *Weekly Return,* June 1966.
* Third week.
† Probably owing to misprints, the figures given in the *Weekly Return* in column (5) do not always correspond to the differences between columns (1) and (4). It has been assumed that the errors occurred in column (5), which has been adjusted.

There is at first sight some evidence of cash withdrawals in the statistics of liquidity of the major banks. As Table 11.7 shows, in the first half of 1965 and again in October, the foreign exchange banks' holdings of cash and liquid assets fell below legal minimum reserve requirements, suggesting liquidity difficulties which may well have originated in withdrawals by depositors. But the evidence is inconclusive since in the last two years the liquidity condition of the banking system came to be entirely dominated by the rate at which the central bank was from month to month adding to the cash holdings of the banks.

To some extent, this had been true even during the 1950's when changes in the liquidity position of the Indonesian foreign exchange banks had reflected a tug-of-war between periodic efforts by the central bank to impose some restraint on bank credit and the monetary effects of government deficit finance. Bank liquidity had been put under pressure by the forced loan provisions of the monetary reform of 1950, by the introduction of the import prepayment system in 1952 and its reinforcement in 1956, by the imposition of liqiud-asset reserve ratio and special account requirements in 1957, and once more by the monetary purge of 1959. On each occasion the effect had been short-lived. Budget deficit finance was almost continuously pumping cash into the system, and more often than not the liquidity crisis caused by credit restraint was soon relieved under political pressures by emergency credits supplied by government banks or directly by government departments.[19] But the banks did not in general borrow directly from the central bank, although the central bank in effect financed credit extended by the foreign exchange banks to help importers meet import prepayment requirements when it agreed to rediscount importers' notes.[20]

In the last two years of the Sukarno regime, the banks themselves became directly dependent on central bank finance. Central bank credit took two distinct forms. One was direct lending to state banks to enable them to finance advances for "approved purposes" under the central bank's system of qualitative control.[21]

19 Cf. Higgins and Hollinger, *op. cit.*, p. 77; Paauw, *op. cit.*, p. 15f; Mackie, "The Indonesian Economy: 1950–1963," *op. cit.*, p. 149.

20 Paauw, *op. cit.*, p. 152.

21 It is not clear whether the amounts shown in Table 11.3, column 9, include only these formal advances or both kinds of credit to banks. Of the total of Rp. 303 million of these advances outstanding at the end of 1965, all but Rp. 9 million had been lent to two of the state banks—Rp. 143 million to BNI Unit IV (Bank Umum Negara) and Rp. 151 million to BNI Unit II (BKT) (Bank Indonesia, *Weekly Return*, June 1966, Table 3a).

The other consisted of a kind of overdraft which the foreign exchange banks enjoyed with the central bank by virtue of the latter's unwillingness to dishonour cheques in the clearing. In effect, the central bank underwrote the foreign exchange banks' clearing debts and in return required the foreign exchange banks to underwrite the debts of their subclearing banks.[22] It was this central bank credit to the commercial banks, together with the still larger volumes of direct central bank advances to the government, that fed the inflation and maintained bank liquidity through 1964 and 1965.

Distribution of Credit

In considering the effects of hyperinflation on the distribution of credit, it is important to bear in mind two facts about the Indonesian banking structure during the 1950's. One is the point made earlier that the banking system which Indonesia inherited from the Dutch was a characteristically colonial one, geared almost wholly to the provision of short-term credit for trade, and foreign trade in particular. Efforts during the 1950's to channel credit towards industrial development, by establishing specialist institutions and through qualitative control of bank advances, had yielded meagre results. The Bank Industri Negara had made some headway by the mid-1950's in industrial financing through loans and direct participation.[23] But the foreign exchange banks, attached to established principles of commercial banking, were content with their traditional business and most reluctant to take on longer-term finance for indigenous enterprises of much less certain credit standing.

Secondly, and partly in reaction to this situation, government credit policy came to be dominated increasingly by political considerations, preference for public over private enterprises, and for national over foreign ones. Especially after 1957, political priorities became more effective in determining the allocation of credit than the attempts of the monetary authorities to enforce economic priorities through selective controls.

[22] In all major centres, the state banks clear through their accounts with branches of Bank Indonesia, while the private banks clear through subclearing arrangements with the state banks.

[23] Cf. Charlesworth, *op. cit.*, pp. 117ff.

The effect of the developing hyperinflation was in a sense to reinforce both these tendencies. On the one hand, by making the whole banking and credit system dependent on central bank finance, it gave far-reaching discretion in the allocation of credit to the political controllers of the central bank. On the other hand, by enormously raising the cost of credit, it virtually limited access to credit, at least within the private sector, to wholly or partially speculative activity.

Neither of these developments can be documented statistically. The available statistics are, for obvious reasons, uninformative about the dispersion of Bank Indonesia funds for extra-budgetary purposes. The available classification of advances by the state and private foreign exchange banks for those years was as we saw, mainly designed to demonstrate compliance by the banks with the central bank's regulations for selective control. There are no statistics at all on the distribution of credit by the nonforeign-exchange banks. But something can be said on the basis of qualitative information.

Much the largest volume of credit, as we saw earlier, went directly from the Bank Indonesia to the government for budgetary and extra-budgetary expenditures. For budgetary expenditures, the departments of the central government drew directly on the central bank under authorisations by the Department of the Budget, although in the last phase these became little more than a formality with little pretence at budgetary control. All other central bank credit appears to have been channelled through the general banking department. It consisted of two parts. One was credit extended to other banks, partly, as we saw, in the form of advances—mainly to the government foreign exchange banks and the state development bank—for approved specific projects and priority sectors, and partly in the form of informal overdrafts. The other was credit granted by the Bank Indonesia for the president's "special projects" and other "vital" purposes. Whatever merit there may originally have been in Muda Dalam's grand conception of the Bank Indonesia as the *bank berdjuang*, the "fighting bank" which would spearhead the direction of credit towards the most urgent needs of national development, it degenerated in 1964 and 1965 into a vehicle for the discretionary use by himself of vast funds for the president's and his own purposes. These funds included not only central bank credit but also the proceeds of special levies such as the *dana revolusi* (for which Muda Dalam was Central Cashier) and the special tax for the trans-Sumatran highway. They were disbursed not only for special projects such as the president's monuments, the great mosque, the luxury hotels, and the Sarinah department store, but also for conferences such as CONEFO and, it is believed, for less official purposes.

The distribution of credit by the foreign exchange banks was in theory subject to qualitative control by the central bank. Until 1964, this had been exercised mainly by limiting the percentages of import prepayment credit which the banks were permitted to grant for more and less essential categories of imports and by selective credit ceilings. Under regulations issued in May 1964, specific proportions were laid down in which government and private banks alike were to allocate credit among three categories: 60 percent to the productive sector (including agricultural production for the domestic market), 20 percent for the export sector (including estates and other producers and export traders), and 20 percent for all other purposes (including imports, housing and other personal loans, etc.). In practice, these regulations proved unenforceable in conditions of hyperinflation.

In 1957 the central bank had been given power to prescribe maximum interest rates on bank advances. For some years the legal maximum was kept at 6 percent per annum. A new regulation in 1960 permitted both state and private banks to charge considerably higher rates, but even these became quite unrealistic as the inflation accelerated. By 1965, with prices rising at 20 percent per month, any bank which charged a much lower rate than this on its advances was virtually giving money away.

The banks evaded legal control of advance rates in a variety of ways. One was to add various administrative charges to the legal maximum advance rates.[24] Some of the banks made profit-sharing

[24] This practice received legal sanction in August 1965 when the state banks were authorised to charge differential advance rates (9 percent per annum for essential production, 15 percent for other production and exports, and 24 percent for other purposes) as well as differential "commissions" ranging from 75 percent *per month* to public sector borrowers for essential

arrangements, lending to traders not at a fixed rate of interest but in return for a 50 percent share in the profits on the transaction. In other cases, banks virtually traded, on their own behalf, stocks held by them ostensibly as clients' collateral being actually their own trading stocks.

How far, if at all, these high rates were charged to borrowers in the public sector is not clear and does not, in any case, matter very much since most of them were no longer subject to any strict accounting control.[25] In the private sector, these high rates rendered the cost of bank credit prohibitive for firms, such as most manufacturers and exporters, who could not cover the cost by selling at prices rising with the general inflation.[26] Most of the smaller textile manufacturers, for example, unable to cover the interest cost of their working capital from the profits of manufacture, took to selling their yarn allocations in the black market.[27]

As access to bank credit for private firms became more than ever a matter of personal connections or political influence with bank officials, those without either were forced to look for finance in the unorganised market where, in the first months of 1966, even "official" interest rates (that is, rates publicly advertised by moneylenders) were running at 15–20 percent per month.[28]

Little concrete information is available about the operations of the numerous private nonforeign-exchange banks in these years, beyond the figures quoted in Table 11.3 for the total volume of

---

production to 2 percent *per month* to private borrowers for nonpriority purposes. The effective rate to the latter had thus become 53 percent per annum.

[25] Much the same may have applied to the state banks themselves. While their administrative costs must have risen greatly (not to mention payment of interest on current account), it is not clear how far they felt compelled to raise their advance rates by the need to avoid losses.

[26] Obviously not all exporters sold their foreign exchange earnings at the official rate; cf. K. D. Thomas, "Price Disparity in Export Trade," *BIES,* no. 4, June 1966, p. 101.

[27] Ingrid Palmer and L. Castles, "The Textile Industry," *BIES,* no. 2, September 1965, p. 43; reprinted as Chapter 9.

[28] This is by no means a record; in Germany in 1923, the market rate on short-term loans is said to have risen to 20 percent *per diem* (Nurkse, *op. cit.,* p. 30).

credit granted. Much of what was said above about the foreign exchange banks probably also holds for the few more substantial nonforeign-exchange banks. The vast majority of the 90–100 officially licenced private banks are believed to have been little more than cover organisations for small groups of traders anxious to hide black market funds or transactions from taxation and other authorities, for party functionaries looking for "deposits," or for Chinese capital looking for a non-Chinese name under which to operate. A favourite device among the first group is said to have been to hide ownership of funds by "depositing" them with, and reborrowing them from, one's own "bank." For this reason, a significant but quite unknown proportion of the not inconsiderable volume of deposits and advances of these private banks recorded in the official statistics may have been fictitious.

Stabilisation, 1966–1969

The abortive left-wing coup of October 1, 1965, was the beginning of the end of Sukarno's rule. General Suharto gradually, during 1966, took over the reins of power and a new government under his leadership began to tackle the enormous task of stabilisation and rehabilitation of the Indonesian economy.[29]

The most urgent need was to secure a moratorium from Indonesia's foreign creditors on accumulated foreign debts estimated at over $2.5 billion and emergency aid to cover a balance-of-payments deficit (excluding debt service) of at least $200 million in 1967. The next most urgent task was to stop, or at least slow down, the still accelerating inflation. During 1966, while the leadership was still preoccupied with the political security of the new regime, a Council of Economic Advisers consisting of five Western-trained university economists, assisted by an International Monetary Fund mission, drew up a short-term stabilisation program.

In October 1966, the first steps were taken to dismantle the complex structure of multiple exchange rates and largely unenforceable trade and exchange controls and move towards a uniform floating exchange rate. In effect, the new BE (export bonus) sys-

29 For more detailed accounts of the developments summarised in this section, see H. W. Arndt's "Surveys of Recent Developments," *BIES,* nos. 4–11 and vol. 5 nos. 1–3.

tem aimed at stimulating exports by allowing exporters to sell their foreign exchange earnings in the free market (subject to varying rates of export tax), while leaving the allocation of scarce foreign exchange, including foreign exchange from foreign emergency credits, increasingly to the price mechanism.

In the compaign against inflation, the first need was to bring some order into the government finances. The obstacles were almost insuperable: greatly impaired central control over government departments and regional authorities, civil and especially military; an enormously inflated establishment of civil and military employees for whom no alternative employment was available; their salaries eroded by inflation to the point where the temptation to corruption was almost irresistible; hence an almost complete breakdown of tax collection including control over smuggling; an ever-mounting financial drain involved in the policy of subsidies to keep down the prices of essential goods and services, such as rice, petrol, sugar, and public-utility charges; and declining taxable capacity with declining production and income in almost every sector of the economy.

During 1966, all of President Sukarno's "special projects" were stopped and virtually all government construction suspended. Some progress was made towards restoring order in government accounts. Late in 1966, for the first time in some years, a budget was drawn up. Budget balance in 1967 was to be secured by stringent control over expenditure and intensified tax collection, heavily supplemented by counterpart funds from foreign credits. In February 1967, public utility charges and some other subsidised prices were steeply increased. Plans were laid for gradual reduction in the government payroll.

These fiscal measures were accompanied by even more drastic monetary ones. Following a provisional central bank directive to state banks in May 1966 to restrict short-term credit selectively and stop all overdrafts and new investment credit, the government in October issued a more detailed set of instructions to the central bank. Severely restrictive qualitative controls on bank credit —none for imports except in special cases, no long-term loans, no overdrafts, no preference for state enterprises, no credit to finance debts to the government—were reinforced by higher official interest rates on bank advances (6–9 percent per month) and by stricter liquid asset reserve requirements upon the banks.

Measured simply by their effect on the rate of price inflation, these measures were remarkably successful. In the ten months until the end of August 1967, prices increased by only 50 percent, in contrast to 1,500 percent in the twelve months to June 1966. A rice crisis in the last months of 1967, caused by a poor dry-season harvest and aggravated by an over-optimistic policy of cutting back rice imports, caused another severe bout of price inflation; between September 1967 and the end of January 1968, the cost-of-living index almost doubled. But P.L. 480 rice shipments filled the gap to the wet-season harvest. From March 1968 to the end of the year, the cost of living rose by only 17 percent and in the first half of 1969 the index remained completely stable. By the end of 1968 exchange rates in both sections of the free foreign exchange market (one for essential imports, the other for less essential goods and services) stabilised and remained constant throughout 1969.

The restoration of price stability within two years from a condition of raging hyperinflation was a notable achievement. The initial effect of the drastic disinflationary measures was inevitably a still further decline in economic activity. Under the impact of the credit squeeze, manufacturing as well as building and construction came close to a standstill, and there were loud complaints from traders, both in private and in state enterprises. Nationalist and xenophobic pressure on the Chinese business community for some months compounded the trouble.

In March and April 1967, the authorities, declaring that conditions warranted a change of emphasis from "checking inflation" to "stimulating production," relaxed restraint. Bank credit was eased; official interest rates were lowered (from 6–9 percent to 4–7 percent a month); prepayment for imports was reduced from 100 to 25 percent, but domestic import-competing industries were given additional tariff protection; and a larger budget allocation for development expenditure, especially roads, was authorised. In July, new foreign exchange regulations sought to give a further stimulus to exports and further protection to import-competing industries by a substantial shift from export to import taxes. A foreign investment law was passed designed to attract private foreign capital to Indonesia, especially for the development of mineral and other natural resources. As evidence of the new attitude towards foreign capital, various foreign enterprises confiscated by the Sukarno government were restored to their foreign owners.

The year 1968 saw the first indications of a revival of domestic production. A favourable season brought a record rice harvest, and favourable trends in world market prices assisted in a 14 percent rise in exports during the year. The industrial sector, especially the important textile industry, began to move forward again, and an improvement in government receipts, both from larger tax revenues and from counterpart funds of large-scale foreign aid, enabled the government to resume development expenditure, especially on restoration of roads, harbours, and other parts of the run-down infrastructure. The share of development expenditure in the central government budget which had fallen to 8 percent in 1966 rose to 19 percent in 1968 and to 37 percent in the 1969–1970 budget. In the second half of 1968, the government instructed the Planning Bureau to formulate a Five Year Development Plan which formally came into effect on April 1, 1969.[30]

The sharp turnabout from hyperinflation to virtual price stability in the space of two years posed difficult, almost unique, problems of monetary management. During the years of accelerating inflation, 1961–1966, the authorities had increasingly lost control of the situation because, on top of barely restrained expansion in the money supply through deficit finance, there had been a flight from money into goods; with waning public confidence in the currency, the demand for money had declined. The drastic stabilisation policies during 1966–1968 had the opposite effect. As confidence gradually returned, the public again became more willing to hold currency and bank deposits. At the same time, the recovery of business activity increased the transaction demand for money. Just as earlier there had been loss of control over the pace of inflation, there was now a danger that the shift in the public's price expectations and demand for money would cause a loss of control over the rate of deflation. Money rates of interest of 5 percent a month which, with an even higher expected rate of price inflation, had represented negative real rates, came to represent

[30] For an account of the Plan, see *BIES,* July 1969, pp. 70–79.

prohibitively high real rates as something like price stability could again be counted upon. A degree of monetary and fiscal restraint which was barely sufficient to hold the line while public confidence was still highly precarious—as the "rice crisis" of late 1967 showed—was liable to become intolerably restrictive in the face of a rapidly rising public demand for money.

The dilemma was substantially resolved during 1967 and 1968 by a combination of strict adherence to formally balanced budgets (which undoubtedly made a major contribution to the restoration of public confidence) with very large further increases in money supply through extra-budgetary channels, mainly central bank credit direct to government agencies, such as the rice procurement agency, and indirectly through the state banks to state and private enterprises. Both in 1967 and in 1968 the money supply (including time deposits) increased by some 135 percent, and by a further 82 percent in 1969.[31] But since these increases barely matched the rise in the public's demand for money balances, they did not interfere with the restoration of price stability. Indeed during 1969 there was increasing concern that expansion of the money supply was lagging behind the rate necessary to support the physically possible rise in business activity.

Table 11.8 (from an unpublished study by Professor J. G. Gurley) lends some statistical support for this concern. It shows that by mid-1969, the real volume of money in Indonesia (the nominal total of currency and bank deposits in the hands of the public, deflated by the Djakarta consumer-price index) had recovered from its 1965 low of Rp. 57 billion to Rp. 187 billion, but at this level was still well below its 1960 peak of Rp. 238 billion. Since real GNP had undoubtedly risen during the decade,[32] it was reasonable to infer that money supply was still insufficient for the normal needs of the economy. While, after years of extreme in-

[31] Bank Indonesia, *Laporan Angka-Angka Minguan no. 631,* February 19, 1970.

[32] Official estimates suggest that GNP at 1960 market prices rose from Rp. 390 billion in 1960 to Rp. 478 billion in 1968, an increase of 22 percent, or 2.5 percent per annum. Since population is estimated to have risen at something like the same rate, there was no net increase in per capita income over the period.

Table 11.8. Money supply in nominal and real terms, 1959–June 1969
(Rp. billion)

Year (end of Dec.)	Money supply* (nominal)	Price index† (June 1969 = 100)	Money supply (real)
1959	0.035	0.017	201.7
1960	0.049	0.021	237.9
1961	0.069	0.040	172.5
1962	0.135	1.100	135.0
1963	0.285	0.250	114.0
1964	0.745	0.630	118.3
1965	2.750	4.800	57.3
1966	22.700	33.000	68.8
1967	54.100	54.000	100.2
1968	128.200	100.000	128.2
1969 (June)	186.900	100.000	186.9

Source: John G. Gurley, "Notes on the Indonesian Financial System," Djakarta, September 1969, mimeo., p. 10.
* Currency outside banks, demand and time deposits.
† Djakarta 62-items index.

stability, there was still need for caution, the greater risk was now one of undue financial restraint on revival of business activity and resumption of development.

Banking Reform

The appalling condition of disorganisation and demoralisation into which the Indonesian banking system had sunk under Sukarno and Jusuf Muda Dalam made banking reform a priority task in the eyes of the new government. New banking legislation was the first to be drafted after the foreign investment law and, after some delay in parliament, was passed late in 1968.

The legislation consisted of eight statutes, one on central banking, one on each of six state banks, and a "basic banking law." The central banking bill reconstituted the Bank Indonesia as a pure central bank, divested of its commercial banking business and equipped with adequate central banking powers but without any radically new features. On the most sensitive issue during the Sukarno era, the degree of central bank autonomy vis-à-vis the government, the new statute was weaker than one might have hoped. Control of monetary policy remained vested in a Monetary Board, consisting of the governor of the bank and up to four ministers (including the ministers of finance and trade) and serviced by officials of the ministry of finance. A potentially helpful safeguard was a new "red-light" clause whereby borrowing by the government from the central bank would be subject to a ceiling fixed from time to time. Although the ceiling would be fixed by the Monetary Board, the formality and publicity attending changes in the ceiling could impose useful restraint.

The two main objects of the reorganisation of the state banks were to undo the grotesque integration of all these banks, together with the central bank, in a single monster institution, and to define the functions of the six banks so as to promote efficiency by a combination of specialisation and competition. There are now eight separate state-owned banks, comprising the five former foreign exchange banks (one of which has been split into two), the state savings bank, and the state development bank. Each of them has been assigned a major area of concentration, but in such a way that in each field there will be scope for competition between at least two banks and that all banks, except the savings bank, will engage both in longer-term financing and in short-term trade and production credit. Table 11.9 shows the structure of the new system.

The basic banking law was in form an enabling act authorising in general terms the establishment of private, state-owned, or cooperative banks of three types: commercial banks, development banks, and savings banks. Of more immediate practical consequence was the section authorising foreign banks to operate once again in Indonesia, either through commercial or development banking branches in Djakarta or by the formation of joint ventures with local banks. Foreign banks were required to pay substantially for the licence to operate in Indonesia ($1 million in commercial banking, $2 million in development banking), the rupiah counterpart of the fee constituting in each case the initial capital of the branch.

A number of foreign banks quickly took advantage of the new opportunity afforded to them. The Bank of America and First National City Bank of New York were the first to open branches in Djakarta. By the end of 1969 eleven foreign banks were operat-

Table 11.9. Structure of state banking system, 1969

New name	Former name*	Main areas of specialisation
Bank Indonesia	BNI Unit I	Central bank
Bank Rakjat Indonesia	(part of) BNI Unit II	Agriculture, livestock
Bank Expor-Impor	(part of) BNI Unit II	Export production, estates
Bank Negara Indonesia 1946	BNI Unit III	Industry, agriculture, export production
Bank Bumi Daya	BNI Unit IV	Export production, estates, mining
Bank Tabungan Negara	BNI Unit V	Savings bank
Bank Dagang Negara	Same	Export production, mining
Bank Pembangunan Indonesia (Bapindo)	Same	Industry and transport

Source: D. Cole, "New Directions for the Banking System," *BIES*, July 1969, pp. 61–62.

* For previous history and names, see above, pp. 359–364.

ing in Indonesia, including four American and one each from Japan, the United Kingdom, Germany, the Netherlands, Thailand, and Hong Kong. They offer significant competition to the Indonesian state banks in foreign trade finance, but also serve as intermediaries for inflow of foreign capital.

Besides the large state banks and the foreign banks, there are still over 100 private Indonesian banks, mostly owned by ethnic Chinese. Many of them have been in severe difficulties in the past three years. Having lost much of their capital in the inflation, they bore the brunt of the credit squeeze and stabilisation which put many of their customers out of business. In August 1967 a banking crisis developed when some private banks which had overlent were unable to meet their clearing debts. When the central bank ordered all private banks to cover their clearing debts within seven days, a run by depositors involved many more banks in difficulties. Twenty-two private banks were suspended and placed under temporary central bank supervision. Those whose affairs were found to be generally in order were granted emergency aid in the form of three months' central bank credit to restore their liquidity, and most of them were subsequently readmitted to the clearing. But the difficulties of the private banks have continued. They have, not without reason, been subject to stringent supervision by the central bank and have enjoyed neither the ample credits nor the regular rediscount facilities which the central bank has made available to the state banks. Until 1968 the private banks had the advantage over the state banks of being free to offer free-market interest rates for deposit money. In October 1968 when the state banks began to offer high rates on time deposits, the private banks lost even this competitive advantage and their share in total banking business declined sharply.

As part of the 1968 general shift of emphasis in economic policy from stabilisation to development, a new set of credit policies was devised which aimed at rehabilitating the role of the banking system in the mobilisation of savings for medium- and longer-term investment. Initially, in October 1968, the state banks were authorised to offer very much higher rates of interest on time deposits, ranging up to 6 percent per month on 12 months deposits; to increase the attractiveness of such deposits, no questions were to be asked as to the source of the money, and the earnings were exempted from wealth and income tax. The central bank offered a subsidy to cover part of the cost of interest payments to the state banks. The move was strikingly successful. Between September 1968 and May 1969, time deposits with the state banks rose from Rp. 2 billion to Rp. 24 billion. With prices reasonably stable and expected to remain so, what had been a realistic level of interest rates earlier was now recognised as too restrictive. From May onwards, deposit rates were progressively reduced to 2 percent a month on 12 months deposits, and the central bank subsidy on new deposits was stopped. The volume of time deposits continued to grow, though at a diminishing rate, to Rp. 34 billion at the end of the year. The experiment demonstrated that the banks were able to attract funds from the public if they paid enough and were thus not wholly dependent on central bank finance.

At the same time, the state banks were assured of large additional funds for investment credit during 1969–1970—Rp. 10 billion in transfers from the development budget and Rp. 15 billion in central bank credits. A program was drawn up under which the state banks were to make available medium-term credit at a minimum lending rate of 12 percent per annum (approximately equal to the expected average cost to the banks of their demand- and time-deposit funds) to be allocated among the private and public sector and different industries as shown in Table 11.10.

Table 11.10. Medium-term credit program, 1969–1970 (Rp. million)

Sector/Program	Government	Private	Total
Agriculture	4,900	5,100	10,000
Food crops	500	2,000	2,500
Estate crops	3,500	2,000	5,500
Fisheries	500	500	1,000
Forestry	200	300	500
Livestock	200	300	500
Industry and Mining	10,380	7,610	17,990
Industry			
Fertiliser, cement, chemicals	2,390		2,390
Textiles	2,280	2,230	4,510
Pulp, paper, printing	1,300	350	1,650
Pharmaceuticals		110	110
Light industries	990	2,520	3,510
Metal industries	2,720	2,400	5,120
Mining (coal)	700		700
Transport and Communications	1,000	1,000	2,000
Total	16,280	13,710	29,990

Source: D. Cole, "New Directions for the Banking System," *BIES*, July 1969, p. 67.

During 1969, the effort to get development investment going again ran into many practical difficulties. Cumbersome bureaucratic procedures and dearth of staff skilled and experienced in drawing up economically and technically sound projects in government departments and agencies caused government development expenditure to lag badly behind the first year of the Five Year Plan incorporated in the 1969–1970 development budget. Similar problems showed themselves in the business sector where new investment was to be financed through the banking system. The banks found that creditworthy projects were slow in coming forward, a reflection of the shortage in Indonesia of people with sufficient business experience and technical and managerial know-how to draw up bankable investment propositions. But applicants for investment credit, in turns, complained about long delays in processing their applications, a reflection of administrative weakness and inexperience inside the state banks.

Bank credit did expand substantially, the state banks alone lending out (net) nearly Rp. 40 billion in the first half of the year; but of this, probably not much more than 5–10 percent consisted of longer-term credit for investment in plant and equipment.[33] In the latter part of 1969, there were encouraging signs that the lag in development spending was being overcome.

Conclusion

As in all other sectors of the Indonesian economy, much has been done in the first three years of the New Order to rehabilitate the banking system. The structure of the system has been rationalised, each component—central bank, commercial, development, and savings banks—being again assigned its clearly defined role. Order has been restored in the relations between the government and the central bank, and the latter has re-established its control over monetary policy. The central bank has also energetically carried out its inspectorate function over the state and private banks, trying to weed out malpractices, securing regular and proper returns, and keeping a watch on the financial soundness especially of the many private banks. Substantial progress has been made towards a more realistic level and structure of interest rates, and in channelling a larger proportion of lending and borrowing transactions through the organised banks.

But as in all other sectors of the economy, there is still a long way to go in adapting the Indonesian banking system and capital market to the tasks which lie before it. Like all other government agencies, the state banks are overstaffed and bureaucratised but short of trained and experienced men. While the banks have found it easier than government departments to raise salaries of key personnel to more reasonable levels, the incomes of the majority of bank employees are still so miserable that standards of integrity are difficult to maintain and enforce. Unavoidably, while so large a part of capital funds for development comes from coun-

[33] *BIES*, November 1969, p. 6

terpart funds of foreign aid, the state banks still lean heavily on the central bank for finance of their own credit operations. Both in this respect, and in the terms on which the central bank makes credit and rediscount facilities available to them, the state banks still enjoy a perhaps excessively privileged position vis-à-vis the private banks. It has been argued that "generally speaking, private bankers are a dynamic group, highly knowledgeable about the business world, and capable of making decisions quickly—while, although there are many exceptions, bankers in the State banks generally have the opposite traits. . . . Private bankers perform such essential functions that any further deterioration in their situation may have unfortunate consequences for Indonesian development." [34]

Outside the banking system, the Indonesian capital market is still embryonic. The bonds issued at various times by the Indonesian government during the 1950's have become almost worthless, and until a decision is reached whether or not to revalue the old debt, the government hesitates to make new bond issues. The stock exchange at Djakarta established in 1952 has been moribund for many years and is unlikely to become effective at least until reform of the company law now in hand makes public issues by domestic companies practicable. Not the least important condition for the development of a capital market is the gradual creation of a tradition of "honest and full reporting of the financial condition of each business firm," [35] and of this there are as yet few signs in Indonesia. Some thought has recently been given to developing a money market, perhaps through the issue of negotiable short-term securities by Bank Indonesia or by the newly formed development bank for Indonesia, a joint venture of the Indonesian government and the Netherlands Overseas Financing Corporation.

Even more important for Indonesia's economic development are other institutional reforms to which little thought has yet been given. Among them are the creation of an institutional framework for the mobilisation of small savings more adequate than the still rather feeble state savings bank; strengthening of the structure of

[34] John G. Gurley, "Notes on the Indonesian Financial System," Djakarta, September 1969, mimeo., pp. 37f.

[35] *Ibid.,* p. 51.

rural credit much of which at present still flows through bureaucratic channels, such as the *bimas* (agricultural extension) program under the Department of Agriculture; better facilities of medium- and long-term credit for development investment in the outer regions, partly perhaps through upgrading of the existing regional development banks; and provision of consumer (especially housing) credit which is at present left almost entirely to the unorganised market.

CHAPTER 12

Pricing of Foreign Exchange in Indonesia, 1966–1967*

BRUCE GLASSBURNER

As a Dutch colony, the Indonesian archipelago fully qualified as an "export economy," i.e., one whose prosperity fluctuated in sympathy with the world prices of rubber, sugar, palm oil, petroleum, and tin. As an independent nation, Indonesia has experienced a dwindling of the absolute and relative importance of her foreign trade. Indeed, at the very outset of her period of independence, the sources of her foreign exchange earnings were in a state of low activity caused by war damage and disruption of market relationships. That lost ground has never been recovered, and postwar events have resulted in further decline. Her prewar positions of strength in sugar and tin have never been regained, and her position of primacy in rubber has passed over to Malaysia. In the 1960's, exports have fallen consistently below ten percent of GNP—roughly in the neighborhood of 6 to 8 percent—with merchandise imports falling slightly below that proportion. A substantial deficit in payments for services has given her a consistent balance-of-payments deficit on current account of $200 million to $250 million annually in this recent period.

* This article first appeared in *Economic Development and Cultural Change,* vol. 18, no. 2, January 1970, pp. 166–187. It is being published here by permission of the editors of *Economic Development and Cultural Change* and by University of Chicago Press. Thanks are due to Suntoro Isman, Stokes M. Tolbert, Donald Snodgrass, for assistance and helpful comment; and to the U.S. Agency for International Development for financial support. The usual disclaimer of responsibility for errors and weaknesses on the part of anyone other than the author is very much in order.

The persistent payments deficit, the awareness of large export potential, and (more importantly in the short run) the need to tax foreign trade heavily in order to maintain anything like an adequate level of government activity, all force economists to direct their attention toward the foreign trade sector in this country in spite of its reduced size. This interest has been heightened since 1966 because of the quite radical movement of the exchange rate policies of the Indonesian government in the direction of liberalization. The primary vehicle of this policy change is the broadening of the market for export bonus (BE) certificates. The central feature of the system is that most exporters are required to surrender virtually all of their foreign exchange earnings and receive marketable certificates (which are claims on the foreign exchange fund) in proportion to earnings as payment. Importers may purchase these certificates directly from exporters or through the organized market in Djakarta, and they may be used to purchase a broad list of essential commodities. The market for the certificates is essentially free. The central bank operates in the market, primarily as a seller, and does so with an eye toward contributing to stability, but this is the extent of control. Government agencies are required (since March 1967) to acquire foreign exchange through this market, using their budgeted rupiah allocations rather than direct foreign exchange allocations. Special certificates for use of foreign aid credits are also sold, but at an administered rate and at a differential vis-à-vis the general BE rate.[1]

In broad outline this system is not new, even in Indonesia. Indeed, a very similar system was inaugurated by the newly established Indonesian government in March 1950, and some version of it, with widely varying degrees of liberalization, has been in operation with occasional interruptions since that time. Three times (in 1950, 1957–1958, and 1964–1965) during that stretch of

[1] The system is a close approximation to the one recently recommended for Pakistan by the author and F. C. Child, in companion articles. See B. Glassburner, "Aspects of the Problem of Foreign Exchange Pricing in Pakistan," and F. C. Child, "A Proposal for Reform of Pakistan's Trade and Payments Control System," in *Economic Development and Cultural Change,* vol. 16, no. 4, July 1968.

time the certificate market was freed, but on each occasion only for short periods. The use of the present type of certificates, which began in a small way in February 1966, has involved free marketing since that date, thus establishing the longest period without pegging, by a substantial margin. All earlier attempts at a free market for certificates ran afoul of political or economic instability or both, while the present system, being accompanied by serious efforts to establish monetary and fiscal equilibrium, appears to have some chance of long life and continued expansion.[2] The similarities between the present system and its predecessors have caused many observers of the Indonesian scene to comment pessimistically that what has failed so consistently before will surely fail again. This prognostication may very well turn out to be correct, but a review of the experience of foreign exchange pricing policy since the abortive coup of September 1965 suggests that things are truly different this time. Unlike the previous attempts to bring the foreign exchange markets under control, this attempt has been marked by a series of successive steps in the direction of increasing liberalization and simplification. Indeed, following the emergency regulations of November 1965, the government became the sole buyer of foreign exchange, at a unitary rate of (old) Rp. 10,000:1 (converted in December 1965 to [new] Rp. 10:1), and all imports were by government or by firms importing for government.[3] Three months later, in February 1966, exporters were extended the concession of a 10 percent BE quota for "hard" exports, and higher rates for less well-established export commodities, as shown in Table 12.1. Quotas were raised again in May 1966, October 1966, and July 1967. When these changes had been accomplished, more than two-thirds of all export proceeds were being marketed through

[2] For the history of the system, see W. M. Corden and J. A. C. Mackie "The Development of the Indonesian Exchange Rate System," *Malayan Economic Review,* April 1962; S. Kanesa-Thasan, "Multiple Exchange Rates: The Indonesian Experience," International Monetary Fund, Staff Papers, July 1966; and the article series "Survey of Recent Developments" in *Bulletin of Indonesian Economic Studies* (*BIES*), June 1965 to date.

[3] Or so intended. In practice this degree of restriction was never attained.

Table 12.1. BE quotas, February through October 1966 and July 1967 (percent)

Category or group*	Feb. 1966	May 1966	Oct. 1966	July 1967
I	10	20	50†	
II	15	60	75	
III	50	100	90	
A				75
B				90

* Category I consisted of primary export commodities with well-established markets abroad, and represented about 75–80 percent of exports by value. The higher categories were items in need of promotion, Category II being less "hard" in the market, but still predominantly primary commodities. Category III consisted of handicrafts and manufactures for the most part. The numeralled categories were "grouped" by the July 28, 1967 regulations. Three items (tea, sisal, and sugar) were moved from the old Category I to Group B, tin was added to the Group A list, but Group A is otherwise the same as old Category I. All other export commodities other than those covered by special regime are in Group B.

† Proportions surrendered from October 1966 until the present are inclusive of the 10 percent ADO (Automatic Exchange Allocation to regional authorities).

the BE market, and 90 percent or more of the proceeds of exports not covered by "special regimes" (see below) were so marketed.[4]

Exporters' Rates

Until the promulgation of the regulations of July 28, 1967, that part of the foreign exchange earned by exporters which had to be surrendered was paid for at the official transactions rate of 10:1. This "exchange rate" has been extremely unrealistic throughout its entire period of effectiveness and became much more so as time passed. However, this progressive overvaluation of the official rate has been increasingly mitigated by the progressive raising of the BE quota. Some notion of the order of magnitude of the *de facto* devaluation which has taken place can

[4] These proportions include the foreign exchange which is surrendered by nonoil enterprises to the Foreign Exchange Fund and marketed by the Bank Indonesia. They exclude the 10 percent allocated to the provincial governments for local development purposes. The magnitude of the foreign exchange proceeds from oil export earnings marketed by the central bank has not been reported.

Table 12.2. Effective exchange rates to exporters,* February through October 1966 and July through October 1967 (in rupiahs per U.S. dollar)

Category	Feb. 1966	May 1966	Oct. 1966
I	13.3	26	55
II	14.95	58	77.5
III	26.5	90	91
BE rate	43	90†	100‡
DPA rate§	45	95	120
Rupiah overvaluation‖ for Category I exports (in percent)	*238*	*265*	*118*

Group	July 1967	Oct. 1967
A	103.5	114.0
B	124.2	136.8
	138	152
	159	167
Rupiah overvaluation‖ for Group A (in percent)	*54*	*46*

* Uncorrected for overprice; see text for explanation.

† Fourth week of the month; *source: Bulletin of Indonesian Economic Studies* (*BIES*), June 1966, p. 8.

‡ October 10, 1966; *source: Business News*, October 12, 1966.

§ February and May DPA rates are estimates based on *Business News* curb rate quotations (*Business News*, August 25, 1967, p. 12); October and July figures are current *Business News* quotations.

‖ DPA rate/Category I rate × 100, all minus 100.

be obtained from the data in Table 12.2. While the DPA[5] rate moved upward from 45, at the end of February 1966, to 167, at the end of October 1967, the proportionate overvaluation was reduced for the large majority of export commodities from an unworkable 238 percent to a relatively modest 46 percent.

The numerical exercise undertaken to complete Table 12.2 overstates the degree of overvaluation at the earliest dates, however, and therefore also overstates the degree of progress toward equilibrium pricing. This is due to the fact that throughout the period concerned, the export price basis of evaluation for application of the BE quota fell below the market price, often by a

[5] The DPA rate (see explanation below) is, to all intents and purposes, a free rate and is used here as an index of equilibrium. It has typically floated at about 3 percent below the curb rate.

very large margin. Since 1964, the realization of proceeds in the form of foreign exchange over and above the so-called "check price" (the evaluation base for application of the BE quota) has been given legal sanction, and such proceeds (called DPA) may be used for transactions abroad and for imports of any type other than the very few which are totally banned. Indeed, throughout 1966, the effective rate, excluding overprice for Category I items (computed as the sum of rupiah proceeds per dollar in the BE market plus Rp. 10 per dollar for the remainder), represented such a preposterous degree of rupiah overvaluation that legal exports were impossible without a substantial overprice, and/or explicitly illegal export procedures.[6]

In interviews with exporters in North Sumatra, the author was told that legal exports of rubber were profitable during this period because the ministry of trade allowed the "check price" to ride far enough below the actual realized price sufficiently to make it so. There are no published sources from which to draw information on the size of this margin. There are three sources of varying degrees of formality, however. A prominent rubber exporter offered the information that in late 1965 and early 1966 the overprice ranged around 25 to 30 percent; in an internal report, the International Monetary Fund (IMF) estimated the average overprice in early 1967 to be 8 percent; and in early August, the ministry of trade announced publicly that the overprice had risen to an average of 27 percent. Table 12.3 shows recalculated effective change rates using these approximations. The results are highly impressionistic, of course, but they do demonstrate quite conclusively that (a) the degree of overvaluation on the export side (and the legal price disparity) has been much less than that indicated by the combination of proceeds from BE certificate sales plus sales to the central bank at the transactions rate, and (b) success in reducing the rate of overvaluation, though very con-

[6] The disparity between domestic prices for export goods and the rupiah value of legal export of those goods has long been officially recognized. The Bank Indonesia used a publicly known formula for its computation. In September 1965, it was calculated at 160 percent of legal receipts. For a brief discussion of this phenomenon, see K. D. Thomas, "Price Disparity in Export Trade," *BIES,* no. 4, June 1966.

Table 12.3. Effective exchange rates to exporters, February 1966 through July 1967 and October 1967, corrected for overprice*
(in rupiahs per U.S. dollar)

Category or group	Feb. 1966	May 1966	Oct. 1966	July 1967†	Oct. 30, 1967‡
I	23	47	71	97	
II	24	69	88	120	
III	32	92	98	134	
DPA rate§	45	95	120	159	167
Rupiah overvaluation‖ for Category I exports (in percent)	*96*	*101*	*69*	*64*	
A					114.0
B					136.8
Rupiah overvaluation‖ for Group A (in percent)					*46*

* Calculation procedure as follows:

$r = t(1 - q)(1 - a) + bq(1 - a) + da$, where
r = effective rate
t = transactions rate
a = proportion of overprice
b = BE rate
q = BE quota
d = DPA rate

Proportion of overprice assumed to be 30 percent in February and May, 25 percent in October, 27 percent in July 1967 before the regulations, and zero after those regulations.

† Before the July 28 regulations.

‡ *Business News*, November 3, 1967. Zero overprice assumed.

§ See Table 12.2, ‖.

‖ DPA rate/Category I (or Group A) rate × 100, all minus 100.

siderable, is considerably less than it appears to be, taking only those proceeds into consideration. The last two columns also show that, with the virtual abolition of overprice earnings, the large increases in BE quotas which took place on July 28 constituted only a modest rise in the effective rate for exporters of those commodities which had been in Categories I and II, and which are now in Groups A and B (i.e., those that were not shifted).[7] However, those moving from old Category III to Group B have actually been subjected to reductions of effective exchange rates.

[7] The immediate devaluation effect was even more modest. Compare column 4, Table 12.3 with column 4, Table 12.2.

In view of these results, it is not surprising that the July 28 regulations were greeted with mixed emotions by exporters. Even those, such as the rubber exporters, whose effective exchange rates were improved by the new regulations, insisted that overprice earnings are so important to them for purposes of doing business abroad that they consider themselves worse off. Delegations from exporters' associations from all over the islands descended on Djakarta to demand partial restitution of the overprice, and it is generally acknowledged that they succeeded. According to one Sumatran delegate, they demanded 5 percent overprice for rubber, but were conceded only 2 percent. At all events, it appears that the main flow of new DPA exchange was substantially restricted by the July 1967 regulations.[8]

Importers' Rates

Private importers, aside from those covered by special regimes, have been exposed throughout this period to fluctuating exchange rates. For those goods which are on the BE list, the price of the U.S. dollar has risen from 43 in early 1966 to approximately 150 in late October 1967—a 2.5-fold increase. For the more luxurious category of goods not on the BE list (which must be imported with DPA exchange) the increase has been slightly greater (2.7-fold). The Djakarta cost-of-living index, the generally used indicator of internal inflation, has experienced a sixfold increase over the same time period. Several explanations for this striking differential have been suggested. First, tariff barriers have been increased. Table 12.4 presents a rough and ready attempt to calculate the changes in the pattern of effective duties, using as bench marks the dates of major changes in tariff policy. Throughout this period, the basic rate ranges have remained as given in the left-hand column. Such changes as have been made have been primarily in the form of an increase of the evaluation base, which

[8] The DPA rate was 15 percent above the general BE rate both at the end of July and the end of August. The differential was only 9.9 percent at the end of October (*Business News* quotations). Presumably this stability and subsequent decline of the differential reflect (a) continued willingness to repatriate accumulated foreign deposits and/or (b) confidence that the overprice would be restored.

Table 12.4. Approximate effective tariff rates 1966–1967 (in percent)

Import categories	Nominal rate range (1)	Feb. 1966 EBR 30/45 = .67* (2)	Prechange Oct. 1966 EBR 30/120 = .25 (3)	Postchange Oct. 1966 EBR 75/120 = .62 (4)	Prechange April 1967 EBR 75/116 = .65 (5)	Postchange April 1967 EBR 90/116 = .78 (6)	Prechange July 1967 EBR 90/160 = .56 (7)	Postchange July 1967 EBR 130/160 = .81 (8)	Oct. 30, 1967 EBR 130/167 = .78 (9)
I	0–5	0–3.35	0–1.25	0–3.1	0–3.2	0–3.9	0–2.8	0–4.5	0–4.3
II	10–15–20	6.7–10–13.4	2.5–3.8–5.0	6.2–9.3–12.4	6.5–9.8–13	7.8–11.7–15.6	5.6–8.4–11.2	8.1–12.2–16.2	7.8–11.7–15.6
III	30–40	20.1–26.8	7.5–10.0	18.6–24.8	14.5–26	23.4–31.4	16.8–22.4	24.3–32.4	23.3–31.1
IV	50–70–100	33.5–46.9–67	12.5–17.5–25	31.0–43.4–62	32.5–45.5–65	39–54.6–78	28–39.2–56	60.8–85.0–121.5†	58.4–81.6–116.6
Average‡	37.5	21.36	9.4	19.8	20.7	24.9	17.8	33.5	32.2

* The 200 percent surcharge which applied to all items prior to the October 3, 1966 regulations is reflected in the EBR (evaluation base ratio) numerators. The EBR is the ratio of the evaluation base rate (in Rp. per U.S. dollar) to the estimated equilibrium exchange rate (the DPA rate).

† Category IV imports were subjected to a general 50 percent surcharge on October 3, 1966. Several items in other categories were also subjected to special surcharges and/or special taxes. The general surcharge is included in these calculations.

‡ Unweighted average of category range midpoints. Failure to weight probably overstates the typical basic duty, but this overstatement is partially compensated by the collection of surcharges and other added taxes on an *ad hoc* basis. Assuming that the relative importance of the several categories remained roughly the same throughout, the averages do indicate the degree of *change* in the height of the tariff barrier. The most egregious misstatement occurs in column 8, in which the 50 percent surcharge carries inordinate weight. However, weighting to calculate tariff barriers presents the special problem that an effective barrier reduces import volume and hence reduces the weights most where protection is most effective. An official of the ministry of trade stated that, by their calculations, the "average tariff increase" effected by the July 28, 1967 regulations was 23 percent. My crude calculation, on the other hand, makes it 88 percent. While the latter is, in some sense, "too high," the former is surely "too low." The reader is advised to split the difference.

has been shifted upward sharply on three occasions, beginning with October 3, 1966. The sharpness of each base increase has given the general impression that effective duties have been moved radically over time, but in fact not a great deal more than restoration of the effective barriers to previous peaks has been accomplished—at least until the most recent change in late July 1967. Even the latter change calls for careful interpretation (see‡, Table 12.4).

Table 12.4, incidentally, points up a serious weakness of tariff policy, namely, the infrequent alteration of the evaluation base. The *raison d'être* for this policy is the same as that for "check prices" in evaluation of exports, namely, that it reduces discretion in evaluation, thereby simplifying administration and reducing opportunities for corruption. However, in a period of substantial inflation, such a policy has obvious drawbacks. The adherence to the (effective) evaluation rate of Rp. 30 per dollar throughout most of 1966 caused a most serious erosion in effective tariff rates, and again between April and July 1967. Furthermore, the evaluation rates have been quite low, even at the time set. The highest ratio of evaluation rate to equilibrium rate at any of the time points in Table 12.4 was .81. The only serious drawback to low evaluation rates is that the nominal rate schedules, even those immediately following readjustment of the evaluation rate, give the illusion of more protection than in fact exists. In the interest of being clear about what the quantitative goals of policy are, and of preventing periodic deterioration of the effective tariff schedule, it would seem to be advisable for the evaluation base to be changed much more frequently (not less often than once per month, perhaps), or even to adopt one of the floating rates as the base. The general BE rate could be used, for example, inasmuch as it represents the effective rate for the largest single category of imports. A possible, quite simple, procedure would be to use the average of the week's BE quotations, lagged one week.

As far as the levels of effective tariffs are concerned, they are quite low by standards established in low-income countries generally. However, it is by no means clear that the tariffs should be higher than they are. At present, Indonesian ability to produce import substitutes is extremely low, and, furthermore, in immediate goals of stabilization require a substantial flow of imports to maintain reasonably low domestic prices; also, the government must be careful not to raise rates much, if any, beyond the point of maximum revenue returns, at least until internal revenues can be increased to the point where such a move can be afforded. Finally, it is an economist's cliche that protective tariffs are inferior, from a welfare point of view, to direct production subsidies as a means of supporting infant industries.

It should perhaps be added, in passing, that the structure of tariffs is more complicated than it should be. Although there are only four tariff categories, there is a total of ten basic rates (including zero). These rates, however, are further complicated by the addition of a surcharge on Category IV, and so-called "excess profits" taxes on many commodities on an *ad hoc* basis. If, as is very often argued, the customs service is painfully weak administratively, and suspect as to integrity, this Byzantine complication should certainly be reduced. Probably no more than three rate categories (i.e., four rates including zero) would be necessary. These rates should be chosen (at least in the short run, when stabilization and budget considerations are of prime importance) with the objective of maximizing tariff revenues. Their present complexity is a by-product of attempting to make the duty system serve three purposes at once, namely, to earn revenues, curtail nonessential consumption, and provide protection. Any cascaded tariff system accomplishes all of these purposes to some extent, but it is impossible to design a system which is optimal in all three senses. If, following experience with a tariff system which is used primarily as a revenue source, it is found that luxurious consumption remains excessive, special internal sumptuary taxes may be levied. Similarly, if there is a clear case for more protection of domestic industry, this may be met by means of direct subsidy.

Inasmuch as duties do not offer an adequate explanation of the slow rate of rise of the effective importers' exchange rates behind the internal price level, the explanation must be sought elsewhere. The most important of these would appear to be the shift of such a large part of the nation's total foreign exchange resources from government control to the free market. Whereas in February 1966, exporters of goods in Categories I and II (which generate nine-tenths or more of total export proceeds) received only 10 and 15 percent of total proceeds in the form of BE, these proportions are now 75 and 90 percent, respectively. Virtually all of the surrendered foreign exchange was directly allocated to state enterprises and the ministries until March 1967, when it was announced that all government-used foreign exchange would have to be purchased with rupiahs on the BE market. The effect of this shift has been to reduce the relative impact of government on the foreign exchange pricing mechanism greatly, for although the addition of government institutions to the demand side of the market added a large price-raising effect, it was much more than counteracted by the supply increase. Whereas government institutions could, beforehand, account foreign exchange at the unrealistically low rate of 10:1, the shift forced them to account at a price ten times higher or more. This, coupled with stringent tightening of rupiah budget allocations, had a distinct braking effect on the foreign exchange market.

Yet another factor which has held back demand for foreign exchange has been the rapid reduction of the rate of increase of bank credit to importers, and the raising of interest rates on such loans to the point where the foreign exchange banks are charging interest rates which are not negative in real terms for the first time in many years. In November 1966, for example, government banks were authorized to raise interest charges to a range of 6 to 9 percent per month, which, with various supplemental charges established effective rates as high as 14 percent per month. There have been (unfortunately) substantial reductions in these rates since that time, by elimination of the supplemental charges (in February 1967) and by reduction of the rate range to 4 to 7 percent in April 1967, and to 3 to 5 percent in June. These rates are to be compared with a 6 percent monthly rate of inflation for the first six months of 1967, declining to less than 2 percent in the second quarter. It is quite possible therefore that borrowers are currently paying 2 or 3 percent per month in real terms—or compound rates of 27 to 42 percent per annum. Even at these rates, the foreign exchange banks are obliged to ration credit.

Finally, the government has introduced the sale of foreign credits to the BE market at a rate which has ranged from six to twenty-one points below the general BE rate. Until August, however, this had little effect, because importers found the "BE-Credit" relatively unattractive even with the discount. In August, the spread was allowed to widen substantially, with the result that BE-Credit (particularly the Japanese) began to move at such a pace that concern was aroused in the international community lest the supply be utilized too rapidly, and that rupiah proceeds from its sale be less than optimal. This surge came at a time, however, when the supply of general BE certificates was temporarily stifled by an export slow-up which fell on the heels of the July 28 regulations.

Summarization: The Pattern of Exchange Rates

As Table 12.5 indicates, the Indonesian exchange rate system, though predominantly a freely floating market system, remains a complex, multiple-rate system. And in addition to this complex

Table 12.5. Exchange rates in effect, end of October 1967*
(in rupiahs per U.S. dollar)

Exporters' rates		Importers' rates‡	
Oil company receipts	85.0	Oil company payments	85.0
Group A exports	114.0†	BE-Credit	131.0
Group B exports	136.8†	General BE	152.0
		DPA rate	167.0

* Based on the general BE rate of 152 on October 30, 1967. The special rates of the hotels, tourist agency, and Garuda Indonesian Airlines are not included.

† Based on the assumption that no overprice is granted. In practice a small overprice will be sustained for most commodities, and perhaps quite large ones for a few commodities, such as coffee, which have special export problems. A 2 percent overprice for Group A items would add about three points to each group's rate.

‡ Actual selling rate to importers. Effective costs to most classes of importers are considerably higher because of the tariff structure.

of buying rates and selling rates, there are several special regimes. Two of these are geographic in nature, namely, the island of Sabang which is a free port on the northern tip of Sumatra, while West Iran (West New Guinea) operates with its own special currency with a unitary exchange rate of 10:1 to the U.S. dollar.[9]

[9] Until late 1963, the Riau Archipelago, which is close to Singapore, oper-

There are also several economic sectors which operate with special rules. The most significant of these is the oil industry, which, when it effects exchanges, does so at a rate of 85:1. The oil companies exchange relatively little currency, however, because they are allowed to utilize their own foreign exchange earnings for purposes of purchasing goods for import, thus operating for such purposes as a free trade area. Furthermore, their royalties, which are substantial (60–65 percent of all profits) do not go into the foreign exchange fund, but are credited directly to the accounts of the state petroleum companies. The amounts involved are not public knowledge, but gross earnings of foreign exchange for the oil companies have been estimated for 1967 at a total of $200 million, or 28 percent of total foreign exchange from exports of goods and services. From this must be subtracted an estimated $60 million for their required imports, and of course not all of the remainder may be regarded as profits. Nonetheless, until July 1967, approximately $140 million of foreign exchange proceeds over and above required imports completely escaped the foreign exchange pricing system which confronts most exporters. Decisions as to its ultimate use were left to the foreign oil companies themselves, and to the directorship of the state oil companies.

This arrangement has recently (in July 1967) been modified. The Indonesian oil companies are now required to deposit foreign exchange payments from foreign oil companies with the central bank, and must surrender rupiahs at the special (85:1) rate when drafts on this account are drawn. The remainder is to be controlled by the central bank, and may be sold as general BE, in the same manner as the foreign exchange surrendered by the ordinary categories of exporters. The modifications constitute a substantial improvement, but the reason for continuation of the 85:1 rate and the special accounting arrangements remain obscure. The same reasoning which led the government to demand of other state enterprises and departments that their foreign exchange re-

ated with the trading freedom of that city, even to the point of using Malayan currency. The Riau area is now formally within the customs area and the legal tender is the rupiah, although it is widely reported that implementation has been considerably less than perfect.

sources be purchased with rupiah earnings (or budget allocations) seems applicable to the state oil enterprises as well. It may be argued that their foreign exchange needs, like those of the foreign oil companies are unusually high, but on the other hand, with a complete monopoly of retailing of petroleum products domestically and a burgeoning export business, they should soon be strong enough to be able to meet the same sort of market test that, say, state spinning and weaving enterprises are forced to meet. Indeed, it is hard to imagine that the present position of the state oil enterprises is not infinitely stronger than that of the textile industries.

There are several other, relatively minor, special arrangements as well. The foreign-operated hotels maintain their own foreign exchange accounting arrangements, and have their own set of exchange rates. In mid-summer, 1967, these rates were 140:1 for accounting of purchases of commodities for import on the hotels' account, and 120:1 in translating tourists' bills into domestic currency. Foreign nationals staying at the hotels are required to pay in convertible foreign currencies, however. Similar arrangements are made for Nitour, the state-owned tourist bureau, and for Garuda Indonesian Airways. The foreign exchange fund of the central bank has no control over the foreign accounts of these institutions, and, indeed, in several cases does not even receive a detailed accounting.

Policy Priorities: The Next Steps

The regulations of July 28, 1967 were the last major changes in exchange pricing regulations. [This statement held true until early 1970.—Ed.] In brief, they consisted of the following: (1) a modest increase in effective exchange rates to most exporters (about 8 percent in Category I at the BE rate in existence at the time of the changes), through increases in BE quotas, was executed (see Table 12.1); (2) much of the implicit tax burden lifted from the shoulders of the exporters was transferred to importers at the same time by means of an increase of 44 percent in the import tax evaluation base, and by adding 50 percent surcharges on Category IV imports; (3) substantial simplification of documentation and clearing procedures was introduced; and (4) prepayment and credit conditions were relaxed for imports using BE-Credit, i.e., marketed foreign aid exchange.

The Indonesian economists and the Indonesian government deserve highest marks for having moved so far so fast toward liberalization and rationalization of their foreign exchange pricing system. It would indeed be difficult to find another example of a major nation which has shown such purposefulness and intelligence in this area.[10] There remain many problems with the system, however, some of which have been introduced above. The most important of these are the following: (1) continued overdependence on revenues from imports and exports; (2) the attendant lowness of effective exchange rates to exporters and strong incentives to smuggle on both the import and export side of the market; (3) a certain amount of unnecessary complication of the exchange rate structure; (4) the continued existence of special regimes, at least some of which can be and probably should be treated under the free marketing system; and (5) overcomplication of the tariff structure, and too infrequent revision of the tariff evaluation base.

Item (1) is understood by the Indonesian authorities, and additional progress will be made in this area in due course. The constraint under which they operate is the time-honored difficulty which most low-income countries have to contend with in the field of internal revenues. In this regard, Indonesia's situation is probably worse than typical. However, as order is brought into the administration of internal revenues and tax reforms are designed and implemented, it should be possible for more burden to be lifted from the export trade, without having to compensate with higher import duties. It remains for the fiscal experts to determine definitively, but it is at least possible that any further attempts to shift the burden from one side of the foreign trade market to the other will yield a reduction in revenues rather than an in-

[10] Contrast this performance, for example, with that of Pakistan in recent years—a nation which has received abundant praise from international trade authorities for its accomplishments. Cf. Glassburner, *op. cit.*, and Child, *op. cit.;* also, Glassburner, "The Balance of Payments and External Resources in Pakistan's Third Five Year Plan," *Pakistan Development Review,* Karachi, Autumn 1966.

crease. Pending solid information on this matter, it would probably not be advisable for Indonesia to attempt to improve exporters' incentives in that way. If this judgment is correct, the pressure on the government to accomplish substantial gains in the internal revenue policy field is reinforced by the need to reduce, or even eliminate, the surrender quotas on exports.

Item (2) is essentially covered by the discussion of item (1). Estimates of the minimal margin necessary to make smuggling profitable in exporting range from 20 to 30 percent—over and above the returns which can be earned by legal exporters.[11] Despite the improvement in the relationship between effective exporters' rates and equilibrium rates, the overvaluation in Group A remains large enough (46 percent in late October 1967) to exceed the smugglers' minimum margin readily (see Table 12.2). On the import side, margins of that order of magnitude (20 to 30 percent), or more, obtain for the high dutied items which may be imported only using DPA exchange. However, for goods on the BE list (i.e., the bulk of basic import needs), the degree of undervaluation relative to the equilibrium rate is too small to cover that range.[12] This should become increasingly true as discipline is introduced into the Djakarta port, which is Indonesia's most important importing facility. Smuggling on both the import and export side will be much more difficult to bring under control, whatever the incentive pattern, in Sumatran ports, which are close to Singapore and which dot a very long coastline.[13]

Item (3) and item (4) are so closely related as to need no separa-

[11] This range was established in interviews with a small, and certainly not statistically significant, sample of Indonesian exporters.

[12] Undervaluation here refers to the extent to which the buying rate plus duty exceeds the free rate. In late October 1967, for example, an item on the BE list dutied at 25 percent would have had an effective rate of exchange of $152(1 + .25) = 190$, or 14 percent above the DPA rate. The "smuggle margin" requires effective importers rates of 200 or more.

[13] The best organized smuggling port, aside from the legalized free trade from Sabang and the still quite open trade of Riau, is said by many observers to be the port of Djambi. All attempts to elicit estimates of the order of magnitude of smuggling through interviews were frustrated. Word of mouth has it that at its worst it was on the order of $200 million per annum, or about 40 percent of the volume of legal merchandise exports excluding oil. The consensus is that it is diminishing.

tion for purposes of discussion. The existence of special rates for the oil companies and for the various tourist and travel-connected institutions appear to have little foundation in economic rationality. As time and contractual relationships make it possible to do so, steps should be taken to bring these enclaves into the BE market system. Item (5) has been discussed above.

A Special Problem: Pricing of BE-Credit

Indonesia has adopted a path in the use of foreign credits which has only been tentatively used by other aid recipient nations, namely, to market it. There are two very good reasons for making this attempt. The first is that it provides an important supplement to the limited revenue raising capabilities of the nation. The second, and equally important reason, is that by submitting the allocation to the market, it is more likely to be channelled to productive uses than would be the case if the decrepit bureaucracy were left to do the job. In short, until internal revenue capabilities are markedly improved, and until there is a planning apparatus of some degree of reliability, direct allocations are inferior to the decisions of private entrepreneurs and the managers of state enterprises. The bulk of the aid provided for the purpose of BE marketing is of the type which can be readily used by established entrepreneurs in the country, namely, raw materials, spare parts, and relatively light equipment.

The attempt has not been without problems. Supplies are fixed for a specific period by the conditions of the loans. Hence there is no automatic supply adjustment in the market place. Thus, pricing is not automatic, but is a matter of administrative decision. Secondly, the goods which may be imported using BE-Credit are limited in two ways, namely, by the typing of the purchase to the specific country whose credits are being purchased, and by specific elimination of items on the BE list by the donor nations. The problem of the Indonesian government is to price the BE-Credit at a level which is attractive and profitable to Indonesian entrepreneurs, and at the same time to reap the maximum amount of rupiah proceeds for government revenue purposes. The problem is complicated by the fact that the cost of use to importers varies with the country whose credits are being used. Thus, it is not (or should not be) just a matter of a single optimal price, but of a set of prices. For if the Indonesian government chooses to set the price low enough to get the full proceeds from the sale of the least attractive credit, it foregoes proceeds from the sale of the more attractive, which could be sold at a higher price. Furthermore, the credits of the country or countries which are most attractive to users will be completely used up long before the end of the tranche period, followed by more rapid use of the less attractive aid.[14] The result would be a lumpiness in the pattern of aid utilization that is not particularly attractive to either the recipient or the donor nations. In short, the various categories of credits are seen by buyers as distinct commodities, and optimal pricing, therefore, calls for differentials in prices.

This line of argument is illustrated in a highly schematic way in Figure 12.1. The four truncated demand functions are intended to represent demand for the credits of four categories of donor, namely, Japanese, German and Dutch, American, and Indian. The functions are truncated because of the fact that no amount beyond that provided in the loan agreements may be sold. The functions are drawn also to reflect the assumption that they are demand elastic, based on the fact that they are close substitutes for other types of foreign exchange which may be purchased in the Indonesian market, particularly general BE.[15] It is important to emphasize that the diagram is schematized to illustrate the relationships, and no attempt is made to achieve cardinal accuracy. It can be seen that if the exchange rate is set at *Of*—the rate which will clear the

[14] This is an oversimplification. Aid carryovers are possible, and there is probably some possibility that full utilization long before the end of a tranche period would make negotiation of additional funds possible. These are minor qualifications, however.

[15] To illustrate the point, assume that the rate of the U.S. BE utilization would have remained the same throughout 1967 had the rate been held at the 132 rate established until early August, and that the spread between the BE-Credit and general BE rates was also not changed during the remainder of the year. At the rate of sale experienced through the end of July, total sales for the year would be $15.1 million, or a shortfall of $14.9. The rupiah proceeds of sales at that rate would be Rp. 1993.2 million. It can be shown that sale of the full $30 million would yield a greater return for any effective rate above 66.4:1. This range (132–66.4) is surely some multiple of the differential that would make all U.S. BE saleable.

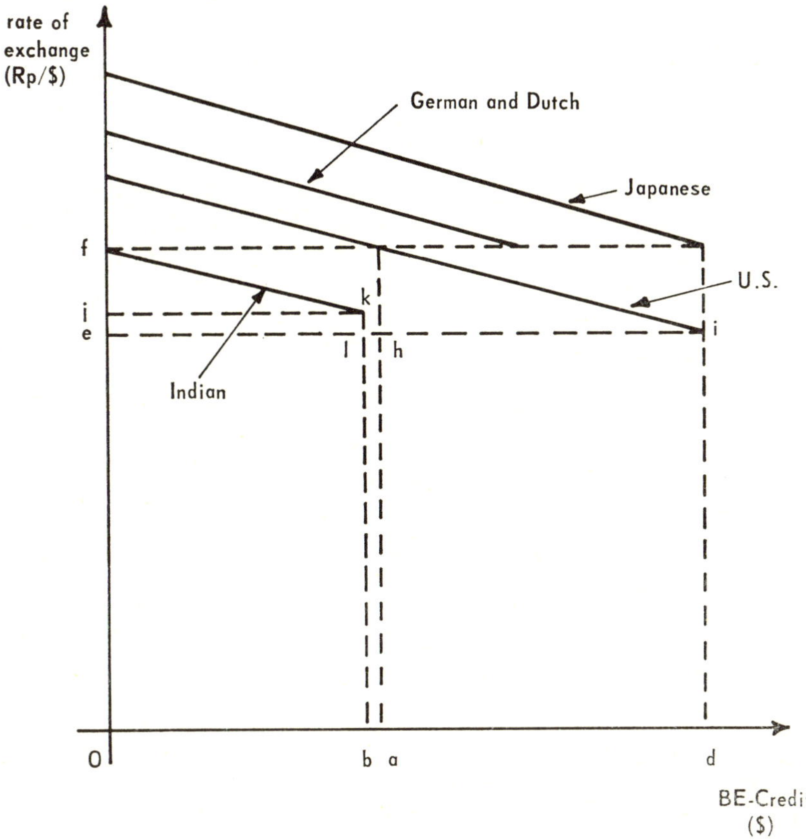

Figure 12.1. Pricing of BE-Credit

market of Japanese, Dutch, and German credits by the end of the calendar year—sales of U.S. credits will be only *Oa,* and Indian credits sales will be zero. The loss in revenues from the sale of the U.S. credits is indicated by the difference in the area of the two rectangles *efgh* and *ahid,* the former being the "loss" from price reduction to the price which would clear American credits and the latter (*ahid*) being the proceeds gained from the additional sales at the lower price. Similarly, Indian credits are potentially capable of yielding *Ojkb* at price *Oj,* their market-clearing price.

As the diagram is drawn, it can be seen by inspection that if one price is chosen it would be best to establish the price to clear the U.S. BE, because all types of credits would then be sold, and the gain from clearing the market of the large block of U.S. credits more than compensates for the proceeds lost from underpricing of the other types. However, if differential pricing is practicable, the optimal solution, from the point of view of maximizing revenues, is to set the price of each at the level which will clear each, i.e., *Oe* for American, *Oj* for Indian, and *Of* for the others. The differentials could rather readily be established by trial and error, and if errors are to be made, perhaps it would be best to err on the low rather than the high side for each, both because it would be well for Indonesia to demonstrate that she can absorb these amounts of assistance if the price is right, and also to give domestic businesses using the imports obtained a relatively advantageous set of prices.[16] The objections raised to multiple prices for BE-Credit are twofold: (1) The nations getting higher prices placed on their credits may object that their exports are being discouraged by unfavorable pricing, while those with the lower prices may find the revelation that their credits are difficult to sell embarrassing; and (2) the Indonesians are under pressure from the IMF to unify exchange rates, and this sort of pricing pattern would mean their proliferation. The former is essentially a diplomatic problem (but none the less serious for that), and the latter involves simply an appreciation of the nature of the problem.

It might very well be possible to deal with problem (1) by making the price differentials effective by means of concessions to buyers rather than by differences in the overt rates. A pattern of concessions already exists, and it could be extended to users of BE-Credit of the several types in discriminatory fashion. For example, prepayment requirements for American and Indian credits could

[16] Low-priced imports also mean increased competition for domestic producers of goods on the BE list. So long, however, as the credits are marketed at near-market-clearing prices, and so long as tariffs on imports produceable domestically are reasonably high, it is difficult to regard this competitive threat as uneconomic. Indeed, it is an openly stated objective of the Indonesian policy-making economists that domestic firms must be subjected to foreign competition with modest protection as part of the economic rationalization process. It goes without saying that few, if any luxuries or semi-luxuries should be importable with BE-Credit. Perusal of the BE list readily shows that, with the possible exception of fine textiles (which are heavily dutied) there are no frivolities.

be relaxed still farther, and perhaps the lending provisions in connection with them could be liberalized. A longer period than the presently allowable three-month term for exporters' credits against BE-Credit could be justified for the United States on grounds of lengthier shipping time than that from Japan. A little imagination could easily provide additional ideas for concessions (import tax credits or deferments, for example).

The government has chosen for the time being to handle the matter by allowing a very large spread to develop between the general BE rate and the (single) BE-Credit rate. The result has been a run, particularly on Japanese credits through the month of August. Sales mounted to a peak of $7 million of Japanese credits per day late in the month. Other types of aid were also moving well, but it was obvious from this experience that, although the late-July point spread between the two rates (six points) was too little to move BE-Credit well, the 19-point spread which developed in August was considerably too much. Further experimentation with this tricky problem is clearly needed, and differential pricing should certainly be given most serious consideration.[17]

Unification of Exchange Rates as a Goal of Policy

As we have seen, the Indonesian foreign exchange pricing system is a system of multiple rates. The economists close to policy decision-making are under considerable pressure, and, indeed, express personal desire, to unify the system as rapidly as is expedient. It will be argued here that the goal should be rationalization rather than unification, and that the two goals converge up to a point, but that, given the objectives of the government and the institutional framework of the system, the presently most desirable involves multiple rates.

The case in neoclassical trade theory for a unitary fluctuating exchange rate is that the acceptance of the equilibrium rate, i.e.,

[17] On October 30, 1967, the government was still selling BE-Credit at 131, 21 points below the general BE market. Japanese and Australian credits were completely gone and Dutch sales on that day were eight times those of the U.S. The $5.2 worth of Australian credits did not reach the market until September 24. Half of it was sold in three days. This very clearly shows how badly differential pricing is needed.

the rate which clears the market, not only satisfies all buyers and sellers quantitatively, but it also establishes a price which reflects the community's evaluation of the resources which flow through the channels of international trade. The attempt, so frequently made, to maintain an official rate which lies below the market equilibrium means excess demand for foreign exchange and windfall profits for those buyers who are fortunate enough to gain access to the limited funds. In order to maintain order in the market and to achieve a socially desirable pattern of allocation of the scarce foreign resources, various rationing devices have to be designed, and special taxes introduced to capture part or all of the windfall. Success in the latter frequently leads to dependence on the revenues earned, so that what evolves is a system which pays exporters less than the equilibrium rate, and (either overtly or through duties) imposes a rate above equilibrium on importers. The revenues are purchased at considerable cost (frequently unrecognized) in most cases, namely, foreign exchange foregone because of the low effective rate to exporters, expenditure of scarce personnel resources in the administration of the system, and inducement to smuggle on the part of both importers and exporters.

There are two primary defenses of the multiple rate system: the argument that the revenues are essential, particularly in countries with limited internal-revenue collection capability; and the fear that elasticities of supply of primary exports and the elasticity of demand for them in the world markets are such that devaluation of the domestic currency to the equilibrium rate may mean a loss of foreign exchange earnings. The logic of the latter argument involves the implicit assumption that there are backward-bending supply curves in terms of foreign exchange earnings for some goods, but not others. If so, and if the points of maximum earnings can be identified, then it follows that separate rates should be established for each category of goods.

The Indonesian system of exporters' rates partially reflects this line of argument. A wedge is driven between importers and exporters in the form of the surrender quota (which equals 100 percent minus the BE quota). The surrendered foreign exchange is sold on the market by the central bank (aside from that portion diverted to provincial governments). Importers must then purchase at a higher effective rate (see Table 12.5). Exporters are grouped into two categories (formerly three), roughly according to their internal supply and external demand elasticities.

On the other side of the market, importers of essential goods may purchase at the relatively advantageous general BE rate, and if they opt for the use of goods provided under foreign aid, the price is still lower. Nonessentials may be purchased, but only with higher priced DPA foreign exchange, generated from "over-price" proceeds, or from balances accumulated in earlier trading arrangements, including capital flight.

Excluding the special regimes from consideration here, there seem to be good reasons for retention of the general pattern, with perhaps some effort to reduce differentials. As we have already seen, the revenue needs of the government are so acute that it probably makes economic sense to continue to sacrifice some foreign exchange earnings (through relatively low price incentives) in order to maintain revenues.[18] This is a short run argument, however, and will cease to have force when and if the Indonesian government succeeds in developing an adequate internal revenue system.

Also, the maintenance of two categories of exports may be defended without resort to the dubious notion of backward-bending supply curves. Export goods which are in a difficult competitive position abroad should be taxed less. In all probability it would be wise to eliminate the present 10 percent ADO (Automatic Exchange Allocation) tax which now exists on Group B. The benefit of the tax is very small (two percent or less of total foreign exchange proceeds), and probably does not justify the hurdle it presents to promotion of higher (supply and demand) elasticity exports.

Serious consideration should also be given to partial restitution of overprice proceeds as a safety valve for the pressures which build up for the import of nonessentials, and as a stimulant to

[18] It is conceivable, of course, that further lowering of effective taxes on exports would both earn more foreign exchange and yield more revenues. Some evidence on the "revenue elasticity" of the export taxation arrangement should emerge in the months following the recent reduction. If it proves striking, a case will then emerge for reduction without compensating taxation elsewhere.

exporters. The DPA exchange which is earned through this channel not only serves the useful purpose of that sort of safety valve, but it is also administratively much easier for both exporters and importers to do business abroad if they have a modest amount of essentially free foreign exchange to work with. Specification of uses of BE for these purposes (clearing of claims accounts, export promotion, services, etc.) may ease the situation, but it is (at least for the present) an administratively much more cumbersome procedure.

Acceptance of this line of argument for the exporters' side of the market means that importers will continue to be faced with at least three rates of exchange, the general BE rate, the DPA rate, and the BE-Credit rate (or rates). It is conceivable that the BE list could gradually be broadened so that the gap between the general BE rate and the DPA rate is progressively reduced, substituting other deterrents to nonessential consumption for the banning of items from the BE list. To do so, however, would probably mean further departure of the BE-Credit rate from the general BE rate, and sharper differences between the BE list and the list of goods which may be imported with foreign credit, unless the donor nations indicate a willingness to similarly broaden their lists of permissible imports. While it would be consistent with liberal economic principles for aid policy to move in this direction, it seems unlikely that the established institutional arrangements of economic aid will make it possible.

If the sole goal of economic assistance were stimulation of the Indonesian economy, a case could be made for making the bulk of nonproject, aid funds available for free marketing without any limitation other than the pattern of duties. However, the motives of the donor nations are mixed, and include a desire to promote their own exports as well as to stimulate the Indonesian economy. For this reason, all such aid, being tied, is more expensive to users than free BE, and much less attractive than DPA. This is further complicated by differences in the domestic price structures of the several countries, differences in the administrative difficulties of utilization, and differences in the lists of allowable imports. Although there may be some hope that the worst of these manifold restrictions will be eased through negotiations, their basic form is probably beyond correction. Hence, BE-Credit pricing will undoubtedly remain a source of multiple rates.[19] One can scarcely resist offering the admonition to the parties responsible for aid policy that this aspect of the pricing problem is one generated by the policy itself, and that efforts should be made to mitigate it wherever and whenever possible.

Conclusion

The effort to liberalize and rationalize foreign exchange pricing in Indonesia has made remarkable strides in the period since early 1966 when the new government began to seek ways out of its deep economic distress. The effort has received, and certainly deserves, the compliments of most observers. However, there are many problems which remain, and there are directions of policy change which should be further explored. These have been discussed in some detail above; they are summarized here:

1. Effective rates to exporters should be raised farther, immediately if experience indicates elasticity of revenue response. Otherwise it should await increased internal revenue collection capability.

2. Further measures should be taken to integrate and normalize the special foreign exchange regimes.

3. A modest proportion of "overprice" proceeds should be allowed—perhaps 5 percent of f.o.b. value—as exporters' incentive and as a "safety valve" for incentives to smuggle.

4. Tariff schedules should be simplified. Four basic rates, including zero, should be sufficient for the combined purposes of revenue yield, sumptuary effect, and protection. The first of these purposes should be given primary consideration.

5. The tariff evaluation base should be allowed to fluctuate with the BE rate, with perhaps some sort of averaging added to simplify administrative procedures, e.g., a weekly announcement, based on the previous week's average of BE rates.

[19] See Child, *op. cit.,* for an analytical anticipation of this sort of difficulty in connection with discussion of possible inclusion of aid credits in the bonus system of Pakistan.

6. BE-Credit should continue to be sold as in the past, but the pricing schedules (or differential concessions) should reflect value differentials to users. An attempt by the donor nations to reduce these differentials would make the problem easier to manage.

7. Progress toward exchange rate unification will have to be made primarily in the area of elimination or reduction of the number of special regimes, and in the continued broadening of the BE list. However, dependence on foreign trade for revenues and the marketing of BE-Credit will require continuation of multiple rates.

PART VI

THE ECONOMY AND ECONOMIC POLICY: PRESENT AND FUTURE

Indonesia enters the decade of the 1970's hopefully, after having weathered economic and political disaster in the 1960's. The last decade splits rather neatly into two parts, with the first six years (1960–1965) dominated by Sukarno and his unsuccessful attempt at social and economic re-ordering. The last four years (1966–1969) have seen a struggle for *Orde Baru* (New Order), under the leadership of a government in which the military plays a very prominent role. In economic policy this effort has been characterized by pragmatism, reliance on professional expertise, and gradualism.

This approach has not been undertaken without risks, nor has it been taken without criticism. It is readily apparent to an outside observer, particularly to an economist, that the distortions and deterioration created over so many years could only be corrected over a comparable number of years. However, to Indonesians, particularly the young, twenty years of independence without economic growth of any significance is enough suffering. Still, the response of the government to its critics has continued to be calm and unhurried—at least in outward appearance. Evidence of this is seen in the fact that although the paper which comprises this section was written in August 1968, it remains essentially correct in early 1970. Some updating comments are called for, however.

The Five Year Plan (REPELITA) for 1969–1973 appeared on schedule in April 1969, and was formally inaugurated with fiscal year 1969–1970. It is a modest plan, in keeping with the tone of governmental leadership. Heaviest emphasis is on creating a new vitality in the agricultural sector—mainly in rice production. The main priority in industry is to be in agriculture-connected activity, such as fertilizer production, milling, and processing. "An Economist in Indonesia," writing in the July 1969 issue of the *Bulletin of Indonesian Economic Studies* (Australian National University Press, Canberra), summarized the theme of the plan as follows: "No major structural changes are envisaged; much of the Plan is concerned with rehabilitation rather than new investment; the economy will still be firmly agriculture-based with no attempt to achieve an industrial 'takeoff'."

Reliance on foreign sources in financing the REPELITA is to be extremely heavy. Seventy-three percent of the total planned expenditure is to come from aid and private foreign investment. The plan was not constructed within a macroeconomic model. Specific sector targets were established and the macroeconomic implications were inferred to provide a rough consistency check. In aggregate terms, the entire program appears very modest indeed. The rate of growth of GNP is projected at approximately five percent per annum, or about 2.5 percent per capita per annum.

Since the writing of this section's paper, the limited success of the stabilization policy reported there has become almost complete success. Food shortages caused a serious price spurt in the winter of 1967–1968, but then, over the last eleven months of 1968, the Djakarta cost-of-living index rose by only thirteen percent. In the first five months of 1969 there was a net increase of only 2 percent. A modest spurt was experienced in the autumn months of 1969, but not so large as to threaten seriously the economists' hopes for "relative stability"—which is defined as an annual rate of inflation of ten percent or less.

The good luck which the conclusion of the paper looked forward to with hope (pp. 191–195) has materialized. Both the dry season crop in 1968 and the wet season crop of 1968–1969 were very good. (Early reports on the dry season crop of 1969 were not optimistic, however.) Rubber prices became strong, reaching a level 40 percent above the 1967 level by mid-year 1969. Tin prices remained fairly good—i.e., stable at roughly the 1967 level—and tin production has recovered to the point that Indonesia is constrained by her quota in the international tin agreement. Oil production has continued to grow vigorously, as predicted.

Professor H. W. Arndt, editor of the *Bulletin of Indonesian Economic Studies,* summarized the situation well in concluding his "Survey of Recent Developments" in the July 1969 issue (cited above). "In Djakarta, and to a less extent also in other cities of Indonesia, there is today an unmistakable sense of relief from the most acute anxieties of the past few years. Life for the ordinary people, especially in the villages of Java and the outer islands, may not be better than in the recent past. But at least it has, generally speaking, stopped getting worse, and there is a good deal more optimism about the future."

CHAPTER 13

Indonesian Economic Policy after Sukarno

BRUCE GLASSBURNER

Indonesia is a fascinating case study for the development economist. She is generally regarded as an underachiever, being far better endowed with resources than Japan or Pakistan, two Asian countries of comparable size, both of which are doing well with their development efforts. She has had an adventure with socialism, at which she failed utterly. She is now placing a frighteningly heavy bet on a handful of economists to bring order out of economic chaos; and these economists have placed their heaviest bets on the revival of the market system.

Following an eight-year postindependence phase of struggles between "development-minded" and "radical" politicians,[1] the latter group emerged dominant in 1958. From 1958 to late 1965, a disastrous pattern of fiscal casualness and overburdening of the economy with military expenditures brought the country an economist's nightmare of hyperinflation, underproduction, and international indebtedness. A brief sketch of the economic performance of Sukarno's attempt at a "Guided Economy" will help to put the problem of the present regime into perspective.

Stagnation in Production

The real national income index of the Central Bureau of Statistics (CBS) implies an average annual rate of output growth of less than 2 percent per annum for the years 1958–1966, i.e., the

[1] Cf. Chapter 2, above.

years which coincide with the period of Sukarno's "Socialisme à la Indonesia." In four of those eight years the NNP growth rate was virtually zero, or even negative. Meanwhile, population grew at a significantly faster over-all rate. Officially, the population growth rate for all of Indonesia was estimated at 2.3 percent at the time of the 1961 census. However, official projections by the CBS are based upon projection equations which treat acceleration of the growth rate explicitly, so that by 1967–1968, the growth rate was being estimated at 2.5 percent.[2] It is quite possible that even this is an understatement in view of the upward revisions of estimates of growth rates which have emerged from recent demographic studies in other Asian nations. However, if we accept these official data as a basis for a conservative estimate of the seriousness of the country's economic problem, we find 1966 per capita real income 3.6 percent below the 1958 level. Thus, even with a substantial recovery in 1967 and 1968, we could not expect much more than reattainment of the 1958 per capita output level by the end of the current year.

We have no data on which to base judgments of what has happened to the nation's capital stock during this period, but it is indubitable that it has declined in major sectors and probably in the aggregate. The deterioration of social overhead capital is readily visible in port facilities, roads, and railways. It is also apparent in shipping, private transportation, and in the irrigation system. The extent to which this has been compensated for by public building construction[3] and by private rural investment is impossible to judge. A reasonable surmise would be that personal consumption standards have been roughly static and that this has been at the expense of major inroads on the capital of the industrialized and commercialized sector.[4]

The growth performance of the several sectors varied widely

[2] Nugroho, *Indonesia Facts and Figures,* Djakarta, 1967, p. 66.

[3] The elaborate public construction program of the Sukarno regime was abruptly interrupted in 1966, and is being only gradually and selectively resumed.

[4] Higgins feels that consumption standards actually rose in the early years of this period. See B. Higgins, ed., *Entrepreneurship and Labor Skills* (monograph series no. 1), Southeast Asia Studies, Yale University, New Haven, 1961, pp. 23–28.

over the period 1958–1966. Agriculture outperformed the economy as a whole by a very slight margin, while the manufacturing sector did little better than maintain a constant over-all level of output. The strongest performances were in mining and quarrying, chiefly oil (6 percent per annum), and in wholesale and retail trade (almost 4 percent per annum). The worst was in banking and finance, the real value of whose output did not grow at all. Strikingly, the value of expenditures on public administration and defense declined in real terms by almost 5 percent per annum.

Inflation

The last of the sectoral growth rates mentioned above highlights the striking example which Indonesia offers of the self-frustration inherent in a government's attempt to mobilize resources through a large inflationary gap. According to Arndt, the real value of the money stock in early 1966 was less than 25 percent of that of the peak reached in 1960. This occurred while the nominal value of the money stock increased by a geometric rate of nearly 50 percent per annum, and this rate was accelerating.[5] The inflation reached its peak in the political transition year of 1966 when the money stock rose in nominal value more than nine times, and the price level, as measured by the Djakarta cost-of-living index, rose sixfold. The heart of the problem, of course, lay in the budget of the central government, aggravated, as the years passed, by subsidy in the form of liberal credit to public enterprises. It was typical in the early 1960's for central bank advances to government to equal half or more of government expenditures.

An important corollary is that the real size of the public sector declined dramatically during this period. It is the common judgment that the rampant budget is the reflection of an overexpanded public sector, an illusion supported by the mushroom growth of public employment and by the spectacular wastefulness of public construction activity and the military establishment. These phenomena mask the fact that the public sector's size was never great, even by Asian standards (expenditures 13 percent of GDP at the

[5] H. W. Arndt, "Banking in Hyperinflation," *Bulletin of Indonesian Economic Studies* (*BIES*), October 1966, pp. 52–54.

1960 peak), and that inflation succeeded only in making it smaller (less than 8 percent of GDP in 1965, and about 3 percent in 1966).[6]

Trade and the Balance of Payments

As recently as 1959, the dollar value of Indonesia's exports was $931 million. By 1966, that total had declined to $685 million.[7] The balance of payments fluctuated widely during these years. There was a favorable current account balance in 1959 of $25 million, and a deficit of $521 million in 1961. The latter figure reflects a very large flow of Soviet assistance in that year, and no other year's deficit was more than half of that amount. However, in 1965, the deficit was $248 million, and the deficit exceeded $200 million five years running, causing the nation's meagre foreign exchange reserve to run down from $313 million in 1960 to $17 million in March 1967.

External Indebtedness

Indonesia has a huge volume of outstanding external debt. According to OECD, scheduled payments for the period 1967–1984 total $2.42 billion—more than three times the nation's total export earnings in 1967.[8] The prevalence of relatively short maturities aggravates the problem to a severity which may be unprecedented in world experience. Rescheduling of a drastic sort is absolutely essential if debt service is not to strangle the country's import potential in the 1970's. Some progress has already been made in this direction—but clearly not enough (see Table 13.1).

Unemployment

Since 1958, Indonesia has undoubtedly experienced a serious increase in unemployment, making the challenge of labor absorption exceedingly difficult to meet. This challenge involves absorption of a substantial idle labor pool, as well as large increments

[6] Estimated from International Bank for Reconstruction and Development (IBRD) sources.

[7] Nugroho, *op. cit.*

[8] Organization for Economic Cooperation and Development, *Projections of Indonesia's Debt Situation,* DD-6, 1st rev., Paris, June 15, 1967.

Table 13.1. Indonesia's debts (in millions of U.S. dollars)

	To the West*				To the USSR		
	Nonrescheduled debt						
Year	Principal	Interest	Rescheduled debt (principal)	Total†	Short-term	Long-term	Total
1968	111.2	17.3		128.5	20.0		20.0
1969	91.4	14.2		105.6	18.2		18.2
1970	75.9	10.3		86.2	13.5	24.8	38.3
1971	60.0	7.7	16.3	84.0		44.6	44.6
1972	41.2	4.5	32.6	78.3		49.5	49.5
1973	23.2	3.1	32.6	58.9		54.5	54.5
1974	18.7	2.2	32.6	53.5		55.0	55.0
1975	14.7	1.6	49.0	65.3		57.8	57.8
1976	9.5	1.1	49.0	59.6		62.7	62.7
1977	6.5	0.6	49.0	56.1		67.7	67.7
1978	5.8	0.4	65.3	71.5		67.7	67.7
1979	3.4	0.1		3.5		72.6	72.6
1980	2.3	0.1		2.4		77.6	77.6
1981	0.5‡			0.5‡	‡	89.1	89.1

Source: Far Eastern Economic Review, 1968 Yearbook, p. 198.

* France, West Germany, Italy, Japan, the Netherlands, the United Kingdom, and the United States.

† Exclusive of interest payments on the rescheduled amounts.

‡ Payments after 1980.

to that pool. The magnitude of the problem cannot be documented; but the order of magnitude can be inferred. The basic figure is the overt unemployment rate given by the census of 1961, which was 5.4 percent of the labor force, or (given the 1961 labor force of 34.6 million), nearly 2 million unemployed. We have no objective indication of what has happened to the incidence of overt unemployment since 1961, although it is a common observation among knowledgeable Indonesians that it has increased. But even if we make the conservative assumption that the proportion of unemployed remained constant from 1961 through 1966, and accept the labor force projections of the Indonesian demographer Tan Goan Tiang, we arrive at an overt unemployment figure for the end of 1966 of 2.15 million persons. Approximately 475,000 of these are urban-based, and heavily disproportionate in the youth-group age brackets. The urban unemployment rate in the 15–19 male age group in 1961 was given in the 1961 census as 25.3 percent. Furthermore, the youth-group age brackets are the most rapidly growing in the total labor force, which may suggest that the problem of incidence of unemployment and its political impact are growing in intensity more rapidly than the above calculation would indicate. Also, the overt unemployment data ignore the incidence and growth of disguised unemployment—a phenomenon which is readily recognized, but seldom effectively defined or measured. The rough figure which has been adopted by Indonesian government officials is 20 percent of the total labor force.

The arithmetic of labor absorption is frightening, particularly if we accept the commonly accepted proposition that the rural sector is labor-saturated and must, therefore, shift its entire labor force increment to new urban-based (or, at any rate, nonagricultural) employment. The tiny urban-based economy employs no more than 14 percent of the labor force. If we calculate the annual increment to the total labor force at the natural rate of population growth, absorption of the increment *alone* requires a growth rate in the urban sector of more than 16 percent per annum, making no allowance for improvement in labor productivity. It is impossible, in this situation, for the policymakers to contemplate anything more than a reduction in the rate of increase in unemployment.

The Chronology of the Coup D'Etat

The extent to which the above state of economic affairs contributed to the political crises of 1965 and 1966 is problematical, but it seems unlikely that it will be regarded by political historians as more than a set of contributing factors—the basic instability of the Sukarno-created political equilibrium being the central fact, with mounting anxiety on the part of the military and conservative elite to the increasing influence of the Communist party, and the failing health of the old president playing central roles.

The initial crisis came with shocking suddenness on the 30th of September 1965, with an (apparently) communist-inspired attempt to liquidate army leadership with a group of murders. The attempt failed, and was followed by several weeks of bloody purges against communists and their associates that brought the country to near-panic and very close to a civil war. Communist cabinet ministers (most of whom literally fled for their lives) were replaced —for the most part by military people. However, the president remained in office, as did many of his old noncommunist associates. *De facto* power shifted quickly to the military leaders and their relatively conservative allies. In March 1966, the Communist party was banned, and in the same month Sukarno, under pressure, granted broad emergency powers to General Suharto. The cabinet was reshuffled in July 1966, and despite criticism of its slowness to act and its domination by the military, it survived until June 1968, when the present cabinet was installed.

President Sukarno held his titles, nominally, following the coup, and continued to struggle to regain meaningful power, but to no avail. The Congress named General Suharto Acting President in March 1967, and forbade Sukarno from undertaking any political activity until new elections could be held. In July 1967, Sukarno's political titles were formally revoked, and Independence Day was celebrated on August 17, 1967 without Sukarno for the first time since the original declaration in 1945. Recently General Suharto dropped the adjective "Acting" from his title, and the promised general elections were postponed for three years.

The Team of Economic Advisers

From the point of view of the professional economist, the most interesting aspect of this political pageant is the role which Indonesian economists have been playing. As early as late 1965, the responsibility for getting the chaotic economy under control fell on the shoulders of Hamengku Buono, the sultan of Djogjakarta. The sultan is completely untrained in economics, and was presumably given this position because of the very high prestige which he commands. He sought assistance from his secretary, who is a lecturer at the Faculty of Economics at the University of Indonesia, who, in turn, brought a team of five colleagues prominently into the pictures as advisers. Of these five, three have Ph.D. degrees from the University of California, Berkeley—products of the Ford Foundation's financed affiliation between Berkeley and the University of Indonesia. The other two also have graduate degrees from American universities.

Subsequently, all five were named members of the president's personal staff, and the acknowledged leader of the group, Widjojo Nitisastro, an economist-demographer, has achieved the equivalent of cabinet status as director of the National Planning Council. Ali Wardhana, once a student of Howard Ellis, was named minister of finance in the new cabinet formed in June. But perhaps the capstone of this emergence of the economists was the naming of the mentor of them all, Sumitro Djojohadikusumo, as minister of trade in the new cabinet. Sumitro was not a member of the original "team of five." [9] Indeed, he was still in exile at the time that the team was formed, having been *persona non grata* for ten years due to his having been vice-president of the rebel government in the attempted coup of 1958. He was returned quietly at the government's request in the summer of 1967.

For many in Indonesia, the name of Sumitro has a special attraction. He was not only the founder of the Faculty of Economics at the University of Indonesia, and its first dean, but he was a member of two of Indonesia's most successful cabinets in the early 1950's and earned a reputation as an economic and financial wizard. He is bold, imaginative, energetic, and articulate. It is to be expected that Sumitro will quickly dispel notions that the government is slow and dull, at least as far as economic policy is concerned. He may, however, suffer from the handicap that miracles will be expected.

The Strategy of the Team of Economists

The Indonesian economists see their task as one that must be accomplished in three phases, namely, stabilization, rehabilitation, and development. These are not regarded as mutually exclusive areas of policy, but rather time periods in which emphasis is to be concentrated. It was hoped that by the end of 1967 the inflation

[9] The team was recently expanded. Its personnel now are: Widjojo Nitisastro, Mohammad Sadli, Subroto, Ali Wardhana, Emil Salim (thus far the original five), Sumitro Djojohadikusumo, Frans Seda (former minister of finance and now minister of communications), and Radius Prawiro (*Business News,* Djakarta, June 21, 1968).

would have been stopped, and that resources would then be available to begin rebuilding the deteriorated infrastructure, and by 1970 a modest beginning on the restructuring of the economy could be hoped for. Inevitably, perhaps, the stabilization phase has taken longer than envisaged, and the battle is still underway. What follows is a description and discussion of the way in which the Indonesians have set about getting off the inflation tiger. The central feature of the stabilization policy was the attempt to neutralize the budget of the central government. The state of the fisc at the time the Suharto government took effective control was such that anything like a balanced budget in the orthodox sense was clearly out of the question. For, despite the fact that government expenditures in 1965 and 1966 were too little to provide adequate government services, revenues from all sources in the two years were 36 percent and 44 percent of expenditures, respectively.[10] It was recognized that, even with Herculean efforts to increase tax revenues, a sizeable deficit was inevitable. The budgeted level of tax receipts for 1967 (49.8 billion rupiahs) was (in money terms) nearly five times the realized tax receipts for 1966 (see Table 13.2). However, it appeared that the very austere level of budgeted expenditures of 81.3 billion rupiahs could be attained only with a planned budgetary gap of nearly 40 percent.

At this juncture basic expertise in economics served the very useful purpose of providing an understanding of the relationship between the balance-of-payments gap and the internal deficit. The two were explicitly integrated in the formal budget by assuming that foreign credits could be acquired and sold in sufficient amount to provide the revenues needed to close the budget gap. Assurances were sought from donor nations that credit flows of that order of magnitude could be hoped for, and on the basis that the aid would be broad and flexible in nature—i.e., of a sort that could be rather generally saleable. Early agreement in principle was attained, and formal pledging followed, albeit with a considerable lag.

The BE System

The proceeds of sale of the foreign credits were to be acquired in a market that was responsive to demand and supply forces. Al-

[10] Office of the Budget, Djakarta.

Table 13.2. The 1967 budget (in billions of rupiahs)

Receipts	Budgeted	Realized*
Direct taxes	10.47	16.08
Indirect taxes	39.33	43.51
Foreign credits	29.50	19.12
Other	2.00	6.72†
Total	81.30	85.43
Expenditures	**Budgeted**	**Realized***
Routine budget	66.7	72.0
Personnel	26.6	32.2
Debt service	13.1	5.1
Other	27.0	34.7
Development budget	14.6	17.3
Special accounts‡		14.4
Total	81.3	103.7

Source: IBRD (International Bank for Reconstruction and Development) Mission and Office of the Budget, government of Indonesia.

* Provisional.

† Includes Public Law 480 (U.S. surplus commodity) credits.

‡ Prefinancing of rice imports and domestic rice procurement. These accounts were liquidated before the end of 1967 in order to put the government on a current year basis in these activities.

though the price at which the credits were to be sold would be determined by the state bank, the price chosen was to be linked with the freely floating price of "general export bonus" certificates, or "general BE." Export bonus schemes of this general nature are not unusual. However, the degree of reliance on the market in the pricing of foreign exchange was substantially greater than it has been in other low-income countries using such schemes, such as were used in Pakistan.[11]

The central feature of the system is that exporters are required to surrender their foreign exchange earnings, and receive marketable certificates (which are claims on the foreign exchange fund) in proportion to earnings as payment. Importers may purchase these certificates directly from exporters (or could, that is, until very recent alterations of the system), or through the organized

[11] Cf. Glassburner, "Aspects of the Problem of Foreign Exchange Pricing in Pakistan," *Economic Development and Cultural Change,* vol. 16, no. 4, July 1968. The description of the Indonesian BE system which follows is largely drawn from Chapter 12 above.

market in Djakarta, and they may be used to purchase a broad list of essential commodities (the so-called BE list). The market for the certificates is essentially free. The state bank operates in the market, primarily as a seller, and does so with an eye toward contributing to stability, but this is the extent of control. Government agencies are required (since March 1967) to acquire foreign exchange through this market, using their budgeted rupiah allocations, rather than direct foreign exchange allocations. Special certificates for use of foreign aid credits are also sold, as indicated above, at an administered rate, and at a differential vis-à-vis the general BE rate.

Until the promulgation of the regulations of July 28, 1967, that part of the foreign exchange earned by exporters which had to be surrendered without BE certificate compensation was paid for at the official "transactions rate" of ten rupiahs per dollar.[12] This "exchange rate" has been extremely unrealistic throughout its entire period of effectiveness, and increasingly so as time passed. However, this progressive overvaluation of the official rate has been mitigated by the increases in the BE quotas, as shown in Tables 12.1 and 12.2. Prior to February 1966, the government had been the sole buyer of foreign exchange, at a unitary rate of 10:1 (rupiahs per dollar), and all imports were by government or by firms importing for government. Three months later, exporters were extended the concession of a 10 percent BE quota for "hard" exports, and higher rates for less well established export commodities, as shown in Table 12.1. Quotas were raised again in May 1966, October 1966, and July 1967. More than two-thirds of all export proceeds are now marketed through the BE market.

Some notion of the order of magnitude of the *de facto* devaluation which has taken place may be obtained from the data in Table 12.2. While the so-called DPA rate[13] (the index of equilib-

[12] The transactions rate was abolished as part of the July 28, 1967 regulations. Thus the proportion of foreign exchange earnings not compensated with BE certificates became a straightforward tax.

[13] The DPA rate is the market rate paid for foreign exchange earned by exporters who received prices greater than the official "check price" for their exported commodities—and also from funds legally repatriated from earlier illegal flight. Those funds command a higher price because their use is not restricted to the commodities on the BE list.

rium used here) moved upward from 45, at the end of February 1966, to 340, in July 1968, the proportionate overvaluation was reduced, for the large majority of export commodities, from an unworkable 238 percent to a relatively modest 51 percent.[14] For less basic types of exports, which presumably face lower elasticities of external demand, the overvaluation is presently only about 26 percent. Private importers, meanwhile, have been exposed to fluctuating exchange rates. For importation of those goods which are on the BE list, the price of the U.S. dollar has risen from 43 in early 1966 to 300 in July 1968, a sixfold increase. For the more luxurious category of goods not on the BE list (which must be imported with DPA exchange) the proportionate increase has been slightly greater (6.5-fold increase),[15] and substantial duties must be paid over and above the payment of the full DPA rate for the exchange.

To sum up, the extremely burdensome implicit taxation of exporters which the fixed, overvalued rate of exchange imposed has been substantially reduced, providing vastly improved incentives to them (though by no means eliminating that problem). Importers have been forced to pay something like market value for their foreign exchange, rather than be either excluded entirely from legal importing or favored by foreign exchange allocations which were accompanied by a huge windfall profit.

The foreign credits which the donor nations provided in support of this liberalization have thus been sold at or near their market value as well. This has served the dual purpose of replacing a very arbitrary and corrupt allocation system with a more rational pricing system while bringing to the government a major source of rupiah financing. A corollary benefit has been that government agencies as well as private firms have been forced to account foreign exchange at the market rate.

Monetary Policy

Although control of the budget was the main pillar of the stabilization policy, success required that the huge unsatisfied

[14] These comparisons overstate the overvaluation of the earlier dates, because of manipulation of the check price. Cf. Chapter 12, above.

[15] The rate of inflation of domestic prices over this period was much greater. See *Ibid.* for discussion of this relationship.

demand for money which had been created by the erosion of the real value of the money stock, be contained in the private sector. It was also highly desirable that new bank credit be allocated in a pattern that would promote the recovery of the production apparatus. In October 1966, the controversial "tight money" policy was announced, declaring as a goal that 90 percent of all new credits must be for the financing of production and/or export. The legal reserve ratio for commercial banks was set at 30 percent. Central bank policy of lending to banks was tightened markedly, meanwhile. Importers were required to advance 100 percent of the value of intended imports to the state bank, plus 50 percent of duties. Interest rates, which had been a nominal 9 percent per annum in the face of 600 percent inflation, were set for three categories of borrowers at rates of 6, 7½, and 9 percent *per month.*

Despite the fact that the absolute increase in the money stock was greater in 1967 than in 1966, the slowdown in the rate of increase which the above set of policies brought about was such a shock to the business community that heavy pressure was brought to bear on government to relax the money reins in 1967. Accordingly, in April 1967, import prepayments were relaxed somewhat, and the interest rate ranges were lowered to 3, 4, and 5 percent monthly. By that time, the rate of inflation had slowed to the point that these rates represented positive real rates—although as the following discussion will show that situation did not last out the year

Other Aspects of the Stabilization Policy

State enterprises—largely public utilities and firms taken over from Dutch private enterprise in the late 1950's—were told publicly in October 1966 that they were to be treated like private enterprises, and that they would have to produce and price competitively. This was a severe dash of cold water for these firms for they had, for the most part, been kept afloat during the guided-democracy years by direct subsidies and/or profits created by favored allocations of foreign exchange and restriction of competition in other forms. Some of these shelters proved harder to dismantle than anticipated, but, in the main, the policy has been implemented.

Foreign private enterprise has been openly invited to invest in Indonesia—a most startling turnabout from the economic xenophobia of the Sukarno years. Aside from the Dutch properties referred to above, most of the foreign enterprises that were nationalized have been returned to their owners. A general financial settlement has been arranged with the Dutch government to compensate for confiscation of Dutch enterprises. A new foreign investment law has been promulgated, offering fast write-offs and other tax concessions.

Price controls, which were ubiquitous (if generally ineffective) prior to October 1966 have largely been done away with. The government still sets prices of petroleum products, electric power, urban transport, and drinking water, but even here an attempt at rationalization has been undertaken. Many of these prices were held fixed for so long during the hyperinflation that they had no meaning. Public utilities prices were increased fivefold in early 1967. They still lag badly behind rises in costs, however.

The Results

It is, of course, much too early to judge adequately the effects of these attempts to re-establish order. It must be said, however, that the "success" has been limited—although viewed in its context, it can be called success of a sort. The Djakarta cost-of-living index, and inflation guage of modest reliability but the best we have, rose by 112 percent in 1967, a compound rate of 6 percent per month. Can this be called success? Over the twenty-four months from December 1964 to December 1966, the compound monthly rate had been nearly 18 percent. The money stock increased in 1967 by 131 percent—a startling figure for a "tight money" period. But in 1965, the rate of increase had been 283 percent, and in 1966 it had been 663 percent. The real value of the money stock increased in 1967 for the first time since 1964—by slightly less than 7 percent. In 1966, the real value of the money stock had fallen by nearly 30 percent.

The attempt at budget balance—i.e., balance in the sense that government revenues of the orthodox type, plus the proceeds of sale of foreign credit were to cover expenditures—ended in a near miss. Revenues and expenditures were budgeted at Rp. 81.3 billion, but estimates of realized expenditure and revenue came to Rp. 103.7 and 85.4, respectively.[16] Thus a deficit of 18 percent of expenditures was realized. The deficit had not been less than 50 percent of realized expenditures since 1962.

The response of the foreign trade sector to the liberalization of trade regulations was modest, but, allowing for the disastrous decline in rubber prices, it was apparently quite respectable. There is a bewildering variety of preliminary estimates of both export and import performance, but the general picture seems to emerge roughly the same from each. Non-oil exports fell slightly short of target in value terms—probably declining slightly from the $490 million level established in 1966. However, oil exports rose by a little more than enough to compensate for that decline. Imports rose, perhaps by as much as $100 million over the 1966 level, so a current account deficit approaching $300 million is the approximate outcome. This can be viewed in two ways, i.e., as the worst deficit, save one, in Indonesia's history, or as a very successful manipulation of finance so as to make the deflationary inflow of imports possible.

It is also too early to report reliably on what happened to production in 1967. The year 1966 had been a good crop year, and the government estimated that a per capita income increase of 1.7 percent had occurred. In 1967, however, the dry season rice crop was poor, and this, added to bad logistical administration, precipitated the food shortage and resumption of inflation that was experienced through the winter months of 1967–1968. One international agency has nevertheless privately estimated that there was quite a respectable increase in per capita real income, but another reports that that is doubtful if per capita income was maintained

[16] These are provisional figures, provided by the Budget Office, Djakarta. *BIES* for February 1968 cites ministry of finance data showing a much smaller total of expenditures, and a deficit of less than 6 percent (*Bulletin of Indonesian Economic Studies,* February 1963, p. 34). The larger part of this discrepancy is due to *BIES'* failure to include the settlement of special accounts. Cf. ‡, Table 13.2, above.

at the 1966 level.[17] Rice production is still the key to economic success in Indonesia. The industrial sector did not respond with vigor to the cold blast of the new competition in Indonesia. All accounts are extremely impressionistic but uniformly indicate that there is no clear evidence that revival has set in.

The 1968 performance is even more difficult to report on, particularly for one who has not been in the country for a year. [See the introduction to Part VI.—Ed.] With the coming of the harvest season in the spring and with the assistance of U.S. agricultural surplus (P.L. 480) shipments, the inflation flare-up of the winter months was put down again. The rate of increase from the end of January through April 1968 was less than 2 percent per month, with prices actually falling in April, according to CBS data. The government continues to be preoccupied with the problem of monetary stability, reasoning that no healthy revival of economic activity can be expected until reasonable price stability is achieved. It is argued that until it becomes more profitable to invest limited funds in productive activity than to speculate in inventories of consumer goods and BE certificates, no real revival can be expected. And until the government's command of real resources is expanded, no major public investment program is possible. The other side of the coin, however, is that the monetary stringency, which the "tight money" policy imposes, hamstrings domestic producers—as does the competition with foreign goods brought on by the liberal import policy.

The 1968 budget is more than 40 percent larger than the 1967 budget (see Table 13.3), and the proportion of total expenditures earmarked for development is much greater. The largest part of the latter is to come from a program of infrastructure rehabilitation financed by the International Bank for Reconstruction and Development (IBRD). Also, the new cabinet is called the development cabinet, and has been charged with producing and undertaking the implementation of a Five Year Plan. The Plan's outline is expected to appear very soon, and assistance has been arranged with the Harvard Development Advisory Service to help with fleshing it out. [Again, see the introduction to Part VI.—Ed.]

17 These estimates are to be found only in the internal reports of these institutions.

Table 13.3. Indonesia's budget 1968, as submitted to parliament on October 16, 1967 (in rupiahs)

Revenue		Expenditure	
I. Routine budget			
Tax	43,000,000,000	Supreme state institutions	1,397,292,131
Customs & excises	36,855,250,000	Departments	93,219,781,100
BE rate balance	10,500,000,000	Nondepartmental bodies	
Profit on petroleum	6,000,000,000	Institutions	568,886,869
Regional development contribution	830,710,000		
Total	97,185,960,000	Total	97,185,960,000
II. Development budget			
Foreign credits	32,700,000,000	Power infrastructure	2,010,230,000
Automatic foreign exchange allocation	8,800,000,000	Social infrastructure	3,161,681,000
		Transport infrastructure	8,558,876,000
Regional development contribution (IPEDA)	4,000,000,000	Government machinery rehabilitation	5,106,739,000
		Irrigation infrastructure	3,072,600,000
		Miscellaneous	23,564,454,000
Total	45,500,000,000	Total	45,459,600,000
Grand total	142,685,960,000	Grand total	142,645,560,100

Source: Department of the Budget, Djakarta.

These measures will take hold only with substantial lags, however, if at all.

Diagnosis

Fundamentally, the medicine of the economic doctors in Indonesia is failing to revive the patient, not so much because the medicine is wrong, but because the illness is so severe and because their luck has been bad. The structural problems created by years of capital consumption and deterioration of economic organization will take years to solve. The president's team of economists gambled that with good weather, reasonably good international markets, and NEP [18] kind of economic policy, and a re-establishment of price stability, production, which was at such a low ebb in 1965, would recover quickly. Probably most neo-classically-trained economists would think along the same lines in the same sort of predicament. The apparent failure of 1967, either to halt the inflation or to stimulate recovery of production, has added another serious hazard, namely, mounting impatience on the part of the politically aware with the heavy reliance of the government on the "economic technocrats." President Suharto's response has been to give two professional economists cabinet status (in June), and to expand the size of his economists' team. However, as he himself has said, they have little time in which to produce results. If 1968's luck should turn out to be as good as 1967's was bad, there is hope that "results" may be shown. However, even if the weather is good and the various agricultural improvement programs take hold well and early, if rubber prices were to recover in the last half of the year (they have at least been stable, if low, for many months), and if the shattered textile industry manages a modest recovery, the problems which will remain will be enough to sober the most optimistic development economist.

[18] The reference is to the "New Economic Policy" (NEP) of the early 1920's in the Soviet Union. Lenin, after it became apparent that the early efforts at communism were premature, freed markets generally as an expedient to restore something like the prewar level of economic activity.

The Economy of Indonesia

Designed by R. E. Rosenbaum.
Composed by Colonial Press, Inc.,
in 11 point linotype Baskerville, 2 points leaded,
with display lines in Optima Semibold.
Printed letterpress from type by Colonial Press
on 60 pound Warren's 1854 Text
with the Cornell University Press watermark.
Bound by Colonial Press
in Columbia Bayside Linen
and stamped in All Purpose Aluminum.